Principles and Pluralist Approaches in Teaching Economics

Towards a Transformative Science

Edited by Samuel Decker, Wolfram Elsner and Svenja Flechtner

Routledge
Taylor & Francis Group
LONDON AND NEW YORK

First published 2020
by Routledge
2 Park Square, Milton Park, Abingdon, Oxon OX14 4RN

and by Routledge
605 Third Avenue, New York, NY 10017

First issued in paperback 2021

Routledge is an imprint of the Taylor & Francis Group, an informa business

British Library Cataloguing-in-Publication Data
A catalogue record for this book is available from the British Library

Library of Congress Cataloging-in-Publication Data
Names: Decker, Samuel, 1990– editor. | Elsner, Wolfram, editor. | Flechtner, Svenja, 1985– editor.
Title: Principles and pluralist approaches in teaching economics : towards a transformative science / edited by Samuel Decker, Wolfram Elsner and Svenja Flechtner.
Description: Abingdon, Oxon ; New York, NY : Routledge, 2019. | Series: Routledge advances in heterodox economics | Includes bibliographical references and index.
Identifiers: LCCN 2019008485 (print) | LCCN 2019010407 (ebook) | ISBN 9781315177731 (Ebook) | ISBN 9781138037687 (hardback : alk. paper)
Subjects: LCSH: Economics—Study and teaching. | Economics—Philosophy. | Pluralism.
Classification: LCC HB74.5 (ebook) | LCC HB74.5 .P75 2019 (print) | DDC 330.071—dc23
LC record available at https://lccn.loc.gov/2019008485

ISBN 13: 978-0-367-78560-4 (pbk)
ISBN 13: 978-1-138-03768-7 (hbk)

Typeset in Times New Roman
by Apex CoVantage, LLC

Principles and Pluralist Approaches in Teaching Economics

This volume is a state-of-the-art compilation of diverse and innovative perspectives, principles, and a number of practiced approaches of fields, courses, and methods of pluralist economics teaching. It fosters constructive controversy aiming to incite authors and commentators to engage in fruitful debate.

The complex economic problems of the 21st century require a pluralist, real-world oriented, and innovative discipline of economics, capable of addressing and teaching those complex issues to students from diverse perspectives. This volume addresses a number of key questions: Which models could be taught outside the equilibrium and optimality paradigm? Which methods could help to improve our understanding of the complex globalized economy? How can qualitative and quantitative methods be combined in a fruitful way to analyze complex economic problems? How can the academic isolation of mainstream economics that has developed over many decades be overcome, despite its attempted transdisciplinary imperialism? What role should knowledge from other disciplines play in teaching economics, and what is the relevance of transdisciplinarity? Through examining these issues, the editors and authors have created a pluralist but cohesive book on teaching economics in the contemporary classroom, drawing from ideas and examples from around the world.

Principles and Pluralist Approaches in Teaching Economics is a unique collection of diverse perspectives on the methodology and applications of pluralist economics teaching. It will be a great resource for those teaching economics at various levels as well as researchers and intermediate and advanced students searching for pluralism in economics.

Samuel Decker is an economist and activist based in Berlin, Germany. He works as a scientific assistant for the online learning platform Exploring Economics (www.exploring-economics.org/en/). He holds a master's degree in Political Economy of European Integration and is an active member of the student movement for pluralism in economics.

Wolfram Elsner was Professor of Economics at the University of Bremen, Germany, from 1995 until he retired in 2016. He has also worked as head of local economic development, head of the Planning Division of the Ministry of Economic Affairs of the State of Bremen, and as director of the State of Bremen government's economic research institute from 1986 to 1995. He was president of the European Association for Evolutionary Political Economy from 2012 to 2016.

Svenja Flechtner is an Assistant Professor of Pluralist Economics at the University of Siegen, Germany. She has been a research assistant at Europa-Universität Flensburg and Freie Universität Berlin. From 2014 to 2018, she was a council member of the European Association for Evolutionary Political Economy.

Routledge Advances in Heterodox Economics

Series Editors: Mark Setterfield

The New School for Social Research, USA

Peter Kriesler

University of New South Wales, Australia

Over the past two decades, the intellectual agendas of heterodox economists have taken a decidedly pluralist turn. Leading thinkers have begun to move beyond the established paradigms of Austrian, feminist, Institutional-evolutionary, Marxian, Post Keynesian, radical, social, and Sraffian economics – opening up new lines of analysis, criticism, and dialogue among dissenting schools of thought. This cross-fertilization of ideas is creating a new generation of scholarship in which novel combinations of heterodox ideas are being brought to bear on important contemporary and historical problems.

Routledge Advances in Heterodox Economics aims to promote this new scholarship by publishing innovative books in heterodox economic theory, policy, philosophy, intellectual history, institutional history, and pedagogy. Syntheses or critical engagement of two or more heterodox traditions are especially encouraged.

Microeconomic Theory
A Heterodox Approach
Authored by Frederic S. Lee, Edited by Tae-Hee Jo

The Economics of Law, Order, and Action
The Logic of Public Goods
Jakub Bożydar Wiśniewski

Advancing Pluralism in Teaching Economics
International Perspectives on a Textbook Science
Edited by Samuel Decker, Wolfram Elsner and Svenja Flechtner

What is Heterodox Economics?
Conversations with Leading Economists
Andrew Mearman, Sebastian Berger and Danielle Guizzo

Principles and Pluralist Approaches in Teaching Economics
Towards a Transformative Science
Edited by Samuel Decker, Wolfram Elsner and Svenja Flechtner

For more information about this series, please visit www.routledge.com/series/RAHE

Contents

Figures

Tables

Contributors

Jonathan Barth is co-founder and Managing Director of the ZOE Institute for future-fit economies.

Frank Beckenbach is a Professor of Pluralist Economics at Cusanus University, Germany.

Karl Betz † was a Senior Lecturer of Economics at the South Westphalia University of Applied Sciences, Campus Meschede, Germany. He passed away in July 2016. His chapter was finished by his colleague **Martin Ehret**.

Samuel Decker works as a scientific coordinator in the Network for Pluralist Economics for the e-learning platform *Exploring Economics*.

Michael Derrer is Lecturer at Lucerne University for Applied Sciences and Arts.

Andreas Dimmelmeier is a Gem Stones Marie Curie doctoral fellow at the University of Warwick and Copenhagen Business School.

Peter Dorman is a Professor of Economics at Evergreen State College, Olympia, WA, USA.

Dirk Ehnts is a research assistant of Dr. Gerhard Schick, a German member of parliament.

Wolfram Elsner is a Professor (retired) of Economics at the Faculty of Business Studies and Economics, University of Bremen, Germany, and a guest professor at Jilin University, China.

Svenja Flechtner is Assistant Professor of Pluralist Economics at the University of Siegen, Germany.

Alan Freeman is a Professor of Economics and Co-director of the Geopolitical Economy Research Group, University of Manitoba, Winnipeg, MB, Canada.

Nils Goldschmidt is a Professor of Contextual Economics and Economics Education at the University of Siegen, Germany.

Hansjörg Herr is Professor Emeritus at the Berlin School of Economics and Law and one of the founders of the Global Labour University.

Frederick Heussner is a PhD candidate at the LMU Munich, Germany.

Johannes Jäger is a Professor and head of the Economics Department at the University of Applied Sciences BFI Vienna, Austria.

Yvette Keipke is a research assistant and doctoral student at the University of Siegen, Germany.

Stefan Kesting is a Senior Teaching Fellow at Leeds University Business School, UK.

Alexander Lenger is an Interim Professor of Economics and Economics Education at the University of Siegen, Germany.

Henry Leveson-Gower is the founder of Promoting Economic Pluralism (PEP, 2016) and is a Fellow of the RSA and a chartered accountant.

Maria Alejandra Madi is Professor Emerita at the Instituto de Economia, UNICAMP, Brazil.

Genna R. Miller is a Lecturing Fellow in the Department of Economics at Duke University in Durham, NC, USA.

Stephan Panther is a Professor of Economics and Interdisciplinary Institutional Research at Cusanus University, Bernkastel-Kues, Germany.

Andrea Pürckhauer coordinated the construction and launch of the platform Exploring Economics as a research associate.

Jack Reardon teaches economics at the School of Business at Hamline University in Minnesota and is Founding Editor of the *International Journal of Pluralism and Economics Education*, Eau Claire, WI, USA.

Oliver Richters is a PhD student at the department of economics at Carl von Ossietzky University Oldenburg, Germany.

Florian Rommel is a research assistant at the Cusanus Hochschule, Bernkastel-Kues, Germany, and a PhD student at the Goethe University Frankfurt.

Christoph Sanders is active in educational work and coordination for the Konzeptwerk Neue Ökonomie (Concept Center for a New Economy), Germany.

Peter Söderbaum is a Professor Emeritus in Ecological Economics, Mälardalen University, Västerås, Sweden.

Elisabeth Springler is an economist and leader of the degree program "European Economy and Business Leadership" at the University of Applied Sciences BFI Vienna, Germany.

Janina Urban is a researcher at the Institute for Societal Development in the field of New Economic Thinking in Düsseldorf, Germany.

Reviewers

The editors wish to thank the following reviewers who contributed to the volume as anonymous reviewers of individual chapters:

Madeleine Böhm
Yannis Dafermos
Charlie Dannreuther
Michael Derrer
Peter Dorman
Sheila Dow
Trevor Evans
Alan Freeman
John Hall
Arne Heise
Hansjörg Herr
Carsten Herrmann-Pillath
Lisa Herzog
Johannes Jäger
Steve Keen
Oliver Kessler
Karsten Köhler
Fabian Lindner
Jens Maeße
Barbara Muraca
Ioana Negru
Marco Raberto
Jack Reardon
Oliver Richters
Malcolm Sawyer
Peter Söderbaum
Pasquale Tridico
Birgit Weber

Towards a pluralist economic education for a transformative science – introduction

Samuel Decker, Wolfram Elsner and Svenja Flechtner

1 Economics and the challenges of the 21st century

In a volume corresponding to the present one, which we edited under the title *Advancing Pluralism in Teaching Economics* (see Decker et al. 2018), the contributors set out how economics as a serious social science can advance our knowledge only as a pluralist discipline – and how this criterion likewise applies to modern teaching and textbook writing. While that volume had a focus on *epistemological* foundations of a potential future pluralist economics, in the present one we will proceed to more *applied* contributions, which cover *principles* (Part I) as well as specific *approaches* (Part II) of pluralist teaching. A final part (Part III) of this volume will generalize again and will reflect on the perspective of economics as a transformative science.

The debate on the shortcomings of mainstream economics and the development of pluralism as a possible alternative may of course not neglect the societal context in which scientific discourse and epistemic change are embedded. As the financial crisis that began in 2008 has illustrated, economics both contributes to and is influenced by developments in the real world. A transformation of the economics curriculum towards pluralism thus needs to be considered against the *manifold crisis symptoms* that have characterized the first two decades of the 21st century. Economic, ecological, societal, and political crises do reinforce each other, and the resulting "new mediocre" of economic growth and its fragility are well recognized even by the established bodies of global governance (see IMF 2015). As a part of that, a political crisis of neoliberalism has taken shape against a globalization obviously gone astray. Billions of people have lost through it at the end of the day, and nationalist, racist, and homophobic political forces, authoritarian politicians, governments, and regimes gain power across the globe and even in the industrialized core countries of neoliberalism. These and other cultural and political changes are seen by some observers as Polanyian "counter-movements" of people against the "marketization" and "capitalization" of their labor, land, money, the redistribution from bottom to top and other conditions of life deteriorating – how misled such reactions ever may be. Inequality levels are at record heights, and entire societies have been left behind by such globalization (Novy 2017).

Those complex challenges of the unfolding 21st century should be met by an active support of democratic-participatory problem-solving through a pluralistic economic discipline. Only the plurality of existing scientific perspectives and paradigms as well as of questions, answers, and recommendations appear to be able to sufficiently inform and inspire public debate, political parties, governments, or social movements to find sustainable economic, ecological, and societal answers to the multiple crises.

As has been discussed in the volume *Advancing Pluralism in Teaching Economics*, mainstream economics has not sufficiently moved towards a pluralist, real-world oriented and innovative discipline – and particularly so in teaching – that would enable students, policy makers, and the public to address the complex challenges. The inclusion of a number of new topics as well as theoretical and methodological elements from behavioral and complexity economics in research cannot conceal the fact that the general state of the discipline's mainstream continues to be critical. Where an open, intense, and diverse discussion on the future of financialized capitalism, globalization, the role of markets, and the environment would be appropriate, a limited set of theories, models, and methods restricts the debate. Where the best solutions to the right questions would be urgently needed to tackle ecological, economic, and social crises, economics students are taught a narrow set of highly standardized "equilibrium" and "optimality" perspectives and "market"-oriented (re-)interpretations as well as pedagogical approaches.

The dominating monism in economics, and particularly so in economics teaching, thus is a barrier to the development of sustainable answers to the multiple crisis, and the rise of backward forces even in the leading capitalist countries reflects this lack of economic pluralism and of knowledge of alternatives. The backward forces address the problems without addressing their causes, and so the multiple crisis worsens and gives rise to even more authoritarian forms of crisis management. The lack of pluralism thus contributes to a crisis of democracy itself. Monism in economics, in other words, appears to be a pressing political problem that necessitates a transformation of economics towards pluralism.

2 A dissolving economics mainstream? Not in education and teaching

In the aforementioned volume corresponding with the present one, we also tackled the thesis of an increasing dissolution, fragmentation, and specialization of the economic mainstream, as forwarded by a number of prominent non-mainstream economists (e.g. Colander 2000, 2010; Colander et al. 2011; Dow 2008; Davis 2016; Fontana 2014; Cedrini and Fontana 2017). We argued that this basically refers to economic research only and holds considerably less for economics education, teaching, and textbook writing. The latter still is a field of monism, dogmatism, and exclusion – still widely underdeveloped as a complex, real-world, and modern scientific discipline.

Economics education and textbook writing have been tackled at all, and critically tackled as a major problem, only in recent years (Elsner 2013, 2017; Schneider and Underwood 2013; Hoyt and McGoldrick 2013; ISIPE 2014). It had been argued for long that, while many mainstream researchers have turned away from simplistic conceptions of optimality and unique predetermined equilibrium in research, and to a more complex understanding of real economies, the discipline has increasingly displayed a "schizophrenia" between research and teaching/ textbook writing (e.g. Elsner 2009).

In *Advancing Pluralism in Teaching Economics*, we also argued that the realization of pluralism in teaching economics faces three challenges: the need for a well-developed and epistemologically founded scientific program, for a true internationalization of economic thought, and for alternatives to the mainstream textbook system. Beyond those challenges that we addressed there, pluralism in teaching economics also faces more applied problems. An obvious problem for pluralism is to show that valuable and insightful alternative approaches do exist. The actually existing plurality of economic thinking still has to be made more visible and virulent. A practical challenge in this respect is the lack of principles of pluralist teaching – it should be made clearer how different paradigms and perspectives can be taught together practically, as classes and syllabi are limited.

In the present volume, accordingly, we proceed to present a number of more applied and practical principles as well as field-related approaches and course syllabi to pluralist teaching. Additionally, we present theories, models, methods, and hands-on course curricula in fields such as

- Political economy
- Macro, monetary, post-Keynesian economics, and income distribution
- Ecological economics and sustainability
- Feminist economics
- Microeconomics, sectoral approaches
- Economics and ethics
- Interdisciplinary and paradigm-comparing approaches to pluralist teaching.

3 The present volume

Part I of this volume ("Principles for teaching pluralist economics") offers systematizations, methods, and experiences of pluralist teaching. Alan Freeman ("The second opinion: an ethical approach to learning and teaching economics") shares his experience of a pedagogical approach to pluralism and heterodox thinking in university courses that he based on the ethical responsibility of the professional economist. The ethical response, he argues, is the pluralist one: the professional should consider a range of different alternative research and policy perspectives. This chapter also draws on the author's experience in government to show how pluralism allows practical questions to be approached ethically. Finally, the approach also implies a guide to curriculum design.

Andreas Dimmelmeier, Frederick Heussner, Andrea Pürckhauer, and Janina Urban ("Making the incommensurable comparable: a comparative approach to pluralist economics education") develop central categories which allow for systematic comparisons between different theoretical perspectives. The meta-theoretical patterns of 10 selected schools of economic thought are then visualized in a comparative way. This highly innovative systematization is grounded in concepts derived from biology, the history of economic thought, the philosophy of science, and international political economy and builds the intellectual basis for the online learning platform Exploring Economics (www.exploring-economics.org/en/).

Stephan Panther ("What can teaching critical pluralist economics gain from 'de-othering' sociology?") argues for the inclusion of an economic sociological perspective into the curriculum, and sketches a course on capitalist markets as an illustration. Karl Betz and Martin Ehret ("Comparing paradigms on a level playing field") develop a one-term introductory course in economics which compares classical, neoclassical, and Keynesian economics. The comparison is done within the same framework (level playing field) so that it becomes obvious which differences are due to the perspective of the paradigm and not just to different ways of modeling.

Michael Derrer ("It needs two eyes to see in perspective: teaching economics through the confrontation of dissenting views") proposes in his short manual-like comment to put one-sided textbooks to use by confronting them with critical texts. Alexander Lenger, Yvette Keipke, and Nils Goldschmidt ("Economic competence, economic understanding, and reflexive judgment: a social theory of teaching teachers of economics") are concerned with economics education in schools, and they discuss how teachers must be educated in universities in order to be able to facilitate an economics education in schools that renders school students able to critically think about the economies they live in.

Part II ("Approaches and building blocks") collects contributions that integrate different schools of thoughts in their teaching practice ("approaches") and/or contain innovative teaching perspectives on the respective school of thought ("building blocks"). Johannes Jäger ("Introduction to critical political economy in a multi-paradigmatic setting") opens the part with a chapter on how to integrate political economy with other paradigms in teaching. His insights are further developed and practically applied by himself and his co-author, Elisabeth Springler, in the following chapter ("Heterodox perspectives in teaching the European integration and crisis: critical political economy and post-Keynesianism"), which contrasts a critical political economy approach with a post-Keynesian approach to teaching European integration.

Peter Söderbaum bundles his long-standing research and teaching experience with ecological economics and pluralism ("Ecological economics in research and teaching: a matter of theoretical and ideological perspective"). Jack Reardon and Maria Alejandra Madi ("Suggestions for incorporating sustainability into the macroeconomics course") develop another concrete course suggestion for some integration of ecological economics and macroeconomics. Jonathan Barth and Oliver Richters ("Demand-driven ecological collapse: a stock-flow fund-service model of money, energy and ecological scale") put forward an example of how different schools in monetary economics and ecological economics can be analyzed and taught in an integrated way by developing economic models that apply the modern macroeconomic approach of stock-flow consistency, combining it in disaggregated, sectoral input-output models. Genna Miller's chapter ("Teaching feminist economics through student-written diaries") provides an instructive example of how non-mainstream paradigms may offer not only highly needed alternative analyses but also innovative pedagogical approaches.

Frank Beckenbach ("Undermining the microeconomic textbook approach: steps towards competitive pluralism") presents microeconomic concepts for teaching that treat the real-world economic complexity differently from the dominant monistic approach. It shows how to gradually exit from that approach by stepwise enhancing the range of phenomena that microeconomics can explain, introducing different basic assumptions and modeling methods. Hansjörg Herr ("Functional income distribution in economic paradigms: the failure of the neoclassical approach and alternatives") shares his rich experience in teaching post-Keynesian economics and focuses on the issue of inequality as a virtual blind spot of mainstream teaching. Dirk Ehnts ("The balance sheet approach to macroeconomics") displays a proposal to rebase macroeconomic teaching on insights of monetary theory. Stefan Kesting ("How to teach ethics and economics to undergraduate students?") contributes a conception of teaching ethics in economics as applied in undergraduate studies at the Leeds University Business School (UK). Peter Dorman ("Addressing controversies in economics instruction through interdisciplinary learning communities: the Evergreen experience") builds on his long teaching experience at an institution that employs interdisciplinary learning communities as its primary pedagogical vehicle. He demonstrates that interdisciplinarity leads organically to a more heterodox approach to economic content.

Considering the transformative capacities of economics, and of a future pluralist economics in particular, we added as a documentation an extract from an overview paper of the UK-based pluralist accreditation initiative *Promoting Economic Pluralism – PEP* by founder and CEO of PEP, Henry Leveson-Gower. In some aspects, PEP appears to be the furthest developed current approach to foster a plural economic teaching and learning (together with, for example, the students' initiative Exploring Economics). PEP's initiatives set up so far have had a surprisingly broad public resonance, and its list of supporters is most impressive, crossing over business, politics, civil society, and academia. The text provided does not originate from academia proper but contributes a perspective from "practice" and practitioners, but the arguments of this text are uniquely well considered and concise. It is a must-know and a perfect complement to the present volume and the endeavors of its authors and editors.

Obviously, these "approaches" to and "building blocks" of future pluralist economics teaching in a number of disciplinary fields – one-field didactical approaches, field-comparing approaches, and paradigm-comparing approaches – presented in this part are still rather selective and by no means piece together a complete picture of the already existing pluralist teaching conceptions and courses in economics. We may sort the contributions to this volume, which have been developed in a diverse practical heterodox space and in fact are multidimensionally interrelated, in a simplifying scheme (Table I.1).

Table I.1 Sorting the contributions to this volume after their thematic focus and field of application

Thematic Focus (Discipline-, Paradigm-, and Field-Related) / *Field of Application (Didactic-, Method-, Course-, and Praxis-Related)*	*Meta-theoretic*	*Inter-disciplinarity*	*Disciplinary*				
			Paradigms Comparing	*Field-Related*			
				Micro Economics	*Macro Economics, Political Economy, Post-Keynesianism, Money*	*Ecology Sustainability, Degrowth*	*Feminist Economics*
Didactic Principles and Approaches	Kesting, Ethics and Economics Freeman, Second Opinion Lenger, Keipke, Goldschmidt, A Social Theory of Teaching Teachers	Panther, De-Othering Sociology	Derrer, Dissenting Views; Dimmelmeier et al., Comparative Approach; Jaeger, Multi-Paradigmatic Perspective	Beckenbach, Micro-Economic Textbook Approach	Jaeger/Springler, Political Economy and Post-Keynesianism in EU-Integration Herr, Income Distribution	Söderbaum, Ecological Economics	
Method-Related:							
Stock-Flow/Input-Output					Richters/Barth, Monetary and Ecological Economics		

Balance-Sheet Approach				Ehnts, Macro-Economics		
Qualitative methods						Miller, Feminist Economics
Course-Related		Dorman, Interdisciplinary Learning Communities	Betz, Comparing Paradigms;	Reardon/Madi, Macroeconomics and Sustainability		
Praxis/ Trans-formative Science	Barth/ Rommel, Trans-formative Economics, Economics and Society; Pluralist study program accreditation (PEP)		Decker, Critical transformative Science		Sanders, Transformation and Degrowth	

While an emphasis of most contributions is *general didactical principles and approaches*, there are two papers anchored in a *specific method* (Barth and Richters, Ehnts), both in macroeconomics (one also in ecology) and two explicitly *course-related*, also in macroeconomics (and in ecology) (Betz, Reardon, and Madi). The chapters discussing general didactical principles and approaches, in turn, have a *comparative focus*, both in *interdisciplinarity* (Panther, Dorman) and *disciplinary paradigm-comparisons* (Freeman, Derrer, Dimmelmeier et al., Jäger). Another subgroup in this horizontal category is related to particular *substantial fields* of economic research and even (pluralist) teaching *courses*, such as *microeconomics* (Beckenbach), *political economy* and *post-Keynesianism* (Jäger and Springler), income *distribution* (Herr), *ecological* economics (Söderbaum), and *feminist* economics (Miller). Another meta-theoretic field, with the potential of a course in a pluralist education conception, is economics and *ethics* (Kesting).

The scheme also indicates potential gaps of pluralist economic education that we will focus on in the conclusion of this book. The perspectives of different schools and the integrated applications to teaching should be considered exemplary, illustrating the richness of economic thought and hopefully stimulating further pluralist teaching developments and experiments. For teaching pluralist economics there exists no ready-made blueprint. The manifold teaching approaches in this volume, rather, should be understood as a compass that may demonstrate the directions for a deliberate transformation of economics. In this sense, this volume presents a recent state of the art of pluralist teaching.

3.1 Towards a progressive, problem-solving transformative science

We have argued that pluralism in economics is fundamental to equip societal cognitive and democratic-participatory processes with the best ideas and solutions to address current multiple crises symptoms and gain new insights for society and its ongoing process of inquiry. The question remains, however, whether teaching diversity and pluralism will suffice to challenge mainstream economics and intervene in society in problem-solving and sustainable ways. A conscious transformation of economics should not only be understood as a change of teaching concepts and contents, but also as a change of the relationship between economics, the economy, environment, and society (e.g. Elsner 2017). The concept of a transformative science, therefore, envisages a pluralist, democratic-participatory economic science that contributes to a progressive, socio-ecological transformation.

The concept of transformative science has been developed since the turn of the millennium and has been previously applied in natural sciences. It proceeds from the assumption that science is always socially embedded and subjected to societal and political boundaries. The latter shape the construction of research questions, their processing in the scientific system, and the societal utilization of research results. Beyond this wide definition of *performativity*, the concept of *transformative* science, as defined by Schneidewind et al. (2016), is accompanied by a political-normative understanding of the role of science in the context of ecological depletion and cataclysmic climate destruction. Instead of masking such social impact of economics and hiding it behind "value-free" algebra, economics should reflect its societal position and impact and utilize it to support transformations towards sustainability. In their call for a "new contract between science and society", for example, 60 German-speaking economists have recently demanded a "transformative economics", which is supposed to operationalize sustainability goals in the realm of the economic-policy system (see Schneidewind et al. 2016).

The contributions in Part III of the volume ("Teaching for socio-ecological transformation: economics as a transformative science?") therefore link the debate on pluralism in economics with the concept of transformative science. Samuel Decker ("Contours of a critical transformative science") refers to the approach of Critical Theory as developed by the Frankfurt School in order to reformulate the approach of transformative economics as a branch of critical social science. Jonathan Barth and Florian Rommel ("Transformative economics – calling for a more conscious relationship between economics and society") elaborate on the performative characteristics of economics and propose concrete strategies for realizing a conscious transformative science. Christoph Sanders ("Tackling the roots: (economic) education for social-ecological transformations and degrowth societies") asks how economic education can contribute to a social-ecological transformation. In our conclusion ("Pluralist economics is taking shape. But further steps have to follow – conclusion"), we point out empty spaces of pluralism and further steps the project of pluralism has to take. Finally, in the documentation mentioned, Henry-Leveson-Gower demonstrates with the initiative PEP that a future transformative economics has a pillar, and a most important one, already in real-world areas, where interests of practitioners in a plural economics have already been clearly articulated.

We consider the selected contributions of the present volume – general principles for pluralist teaching, more applied pedagogic conceptions, and the broader transformational impact of economics – only as a stepping stone in a debate on *the transformation of economics and on economics as a transformative science.* Like teaching pluralism, transformative science is no monolithic concept supposed to replace existing paradigms. It is supposed, rather, to foster cooperation among diverse schools, paradigms, disciplines, and political specters in order to transform the social sciences and to contribute to the social-ecological transformation needed in the multiple crisis of capitalist globalization. We hope to have provided with the present volume a pertinent source of approaches to a pluralist economics and to a transformative economic discipline, which will help building more fruitful, broader, and longer-run societal problem-solving capacities.

Acknowledgments

We are thankful to our co-organizers and the funders of the conference "Teaching Economics in the 21st Century", from which this volume emerged. The conference took place at the Berlin School of Law and Economics on 26–28 November 2015. It was jointly organized by the Institute for International Political Economy (IPE), Forschungsstelle für wissenschaftsbasierte gesellschaftliche Weiterentwicklung (FGW), Netzwerk Plurale Ökonomik, the World Economics Association (WEA), the European Association for Evolutionary Political Economy (EAEPE),

Arbeitskreis Politische Ökonomie (AK PolÖk), the Research Network Macroeconomics and Macroeconomic Policies (FMM), and Vereinigung für Ökologische Ökonomie (VÖÖ). Furthermore, we are thankful to Anne Lödige and Kevin Rösch for helpful assistance with the editing of individual chapters.

References

Cedrini, M. and Fontana, M. (2017): "Just Another Niche in the Wall? How Specialization Is Changing the Face of Mainstream Economics", *Cambridge Journal of Economics* 42(2), 427–451.

Colander, D. (2000): "The Death of Neoclassical Economics", *Journal of the History of Economic Thought* 22(2), 127–143.

Colander, D. (2010): "Moving Beyond the Rhetoric of Pluralism: Suggestions for an 'Inside-the-Mainstream' Heterodoxy", in Garnett, R. F., Jr., Olsen, E. and Starr, M. (eds.), *Economic Pluralism*. New York and Abingdon, UK: Routledge, 36–47.

Colander, D., Holt, R. and Rosser, J. B. (2011): "*The Complexity Era in Economics*", *Review of Political Economy* 23(3), 357–369.

Davis, J. (2016): "Economics Imperialism versus Multidisciplinarity", *History of Economic Ideas* 24(3), 77–94.

Decker, S., Elsner, W. and Flechtner, S. (eds.) (2018): *Advancing Pluralism in Teaching Economics: International Perspectives on a Textbook Science*. London and New York: Routledge.

Dow, S. (2008): "Plurality in Orthodox and Heterodox Economics", *Journal of Philosophical Economics* 1(2), 73–96.

Elsner, W. (2009): "Market and State", *International Encyclopedia of Public Policy* 3, 367–386.

Elsner, W. (2013): "State and Future of the 'Citadel' and of the Heterodoxies in Economics: Challenges and Dangers, Convergences and Cooperation", *European Journal of Economics and Economic Policies: Intervention* 10(3), 286–298.

Elsner, W. (2017): "Complexity Economics as Heterodoxy: Theory and Policy", *Journal of Economic Issues* 51(4), 939–978.

Fontana, M. (2014): "Pluralism(s) in Economics: Lessons from Complexity and Innovation", *Journal of Evolutionary Economics* 24(1), 189–204.

Hoyt, G. M. and McGoldrick, K. M. (eds.) (2013): *International Handbook on Teaching and Learning Economics*. Cheltenham, UK and Northampton, MA: Edward Elgar.

IMF International Monetary Fund (2015): *Lagarde: Prevent "New Mediocre" from Becoming "New Reality"*. IMF-World Bank Spring Meetings, IMF Survey, April 9, www.imf.org/external/pubs/ft/survey/so/2015/NEW040915A.htm, accessed 1 February 2017.

ISIPE (2014): "International Student Initiative for Pluralism in Economics", *An International Student Call for Pluralism in Economics*, www.isipe.net/, accessed 2 January 2017.

Novy, A. (2017): "Emancipatory Economic Deglobalisation: A Polanyian Perspective", *Revista Brasileira de Estudos Urbanos e Regionais* 19(3), 558–579.

Schneider, G. and Underwood, D. (2013): "Introduction to Teaching Social Economics", *Forum for Social Economics* 42(1), 1–4.

Schneidewind, U. et al. (2016): "Transformative Wirtschaftswissenschaft im Kontext nachhaltiger Entwicklung", *IÖW* 31(2), *S*, 30.

Schneidewind, U., Singer-Brodowski, M., Augenstein, K. and Stelzer, F. (2016): *Pledge for a Transformative Science: A Conceptual Framework*. Wuppertal Papers No. 191, http://nbn-resolving.de/urn:nbn:de:bsz:wup4-opus-64142, accessed 1 February 2018.

Part I

Principles for teaching pluralist economics

1 The second opinion

An ethical approach to learning and teaching economics

Alan Freeman

1 Introduction: economics, pluralism, and the right to a second opinion

The chapter suggests that the best way to introduce students to the pluralist method in economics, and thereby heterodox alternatives to the mainstream, is to focus on the ethical responsibilities of the professional economist. Teaching and learning can then be organised around the principle that the economist, analogously with the health practitioner, has a duty to reduce the risk of harm.

As first suggested in Freeman (2015), the primary way in which economists do harm is by unjustifiably claiming that their analyses or recommendations are true when these have not been validated by testing them against alternative explanations of reality. This practice occurs because economics, unlike any other branch of the sciences, adheres to the monotheoretic fallacy (Freeman 2015) that we can develop an adequate understanding of an object of study by pursuing a single theoretical approach, based on a single set of presuppositions, without considering other approaches.

This denies the public the 'right to a second opinion', accepted in health care and other human sciences. This is the right to be informed of all those possible analyses which would lead to alternative courses of action to that recommended by the expert, allowing it the autonomy to make its own informed decisions based on the combination of the advice given, its own experience, and its own requirements.

Monotheoreticism demonstrably leads to false analyses, confirmed by the experience of structural readjustment, shock therapy, the financial crash of 2008, and other areas (DeMartino 2011; Earle et al. 2017; Freeman 2009). This leads to harm because the public either adopts, or consents to, policies that make things worse than they could have been, had alternatives known at the time been adopted in their place. Economists bear responsibility for this harm if they have made unjustified claims of truth, misleading the public into placing trust in their analyses and the courses of action that flow from them.

The primary duty of the economist is to avoid doing harm in this way. To fulfil this duty, the would-be economist must be aware of and capable of deducing, presenting, and clarifying the range of alternative explanations of reality that are relevant in deciding on the courses of action at issue. This practice, called pluralism, is already known to be a scientific requirement in economics (Freeman 2015) because, unless alternative relevant explanations of observed reality have been considered, we cannot justifiably claim that one single explanation has been validated. We can now further clarify that pluralism is not only valid on the grounds of methodology and epistemology, as recognised in the literature and elucidated in many contributions to this volume, but also constitutes an *ethical* duty of any practicing economist – including its teachers and researchers – precisely because it is unethical to inspire trust in a statement that scientifically does not merit it when that trust leads to harm.

No claim is involved that the alternatives are automatically right, or that the public will necessarily make the correct decision, any more than a doctor asserts that patients are better able to cure their conditions than health practitioners. The point is simply that the risk of 'econogenic' harm – harm caused by economists – is greater if the public, or the client, is not informed of the alternatives, just as the risk of iatrogenic harm – harm caused by doctors – is greater if the patient is not informed of the alternatives.[1]

Just as a professional doctor will say, 'I diagnose cancer for which the currently recommended treatment is a combination of surgery and chemotherapy, but there are known risks associated with this; you should consider the following possible alternative treatments', the economist should be able, and required, to say things such as 'I diagnose excessive government spending for which the currently recommended prescription is a combination of austerity, cuts in government spending, deregulation, and privatisation. However, you should consider the alternative diagnosis that the economic problems stem from insufficient government income caused by idle economic capacity, and various alternative prescriptions that this view leads to, such as monetary and fiscal stimuli financed by appropriate taxes and responsible borrowing'.

This principle also governs the equivalent heterodox statement, which might run something like, 'I diagnose inadequate levels of economic activity for which there are a number of prescriptions including monetary stimulus, fiscal demand stimuli, and direct government investment in new capacity, all of which should be considered. However, there are a number of alternative theories, for example that the underlying problem is the lack of controls on government spending. Prescriptions would then range from reigning in the excess to outsourcing inefficient government functions to the private sector'.

The idea that the responsibility of the economist is to propose a range of possible alternatives, along with the reasons for preferring one over the other, is hence, as increasingly recognised, a systemic and comprehensive antidote to the reigning logical positivist idea that the economists' responsibility is to be 'technically competent' in prescribing a single package of policy options derived from the single theoretical framework of prevailing orthodoxy.

This chapter makes a further proposal: that pluralism, thus defined, is not merely superior as a practice but as *pedagogy* – a means of enabling the student to learn. That is to say, it is a better way to learn and (therefore) a better way to teach.

2 Pluralism as pedagogical best practice

Because pluralism is thus a general principle applying to all of economics, not just an antidote to orthodoxy, we can evolve and assess general pedagogic methods in economics based on it. The novelty of this chapter's approach, as noted above, is that it treats monotheoreticism as an ethical in addition to a scientific failure; pluralism thus constitutes an ethical duty.

This approach provides a pedagogical reason for pluralism, a rather critical point. Much pluralist writing on education starts from epistemological or methodological bases for pluralism and then addresses the problems arising from the entrenched resistance of course designers from within the subject. The pluralist pedagogue, in any subject, is often up against the unwritten convention that the subject specialists 'know' what is to be taught, so that the only problem is how to teach it. Why 'waste time' familiarising students with what is 'known' to be untrue? The informed pedagogical answer is, of course, that even if we are 100% certain of our present knowledge, it is only by encountering ideas that contradict said knowledge that the student can learn. A yet more precise answer is that in any case, the student is tasked not merely with acquiring some fixed thing called 'knowledge' but with learning how to generate new knowledge, which requires her to be capable of interrogating ideas critically and experimenting with alternatives.

Economics presents a further damaging twist to this uninformed prejudice. Uniquely, the subject specialists define 'knowledge' of the subject as mastery of a single legitimate methodological approach. The case for reform thereby appears internal to the subject, leading to a permanent uphill battle. As Dow (2009, 53) puts it:

> When the impression has been created that there is only one legitimate approach to economics (within which there may be differences of theory and method, but not methodology), it is hard to get across a methodologically-pluralist approach.

Ethical responsibility is a different starting point: it is a generic curricular requirement. It follows from the fact that the student, when she becomes a practitioner, will have influence in society, which she should know how to exercise responsibly. The conduct of experts is as important as the expertise itself – otherwise the infamous Josef Mengele, who justified lethal experiments in the death camps on the grounds that the knowledge gained would contribute to medical science, should be celebrated as a pioneering investigator. Ethics is, for precisely this reason, increasingly recognised as a generic requirement of learning at the higher education level, indeed especially – and interestingly – in technological subjects (Fry et al. 2009, 295–296). A growing number of universities publicly and explicitly state (see e.g. Sheffield 2011) that any and every student that graduates from the university will be ethically aware and competent.

This point is poorly understood and therefore worth establishing at greater length. In 2007 the Association for Heterodox Economics (Freeman 2007), in response to an exercise by the UK's Quality Assurance Agency (QAA), compared benchmarked curricula in a range of subjects and found that economics was alone in omitting any requirement for diversity. The point is stark when these benchmarks are studied. The following extracts are taken from the responses of the other subjects.

> **Theology**
>
> Given that constant new development has been the characteristic of the field of TRS [Theology and Religions Studies] since the latter half of the twentieth century, both in the UK and elsewhere, it is vital that any definition of the subject does not constrain future innovation . . . Much of the excitement of the discipline lies in its contested nature.
>
> **Accountancy**
>
> [K]nowledge and understanding of some of the alternative technical languages and practices of accounting (for example, alternative recognition rules and valuation bases, accounting rules followed in other socio-economic domains, alternative managerial accounting approaches to control and decision-making) . . . the ability to critically evaluate such theories and evidence.
>
> **Earth sciences**
>
> It is stressed that the examples which follow should not be taken as prescriptive but are presented to illustrate the variation in emphasis from subject areas which can be described as natural sciences-based to those characterised as more social sciences or humanities-based.
>
> **History**
>
> We have seen our task as the following: to lay out criteria for judging the suitability and adequacy of single-honours degree courses in history; to do this in a way that is as specific as possible without undermining the principle that there are many different suitable and adequate ways of constructing and making available the great richness and diversity of history; to do it in a way that recognises also the need for adaptability to new academic developments in the field, and innovations in course structures and teaching methods.
>
> **Geography**
>
> The breadth of geography means that many of its core constituents can be approached through a number of routes, and so any attempts at prescription must be discarded; institutions offering degree programmes in geography must be free to decide upon the details of content and organisation. A valued characteristic of the discipline is its plurality of ways of knowing and understanding the world, and the depth to which individual specialisms are studied will vary according to the nature of specific departments.

The AHE's report (Freeman 2007, 8) concluded that

> Faced with a benchmark less critical of its prescriptions than theology and which attaches less importance to diversity than accountancy, it is hard to accept that iterative reform is a practical procedure. This is why we consider a complete rethink to be necessary. Such a complete rethink should review the QAA statements of the whole of the peer disciplines with which, it is recognised in the statement, economists should be able to interact.

In short, the problematic can and should be reversed: pluralism is a requirement of good curricular practice which is generally recognised in other subjects, and economics sticks out like a very sore thumb. The problem of economics course design is not 'introducing' pluralism into the curriculum against the received wisdom of the subject specialists but bringing the teaching of the subject into line with recognised modern curricular principles.

This becomes clearer the more we study the issues involved in curriculum design. A central such problem, evident in alternative curricula which adopt the mantle of heterodoxy while discarding pluralism (see Coyle 2012; INET 2011 and the critical response from Morgan et al. 2014), is an issue I will term the 'pluralist selection problem' or 'selection problem' for short:[2] which, out of many alternative approaches, should be presented in a course, and how much weight should be assigned to each of them?

First, an ethical standpoint resolves this problem in a strikingly clear manner. The approaches that should be included are those which the would-be economist needs to know, in order to identify the alternatives relevant to the problems she will be called on to answer. These are of two types. Some are more or less directly relevant to a practical question, such as trade policy, public choice, or fiscal policy. In each such field, the range of options which lead to clearly different conclusions is usually limited and accessible.

Second, the student needs to be familiar with the 'underpinnings' – the theoretical foundations – of such options. To understand the rationale for a state-led development theory, for example, the economist cannot make do with a concept of trade rooted in the theory of comparative advantage; she needs to be familiar with theories of uneven development, unequal exchange, and so on, not to mention the theoretical frameworks usually employed to understand the state's potential developmental role, notably Keynesian, Marxist, and institutionalist theories. It is not difficult to see that with a little thought and application, this can lead to a well-grounded curriculum offering a range of specialisations to the student, without in any way constraining her to master one single body of theory or one single set of technical skills.

The approach thereby resolves, in a quite satisfactory way, the problem of rationale. This arises, among other reasons, because it is hard for students to know, in advance of receiving tuition, why the material being presented is relevant. This is especially important in economics, when much teaching of a highly technical nature is simply presented to the students without any real explanation of what it is for, leading to frequently repeated and probably legitimate objections, especially from students, that the focus on mathematics technique is at best an obstacle, and at worst a substitute, for discussing the real world (Lawson 2006; PAE 2016; PCES 2015; RE 2017).

The problems of selection and rationale intersect when students have to navigate through a curriculum structure and make their own selections about which subjects to specialise in. The ethical approach, I will argue, provides a practical approach to both problems and, thereby, a coherent general framework for pluralist curriculum design.

3 Economics, the non-specialist, and the cult of the expert

In this middle section of the chapter, I will try to explain the relation between the 'ethical approach to pluralist economic pedagogy' and the various traditions from which it emerges. This is needed, I think, both because the history of any theory is an important element of its development, and because the approach as far as I know is novel, which can be an obstacle to acceptance, unless I can convince my readers that it is a synthesis of existing work, not a replacement, and that it both preserves the most important elements of what went before, and addresses one or two critical problems that these prior traditions have noted as important but have not solved to their own satisfaction.

This chapter draws on a 15-year history of research on the place of pluralism and heterodoxy in economics (Lee 2007; Lee and Harley 1998; Lee et al. 2013) and the adverse consequences of its absence (Chick and Dow 2001; Dow 2009; Freeman 2009; Freeman et al. 2014; Earle et al. 2017), leading to a wide range of student movements for pluralism across the world (see ISIPE 2015; RE 2017 for comprehensive lists). This has been accompanied by an impressive literature on pluralist pedagogy (Denis 2009; Groenewegen 2007; McGoldrick 2009; Mearman 2011; Morgan et al. 2014; Negru 2010; Reardon 2009, and many others).

The idea of an ethical approach to pedagogy, I believe, constitutes a potentially pathbreaking extension of this tradition. I attempt to integrate it into the pioneering work of DeMartino and McCloskey (2015), and their co-workers and predecessors (Zingales 2013; Thompson 1983, 1987; see also DeMartino 2011; Amy 1984) for which pluralism is not (yet) a central focus, but which has put the issue of ethical conduct at the forefront of recent debates in the United States, with considerable success.[3]

For those in the 'pluralist-heterodox' stream, a focus on ethics can seem a departure or even a diversion. I will argue, however, that it makes sense of pluralist methodology in a way that has been to some extent obstructed by a focus on technical details until now. An ethical approach grounds the need for pluralism in the actual social function of economists today; it asks, 'How can one be a good economist?'

As a result, an ethical approach explains to the non-economist why pluralism is required and why society should demand it. The moment one asks what makes for good economists, one has to ask, 'What kind of economists does society need?'

This starting point has many advantages: not least, it explains the importance of disputes whose technical complexity appears, to the non-specialist, to be too difficult to warrant meddling with.

It should, I hope, be clear why non-specialist perceptions are relevant to pedagogy: every student of economics starts her professional life as a non-specialist. A beginning student is almost by definition a person whose state of knowledge should be assumed to be no different from that of an ordinary member of the public. The student who sets out to be a good economist therefore faces a set of problems not that different from a non-economist who would like to know how to tell good economists from bad ones, preferably before experiencing their ministrations.

The common factor is that in both cases, the person needs to know why it could be important to study a particular approach or theory. Most difficult of all, for such a person, is to understand why one has to study more than one particular approach.

This reaction produces bafflement among heterodox economists understandably frustrated by the actions of funders and providers who support, defend, and award prizes to teachers of economic theories that they know in their heart of hearts have got things seriously wrong. Discussions with public servants, education providers, and practical business people reveals deep unease about the profession.[4] What explains their reluctance to confront its weaknesses?

Certainly, a non-ignorable factor is the regulatory capture of economics by private interests (Freeman 2009; Zingales 2013). It is convenient, for politicians, bankers, and corporate providers alike, to have economic experts who can help them justify otherwise unpopular policies. This is, however, not the only problem: non-specialists find it difficult to involve themselves because mainstream-heterodox controversies are actually hard to understand. An increasingly angry section of the public may accept that neoliberalism, in addition to destroying social services, causes rising inequality and various other social evils, but far fewer have grappled with the case for government involvement in investment. This accounts for the paradox that a big section of the American working classes, exasperated with the corrosive neoliberalism of the Democrats, has voted to replace it with the explosively destructive neoliberalism of Donald Trump.

The 'difficulty' of understanding economic disputes is a considerable problem for heterodoxy because the lay public, faced with a bewildering mass of technical and often obscure arguments, naturally reacts by expecting the experts to sort it out for themselves. The problem is that economics has proven incapable of doing just that, which is why a public intervention is required. However, even if the public wants to change economics, it needs to be able to understand, in non-technical terms, the difference between good and bad economic practice in order to promote the good and root out the bad.

The basic pluralist response to the non-specialist question, 'How do I tell a good economist from a bad one?' is that monotheoretic practice is a sure sign of an unprofessional economist, unconditionally bad, and likely to end in tears. As for what is good, while pluralism is not a guarantee of merit, it is a precondition of it. The case for this answer is not, however, as transparent as we pluralists like to think. Superficially, it conflicts with what we expect of an expert. If you hire a builder to make a house, you don't expect him to make two of them. When the lay public has a technical question, we are superficially inclined to think it has a single answer, or at least a single 'best' answer, and equally superficially it appears that this is what experts are for. Of course, we get annoyed if the answer is wrong, but the natural response of the non-specialist is to expect one right answer, not two.

It is at this point that two important strands of the new thinking intersect. The first, which DeMartino has inserted into the discussion on ethical conduct, is an earlier critique of the 'neutral' advisor (Amy 1984; Thompson 1983, 1987). Expertise is paid for, which leads directly to the question, 'Is the client paying for the expert, or for the answer?' In a system where one set of answers gets the funding, and the awkward answers don't, the expert is not playing a neutral role. Regulatory capture is relevant here; this is why, given the role of Big Pharma, the responsibility of the expert is of particular concern in medicine.

Whether neutral advice is existentially possible is a philosophically complex question. But we can set aside these complexities by noting that actually, we don't really like experts to give a single answer. Even when we take such simple advice as the salesperson's recommendation for a washing machine, a car, or a computer, we expect a knowledgeable account of the field. When we hire plumbers, engineers, architects, or lawyers, the first thing we check out these days are the rating pages.

In short, the function of an expert is not to give us an answer but to help us make an informed choice. But the need for a diversity of opinions does not stop when we hire the expert. We don't expect an architect to dump a plan on our lap with the words 'take it or leave it, my invoice is in the post'. In a session with a lawyer, a doctor, or even an accountant, we expect and we get advice on the range of possibilities. In health, as DeMartino points out, the principle of 'patient autonomy', meaning the need to ensure the patient is involved in decision-making in an informed way, is widely recognised. Indeed, in the world of expert services the more expensive the purchase, the more choice is offered. When hiring economic expertise that pays for the future of a country, a little bit of consumer sovereignty would not go amiss.

In short, *quaesitor oeconomica*, the idealised economic expert, is as mythical as *Homo oeconomicus*, the idealised economic agent. Indeed, when it comes to the control of our own bodies, we are less inclined to trust the expert unquestioningly than when fixing the plumbing. In the field of health, the public is not only familiar with many issues but actively seeks knowledge, as can be seen from the wealth of medical websites, forums, and treatment alternatives. People do not just desire more than one answer, but if anything, insist on it. If, therefore, we explain the reason for pluralism in these terms – that is, to argue that in matters of economic health the right to a second opinion is just as essential as in private health – we are making an argument that can be understood. There is a solid, non-specialist case for pluralist practice and therefore an equally solid case for pluralist teaching.

4 Selection, rationale, and progression: confronting the fallacy of imposed choice

The relevance of ethical responsibility to pedagogy now takes a recognisable shape. The fundamental thing we want from our economists is that, confronted with any real-world problem, they will assist and permit us to minimise the risk of embarking on economically harmful courses of action. To this end, we want them to help us make informed judgements. This in turn requires the economist, just like the doctor, to report not just the one single recommendation of the economic authorities but to inform us about the relevant alternatives.

As noted, an immediate consequence is that the ethical approach offers an answer to the selection problem. In a report on economic development, for example, the ethical duty is not to present an exhaustive intellectual account of all known theories of commerce. It is a duty to consider notable alternatives to the view that is presented as the principal conclusion of the reporter. So if the reporter advocates the structural adjustment doctrine of deregulation, full trade liberalisation and privatisation, she or he has the duty to ensure the reader may access and study the alternatives and principal objections by directing the reader to their sources, such as the 'other canon' and developmental literature. Equally, a reporter who advocates capital controls, state-led investment, and national economic sovereignty should ensure the reader is aware of significant mainstream critiques of the heterodox conclusions drawn.

The duty is not 100% symmetric. Since the mainstream literature is generally more accessible to the normal reader, it is more important for a heterodox writer to address mainstream critiques than draw the reader's attention to a vast literature with which she is doubtless familiar.

Nevertheless, in each case, the duty is what I would term 'emancipatory'; the reader must be *freed* to make her own judgement, and to this end the writer must provide access to the information relevant to that judgement. This is entirely consistent with the liberal democratic concept of 'informed choice'. Dow rightly informs us that to a choice between one single option and nothing at all is not, in any meaningful sense, a choice. But the injury is multiplied a hundredfold if the reader is compelled to make her choice in total ignorance of the options.

This implies a further duty to present these alternatives 'fairly' – in such a way that the audience understands the reasons behind them, which includes their theoretical underpinnings. It follows, as night from day, that the student must be familiar with these underpinnings: she must be equally conversant with Ricardo's theory of comparative advantage and the theories of uneven development and unequal exchange.

In order to see the relevance of this approach, and rebut the commonplace and, one must say, vulgar and trivial objections that meet this simple idea, let us consider three related alternative solutions which I will call the *fallacy of limited time, the fallacy of recognised authority*, and *the fallacy of necessary complexity*. These are all variants of the fallacy of imposed choice, the notion that we can deduce the choice to be made from the fact that it has to be made.[5]

We begin with the ur-fallacy of limited time, as articulated by Samuelson (1987, 52):

> Shortly after 1930 economics burst out into new life. At least four revolutions erupted: the monopolistic competition revolution, the Keynesian macro revolution, the mathematicization revolution, and the econometric inference revolution. Graduate students need at least 4 hours a night of sleep: that is a universal constant. So something had to give in the economics curriculum. What gave, and gave out, was History of Thought.

The problem is this: the fact that time is in limited supply tells us nothing about how to use it. One might as well say that because it takes a long time to understand the skeleton, bone doctors should be exempt from studying the pelvis. If an idea is required for mastery of the subject, it should be taught.

In common with all variants of the fallacy of imposed choice, Samuelson's argument makes a problem out of something unproblematic. It ignores the standard curricular solution to the limitations of time, namely progression. That which cannot be absorbed in a 101 course must be taught in a 201 course. There is no reason at all, having selected two or more approaches to fiscal policy, trade theory, monetary theory, the economics of finance, or the theory of agent behaviour, not to teach each approach to an elementary level in year one, an intermediate level in year two, and an advanced level in year three. If things are really that difficult (and we strongly suspect they are not), the profession could require fully trained economists to take extra years in masterships, doctorates, or habilitations, or like doctors or lawyers to take articles in recognised practices before being declared fit to unleash on the public.

All the revolutions in Samuelson's heaven, plus the unaccountably omitted revolutions of input-output analysis, optimal path theory, conjunctural analysis, and planning theory, all originating in Russia in his day, can be taught together with their history, provided one only allows the student to study each at the due level of complexity required of a systematic progression in knowledge and understanding.

This illustrates the fallacy in all limited choice arguments: they claim that when circumstances force us to make a choice, we can work out what to do by the fact of being forced. But choices have to be made on grounds that stand on their own. Even if we don't know the full answer, the correct choice is neither 'what we have always done' nor 'what the authorities recommend' but a method of enquiring into the options in a coherent and consistent way. This is exactly what an ethical approach provides.

It will help to explore some common defences of monotheoretic practice, especially those offered under the mantle of pluralism. Vromen (2007, 72f) deserves especial attention for the unity of purpose involved in conjoining two specious prejudices in a single harmonious trope.

> I believe that it is better that students get a solid training in a particular school, tradition, and approach than that they only touch upon, in a rather facile way,

> various schools and approaches. And it seems obvious to me that this particular school, tradition and approach should be the one that is dominating the discipline.

The basic error is aptly addressed by Tucholsky (1995 [1927]):

> Laß dir von keinem Fachmann imponieren, der dir erzählt: 'Lieber Freund, das mache ich schon seit zwanzig Jahren so!' – Man kann eine Sache auch zwanzig Jahre lang falsch machen.[6]

The test of a scientific theory is whether it works, not who likes it. On the admission of the leading practitioners of economics themselves, of which Greenspan's confession (Norris 2008) is only the most famous among many post hoc admissions, an unacceptable proportion of mainstream recommendations have failed to produce the promised outcomes and have caused great damage and hurt. In contrast, alternatives – notably the Chinese economic approach – perform as well or indeed better than the 'tradition[s] dominating the mainstream'.[7] If an explanation works, the student should be aware of it. If it works better than the alternatives, the student should be competent in it. If it is known to lessen the risk of harm, the student should be proficient in it.

There are thus no special grounds for favouring the existing authorities over their critics and indeed, there are substantial grounds for the opposite. But another interpretation of the argument offers itself: perhaps Vromen means that the authorities are the best guide to their own critics? This is a very common but reprehensible response to heterodox economists who point out that biased peer review is inevitable if their papers are judged by their opponents.[8]

The underlying argument is that even though orthodox economists disagree with heterodox approaches, they have mastered techniques, skills, methods of learning, or methods of analysis which equip them better than anyone else to judge their critics.

Unfortunately, it is equally possible that we critics have mastered techniques and so forth which equip us better than anyone else to judge the authorities. Authority provides no logical ground for choice. It presents a symmetric issue – two or more points of view equally qualified to comment on each other – as if it were an asymmetric issue, so that somehow one particular view is uniquely better qualified to comment on everyone else. In particular, there is no justification for supposing that an entrenched majority is more likely to be right (about anything) just because it is entrenched. Indeed, if anything, history suggests that the newly arrived minority, having grappled with the failings of its predecessors, frequently grasps the errors that led to these failings first, and better, than the established authorities.

The argument from necessary complexity[9] is a further variant. The adroitly understated underpinning of Vromen's statement is the idea that entrenched authority is best qualified to educate because difficulty is inherent in the subject. Attempts to present alternatives would be 'facile', because given this inherent difficulty, the best option is a master-apprentice relationship ceding pride of place to those who have grappled longest with the subject matter.

Apart from the facts that as noted, critics grapple harder, and that many would consider it equally facile to present the neoclassical arcana in less than a lifetime, there is no necessary relation between complexity and validity. To the contrary, complexity, however defined, normally arises when a paradigm is stretched beyond its capacity to explain what is seen. Most important advances in science are acts of simplification, which achieve their results by cutting through unwonted complexity, rendering it unnecessary. Pre-Galilean mathematical astronomy was very complex (see Lattis 1995), however this was because the Sun does not go around the Earth, not because the complexity solved anything useful.

The true difficulty of knowledge consists only in making the required leaps, at the appropriate time, from old ways of thinking to the new. The argument from recognised authority does not resolve the problem of difficulty but perpetuates it by venerating obstinate resistance to the obvious.

Again, the fallacy is a device for avoiding the essential symmetry in the relation between conflicting views. It is an attempt to 'pre-select' one particular alternative on no logical or evidential grounds. Actually, there is no reason students should not be given an equal exposure, in a course on international economics, trade, or development, to theories that have evolved from Ricardo's theory of comparative advantage, and those such as unequal exchange or dependency theory that arise from the theory of uneven development, and there is nothing 'facile' in providing proper systems of curricular progression to ensure that, at each stage, the student grasps the principles of each to the level required of the qualification.

What is facile is to suggest that one approach should be prioritised over the other because it happens to be more complicated. This is of no use at all if the reason for its complication is that it is wrong. The technically difficult developments of Ricardo's theory of comparative advantage, such as the Heckscher-Ohlin trade theory or the factor-price equalisation theorem, are certainly more sophisticated mathematically but are equally at variance with the known facts of both development and national inequality. The fact that they are harder to understand is no basis for dropping other less complex theories which, whatever their limitations, furnish at least some basis for understanding the immense and growing disparities in national income that dominated the 20th century. It might mean adding a second unit where advanced student can study the controversies in more depth, but as a justification for a monotheoretic curriculum, neither the shortage of time nor the requirement of expertise holds any water at all.

5 Concluding remarks: on the practicality of pluralism

At that point in every long intellectual journey when things 'fall into place', two contradictory phenomena make their appearance. Of these, the more important is that many of the things which have appeared difficult or intractable suddenly become easy. Once it is recognised that it is impossible to teach any subject without an ethical standpoint, the rationale for doing it in economics becomes completely unproblematic. Once we realise that the positive-normative distinction so beloved of economists stands in quicksand, as soon as we recognise the simple fact that economists get things wrong, the neutrality of the expert sinks without trace. Once we realise that monotheoretic practice wilfully increases the risk of wrong judgements, it becomes clear that it constitutes a derogation of ethical responsibility. Once the ethical standpoint is adopted, the 'pluralist selection problem' ceases to exist. And so on.

At the same time, other things we once thought were simple turn out to be much more complicated than we imagined. In particular, the vexed question, 'Do economists lie?' turns out to be a lot more complicated than it appears at first sight. Sometimes they definitely do, and brazenly so; this particular investigation will certainly not be complete until historians of thought have picked over the conduct of the two renowned economists who gave Iceland a clean bill of health just before its crash for a fee approaching half a million dollars (see Wade and Sigurgeirsdóttir 2013); it would be reasonable to ask whether, having made history as the only country to jail its miscreant bankers, Iceland has a case also for indicting their accomplices, or at least asking for its money back.

That said, lying is not the problem. As DeMartino notes, the great majority of economists are earnestly concerned about their integrity and try to conduct themselves according to what they believe, from their training, is professionally correct. The problem is what their training tells them: it trains them to claim that the things they say are true when there is no sound basis for doing so. This is not lying, but neither is it telling the truth. To make a complex matter yet more complicated, it cannot even be described as a falsehood. To paraphrase Lincoln,[10] some things they say are true most of the time, and most things are true at least some of the time, but almost nothing they say is true all the time. They are not necessarily wrong, which is what we would need to confirm to describe them as falsehoods. But they are also not right. They are not 'true statements' in the normal sense of the word, as something that we can rely on when making a decision.

What's wrong with them is that we don't in fact know whether they are true or not, because we haven't exercised the due diligence that genuinely scientific practice demands. Even this is an inadequate description of the problem, because specialists other than economists will frequently make statements that are 'likely but unconfirmed' or 'the best we can do in current circumstances'. The real problem is that economists are educated to claim that their findings are true when they have no right to do so and, importantly, when no other profession would dare make such claims before checking out their power to explain reality against the power of the alternatives. To put it another way, these statements are very far from the best that can be done and are not merely unconfirmed but unchecked, which is a rather different matter.

In Freeman (2015), I coined the term 'untruth' to describe a statement that is portrayed as true when the basis for this claim does not exist. This however conveys the whiff of falsehood or falsification, which is, as explained above, not what's at stake. The term 'non-truth' might more neutrally convey the idea. At this point, however, there is a different direction to go in, which arises from my private response to post-modernist colleagues who object that the concept of untruth implies a concept of truth. I don't think this is so, but it may help to pose the matter in terms of unjustified trust or confidence.

Economics makes claims, for statements about the real world, which leads its listeners to trust the claims and act on them. Sometimes, this trust might be justified – I don't rule that out. The problem is that, in the dismal history of the subject, practicing economists habitually and regularly inspired unjustified trust, and great harm has resulted. The ethical duty of the economist is then to minimise the risk of unjustified trust, for which of course pluralism is the remedy.

This being so, I conclude by insisting that this chapter is a starting point, not a finished work. I have shown how to approach the solution of the selection problem, which is not the same as solving it. I have suggested how we can, and should, seek to convince the providers of economics education that they need to intervene in the way economics curricula are constructed – something they are always unwilling to do – because current practice violates general curricular principles for which they are responsible. I haven't shown how to win the argument; I've just supplied what I think is a better argument.

I cannot predict if the argument will be won, and I believe that, in the profound sense of Keynes, the outcome of the argument is uncertain. This arises from a Heisenbergian circumstance, namely we are ourselves both the observers and agents of our own condition. 'Economics', conceived of as something marginally more profound than 'what economists do', is an *institution*. It is a material entity, sustained by an unholy combination of state, academic, and financial sources, which employs upwards of 50,000 diligent intellectuals worldwide,[11] principally in occupations in which job security consists – not to put too fine a point on it – of toeing the line. The principal function of this institution is to provide justifications for the policies that its financiers wish to implement. However, it has a secondary function, which is to set limits on the imprudent social consequences of an over-enthusiastic implementation of these same policies. The institution has a residual instinct for survival, however suicidal its recommendations have been for some time. The question is whether this instinct will be sufficient to offer some kind of resistance to the abusive practices its patrons have successfully imposed upon it.

The prospects are not bright. To advocate too stridently for pluralism is to put oneself, like Luther, on the wrong side of where that line is currently drawn by the mere blasphemous act of demanding that a truly free citizen must be allowed freely to interpret the alleged 'will' of the market – and, by revolutionary implication, seek political institutions capable of supplanting the will of free humans for the whims of a market economy.

However, the line itself is drawn by material forces. Even those who finance the institution of economics are keenly aware of their love child's limitations and, like all good risk-taking capitalists, recognise the need for a plan B.

I therefore think that, subject to the impulse of an informed resistance, a tipping point has been reached: I think a pluralist curriculum is a practical proposition; in a number of institutions progress is being made towards it. I think in the not too distant future, consistently and coherently pluralist economics curricula will be put in place in one or more institutions, in discussion and agreement with the administrations in those universities, which will serve as a beacon, because they will show that it is possible to do things differently, and because the results will be better. A number of things will then happen. Employers will take notice and begin to seek out students from these institutions. Countries ill-served by orthodoxy will (perhaps surreptitiously, but hopefully brazenly) promote centres of learning in which pluralism is openly recognised as the most likely source of useful policies. Universities will become proud of their distinctive pluralist economist departments, which will make a difference in many things. And, not least, the students of these institutions will make their way into the world, beat the pants off the monotheoreticists in their cohort, and serve as the best possible proof of the pluralist ideal: by making it work.

Notes

1 See DeMartino (2011) for a full definition and explanation of iatrogenic and econogenic harm.
2 Curriculum theory generally deals with the selection of subject matter under the heading 'syllabus', but the phrase 'syllabus problem' somehow fails to get the point across.
3 While I fully acknowledge these contributions, responsibility for my interpretation and presentation of them (including errors) is of course my own.
4 See, for example, the introduction to PCES 2014 by Andrew Haldane of the Bank of England, or Queen Elizabeth's well-known question to the director of the London School of Economics' (LSE's) economics department (Pierce 2008). Freeman (2009) gives a fuller list. Concern among economists themselves is extensive: membership of the pluralist World Economics Association (WEA 2017) reached 13,500 by 2017; see also AIRLEAP (2017).
5 This critical treatment of these responses might seem in violation of pluralism. The pluralist duty is however to *present* the alternatives, not to present them favourably. The reader must be able to form an independent judgement; that is why I provide original text, citations, and interpretations of the reasoning behind the arguments I criticise. That's what pluralism consists of. Today's monotheoretic economist does not even mention, let alone give access to, the alternatives to his own views.
6 'Don't let any expert impress you by explaining "Dear friend, I've been doing it this way for twenty years!" You can also do something wrong for twenty years'.
7 The economic theories of Deng Xiaoping, arguably the most successful of modern times, are virtually absent from mainstream curricula. See Ross (2014). See Reinert (2007) for a systematic account of the alternative 'canon' to the mainstream, and Reinert and Ghosh (2016) for a broad exposition of heterodox development theory.
8 See Lee (2002) for an informative account of the history of the UK Association for Heterodox Economics, formed precisely because the Royal Economics Society insisted (and still insists) that mainstream reviewers are best equipped to pass judgement on heterodox papers they profoundly disagree with. See also Gans and Shepherd (1994) on the extraordinary incidence, in economics, of papers being rejected and going on to become classics and win prizes.
9 A referee has kindly suggested I should address the complex issue, 'What is complexity?' I would love to. However, in this chapter I address a fallacy, that of 'necessary complexity'. I limit myself to clarifying its erroneous consequences. It is up to those responsible for the fallacy to dispel its conceptual origins.
10 I attribute to Lincoln in deference to popular belief. On the accuracy of this belief, see http://historynewsnetwork.org/article/161924.
11 A back-of-the-envelope estimate based on US figures in DeMartino (2011).

References

AIRLEAP (Association for Integrity and Responsible Leadership in Economics and Associated Professions) (2017): "Home Page", www.airleap.org, accessed 20 January 2017.

Amy, D. J. (1984): "Why Policy Analysis and Ethics Are Incompatible", *Journal of Policy Analysis and Management* 3(4), 573–591.

Chick, V. and Dow, S. C. (2001): "Formalism, Logic and Reality: A Keynesian Analysis", *Cambridge Journal of Economics* 25(6), 705–721.

Coyle, D. (ed.) (2012): *What's the Use of Economics?* London: London Publishing Partnership.

DeMartino, G. (2011): *The Economist's Oath: On the Need for and Content of Professional Economic Ethics*. Oxford: Oxford University Press.

DeMartino, G. and McCloskey, D. (eds.) (2015): *The Oxford Handbook of Professional Economic Ethics*. Oxford: Oxford University Press.

Denis, A. (2009): "Pluralism in Economics Education", *Editorial in International Review of Economics Education* 8(2), December, 6–22.

Dow, S. C. (2009): "History of Thought and Methodology in Pluralist Economics Education", *International Review of Economics Education* 8(2), December, 41–57.

Earle, J., Moran, C. and Ward-Perkins, Z. (2017): *The Econocracy: The Perils of Leaving Economics to the Experts*. Manchester: Manchester University Press.

Freeman, A. (2007): "Catechism versus Pluralism: The Heterodox Response to the National Undergraduate Curriculum Proposed by the UK Quality Assurance Authority", http://mpra.ub.uni-muenchen.de/6832/, accessed 20 January 2017.

Freeman, A. (2009): "The Economists of Tomorrow: The Case for a Pluralist Subject Benchmark Statement for Economics", *International Review of Economics Education* 8(2), December, 23–40.

Freeman, A. (2015): "First Tell No Untruth", in DeMartino and McCloskey *op. cit.*

Freeman, A., Chick, V. and Kayatekin, S. (2014): "Introduction", in Freeman, A., Chick, V. and Kayatekin, S. (eds.), *Whig History and the Reinterpretation of Economic History*. Special edition of the *Cambridge Journal of Economics* 38(3), May.

Fry, H., Ketteridge, S. and Marshall, S. (2009): *A Handbook for Teaching and Learning in Higher Education*. 3rd edition. London: Routledge.

Gans, J. S. and Shepherd, S. (1994): "How Are the Mighty Fallen: Rejected Classic Articles by Leading Economists", *Journal of Economic Perspectives* 8(1), March, 165–179.

Groenewegen, J. (ed.) (2007): *Teaching Pluralism in Economics*. Cheltenham, UK: Edward Elgar.

INET. (2011): *Building a Global Community of New Economic Thinkers: Inaugural Annual Report 2010–2011*. New York: INET, http://ineteconomics.org/sites/inet.civicactions.net/files/inet-annual-report-2010-2011.pdf

ISIPE (International Student Initiative for Pluralist Economics) (2016): "An International Student Call for Pluralism in Economics", www.isipe.net/open-letter/, accessed 20 January 2017.

Lattis, J. M. (1995): *Between Copernicus and Galileo: Christoph Clavius and the Collapse of Ptolemaic Cosmology*. 1st edition. Chicago: University of Chicago Press.

Lawson, T. (2006): "The Nature of Heterodox Economics", *Cambridge Journal of Economics* 30(4), 483–505.

Lee, F. (2002): "Early History of the Association for Heterodox Economics", Published on the AHE, http://hetecon.net/?page=about&side=early_history_of_the_ahe, accessed 21 January 2017.

Lee, F. (2007): "The Research Assessment Exercise, the State and the Dominance of Mainstream Economics in British Universities", *Cambridge Journal of Economics* 31(2), 309–325.
Lee, F. and Harley, S. (1998): "Peer Review, the Research Assessment Exercise and the Demise of Non-Mainstream Economics", *Capital and Class* (66), 23–53.
Lee, F., Pham, X. and Gu, G. (2013): "The UK Research Assessment Exercise and the Narrowing of UK Economics", *Cambridge Journal of Economics* 37(4), 693–717.
McGoldrick, K. M. (2009): "Pluralism and Economic Education, Promoting Change: Past, Present, and Future", in Garnett, R., Olsen, E. and Starr, M. (eds.), *Economic Pluralism*. Abingdon, UK: Routledge, 221–225.
Mearman, A. (2011): "How Should Economics Curricula Be Evaluated?", *International Review of Economics Education* 10(2), 50–62.
Morgan, J., Philp, B., Cronin, B., Bigo, V., Chick, V., Desai, R., Ekeland, A., Freeman, A., Hermann, A., Lee, F., Mearman, A., Negru, I., Olsen, W., Reardon, J. and Wells, J. (2014): *Pluralism, Heterodoxy, and the Prospects for a New Economics Curriculum: Assessing the Potential of INET, "What's the Use of Economics", and the CORE Project*. Association for Heterodox Economics, February.
Negru, I. (2010): "Plurality to Pluralism in Economics Pedagogy: The Role of Critical Thinking", *International Journal for Pluralism in Economics Education* 1(3), 185–193.
Norris, F. (2008): "Greenspan's Lament", *New York Times*, 28 October.
PAE (2016 [2000]): "Lettre ouverte des étudiants en économie", *Le Monde*, 17 June, www.autisme-economie.org, accessed 31 December 2016.
PCES (Post-Crash Economics Society) (2015): *Economics, Education and Unlearning: Economics Education at the University of Manchester*. With a foreword by Andrew Haldane (Bank of England). London: PCES.
Pierce, A. (2008): "The Queen Asks Why No One Saw the Credit Crunch Coming", *The Daily Telegraph*, 5 November.
RE (Rethinking Economics) (2017): "Home Page", www.rethinkeconomics.org/, accessed 20 January 2017.
Reardon, J. (ed.) (2009): *Advances in Heterodox Economics*. London, UK and New York: Routledge.
Reinert, E. (2007): *How Rich Countries Got Rich . . . and Why Poor Countries Stay Poor*. London: Constable.
Reinert, E. and Ghosh, J. (2016): *Handbook of Alternative Theories of Economic Development*. Aldershot, UK and London: Edward Elgar.
Ross, J. (2014): *Deng Xiaoping: The World's Greatest Economist*, www.china.org.cn/opinion/2014-08/22/content_33303318.htm
Samuelson, P. (1987): "Out of the Closet: A Program for the Whig History of Economic Science: Keynote Address at History of Economics Society Boston Meeting, June 20, 1987", *Bulletin of the History of Economic Thought* 9(1), 51–60.
Sheffield University (2011): *Student Attributes*, www.sheffield.ac.uk/sheffieldgraduate/studentattributes, accessed 20 January 2017.
Thompson, D. F. (1983): "Ascribing Responsibility to Advisors in Government", *Ethics* 93(3), 546–560.
Thompson, D. F. (1987): *Political Ethics and Public Office*. Cambridge, MA: Harvard University Press.
Tucholsky, K. (1995 [1927]): *Schnipsel*. Hamburg: Rowohlt.
Vromen, J. (2007): "In Praise of Moderate Plurality", in Groenewegen, J. (ed.), *Teaching Pluralism in Economics*. Cheltenham: Edward Elgar, 64–94.

Wade, R. and Sigurgeirsdóttir, S. (2013): "How to Discredit a Financial Regulator: The Strange Case of Iceland", *TripleCrisis*, http://triplecrisis.com/the-strange-case-of-iceland/

WEA (World Economics Association) (2017): "Home Page", www.wea.org, accessed 20 January 2017.

Zingales, L. (2013): "Preventing Economists' Capture", in Carpenter, D. and Moss, D. (eds.), *Preventing Regulatory Capture: Special Interest Influence and How to Limit It*. Cambridge: Cambridge University Press.

2 Making the incommensurable comparable

A comparative approach to pluralist economics education

Andreas Dimmelmeier, Frederick Heussner, Andrea Pürckhauer and Janina Urban

1 Introduction

Demands for change in economics have become prominent since the financial crisis of the late 2000s. While criticisms of the discipline had been levelled from within the heterodox community in economics for a long time (see e.g. Hodgson et al. 1992; Mäki 1997; Dow 2004; Fine and Milonakis 2009; Hodgson 2009; Lee 2011; Kapeller 2012), the financial crisis not only reinforced these criticisms but expanded their range. Critical voices have subsequently been raised from within the mainstream of the discipline (e.g. Krugman 2009), by economic policy makers (e.g. Blanchard et al. 2010; Turner 2012; Haldane 2017) and by the wider public, as in Queen Elizabeth's well-known address at the London School of Economics (Pierce 2008).

Students of economics also joined the debate. Building upon previous activities, such as the post-autistic movement in the 2000s, student initiatives formed in many parts of the world demanding economics education that is committed to the ideal of pluralism in theories, methods and disciplines (ISIPE 2014). While their critique also highlights the potential consequences of mainstream research for society, their main focus lies on changing economics education. Regarding economics teaching in higher education, the narrowing-down of economics education to the neoclassical theory can be exemplified by the notion of a few economics textbooks becoming the standard for teaching in many parts of the world (van Treeck and Urban 2016). The existence of pluralist teaching materials (e.g. Snowdon et al. 1994; Earl 1995; Dow 1996; Himmelweit et al. 2001; Earl and Wakeley 2004; and more recently Groenewegen 2007; Reardon 2009; van Staveren 2011; Jäger and Springler 2012; Mixon and Cebula 2014; Elsner et al. 2015) could not contribute to changes in economics education on a larger scale (Earl 2010, 219). Recent research confirms the notion that economics teaching all over the world – with regards to university curricula – is far from being pluralist (Wigstrom 2010; Thornton 2012; PEPS Economie 2014; Beckenbach et al. 2016; ISIPE forthcoming). More recent intentions to bring plurality into teaching, like the Curriculum Open-Access Resources in Economics (CORE) project developed inter alia by Wendy Carlin and Samuelson Bowles, have been criticized by the student movement for only including extensions from an otherwise mainstream approach.

The aim of this chapter is to propose a vision of pluralist economics that can be relevant for learning and teaching, online and offline, as well as potentially guiding research endeavours. While it is not our intention to define once and for all what a pluralist education in economics entails, we aim to develop frameworks in which the diversity of perspectives and methodologies are structured in a way that reflects the complexity of the issue but remains comprehensible. In our view, a comparative approach that sets diverse perspectives in relation to one another is the most feasible way of developing such a framework. Even though research on pluralist education in economics and its impact is scarce, the existing literature emphasizes the importance of comparisons and strong (or even caricatured or ideal type) contrasts between theoretical perspectives (Harvey 2011; Mearman et al. 2011). First case studies suggest that a pluralist teaching method, which offers a comparison among different economic perspectives – sometimes referred to as the 'contending perspectives model' – has the potential to strengthen students' ability for critical thinking (Barone 1991; Elsner 2006; Mearman et al. 2011; Cooper and Ramey 2014). Demands from economics students similarly emphasize the importance of a comparative assessment of economics alongside problem-based learning (Cambridge Society for Economic Pluralism 2014; PEPS Economie 2014).

We survey 10 economic schools of thought present in contemporary academic research and discourse and set out to present them in a common and comparable framework. To do so we developed a typology based on meta-theoretical considerations that have been used in extant comparative research regarding different schools of thought or paradigms such as the ontological, epistemological, methodological, political, axiological and theoretical characteristics of different schools of thought (Dobusch and Kapeller 2012; Dutt 2014). Subsequently more fine-grained questions regarding the meta-theoretical fields were given to students with knowledge in the respective schools of thought, who then produced texts grounded in the literature of the perspective, which provide tentative answers to the questions. Each text was then reviewed by a senior academic who is either a representative of the respective school of thought or has a reputation for having studied it thoroughly. Lastly, answers were coded, compared and sorted for graphical representation. This typology forms the basis for the 'orientation' part of the learning platform Exploring Economics and also provides an ordering scheme by which massive open online courses (MOOCs), video lectures, graphics and articles on economic issues can be searched.

This paper is structured as follows. Section 2 covers concepts of different scientific fields which are especially concerned with typologies. The criteria established are then applied to economics. In Section 3, the typology is presented that compares different schools of thought ('perspectives') according to their epistemological, ontological, axiological and methodological stances. The connections between the perspectives according to the criteria established leads to some results regarding the nature of these theories in Section 4, and final conclusions are drawn in Section 5.

2 Searching for a typology of economic schools

2.1 Developing a typology

The branch of science in which typologies, systematizations, taxonomies and the like are most frequently used is biology or, more specifically, zoology. This is due to the fact that natural scientists have to deal with organizing millions of species in comprehensible and manageable categories. Historically in zoology there have been two broad traditions of classification. The first tradition in this field, also called the old systematics, started with Aristotle and was further developed by the Swedish naturalist Linnaeus in the 18th century. The old systematics departs from a Platonian '(ideal) type philosophy', where categories are developed a priori and the analyzed objects are static. Furthermore, the employed categories must be exhaustive and mutually exclusive. The new systematics, developed mostly in the 20th century, by contrast has traded off the philosophical consistency of the old systematics for greater descriptive accuracy and greater compatibility with evolution. Hence, instead of ideal types, larger samples of species are measured, with the use of statistics and considerations on context such as ecology, geography and genetics being included. Due to the implications of evolution, mutually exclusive categories are abandoned and sometimes replaced by overlapping, hybrid or 'fuzzy' categories (Mayr et al. 1953; see also Mearman 2010).

Applying these insights to the classification of economic schools, we opted for starting with an old systematics approach, mostly for pragmatic reasons. Still, one has to take seriously that evolutionary development as well as the fluidity and fuzziness of categories are also important issues in the (eco)system of economic theorizing (Dequech 2007). Therefore, in our approach we aim to transcend strict binaries, where possible, and develop middle categories (see also Goertz and Mahoney 2012, chapter 13 on the development of such middle categories in social science research). Another important consideration that has to be made regarding the classification in human societies is the potential of typologies to be performative, either in an emancipatory or a repressive way. An example of the former is the Nursing Interventions Classification that highlighted formerly ignored work, while the typology of race developed by the South African apartheid regime is an example of the latter (Mearman 2010, 11). Against this background it is important to reflect upon the potential effects of the typology suggested herein. One tentative deficiency is a bias toward 'Western traditions' in economic thought, which therefore fails to address calls for a decolonialization of economics. In an expanded version of this typology we will hopefully be able to include further categories.

2.2 Deriving a typology for economic thinking

The first step in developing a typology for economics is to reflect on what would be the 'types'. A look into the literature on comparative approaches to economic theorizing suggests that schools of thought – which we will also call 'perspectives' subsequently – are a good starting point. Relying on the Kuhnian idea that there is a scientifically legitimate role for differences in theorizing in the face of epistemological uncertainty, scholars such as Deirdre McCloskey and Sheila Dow have found it useful to refer to schools of thought as concepts for communication and exchange (McCloskey 1990; Dow 2004, 277, 281, 283). Even though according to Thomas Kuhn (1996) a strict commensurability of scientific paradigms is impossible, since each paradigm can only be judged in its own terms, other philosophers of science such as A. F. Chalmers (2009) have argued to the contrary. Different paradigms might refer to the same object of inquiry and hence be compared in terms of either objective or intersubjective knowledge about such a given object. Indeed, Kuhn himself later acknowledged the possibility of communication between paradigms by means of 'translation' (Dow 1990, 2004, 279, 287).

Proceeding along the line of economic perspectives, we have to assess what exactly makes up an economic perspective. This requires:

1 The selection of 'perspectives', which
    - Entails a principled identification of perspectives that are (a) important for the discussions in the field of economics and (b) sufficiently different in their assessments to make a comparison meaningful;
    - Entails a distinction in form and content rather than historical – sociological terms;
    - Is broad enough to capture the essence of (ideal-typical) perspectives.
2 The selection of categories, which
    - Allows for systematic comparisons between perspectives;
    - Can be applied to each of those perspectives and will give the reader a sufficiently clear idea about their fundamental differences – these categories have to be able to make meaningful statements about (almost) all of the surveyed perspectives;
    - Are able to highlight the differences that have historically been relevant in the debates of the economic discipline, the social sciences and society more broadly.

2.3 Review of relevant research

The academic traditions within economics that are pluralist-comparative in orientation, and henceforth can provide an entry point for our analytical project are the history of economic thought, the philosophy of economics and international relations/international political economy.

2.3.1 History of economic thought

In the history of economic thought, a common way of approaching the subject is to trace the development of economic theorizing by chronologically examining the work of renowned scholars. Another often-used approach rests upon the identification of sociologically defined schools of thought and the recasting of historical debates between those different perspectives and their intellectual and institutional development (see for example the contributions to Morgan and Rutherford 1998; Milonakis and Fine 2009). These practices are common in other (pluralist) disciplines such as sociology and – when aiming at pluralist economics education – constitute a great improvement over standard economic teaching.

However, certain shortfalls are also apparent. First, the differentiation of perspectives as 'schools of thought' is often based on historical association or affiliation, that is, sociological categories, rather than theoretical content or meta-theoretical orientations and is hence rather unsystematic. Second, the comparison of different schools of thought is often embedded in the debates between contending schools, which means that the focus is usually laid on specific theoretical propositions (or even policies), rather than meta-theoretical or methodological differences.

2.3.2 Philosophy of economics

Research grounded in the philosophy of economics often expands beyond sociological classifications and specific theoretical disputes by adding more methodological and meta-theoretical questions. As Sheila Dow observes, during the second half of the 20th century differentiations among schools, which had initially been focused on theoretical differences – such as in the early discussion of the capital controversy that was thought to be fought inside a common methodological framework – gradually carried over to a higher level as it was revealed that differences in understanding were rooted in 'methodological, epistemological and ultimately ontological differences' (Dow 2004, 277). David Dequech (2007, 288, 300) labels this analytical approach 'intellectual' insofar as it stresses common theoretical and to some extent also methodological convictions and is as such different from sociological classifications. However, many scholars so far have employed ad hoc categorizations that are based on their own experiences or the self-identification of scholars (see Hirte and Thieme 2013, 9, for a synopsis of such categorization efforts). Another problem with research that compares economic perspectives in terms of higher-order categories derived from the philosophy of science is that it is often dedicated to comparing a mainstream or orthodoxy with an opposing non-mainstream or heterodoxy, or alternatively comparing one contending perspective with the neoclassical school. So far, the most rigorous and comprehensive categorizations we are aware of have been developed recently by Amitava Krishna Dutt, who has analyzed neoclassical economics and some competing perspectives according to their ontological, epistemological, methodological, normative, prescriptive and theoretical dimensions (Dutt 2014), and by Leonhard Dobusch and Jakob Kapeller, who present a similar approach (Dobusch and Kapeller 2012). To our knowledge, no categories have been developed that gauge meta-theoretical questions for all or most economic schools of thought.

2.3.3 International political economy

In addition to the analysis examined so far, drawing upon a method commonly used in the neighbouring discipline of international relations (IR) as well as the more closely related discipline of international political economy (IPE) offers important insights. Although especially parts of the so-called American IPE have increasingly become dominated by rational choice theorizing and econometrics, IPE is committed to a political vision of the economy which is reflected in a multi-perspectivist understanding of academic reasoning (Cohen 2007). Furthermore, the dominant narrative in IPE is heavily influenced by the neighbouring and often overlapping field of IR. Following the success of social constructivism in the 1990s, research in IR has been understood as a discipline characterized by contending perspectives, while staying committed to a 'rationalist' understanding of 'scientific progress'. This means that the existence of different paradigms is regarded as a necessary and enduring condition for evaluating the plausibility of explanations with regard to a complex and changing reality. Reflecting these traditions, the didactic method of both IR and IPE is comparative, which is due to the fact that these traditions explicitly emphasize a multi-perspective way of approaching their subject of inquiry. The method of comparison used in those disciplines makes reference to ontological, epistemological concepts as well as to preferred methods and central axioms of each theoretical perspective (e.g. realism, liberalism, Marxism, constructivism, feminism). As one introductory IPE textbook states:

> All theories in IPE incorporate foundational assumptions about how the world works and what there is to know about it, for without such assumptions they would be empty of both content and explanatory value. The goal for students of IPE is not simply to recognize what these foundational assumptions are with respect to different theoretical perspectives. It also involves the more challenging job of assessing the explanatory or normative value of different theoretical perspectives in relation to empirical evidence, while avoiding the problem of selection bias.
>
> (Broome 2014, 2)

In broad terms, the goal of our enquiry can be described as offering a similar guidance adapted to the needs and idiosyncrasies of economics.

3 The typology for a comparative approach to pluralist economics education

Drawing on the history of economic thought and combining the concepts of the philosophy of economics and IPE with the requirements of establishing a typology, we present economic perspectives and categories and explain their selection. We aim at taking a meta-perspective on economic theories as well as relying on the general familiarity of the researchers and contributors with the underlying (and often implicit) categories. The selection method is thus based more on a pragmatic understanding than on a clearly defined procedure.

3.1 Perspectives

The literature from the history of economic thought as well as the discussions based on the philosophy of science from within the economics discipline and from the outside make it possible to group a total of 10 broad perspectives, each of which is more or less sub-differentiated. Different combinations of three to seven of these perspectives are presented in historical (Colander et al. 2004; Milonakis and Fine 2009), methodological and philosophical (Lee 2011, 544; Dobusch and Kapeller 2012, 1037), sociological (Pahl 2011) and empirical, that is, survey design (Frey et al. 2010, 319; di Maio 2013) work. Sequencing these perspectives on the basis of their unit of analysis (going from small to large), the following list ensues:

1. Behavioural economics
2. Austrian economics
3. Neoclassical economics
4. Feminist economics
5. Marxist economics
6. Institutional economics
7. Post-Keynesian economics
8. Evolutionary economics
9. Complexity economics
10. Ecological economics.

3.2 Categories[1]

3.2.1 Ontology

3.2.1.1 CENTRAL ECONOMIC PROBLEM

Ontology is the scientific philosophical field which is concerned with the study of 'what is'. Applied to economic knowledge, we can pose the question: which is the central, independent or even exogenous problem (or entry point) that must be analyzed in theory and answered by policy measures? The relative emphasis of one problem or dynamic inside a theoretical framework often acts both as a magnifier and as a blinder for other dynamics (Moldaschl 2015). Or as Stephen Resnick and Richard Wolff (2006, 7) put it, such concepts are entry points which open the analysis for gauging reality and close it at the same time. Morgan Marietta and Mark Perlman describe central economics problems as culturally and historically enduring frameworks or legacies that shape the theories developed and their reception in society (Marietta and Perlman 2000). As such they are not unlike Max Weber's famous 'switchmen', who create certain world images and prescribe political actions based on them (Weber 1946, 280). While historically there has been an ample variety of such concepts, most of which probably have a justified claim to describe an important part of the reality connected to economic activity, we chose to focus on four 'economic problems' in particular.

Marietta and Perlman (2000, 156), after doing a historical survey, present scarcity as one of the most prominent central economic problems that inter alia Malthus, Smith, Ricardo, Hicks and Samuelson were concerned with. Dobusch and Kapeller also name scarcity as one central economic problem and regard it as mainly addressed by the neoclassical paradigm. For the Keynesian school of thought, they identify unemployment as the central economic problem (Dobusch and Kapeller 2012, 1039). Uncertainty, though, appears to be a more general and appropriate identification of the central problem in the theorizing not only of Keynes but also of Schumpeter, Arrow and many more (Marietta and Perlman 2000, 156). We furthermore include the pre-ontological category of change, as suggested by Dobusch and Kapeller (2012, 1039), in our scheme for gauging key elements present in older research fields such as institutional economics and in more recent ones such as evolutionary and complexity economics. Additionally, a strong legacy is present in social or governmental order, as it is found in the thinking of Aristotle, Hobbes, Marx, Schmoller or Sen (Marietta and Perlman 2000, 156). We have not included this category because we did not find it to be commensurate with the categories introduced before, but it remains potentially relevant for further categorization efforts. Our last category is dominance, which might also be referred to as differentials in power. The importance of the dominance of one group over others in an economic context and the associated struggles can be found in Marx and Engels (inter alia1848[1967]) as well as in theories addressing the colonial (e.g. Galeano 1971), gendered (e.g. Folbre 1994), and cultural as well as institutional (e.g. Veblen 1899) dimensions of the economy.

3.2.1.2 MAIN UNIT OF ANALYSIS

The next ontological category deals with the main unit of analysis, meaning the 'things' that drive economic processes and the level of analysis which henceforth is regarded as the most adequate for analysis. Dobusch and Kapeller (2012, 1039) present a differentiation between the micro level and individuals as main units of analysis, the meso level with institutions, emergent phenomena and interactive processes and the macro level with economic aggregates. Concerning this matter, Ha-Joon Chang (2014: 166–169) refers to individuals, classes and institutions as central units of analysis. Building on these existing categorizations and the elaborations of the different perspectives, our categorization includes individuals on a micro level, groups (class, gender, race) and institutions on a meso level and systems (including biosystems) on a macro level.

3.2.1.3 HUMAN NATURE AND REDUCTIONISM

Diverging ideas about what lies at the core of human nature have been central to most philosophical and political considerations. Ha-Joon Chang (2014, 166–169) compares different schools of thought according to their understanding of individuals as selfish, rational, boundedly rational or layered (instinct – habit – belief – reason). Dimitris Milonakis and Ben Fine show how the understanding of human nature in the neoclassical school of thought has changed strongly over past centuries (e.g. from Mill's ethical to Bentham's hedonist utilitarianism). They also reveal how the relevance of context decreased with successive neoclassical thinkers who later strongly engaged in mathematical formalization (Milonakis and Fine 2009). Both Steve Keen and Philip Mirowski argue that economists came to follow an atomistic understanding of society and economy, similar to how physicians described the world at the beginning of the 20th century. They regard this way of theorizing as mostly outdated, since the natural sciences then recognized and theorized that systems work in complex and unstable rather than mechanistic ways (Mirowski 1992; Keen 2011, 187–192, 223–225). While we include a continuum of an atomistic to contextual conceptualization of the world in our categorization, we leave the understanding of human nature to be described by each school of thought for gauging diversity and evolution.

3.2.1.4 CONCEPTION OF TIME

Another central difference between the economic schools of thought lies in whether time is regarded as affecting economic outcomes historically, logically or not at all in the long term. Steve Keen points to the specialty of neoclassical economics to capture economic processes in states of equilibrium, with the assumption that changes in the determining variables during the 'adjustment' process do not affect the outcome. In contrast to this, most social scientists understand the economy as a continuous process, non-reversible and with constant change (Hodgson 2001). Recent attempts to depict and quantify such dynamics and path dependencies have employed computer simulations and more complex mathematics (Keen 2011, 195–220). Our categorization thus involves the scale of static, a middle category, and dynamic.

3.2.2 Epistemology

3.2.2.1 LINK BETWEEN SCIENTIFIC INQUIRY AND THE REAL WORLD

The question of 'correspondence' between the concepts used in scientific discourse and the real world has been around since the times of classical philosophy and resembles the discussions on universalism versus nominalism. In the social sciences, a more contemporary debate ranges around the questions of whether a theory can grasp the world in a realistic fashion or whether theory is constructivist, thus having an impact on the things it observes and theorizes. Albeit issues of social construction are prominent in other disciplines like anthropology, political science and sociology (see Hacking 1999 for an overview), in economics the theme has not been of much concern. Arne Heise (2016, 10), referring to the work of Mäki, summarizes the non-constructivist, that is, realist position, often used and seldom problematized in economics, as the 'one world–one truth' principle. This means that there is only one reality and that humans are capable of referring to this reality and communicating it without much complication. The opposing view holds that referring to the objective reality in the social sciences is impossible and that communication is only possible by referring to human-made constructions (Sayer 2000, 33). Meanwhile, a middle category is provided by those such as critical realists or moderate social constructivists, who acknowledge the possibility for science to refer to the real world yet at the same time emphasize the fallibility of scientific knowledge and its situatedness inside a social context (Sayer 1992; Lawson 2006; Heise 2016).

3.2.2.2 OBJECT- OR PERSPECTIVE-DRIVEN THEORY

This question might be conceptualized in a somehow similar way to the discussions on whether a research question is substantive, that is, addressing a particular puzzle of societal relevance, or analytic, that is, addressing a particularly relevant gap inside a theoretical framework (Sil and Katzenstein 2010, 418). In addition to developing its analytical framework, in our view, a perspective-driven theory seeks to expand its reach to other fields or objects, as can be seen in the discussions on economic imperialism (Fine and Milonakis 2009). Hence a perspective-driven theory is rooted in a certain way of theorizing that can be applied to any object, whereas in an object-driven theory an object determines the interest of the perspective and then multiple ways of understanding and explaining the object are employed. Lawson (2006, 2013) has, for instance, prominently characterized neoclassical economics as a school of thought that defines itself through a perspective or a thinking style, that is, mathematical modelling. Similarly, Milonakis and Fine in their reconstruction of the Methodenstreit identify a preoccupation with perspective with the marginalists, who sought to establish a theory that could serve as a template for explaining all economic phenomena (Milonakis and Fine 2009, 94–96). The German Historicists' eclecticism regarding methods, on the other hand, as well as their interest in the development of historically specific institutions of socio-economics makes them the ideal type for an object-driven paradigm (see Hodgson 2001, 59–61 and Rieter 2002, 136–137 for persistent themes that were important to the school's research).

3.2.3 Methodology and methods: preferred analytical methodology and preferred means of hypothesis generation

While there are different usages of the term methodology in social science, for our purpose we follow the definition by Arne Heise, who identifies methodology as the rules or the understanding which is employed to demarcate what counts as justified knowledge (Heise 2016, 20). This contrasts with equating methodology with the concrete methods employed, even though different methodological understandings will privilege certain methods as more reliable. Reflecting on methodology, we separate on the theoretical level between a formalistic and a broad reasoning (Dow 1990) approach, while on the empirical level we differentiate between a standardized and prescriptive framework and an idiosyncratic and context-dependent framework. Regarding the use of concrete methods, we have chosen to include the common differentiation between inductive and deductive hypothesis generation. Though both are central parts of theory generation (under a positivist vision of science), the neoclassical school of thought especially turned to 'test' their axioms quantitatively, and to develop a negligence towards inductive and qualitative approaches (Morgan and Rutherford 1998).

3.2.4 Axioms: core or paradigmatic concepts of the perspective

Axioms in the understanding advanced here refer to central themes that guide research. As such they are unlike hypotheses or theories that are developed in accordance with empirical observations and tested against empirical data. Instead, they are more like hunches or heuristics that guide the formulation of hypotheses. Our understanding is derived from the work of Imre Lakatos, who differentiates between negative heuristics (unfalsifiable axioms) and positive heuristics (strategies for how to develop more elaborate hypotheses from axioms) as the preanalytic 'hard core' of a paradigm (Lakatos 1978). Terminological expressions, on the other hand, are not self-evident statements but rather certain codes and concepts that are typically employed within a perspective. Whereas Dobusch and Kapeller, from whom we take the inspiration to include the axiological and terminological dimensions of different paradigms, develop a separation between the two (Dobusch and Kapeller 2012, 1039), we chose to group those two dimensions together because we found it difficult to come up with a crisp separation for each of the analyzed perspectives and chose not to impose an arbitrary boundary.

3.2.5 Ideology/values

Ideals refer to normative convictions that describe which things are considered to be 'good' in the realm of economics. Politics or policies, on the other hand, are concrete measures that are considered to bring the economy into a normatively 'better' state. In practice, statements and opinions often include both values and policy suggestions. Since many theories in the social sciences go beyond description in their ambition but conclude that the attainment of certain characteristics or states of the economy are desirable, it was possible to identify a list of normative goals as well as concrete policy suggestions associated with each of the perspectives.

4 Results and limitations

4.1 Results

The categorization in combination with the content of the perspective web-pages which have been academically reviewed are visualized in infographics. Aggregating the information of these graphics helps to draw some general conclusions on the ecosystem of economic schools of thought. We developed an aggregate measure of the similarities of the perspectives by surveying the nine infographics, where perspectives are put into categories and assigned a score of 1 for each time two perspectives are inside the same category. This means that scores for one perspective in relation to another range from 0 to 9. With 10 perspectives in total, 45 relationships can be studied. The results of this coding of the links between the perspectives are graphically displayed in Figure 2.1, which was made using R's igraph package.

As can be evidenced from Figure 2.1, the network is very connected, with graph density equalling 0.93. All but four perspectives have at least one commonality with all other perspectives. Of those four, feminist and behavioural economics have eight connections each, whereas neoclassical and institutional economics are the most isolated, with seven connections each. Focusing on these last two for the moment, one can observe that neoclassical economics fails to engage with approaches that emphasize analysis of group and macro phenomena as well as dynamism. Hence there are no connections to feminist and institutional economics, while the connection scores to both evolutionary economics and Marxian political economy are only equal to 1.

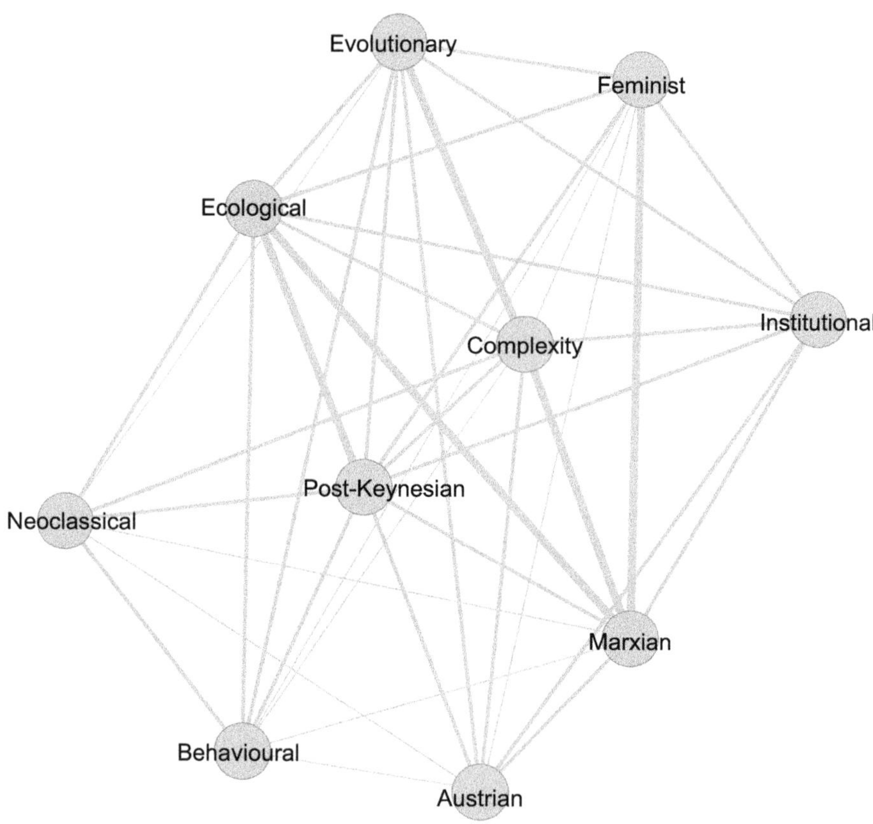

Figure 2.1 Network of perspectives

Source: Own representation.

The relative isolation of neoclassical economics in meta-theoretical terms when compared to mostly heterodox schools is something that has also been emphasized by Tony Lawson (2006, 498). Institutional economics, on the other hand, owes its relative isolation to the eclecticism and inductivism that it displays regarding methodological standards. This isolates the perspective completely from schools of thought that connect a methodological and epistemological natural science ideal with microfoundations (behavioural and neoclassical, score = 0) and leads to lower scores in relation to macro perspectives that equally follow a more rigid methodology, such as post-Keynesian and ecological economics.

Apart from looking at the absence of connections, it is also interesting to look at the strongest meta-theoretical similarities, evidenced by the thickest lines in the network. The greatest score of 8 was given to two connections only, namely the one between Marxian political economy and feminist economics and to post-Keynesian and ecological economics. The first association is not surprising, since there are historical connections between the two perspectives and the Marxian political economy perspective web-pages also incorporate elements from a broader social science use of Marxian theory. The second association, however, is somewhat surprising and can mostly be attributed to the perspectives having a macro focus and a historicized and dynamic understanding of economics while at the same time largely rejecting constructivism. Other strong connections with scores of 7 can be found between Marxian political economy and ecological economics as well as between feminist and evolutionary economics.

Leaving the description of aggregate similarities and differences aside, we now focus on the position of single perspectives. First, it becomes apparent that behavioural economics is situated in the middle category in 5 of the 7 infographics that have such a middle category (e.g. reductionism, dynamics, hypothesis generation). The most interesting of these comparisons is the perspective-driven versus object-driven theory comparison, where behavioural economics is the only school of thought that was not sorted into one of the extremes. This, according to the perspective web-pages, is due to an ongoing debate on whether the description of human behaviour or a certain conception of rationality and decision-making should guide research. In behavioural economics those tensions exist between the focus on the object of economic decisions and the affiliation to established (neoclassical) theories. It can be inferred from its overall middle position that behavioural economics is still a contested field uniting many different approaches under its umbrella. Another interesting finding is that Austrian economics is the only perspective that was coded as being constructivist. Whereas constructivism and the focus on cultural phenomena are often associated with post-positivist scholarship of social scientists of a left-wing persuasion, the radical subjectivism of the Austrian school and its hermeneutical methodology puts it into this category.

Taking the central economic problem of the perspectives into consideration, uncertainty and change result as the most frequently theorized legacies, while scarcity and dominance are also very relevant concepts. It stands out that the neoclassical school of thought ideal type is only related to 'scarcity' as its main constituency (Figure 2.2). Next to scarcity, behavioural and Austrian economics theorize against

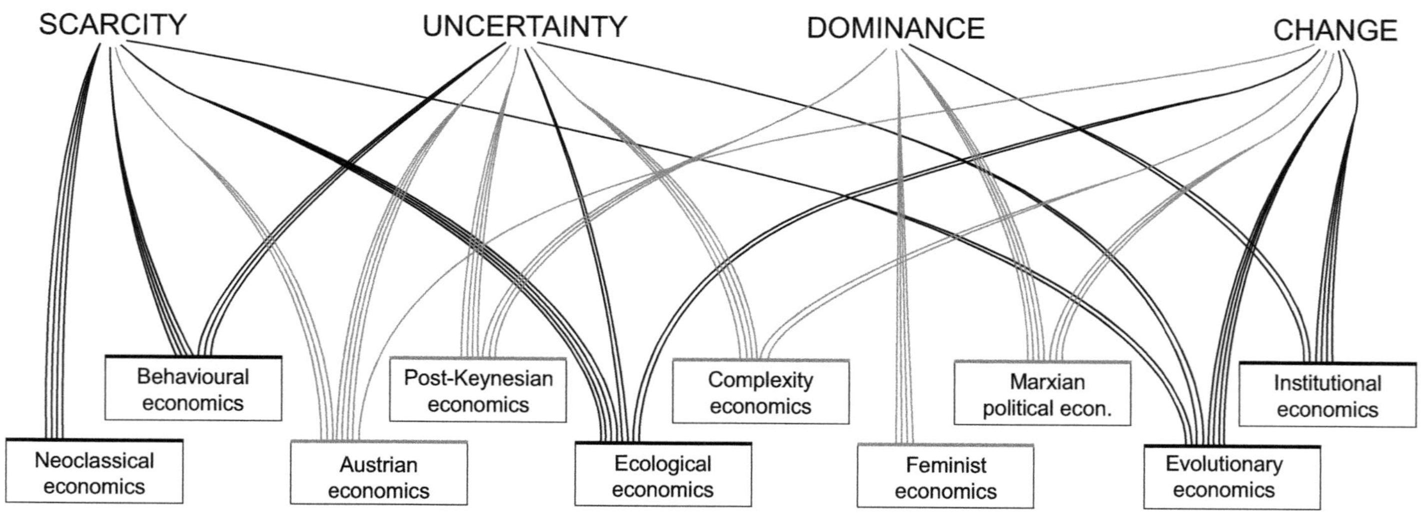

Figure 2.2 Which problem or problems are central to the economy?

Source: Own representation.

the background of insecurity (and change). Gauging scarcity related to the limits of the ecosystem, ecological economics is furthermore constructed around the problems of uncertainty and change. Departing from a socially more conscious approach, Marxian, feminist, post-Keynesian and institutional economics view inter alia dominance as the central economic problem (Critical Theory approach), whereas the other theories with their focus on addressing uncertainty or scarcity rather represent a 'problem-solving' approach (Cox 1981, 128).

Answering the question from which 'thing' inquiry should start, if knowledge about the economy is to be acquired, most perspectives regard either institutions and systems or individuals as central (Figure 2.3). To the former position belong institutional economics, complexity economics and ecological economics, which are mainly concerned with the creation and durability of formal and informal rules and regulations, or ecosystems. The driving forces of the economy are gauged to be groups, institutions and systems, or more specifically classes, production and consumption regimes, and capitalism in Marxian and post-Keynesian economics. Much in contrast to this, neoclassical economics with its representative agent and firm, behavioural economics, inter alia with borrowing from psychology and Austrian economics with its source, ascribe the course of economic development to individual behaviour. Evolutionary economics is positioned between groups and institutions because it holds that processes on the macro level can only be explained by reference to the meso level. In feminist economics, different perceptions and rights of groups are the focus of analysis, although their (re-)creation and (re-)production through institutions and systems are also analyzed by some strands of this school of thought.

Figure 2.4 presents the results of the question whether a perspective is perspective- or object-driven. Three perspectives can be considered as object-driven, namely feminist economics, institutionalist economics and evolutionary economics. Feminist economics focuses on the object's gender and gender relations and

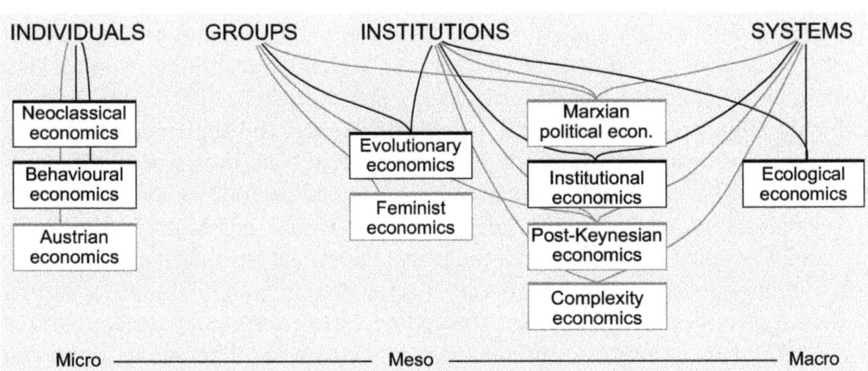

Figure 2.3 Which 'thing' should inquiry start from if we want to acquire knowledge about the economy?

Source: Own representation.

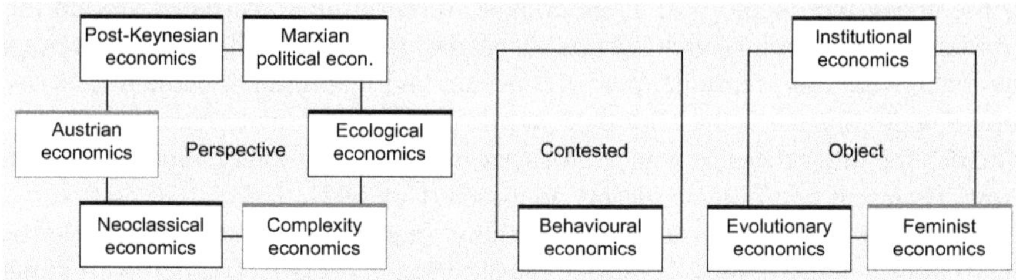

Figure 2.4 Does the perspective apply a certain mode of thought, generally, or study a focused object?

Source: Own representation.

does so from a variety of perspectives, including neoclassical methods. Institutional economics focuses on social and legal institutions, and evolutionary economics focuses on change processes such as growth, institutional or technological change, and development. Five perspectives are considered to be perspective-driven, including neoclassical economics for regarding economic phenomena with the pre-ontological concepts of scarcity, decision and efficiency or applying a 'modelling approach', or Austrian economics which emphasizes the importance of the economic principle and subjectivism. Also, Marxian political economics is considered to be perspective-driven, since it applies pre-ontological concepts (e.g. theories of power and hegemony or dialectical materialism) to different realms of the economy.

4.2 Limitations

A few limitations and potential shortcomings should be noted. First, it might be useful to think of the results as a representation of the way we chose to conceptualize the different schools of economics instead of a factual description of their true nature. This means that on the one hand commonalities and differences rest on the non-exhaustive means of comparison, which we identified by surveying work in the philosophy of science and economics, the history of economic thought and international political economy. Certain differences and similarities that could have been constructed by taking a different approach are thus potentially omitted. On the other hand, the comparison can only be as good as the perspective web-pages. By having sought academic review, we are confident that we have captured important parts of each of the perspectives, yet omissions and errors are still possible. Second, a further source of errors lies in the coding or the sorting of the perspectives into categories. The coding was performed by a team of three coders with backgrounds in different parts of economics. Though we think that subjective bias was reduced by revising the coding on multiple occasions, the procedure fell short of best practices advocated by scholars engaging in qualitative codings of texts (e.g. Campbell et al. 2013). Lastly, a more practical limitation is that the coding for complexity economics could not be done appropriately, since the production of the perspective web-pages was delayed. Still, categories were assigned to the perspective based on the background knowledge of the coders, but these are far less reliable than those of the other perspectives.

5 Conclusions

The chapter has developed a typology of the different schools of economics by drawing from a range of literature including the history of economic thought, economic methodology, the philosophy of science and international political economy. The resulting conceptualization offers a tool for the teaching of pluralist economics according to a contending perspectives method, emphasizing the different underlying assumptions and meta-theoretical positions of some of the most prominent schools of thought in economics. Even though one has to be cautious regarding the categorization and development of ideal types, the results apart from their educational purpose do arguably also provide some analytical insights. As the discussion of the results shows, meta-theoretical commonalities and differences can be traced by applying the typology. Such an approach holds promise of adding value to discussions in the history of economic thought as well as to recent contributions in international political economy, which so far have mostly relied on network theoretical and genealogical methods to visualize the spread and impact of different economic ideas (Ban 2016; Ban et al. 2016).

Note

1 The categories move from the 'foundational' and abstract (ontological) to the practical dimension processes and the macro level with economic aggregates. Concerning this matter, Ha-Joon Chang (2014, 166–169) refers to individuals, classes and institutions as central units of analysis. Building on these existing categorizations and the elaborations of the different perspectives, our categorization includes individuals on a micro level, groups (class, gender, race) and institutions on a meso level and systems (including biosystems) on a macro level.

References

Ban, C. (2016): *Ruling Ideas: How Global Neoliberalism Goes Local.* New York: Oxford University Press.

Ban, C., Seabrooke, L. and Freitas, S. (2016): "Grey Matter in Shadow Banking: International Organizations and Expert Strategies in Global Financial Governance", *Review of International Political Economy* 23(6), 1001–1033.

Barone, C. A. (1991): "Contending Perspectives: Curricular Reform in Economics", *The Journal of Economic Education* 22(1), 15–26.

Beckenbach, F., Daskalakis, M. and Hofman, D. (2016): *Zur Pluralität der volkswirtschaftlichen Lehre in Deutschland: Eine empirische Untersuchung des Lehrangebotes in den Grundlagenfächern und der Einstellung der Lehrenden.* Weimar: Metropolis.

Blanchard, O., Dell'Ariccia, G. and Mauro, P. (2010): *Rethinking Macroeconomic Policy.* IMF Staff Position Note SPN/10/03, www.imf.org/external/pubs/ft/spn/2010/spn1003.pdf, accessed 31 January 2017.

Broome, A. (2014): *Issues and Actors in the Global Political Economy*. Basingstoke, UK: Palgrave Macmillan.

Cambridge Society for Economic Pluralism Report (2014): *CSEP Survey of Economics Students: Is It Time for Change at Cambridge?*, www.cambridgepluralism.org/uploads/1/7/4/9/17499733/report_v14_w.appendix.pdf, accessed 31 January 2017.

Campbell, J. L., Quincy, C., Osserman, J. and Pedersen, O. K. (2013): "Coding in-Depth Semistructured Interviews: Problems of Unitization and Intercoder Reliability and Agreement", *Sociological Methods and Research* 42(3), 294–320.

Chalmers, A. F. (2009): *What Is This Thing Called Science?* 3rd edition. Buckingham, UK: Open University Press.

Chang, H. (2014): *Economics: The User's Guide: A Pelican Introduction*. London: Pelican Books.

Cohen, B. J. (2007): "The Transatlantic Divide: Why Are American and British IPE So Different?", *Review of International Political Economy* 14(2), 197–219.

Colander, D., Holt, R. and Rosser, B., Jr. (2004): "The Changing Face of Mainstream Economics", *Review of Political Economy* 16(4), 485–499.

Cooper, B. and Ramey, E. A. (2014): "Pluralism at Work: Alumni Assess an Economics Education", *International Review of Economics Education* 16, 63–72.

Cox, R. W. (1981): "Social Forces, States and World Orders: Beyond International Relations Theory", *Millennium: Journal of International Studies* 10(2), 126–155.

Dequech, D. (2007): "Neoclassical, Mainstream, Orthodox, and Heterodox Economics", *Journal of Post Keynesian Economics* 30(2), 279–302.

Dobusch, L. and Kapeller, J. (2012): "Heterodox United vs. Mainstream City? Sketching a Framework for Interested Pluralism in Economics", *Journal of Economic Issues* 46(4), 1035–1058.

Dow, S. C. (1990): "Beyond Dualism", *Cambridge Journal of Economics* 14(2), 143–157.

Dow, S. C. (1996): *The Methodology of Macroeconomic Thought: A Conceptual Analysis of Schools of Thought in Economics*. Cheltenham, UK and Northampton, MA: Edward Elgar.

Dow, S. C. (2004): "Structured Pluralism", *Journal of Economic Methodology* 11(3), 275–290.

Dutt, A. K. (2014): "Dimensions of Pluralism in Economics", *Review of Political Economy* 26(4), 479–494.

Earl, P. E. (1995): *Microeconomics for Business and Marketing: Lectures, Cases and Worked Essays*. Aldershot, UK and Brookfield, VT: Edward Elgar.

Earl, P. E. (2010): "Economics Fit for the Queen: A Pessimistic Assessment of Its Prospects", *Prometheus* 28(3), 209–225.

Earl, P. E. and Wakeley, T. (2004): *Business Economics: A Contemporary Approach*. London: McGraw Hill.

Elsner, W. (2006): "Heterodoxe Ökonomik und ihre Einbeziehung in eine pluralistische Lehre", in Duermeier, T., Egan-Krieger, T. V. and Peukert, H. (eds.), *Die Scheuklappen der Wirt-schaftswissenschaft. Postautistische Ökonomik für eine pluralistische Wirtschaftslehre*. Marburg: Metropolis, 145–160.

Elsner, W., Heinrich, T. and Schwardt, H. (2015): *The Microeconomics of Complex Economies: Evolutionary, Institutional, Neoclassical and Complexity Perspectives*. Amsterdam: Elsevier.

Fine, B. and Milonakis, D. (2009): *From Economics Imperialism to Freakonomics: The Shifting Boundaries between Economics and Other Social Sciences*. London: Routledge.

Folbre, N. (1994): *Who Pays for the Kids? Gender and the Structures of Constraint*. Vol. 4. London: Routledge.

Frey, B. S., Humbert, S. and Schneider, F. (2010): "What Is Economics? Attitudes and Views of German Economists", *Journal of Economic Methodology* 17(3), 317–332.

Galeano, E. (1971): *Las venas abiertas de América Latina*. Mexico: Siglo XXI Editores.

Goertz, G. and Mahoney, J. (2012): *A Tale of Two Cultures: Qualitative and Quantitative Research in the Social Sciences*. Princeton, NJ: Princeton University Press.

Groenewegen, J. (ed.) (2007): *Teaching Pluralism in Economics*. Cheltenham, UK and Northampton, MA: Edward Elgar.

Hacking, I. (1999): *The Social Construction of What?* Cambridge, MA: Harvard University Press.

Haldane, A. (2017): "Chief Economist of Bank of England Admits Errors in Brexit Forecasting", *The Guardian*, www.theguardian.com/business/2017/jan/05/chief-economist-of-bank-of-england-admits-errors, accessed 31 January 2017.

Harvey, J. T. (2011): "Student Attitudes toward Economic Pluralism: Survey-Based Evidence", *International Journal of Pluralism and Economics Education* 2(3), 270–290.

Heise, A. (2016): *Pluralismus in den Wirtschaftswissenschaften: Klärung eines umstrittenen Konzepts*. IMK Study, No 47.

Himmelweit, S., Simonetti, R. and Trigg, A. (2001): *Microeconomics: Neoclassical and Institutional Perspectives on Economic Behaviour*. Boston: Cengage Learning.

Hirte, K. and Thieme, S. (2013): *Mainstream, Orthodoxie und Heterodoxie: Zur Klassifizierung der Wirtschaftswissenschaften*. ZÖSS Discussion Papers.

Hodgson, G. M. (2001): *How Economics Forgot History: The Problem of Historical Specificity in Social Science*. London and New York: Routledge.

Hodgson, G. M. (2009): "The Great Crash of 2008 and the Reform of Economics", *Cambridge Journal of Economics* 33(6), 1205–1221.

Hodgson, G. M., Mäki, U. and McCloskey, D. N. (1992): "Plea for a Pluralistic and Rigorous Economics", *American Economic Review* 82(2), 25.

ISIPE (2014): *An International Student Call for Pluralism in Economics*, www.isipe.net/open-letter/, accessed 1 February 2017.

ISIPE (forthcoming): *International Survey on Pluralism in Economics, Excerpt from the Survey Online*, http://pepseconomie.wixsite.com/isipe/international-survey, accessed 1 February 2017.

Jäger, J. and Springler, E. (2012): *Ökonomie der internationalen Entwicklung: Eine kritische Einführung in die Volkswirtschaftslehre*. Wien: Mandelbaum Verlag.

Kapeller, J. (2012): *Modell-Platonismus in der Ökonomie: Zur Aktualität einer klassischen epistemologischen Kritik*. Frankfurt am Main: Peter Lang, Internationaler Verlag der Wissenschaften.

Keen, S. (2011): *Debunking Economics: The Naked Emperor Dethroned?* New York: Zed Books.

Krugman, P. (2009): "How Did Economists Get It So Wrong?", *The New York Times*, http://www.nytimes.com/2009/09/06/magazine/06Economic-t.html, accessed 31 January 2017.

Kuhn, T. S. (1996): *The Structure of Scientific Revolutions*. 3rd edition. Chicago: University of Chicago Press.

Lakatos, I. (1978): *The Methodology of Scientific Research Programmes: Philosophical Papers*. Vol. 1. Cambridge, UK: Cambridge University Press.

Lawson, T. (2006): "The Nature of Heterodox Economics", *Cambridge Journal of Economics* 30(4), 483–505.

Lawson, T. (2013): "What Is This 'School' Called Neoclassical Economics?", *Cambridge Journal of Economics* 37(5), 947–983.

Lee, F. S. (2011): "The Pluralism Debate in Heterodox Economics", *Review of Radical Political Economics* 43(4), 540–551.

Maio, M. D. di (2013): "Are Mainstream and Heterodox Economists Different? An Empirical Analysis", *American Journal of Economics and Sociology* 72(5), 1315–1348.

Mäki, U. (1997): "The One World and the Many Theories", in Salanti, A. and Screpanti, E. (eds.), *Pluralism in Economics*. Cheltenham, UK and Northampton, MA: Edward Elgar, 37–47.

Marietta, M. and Perlman, M. (2000): "The Uses of Authority in Economics", *American Journal of Sociology and Economics* 59(2), 151–189.

Marx, K. and Engels, F. (1848 [1967]): *The Communist Manifesto*, S. Moore (trans.). London: Penguin Books.

Mayr, E., Linsley, E. G. and Usinger, R. L. (1953): *Methods and Principles of Systematic Zoology*. New York and London: McGraw Hill.

McCloskey, D. N. (1990): "Storytelling in Economics", in Lavoie, D. (ed.), *Economics and Hermeneutics*. London: Routledge, 61–75.

Mearman, A. (2010): "What Is This Thing Called 'Heterodox Economics'?", *Econpapers* (1006).

Mearman, A., Wakeley, T., Shoib, G. and Webber, D. (2011): "Does Pluralism in Economics Education Make Better Educated, Happier Students?", *International Review of Economics Education* 10(2), 50–62.

Milonakis, D. and Fine, B. (2009): *From Political Economy to Economics: Method, the Social and the Historical in the Evolution of Economic Theory, Economics as Social Theory*. London and New York: Routledge.

Mirowski, P. (1992): *More Heat Than Light: Economics as Social Physics: Physics as Nature's Economics*. Cambridge, UK: Cambridge University Press.

Mixon, F. G. and Cebula, R. J. (2014): *New Developments in Economic Education*. Cheltenham, UK and Northampton, MA: Edward Elgar.

Moldaschl, M. (2015): "Paradigmatisches Lernen", in Hedtke, R. (ed.), *Was ist und wozu Sozioökonomie?* Wiesbaden: Springer VS, 339–369.

Morgan, M. S. and Rutherford, M. (eds.) (1998): *From Interwar Pluralism to Postwar Neoclassicism*. Durham, NC: Duke University Press.

Pahl, H. (2011): "Die Wirtschaftswissenschaften in der Krise: Vom massenmedialen Diskurs zu einer Wissenssoziologie der Wirtschaftswissenschaften", *Schweizerische Zeitschrift für Soziologie, Sonderheft The Global Economic Crisis: Perceptions and Impacts* 37(H2), 259–281.

PEPS Economie (2014): "The Case for Pluralism: What French Undergraduate Economics Teaching Is All about and How It Can Be Improved", *Journal of Pluralism and Economics Education* 5(4), 385–400.

Pierce, A. (2008): "The Queen Asks Why No One Saw the Credit Crunch Coming", *The Daily Telegraph*, www.telegraph.co.uk/news/uknews/theroyalfamily/3386353/The-Queen-asks-why-no-one-saw-the-credit-crunch-coming.html, accessed 1 March 2017.

Reardon, J. (ed.) (2009): *The Handbook of Pluralist Economics Education*. London: Routledge.

Resnick, S. A. and Wolff, R. D. (2006): *New Departures in Marxian Theory*. London and New York: Routledge.

Rieter, H. (2002): "Historische Schulen", in Issing, O. (ed.), *Geschichte der Nationalökonomie*. München: Verlag Franz Vahlen.

Sayer, R. A. (1992): *Method in Social Science: A Realist Approach*. London and New York: Routledge.

Sayer, R. A. (2000): *Realism and Social Science*. London: Sage.

Sil, R. and Katzenstein, P. J. (2010): "Analytic Eclecticism in the Study of World Politics: Reconfiguring Problems and Mechanisms across Research Traditions", *Perspectives on Politics* 8(2), 411–431.

Snowdon, B., Vane, H. and Wynarczyk, P. (1994): *A Modern Guide to Macroeconomics: An Introduction to Competing Schools of Thought*. Aldershot, UK and Brookfield, VT: Edward Elgar.

Thornton, T. (2012): "The Economics Curriculum in Australian Universities 1980 to 2011", *Economic Papers: A Journal of Applied Economics and Policy* 31(1), 103–113.

Turner, A. (2012): *Economics after the Crisis: Objectives and Means*. Cambridge, MA: MIT Press.

Van Staveren, I. (2011): *Economics after the Crisis: An Introduction to Economics from a Pluralist and Global Perspective*. New York: Routledge.

Van Treeck, T. and Urban, J. (eds.) (2016): *Ökonomie neu denken: Blinde Flecken der Lehrbuchökonomie*. Berlin: Irights.

Veblen, T. (1899): *The Theory of the Leisure Class: An Economic Study in the Evolution of Institutions*. New York: B. W. Huebsch.

Weber, M. (1946): *Essays in Sociology*. New York: Oxford University Press.

Wigstrom, C. W. (2010): *A Survey of Undergraduate Economics Programmes in the UK*, www.ineteconomics.org/uploads/downloads/existing_undergrad_econ_curriculum_UK.pdf, accessed 1 February 2017.

3 What can teaching critical pluralist economics gain from "de-othering" sociology?

Stephan Panther

1 Introduction

The wonderful and by now famous satirical piece by Axel Leijonhufvud, "Life among the Econ" (Leijonhufvud 1973, 327) still describes quite well the fundamental state of affairs between economics and sociology.[1] A state of affairs that has existed throughout the history of the two academic disciplines, with variations in mutual distance and dislike, but essentially unchanged. It seems so entrenched that it appears to be shared to some extent even by some economists in the pluralist camp (see e.g. Heise 2016, 22). It almost appears as if the economist to some extent is an economist by not being a sociologist, and indeed, the sociologist is a sociologist by not being an economist.

In the following pages I first characterize this relationship as two scientific communities "othering" each other and follow this through a sketch of the history of the two disciplines. I then argue that economic sociology and heterodox economics have both been active in those areas that the narrow(ing) focus of mainstream economics has left barren, and have been active in a complementary way. Third, I explore the consequences this has for teaching pluralist economics.

2 Economics and sociology – a pair tied to each other by othering each other

Looking at this situation through the lenses of those social scientists who theorize processes of identity formation and identity maintenance in human collectivities, the concept of "othering" is offering itself to grasp what is happening between these two scientific disciplines.[2] Spivak (1985) is usually credited with using the term systematically for the first time.[3] She distinguishes three dimensions of othering:

- A claim of the "us" to have superior power;
- The construction of the "other" as being pathologically or morally inferior;
- The claiming of knowledge and technology to be under the command of "us".

Thus "othering" is a process by which human collectivities demarcate themselves, ascribing positive characteristics to "us" and negative characteristics to "them", claiming superior power and knowledge for themselves. Applying this to scientific disciplines, whose bread and butter after all is the generation of knowledge, makes the third component somewhat redundant since in this context the first and the second dimension will also be claims within the realm of knowledge production.

It is not difficult to come up with citations illustrating the above for the relationship between economics and sociology. Thus Richard Swedberg (1990, 8–18), in a short sketch of the history of the relationship of the two disciplines still well worth reading, points out how Auguste Comte (1798–1857), who used the term "sociology" for the first time in his "Cours de Philosophie Positive", repeatedly refers to economics as that "alleged science" (Swedberg 1990, 9). And he cites the economist Frank Knight (1885–1972) as saying "sociology is the science of talk, and there is only one law in sociology. Bad talk drives out good talk" (Swedberg 1990, 15).

This relationship has had a history which on the one hand reveals different kinds of "othering", and on the other hand helps to understand its dynamics. Sociology had to find its place in academia at a time where economics, or "political economy" as it was called then, already was an established discipline. Contrary to what one might expect and contrary also to what the above citation from Comte might suggest, when sociology was established as an academic discipline in the late 19th and early 20th centuries,[4] several leading figures were active in both economics and sociology. The list of names is impressive: John Commons, Vilfredo Pareto, Joseph Schumpeter, Thorstein Veblen, Max Weber. Note, however, that all of these except for Pareto were associated either with the German historical school or with American institutionalism – schools of thought soon to be marginalized in economics.

Indeed it was Pareto who provided the conceptual scheme, which can describe well the first phase of "othering" between the two disciplines. He proposed that economics was to deal with "logical" (i.e. rational) behavior, while sociology was to deal with "non-logical" (i.e. irrational) behavior. This division of labor has been described (especially for American sociology) as "the pact" and has been in place roughly from the 1920s up to the 1980s. It has a double significance. First of all, it leaves the study of the production, distribution and consumption of goods and services to economics as an academic discipline and keeps sociology out of it. At the same time, it defines economics by the rational actor model (i.e. a methodological stance), soon to be enshrined by the famous definition of economics by Lionel Robbins.[5] Modernity being the age of rationality, sociology had been othered by economics, and so had those schools of thought of economics which did not fit into the scheme – even if the process took some decades to develop into an all-out victory.

That all-out victory was essentially complete when economics had been turned into a science dominated by deductive reasoning, mathematical modelling and quantitative empirical techniques by the end of the 1970s. And it is then when the relationship between sociology and economics changes once again when economics breaks "the pact" and attacks. Following the logic of defining economics by the rational choice model, economic imperialism gains more and more ground. Economics, defined by its methodological stance and not by its substantive research area, claimed to have a model of behavior applicably to any kind of human action, an idea epitomized by Gary Becker: "The economic approach to Human Behaviour " (Becker 1976).

It took some time for sociology to react. However, starting with the papers[6] by Harrison White (1981) and Mark Granovetter (1985), sociology counterattacked by (re)opening the field of economic sociology,[7] a field which turned out to be extremely successful in the last three decades:

> We are now almost 35 years into the era of modern economic sociology if one takes the publication of Harrison White's 1981 paper entitled "Where do markets come from?" as the origin point. The field has literally gone from nowhere to being one of the central fields in sociology. [. . .] Mark Granovetter's (1985) paper is the most cited paper in the post-war era.
>
> Fligstein (2015, 301)

It is interesting to see that in this situation of renewed crossover into each other's fields the relationship between economics and sociology and economics was not all-out hostile. The new economic institutionalism, especially in the variety represented by Douglass North, appeared to open up to sociological ideas. And the new economic sociology in turn certainly was taking especially new economic institutionalism seriously. For a time, especially in the so-called social capital debate, whose heyday can probably be dated between 1995 and 2005, we saw the first scientific debate crossing the boundaries of economics, political science and sociology – or so it seemed. Looked at from today, it appears that while there was and indeed is considerable cross-referencing, the willingness and/or the ability to really transcend one's own disciplinary borders trying to understand the other discipline from within, from its own disciplinary premises, has remained very limited. This is particularly true for the economic side of the schism.

A look at the recently published *Handbook of Social Economics* (Benhabib et al. 2010) part of the highly prestigious Elsevier Handbooks of Economics series, is revealing. Looking at the table of contents, chapter headings like "Social Norms and Preferences", "Social Construction of Preferences: Advertising", "The Economics of Cultural Transmission and Socialization" and "An Overview of Social Networks and Economic Applications" clearly testify that at least for those active in this field of research, mutual ignorance at least of topics cannot be claimed any more at the part of those mainstream economists who are working at this side of David Colander's edge.[8] However, the following citation from the introduction to the handbook makes clear the need to define an economist by his adherence to rational choice and methodological individualism – and more generally, by not being a sociologist:

> *Social economics* is the study, with the *methods of economics*, of social phenomena in which aggregates affect individual choices. Such phenomena include, just to mention a few, social norms and conventions, cultural identities and stereotypes, peer and neighbourhood effects.

> A central underpinning of the methods of economics is methodological individualism. In particular, explanations based solely on group choice are unusual and aggregates are generally studied as the result of individual choices. Furthermore, the methods of economics rely mostly, although not exclusively, on a rational choice paradigm. *Social economics* is to be distinguished therefore from *Economic sociology*, which may be thought of as the study, with the methods of sociology, of economic phenomena, e.g., markets. Although there is increasing overlap in these areas of study as it is quite evident in some of the chapters that follow, they are still quite complementary.
>
> (Benhabib et al. 2010, xvii, emphasis in original)

Thus mainstream economics and economic sociology are heavily engaged in toiling the same fields, but doing so competitively. And just as sociology was relegated to the non-economic during "the pact" in the same move by which schools of thought in economics other than rational choice began to be marginalized by what today is the mainstream, those same schools of thought engaged in the struggle for pluralism today have, I will argue, a natural ally in economic sociology.

3 What has been othered by the mainstream (and is dealt with in heterodox economics and economic sociology)?

What topics have been systematically excluded by mainstream economics, which have in turn been emphasized by the various heterodox schools and should therefore be core elements in a pluralist curriculum of economics? The notion of methodological individualism abstracts from the fundamentally social nature of human actors and their actions. While the sum of the actions by actors in the economy will have a feedback effect in these models as well (such as via the price in a market), this feedback will never affect the actor as such, his preferences or her view of her world; it is not a constitutive feedback loop. By way of contrast, this constitutive feedback from the social to the individual has been central to both to the original institutionalism and economic sociology.

This is closely connected to the absence of the idea of emergence in the economic mainstream (i.e. the idea that higher level social aggregates [organizations, states, the macroeconomy]) display characteristics that are non-reducible to the characteristics of the individuals they "consist" of. This idea is central to post-Keynesianism in its rejection of the idea of microfoundations and to complexity economics. While not being central to economic sociology, it is deeply engrained in sociology.[9]

Again closely related to the absence of constitutive feedback loops, the economic mainstream has lost the idea of historical specificity.[10] Economic action is always based on the interpretation of the situation by the actors, which in turn cannot be separated from the historically contingent images of the world these actors have. Historical specificity is central again to both institutional economics and economic sociology.

Investigating a bit more deeply into the manner in which mainstream economics bypasses this issue leads us further on. In its arguably theoretically most advanced variety, game theory, the notion of common knowledge is central and implies nothing less than 100% agreement on the interpretation of the situation by the actors.[11] This defines away the need of actors to interpret a situation each time they enter one, which implies that this interpretation of the situation may differ between the actors in a situation. A common understanding, if achieved, is as much a result of interaction as a condition for it.

This constant need of interpretation of the situation and the negotiation of the meaning of a situation between the actors is the source of constant (potential for) change. And it is this conceptual, interpretative or deep change – in contrast with change as the accumulation of some factors – which mainstream economics cannot handle. This is on the one hand another aspect of the loss of history; on the other hand, it is one foundational reason of "real uncertainty" again central to post-Keynesian economics. In a world in constant need of interpretation, the occurrence and even more so the repeated occurrence of what has not been interpreted so far or indeed has not been foreseen as being possible causes of "real uncertainty". Original institutionalism knows that reducing real uncertainty by making the world interpretable is a central function of institutions.

The need for constant interpretation and negotiation of meaning is at the heart of many approaches of economic sociology, not least of field theoretic accounts of markets, which we turn to further below as well as to the sociological analyses of consumption.

All of the above taken together has more recently been aptly summarized as the contrast between an open systems view of social reality and social science (taken by economic sociology and heterodox economics) versus a closed systems view (taken by mainstream economics, prominently so by Dow and Chick [2012] for example). The latter add at least one necessary condition for an open social system which is not clearly connected to the above but constitutes an additional issue neglected by mainstream economics: the embeddedness of social structures in more-encompassing ones, with continuous interaction between them (Dow and Chick 2012, 182). Embeddedness in turn has indeed been the most central idea of the new economic sociology ever since the publication of Mark Granovetter's seminal paper.

It is, however, somewhat curious that not more has been published in economic sociology on another important shortcoming of mainstream economics: the relative neglect of distributional issues, analytically and also normatively (i.e. concerning issues of distributional justice). Here indeed, taking up the French tradition following Bourdieu and especially the idea of field theory could provide a theoretical framework which integrates embeddedness issues and distributional issues right from the start. While a social field, as conceived by Bourdieu, is specifically defined by the array of mutual relationships actors have and are aware of, it is also by definition an arena of struggle for positions and for the definition of the rules of the game in the field. Thus contestation here is intrinsic and distributional issues arise naturally.[12] Taking up the conceptualization of markets as fields could provide a way of thinking about distributional issues beyond abstract normative considerations on the one hand and the artificial environment of the experimental lab on the other.

Moving away from theory to empirical research, the mainstream has embraced quantitative empirical techniques almost exclusively, testing hypotheses generated deductively from mathematical models, until recently almost entirely on pre-collected data. Qualitative research has been absent. This is not really surprising since for all its heterogeneous research traditions, qualitative research has always been seen as an alternative way to generate hypotheses by directly observing or talking to those engaged in a particular social situation, eager to learn about the interpretations actors have of that situation, regularly unveiling the heterogeneity between them.

Especially at the borders between sociology and political science, other methods have been developed for macro-social contexts favoring the case study as a means to delve into the special features of single macro units like countries, regions, firms and so forth (Blatter and Haverland 2014). Both case studies and more traditional qualitative methods have been employed successfully in economic sociology, being standard fare in its home discipline. I do believe there is extremely much to be learned by economics on this account.

Overall it should have become clear that the situation has not changed fundamentally since economics began to be identified with the rational choice approach in the interwar years: by this narrowing of perspectives both heterodox economics and sociology have been othered, and have both theorized those features of the economic excluded by the narrow mainstream vision. They have done so with varying emphasis and are thus highly complementary efforts.[13]

4 Consequences for teaching a pluralist economic curriculum

4.1 General considerations

In several publications Sheila Dow has fleshed out a clear case for pluralism from open systems thinking in economics.[14] Also, on theoretical grounds she favors a pluralism which does not embrace a postmodern "anything goes" but a pluralism structured around "schools of thought, in which the boundaries which define schools are provisional, semi-permeable and possibly overlapping" (Dow and Chick 2012, 194).

On several occasions she has also spelled out the consequences this has for teaching economics. A recent statement is Dow (2013), which we refer to in the following. She emphasizes how a curriculum based on a structured pluralism has to motivate and enable students to digest a set of materials which by its very nature is incommensurate (i.e. it represents distinct and at best incompletely compatible visions of the economy). At the same time, students need to develop what she calls "judgment": the ability to use the distinct approaches for particular applications in research and policy. (Simple) models should be part of the program, but in a situated manner: accompanied by a discussion of those factors left out of the model in order to be able to close the analysis. Students interested in making their mark in the real world will be best able to be motivated and successful in such a program.

Based on her own biography and experience, she sees this best realized in a curriculum which starts with philosophy as a grounding for all subjects. Moreover, all subjects should be taught with explicit reference to their history. Furthermore she pleads for interdisciplinary openness, making explicit reference to sociology and psychology.

When looking for predecessors to this view, one might be surprised to find a very similar vision expressed by Joseph Schumpeter on the first pages of his monumental *History of Economic Analysis* (Schumpeter 1954, 12–21). Economics, Schumpeter writes, is to be seen as consisting of four major areas: economic history, statistics, economic theory and economic sociology. Economic history, which he singles out as most important,[15] he sees as comprising both "economic" and "institutional" facts. And while he does not explicitly mention the history of economic thought, he emphasizes how economic history leads to the realization that "the economist himself is a result of his own *and all preceding* time" and thus "economic analysis and its results are certainly affected by historical relativity and the only question is how much" (Schumpeter 1954, 13, emphasis in original).

Schumpeter's understanding of statistics and theory are very much what we expect them to be. However, very much in line with the above, for all his fascination for deriving hypotheses from abstract models, Schumpeter clearly favors a method of theory formation starting with observation and then going down the path of increased abstraction, in effect nesting models in a larger set of experience (Schumpeter 1954, 15–20).

Schumpeter's concept of economic sociology, then, is underlining the meaning he already gave to the field of economic history by emphasizing the role of institutions. In modern parlance, the importance of economic sociology is based on the social embeddedness of the economy, economic sociology giving us the knowledge to understand the habits, cognitions and motives economic actors have at any one particular place and time.

But maybe I am overinterpreting Schumpeter here. This matters when looking at the question how to integrate economic sociology into a curriculum. One can read Schumpeter, certainly more than Dow, as saying that economic sociology provides additional contextual information for economic theory which can be used to calibrate the models without changing their inner workings – a weak form of historic specificity. In this case economic sociology could be added into a pluralist curriculum as a separate course, module, or the like, perhaps integrated into an interdisciplinary course on institutional analysis.

If, however, one is convinced, as I have argued above, that economic sociology provides an additional perspective to the way we think about the economy, contextualizing economic theory in a way that affects the inner working of a "model", then it would have to be mainstreamed. That is, it should contribute an additional perspective on the substance of courses taught in the curriculum, sometimes more and sometimes less central.[16]

In the following I will sketch how such mainstreaming could work for one central substantive field of economics: the study of markets.

4.2 A substantive example

Markets are a central component of capitalist economic systems. A course on theories of markets would start by describing a specific market in detail in its structure and in one or more episodes, followed by the exposition of general approaches to their theoretical analysis, some of which could then be analyzed in depth subsequently.

Such an architecture has the benefit of the specific, hands-on, real-world example for it. It also presents the challenge of presenting an initial picture of a market which contains elements of all the theoretical approaches. This may well be an overwhelming task or simply make the example extremely difficult to understand. Alternatively, one could start with a real-world media exposition of a market and then proceed by adding details corresponding to each theoretical approach as these are explained during the course.

My candidates for theoretical approaches to be dealt with would be the mainstream, evolutionary economics, innovation systems and economic sociology. In a general exposition of the mainstream approach, a skillful balance would have to be struck between correctly focusing on the dominance of price competition in that perspective and not hiding efforts to handle quality competition and innovation. Central messages could be the character of perfect competition as a limiting case and the incentives for firms to avoid price competition wherever they can.[17] Also it should be stressed how in such an analysis a 100% identical vision of the market situation by market actors is assumed (common knowledge).

Nelson and Winter (1982) are still a good starting point for representing an evolutionary theory of markets, where firms are a collection of organizational routines and markets the selection environments. Here I would stress the continuous heterogeneity of firms even in stationary periods of markets.

The literature on innovation systems is central because of its clear focus on what I do believe to be the most decisive characteristic of modern markets – their character as innovation machines. While the literature on national innovation systems is not a good fit for a course on markets, the literature on sectoral or technological innovation systems is (see e.g. Bergek et al. 2008). It should highlight the intricate interplay of knowledge development, entrepreneurial experimentation, the coordination between (potential) market participants on the direction of technological search, the mobilization of financial, skill and other resources, legitimation and more for a market for a new product to be generated. These activities involve firms, civil society, politics and the state.

And economic sociology? In their recent survey on economic sociology, Fligstein and Dioun (2015) distinguish four theoretical strands in economic sociology: the network approach, neo-institutionalist work, a political economy approach and what they call market devices and performativity.[18] The network approach, pioneered by Mark Granovetter's early article, has been most fundamentally associated with the early work in economic sociology. It has been successfully imported into economics and has become somewhat standard fare in institutional economics. In a course I would probably give it some initial space and possibly work on it deeper because of its integrative features. However, it would also be essential to emphasize the distinguishing feature of sociological thinking on networks: ongoing network relations shape the actors themselves; relations are not merely an external add-on.

Neo-institutionalist work emphasizes the role of cognitive frames in markets as well as the idea that market participants constantly observe each other's behavior. This increases the likelihood of herding behavior just as much as the formation of cartels or conflict. Fligstein and McAdam (2012) have recently integrated the neo-institutionalist perspective with Bourdieu's theory of fields to provide a fairly general framework. Actors constitute a field by their position within it. There is a common understanding of what is at stake, what the rules are and who occupies which positions. The more unsettled the field, the greater is the heterogeneity of understanding and the visions and interpretations are haggled over as part of the struggle for dominance in the fields. Institutional entrepreneurs exploit the social need for identity and orientation through meaning making as fundamental needs of human actors trying to orient themselves in a field where both cooperation and conflict are options.

By the term "political economy perspective" Fligstein and Dioun (2015) denote the work on comparative capitalisms. Here the interplay of the state, interest groups and firms is analyzed and compared between different countries, initially only in the high income range.[19] Complementarity between institutions as well as durable socio-political coalitions is seen to shape the institutions in which markets are embedded.

Finally, recent work has focused on the creation of markets. Special emphasis has been given to the role of conventions to create products, their qualities and their prices as well as to the role of economic theory itself to create and shape markets and the behavior of the agents in them (performativity).

Teaching all of these perspectives together in a single course might create too much complexity. If pressed to restrict myself to only one of the four perspectives, I would teach Fligstein's field theory. It nicely emphasizes what economic sociology is best in: the role of power struggle, the endogeneity of the cognitive and normative concepts to the dynamics of the field, and the dynamics of the field itself and its fundamental heterogeneity.

If there is room for two perspectives, any of the other three could be taught together with Fligstein's approach. The connections are closest with the work on the creation of markets, which is complementary on the dynamic part, and with the comparative capitalisms approach, which in a sense is climbing up into a macro perspective starting from institutions in different market and non-market spheres. The network perspective, finally, would emphasize the structure of the relations in the field and its effects.

On a slightly provocative note, one could say that overall economic sociology provides a conceptual and in some part analytical frame which has room for all of the approaches discussed before and adds some emphasis on its own. It would be a very fitting capstone for a course starting out from the static visions of competition of mainstream analysis to an ever more dynamic understanding of markets.

5 Concluding remarks

Economics and sociology have not only followed separate paths starting in the 1920s but they have also othered each other, each claiming the high ground of theoretical supremacy. This has its origin in the same process which othered heterodox approaches in economics – the increasing identification of economics with a single methodological position: methodological individualism and rational choice. From the 1980s onwards, both disciplines have been toiling each other's core substantive fields of interest, economic sociology providing an additional perspective on core economic phenomena. A pluralist economic curriculum thus should include economic sociology as a rich and dynamic source of ideas, concepts and evidence. Ideally such integration should be done via the mainstreaming of an economic sociological perspective, as I have sketched for a course on markets. Organizationally this might very well invite the experiment of co-teaching in several courses, something we should love as academics, even if university administrators do not like it all that much. It's a worthwhile investment.

Notes

1 This might no longer be true for the relationship between political science and economics. However this might also be a misperception insofar as it simply reflects the fact the economic imperialism has been so much more successful in political science compared to sociology. An economist therefore has no need to distance herself from political science since the part of political science she relates to cannot be methodologically separated from economics.

2 So indeed Ayel Leijonhufvud, by couching his satire as an anthropological study, was 100% on the right track.

3 Hegel is frequently cited as an early predecessor, and Simone de Beauvoir's *The Second Sex* (Beauvoir et al. (1949 [2009])) and Edward Said's *Orientalism* (Said 1978) are considered key early contributions in substance. According to a brief search on Google Scholar (4 August 2016), the term "othering" was used in the title of scientific publications 65 times in 2012, 78 times in 2013, 93 times in 2014 and 96 times in 2015. This does not make it an academic terminological "superstar", but it is testimony to a steady stream of research.

4 In 1892 the department of sociology was founded at the University of Chicago; in 1895 Durkheim established the first sociology department in France; in 1904 the first sociology department was founded in the UK (London School of Economics); and in 1919 the first chair of sociology was established in Germany. See Kruse (2012).

5 "Economics is the science which studies human behaviour as a relationship between ends and scarce means which have alternative uses" (Robbins 1932, 15).

6 In France, Pierre Bourdieu opened up similar lines of inquiry, the reception of which in the English-speaking world underwent a serious upturn during the 1980s. For an example of a full-blown application to an economic topic, see e.g. Bourdieu and Steinrücke (2002).

7 For a similar view with explicit reference to Becker, see Smelser and Swedberg (2005a, 14).

8 Even though this probably means wearing owls to Athens: David Colander (Colander et al. 2004) in a frequently cited book mapped out the increasing diversity in mainstream economics, coining the term "edge" for those economic research programs close to heterodox approaches but accepted by the economic mainstream.
9 Sawyer (2001) has been generative of a renewed debate on the issue in sociology.
10 Hodgson (2001) is a classical treatment.
11 Herbert Gintis summarized the issue as follows: "We saw [. . .] that both individual characteristics and collective understandings, the latter being irreducible to individual characteristics, are needed to explain common knowledge. It is for this reason that methodological individualism is incorrect when applied to the analysis of social life". (Gintis 2009, 162).
12 Kluttz and Fligstein (2016) is a recent survey of the state of the art in sociological field theory. See also section 4.2.
13 A detailed argument along highly similar lines can be found in Labrousse (2014).
14 See e.g. Dow (2004, 2007, 2016).
15 "If, starting my work in economics afresh, I were told that I could study only one of the three [in an early version of the manuscript, Schumpeter had not included economic sociology, S.P.] but could have my choice, it would be economic history, that I should choose" (Schumpeter 1954, 12).
16 Explorations of how an integrated "socio-economic" perspective might look can be found in Hedtke (2015). See also again Labrousse (2014).
17 Such a perspective is for example taken in the treatment of the mainstream in Elsner et al. (2015).
18 Swedberg (2007) and Portes (2010) are systematic expositions of economic sociology. Smelser and Swedberg (2005b) is a comprehensive handbook.
19 Morgan (2011) is a comprehensive handbook.

Bibliography

Beauvoir, S. de, Borde, C. and Malovany-Chevallier, S. (1949 [2009]): *The Second Sex*. London: Jonathan Cape.

Becker, G. (1976): *The Economic Approach to Human Behavior*. Chicago: Chicago University Press.

Benhabib, J., Jackson, M. O. and Bisin, A. (2010): *Handbook of Social Economics*. Amsterdam and London: North Holland (Handbooks in Economics).

Bergek, A., Jacobsson, S., Carlsson, B., Lindmark, S. and Rickne, A. (2008): "Analyzing the Functional Dynamics of Technological Innovation Systems: A Scheme of Analysis", *Research Policy* 37(3), 407–429.

Blatter, J. and Haverland, M. (2014): *Designing Case Studies: Explanatory Approaches in Small-N Research*. Basingstoke and Hants: Palgrave Macmillan (Research Methods Series).

Bourdieu, P. and Steinrücke, M. (eds.) (2002): *Der Einzige und sein Eigenheim*. Hamburg: VSA-Verlag.

Colander, D. C., Holt, R.P.F. and Rosser, J. B. (2004): *The Changing Face of Economics: Conversations with Cutting Edge Economists*. Ann Arbor: University of Michigan Press.

Dow, S. C. (2004): "Structured Pluralism", *The Journal of Economic Methodology* 11(3), 275–290.

Dow, S. C. (2007): "Pluralism in Economics", in Groenewegen, J. (ed.), *Teaching Pluralism in Economics*. Cheltenham, UK: Edward Elgar, 22–39.

Dow, S. C. (2013): "Teaching Open-System Economics", in Jespersen, J. and Madsen, M. O. (eds.), *Teaching Post Keynesian Economics*. Cheltenham, UK: Edward Elgar, 73–87.

Dow, S. C. (2016): "Consistency in Pluralism and the Role of Microfoundations", in Courvisanos, J., Doughney, J. and Millmow, A. (eds.), *Reclaiming Pluralism in Economics: Essays in Honour of John E. King*. London: Routledge, 32–46.

Dow, S. C. and Chick, V. (2012): "The Meaning of Open Systems", in Dow, S. C. (ed.), *Foundations for New Economic Thinking: A Collection of Essays*. Basingstoke, UK: Palgrave Macmillan, 178–196.

Elsner, W., Schwardt, H. and Heinrich, T. (2015): *The Microeconomics of Complex Economies: Evolutionary, Institutional, Neoclassical, and Complexity Perspectives*. Amsterdam and Boston: Academic Press.

Fligstein, N. (2015): "What Kind of Re-Imagining Does Economic Sociology Need?", in Aspers, P. and Dodd, N. (eds.), *Re-Imagining Economic Sociology*. Oxford: Oxford University Press, 301–315.

Fligstein, N. and Dioun, C. (2015): "Economic Sociology", in Wright, J. D. (ed.), *International Encyclopedia of the Social & Behavioral Sciences*. Amsterdam: Elsevier, 67–72.

Fligstein, N. and McAdam, D. (2012): *A Theory of Fields*. Oxford: Oxford University Press.

Gintis, H. (2009): *The Bounds of Reason: Game Theory and the Unification of the Behavioral Sciences*. Princeton, NJ: Princeton University Press.

Granovetter, M. (1985): "Economic Action and Social Structure: The Problem of Embeddedness", *American Journal of Sociology* 90, 481–510.

Hedtke, R. (ed.) (2015): *Was ist und wozu Sozioökonomie?* Wiesbaden: Springer Fachmedien.

Heise, A. (2016): *Pluralism in Economics: Inquiries into a Daedalean Concept*. Discussion Papers 51. University of Hamburg, Centre for Economic and Sociological Studies (CESS/ZÖSS).

Hodgson, G. M. (2001): *How Economics Forgot History: The Problem of Historical Specificity in Social Science*. London: Routledge.

Kluttz, D. N. and Fligstein, N. (2016): "Varieties of Sociological Field Theory", in Abrutyn, S. (ed.), *Handbook of Contemporary Sociological Theory*. Cham: Springer International Publishing (Handbooks of Sociology and Social Research), 185–204.

Kruse, V. (2012): *Geschichte der Soziologie*. Konstanz: UVK Verl.-Ges.

Labrousse, A. (2014): "Comment l'economie politique peut s'inspirer de la sociologie et renouer ainsi avec de traditions délaissées, mais fécondes", *La Decouverte – Revue Française de Socio-Économie* 13(1), 225–240.

Leijonhufvud, A. (1973): "Life among the Econ", *Western Economic Journal* 11(3), 327–337.

Morgan, G. (ed.) (2011): *The Oxford Handbook of Comparative Institutional Analysis*. Oxford: Oxford University Press.

Nelson, R. R. and Winter, S. G. (1982): *An Evolutionary Theory of Economic Change*. Cambridge, MA: The Belknap Press of Harvard University Press.

Portes, A. (2010): *Economic Sociology: A Systematic Inquiry*. Princeton, NJ: Princeton University Press.

Robbins, L. (1932): *An Essay on the Nature and Significance of Economic Science*. London: Palgrave Macmillan.

Said, E. W. (1978): *Orientalism*. New York: Pantheon Books.

Sawyer, K. (2001): "Emergence in Sociology: Contemporary Philosophy of Mind and Some Implications for Sociological Theory", *American Journal of Sociology* 107(3), 551–585.

Schumpeter, J. (1954): *History of Economic Analysis*. New York: Oxford University Press.

Smelser, N. J. and Swedberg, R. (2005a): “Introducing Economic Sociology”, in Smelser, N. J. and Swedberg, R. (eds.), *The Handbook of Economic Sociology*. Princeton, NJ: Princeton University Press, 3–25.

Smelser, N. J. and Swedberg, R. (eds.) (2005b): *The Handbook of Economic Sociology*. Princeton, NJ: Princeton University Press.

Spivak, G. C. (1985): “The Rani of Sirmur: An Essay in Reading the Archives”, *History and Theory* 24(3), 247–272.

Swedberg, R. (1990): *Economics and Sociology: Redefining Their Boundaries: Conversations with Economists and Sociologists*. Princeton, NJ: Princeton University Press.

Swedberg, R. (2007): *Principles of Economic Sociology*. Princeton, NJ: Princeton University Press.

White, H. (1981): “Where Do Markets Come from?” *American Journal of Sociology* 86, 517–547.

4 Comparing paradigms on a level playing field

Karl Betz with Martin Ehret[1]

1 Introduction

There is not just one economic science, but there are different paradigms – classical, neoclassical and Keynesian – with very different views of the functioning of the economic process. Different paradigms imply different perceptions of the same phenomena. Coming from a neoclassical perspective, you are led to interpret unemployment as voluntary and the unemployed turn from victims to culprits of unemployment. This leads to quotations such as, "Where is the fairness for the shift-worker, leaving home in the dark hours of the early morning, who looks up at the closed blinds of their next-door neighbour sleeping off a life on benefits?" (George Osborne 2012, see *Economist* 2015) or to EU estimates such as a Non Accelerating Inflation Rate of Unemployment (NAIRU) (i.e. full employment) of 20% for Spain (Gechert et al. 2015).

As adherents to different paradigms experience different phenomena differently (paradigms are worldviews after all, so small wonder that proponents of different approaches see different "worlds", or realities), different paradigms provide different explanations – it is your experience after all, which the theory, (a) forms and (b), is called upon to explain. I therefore argue that it is important to demonstrate the different foundations of these paradigms in an introductory course. This can be done within the same framework so that it becomes obvious which differences are due to the perspective of the paradigm and not just to different ways of modelling, so that the students from the start get an idea why different economists can reach different conclusions and have a fair chance to decide for themselves which approach seems more reasonable for them.

In what follows, I give a short outline of a one-term introduction to economics, in which I try to do that. For *price theory* (*micro*) I use a simple (one-good) production price model and the factor price frontier (fpf). For *income and employment (macro)*, the three approaches are compared using the production function which connects the labour market and the goods market of the income-expenditure model. In both contexts I discuss the difference between the three approaches, the differing equilibria and the differences in the comparative static results. At the start of the course the market diagram is presented – not because the critique of it is not valid (see Keen 2011), but just to make the students familiar with the concepts of excess supply and demand and the directions of price reaction.

2 Price theory

In his 1982 essay “The Neo-Ricardians”, Hahn rebukes the Sraffian critique of the neoclassical model by showing that the production price model is a special case of a price system in which supply has adjusted to demand, so that the vector of relative prices remains constant over different periods (Hahn 1982, 359, 364). His reasoning, however, identifies the production price model as a viable model for a long-term neoclassical price system (balanced growth). So the production price system can safely be put to use to compare the properties of (long-term) classical, neoclassical and Keynesian price theory.

2.1 Long-run equilibrium

To compare the difference in price theory, the most simple version of a production price model, a one-good economy is sufficient. A single output good is produced with a units of the same good and l unit of labour as inputs. Let p denote the price of the good, w the (nominal) wage rate and r the rate of profit (or $1 + r$ the rate of return). Then the price system is given with

$$a \cdot (1+r) \cdot p + l \cdot w = p \Leftrightarrow p = [1 - a \cdot (1+r)]^{-1} \cdot l \cdot w$$

given the technology, the input coefficients a and l are known. This leaves us with three unknowns (p, r and w) and one equation. One unknown can be eliminated by the choice of the numeraire; for instance use w, the wage unit, as numeraire. Then we need to know just the rate of profit r or the real wage rate w/p to determine p.[2] But these depend on each other, as expressed in the factor price frontier (fpf). Dividing the production price system by p yields:

$$a \cdot (1+r) + l \cdot w/p = 1$$

So the whole price system is solved if either the real wage rate or the rate of profit is explained. This observation allows to explain the basic difference between the price theory of the three paradigms.

Classical economics: Labour is just some other reproducible commodity. So its price is determined by its costs of reproduction – the amount of goods and labour needed to (re)produce one unit of labour. Let these coefficients be denoted by the index l. Then

$$a_l \cdot p + l_l \cdot w = w$$

is the additional equation which determines w/p (labour is not produced by capitalists, so the rate of profit is zero). At this wage rate the supply of labour is perfectly elastic – just as is the supply of any other commodity at its (re)production price.[3]

This reasoning is illustrated by the dashed line in Figure 4.1: given the input coefficients and w/p, the rate of profit (and the complete vector of relative prices) is determined.

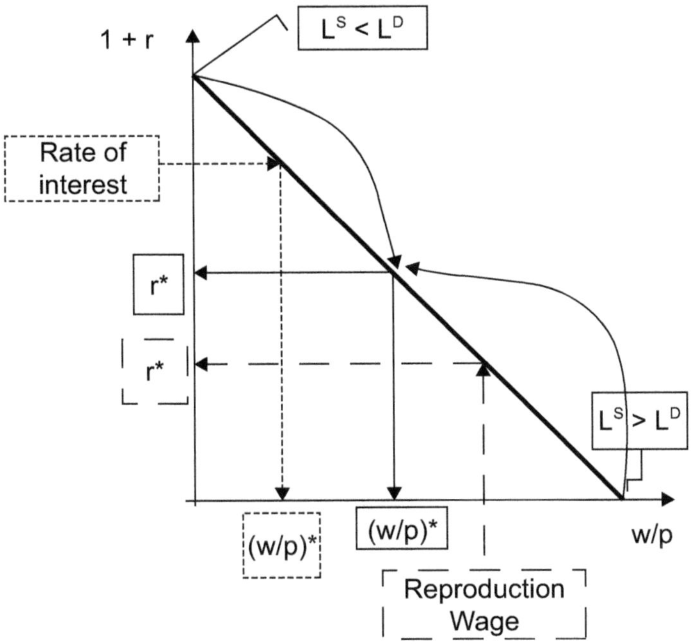

Figure 4.1 Closing the degree of freedom of the fpf

Keynes: The rate of interest is determined in the credit and asset markets. The rate of profit in turn is determined by the rate of interest. "Capital . . . is kept scarce because of the competition of the rate of interest on money" (Keynes 1936, chapter 16). What emerges is the real wage rate (and the complete vector of relative prices;[4] see dotted lines in Figure 4.1).

The neoclassical solution: Consider the maximum rate of return. Here the demand for labour will be high while the supply of labour will be zero, as the real wage rate is zero. So at this point we find an excess demand for labour, which will induce (real) wages to increase with the rate of profit decreasing. At the other extreme, when the rate of return is zero, the real wage rate reaches its maximum. Here at least some amount of labour services will be offered, while the demand will be zero. Hence there will be an excess supply, real wages will fall and the rate of return will increase. Now suppose that the excess demand function for labour decreases monotonously. Then there must be one combination (r^*; $(w/p)^*$) at which the labour market clears, so that there is no further tendency for the factor prices to change (see solid lines in Figure 4.1). So r^* and $(w/p)^*$ are determined by the equilibrium of the factor markets. (As a further unknown (employment) is derived, the system has one additional degree of freedom, so it is not overdetermined.) This reasoning also implies that neoclassical price theory requires the assumption of (the necessary conditions for the market process to lead to) full employment.

Table 4.1 Synopsis (price theory)

	Given	*Determined*
Classical economics	Reproduction wage	Rate of profit
Neoclassical economics	Factor supply	r^*, $(w/p)^*$, L*
Keynesian economics	Rate of profit	Wage rate

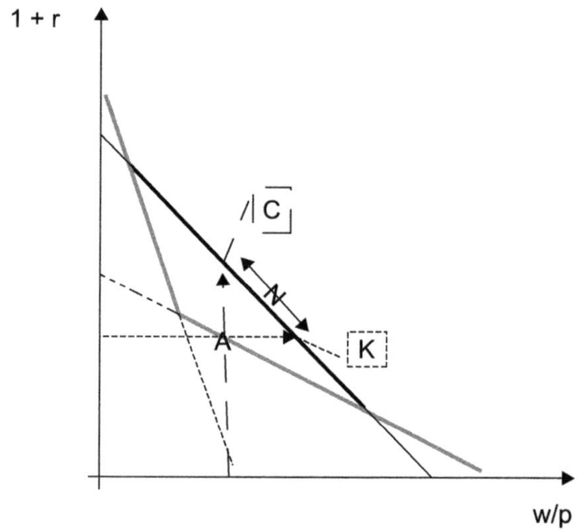

Figure 4.2 Technological progress

Note: With the introduction of a new technology, a part of the original enveloping curve becomes obsolete, as superior factor price combinations become feasible (solid black line).

2.1.1 *Comparative statics*

The fpf can furthermore be used to do comparative statics. One obvious application is the analysis of changes in factor prices. This, however, is straightforward, so that in this section only three applications are discussed: technological progress, taxes and environmental policy. If there is more than one technique, then each of these has its own fpf and the fpf of the society is the envelope of the individual fpfs[5] (the fpf in Figure 4.2 therefore is not drawn as a straight line). Comparative statics can discuss which consequence changes in the envelope of the fpfs imply for factor prices.

2.2 *Technological progress*

Technological progress implies that some new fpf emerges which, at least in part, runs above the old enveloping curve (grey curve in graph 2). Suppose the economy starts in point A.

Classical economics: As the real wage rate is given, an outward shift of the fpf will raise the rate of profit (Marx's production of relative surplus value; Marx, 1859 [1974], 1867 [1974]). The new factor prices are found at point C (vertical dashed line).

Neoclassical economics: The new factor price combination will lie on the new fpf in the triangle above the former equilibrium point. Both the wage rate and the rate of profit will rise – although without additional information about L^S and L^D the exact magnitude of these changes can't be decided (solid arrow; $N = \overline{CK}$).

Keynesian economics: As *r* is given, the real wage rate will rise (horizontal dotted lines) and the system will end up in point K.

2.3 *Tax incidence*

Taxes imply that a part of the output accrues to the state and therefore is no longer available for factor remuneration. This can be represented by an inward shift of the fpf. I mention in passing that the fpf shifts the focus of attention to the consequences for income distribution while the discussion in the market diagram focuses attention to the relative incidence for sellers and buyers. The former is more meaningful than the latter, since everyone has to sell in order to be able to buy, while you don't need to be a capitalist in order to sell your labour services (and in general you are not, as the net assets of the lower two quintiles of the wealth distribution are negligible to negative in most capitalist societies) (Piketty 2014, chapter 10; OECD 2015).[6]

Classical economics: Never mind which form of taxation is implemented; taxes are paid out of profits. (This of course changes, when rents enter the model.)

Neoclassical economics: The new factor price combination will lie in the triangle ACK below the former equilibrium point. Both the wage rate and the rate profit will be affected.

Keynesian economics: As *r* is given, only the real wage rate will be affected. The tax burden is borne by workers.

2.4 *Environment*

Both pollution and abatement have the same consequence: some formerly feasible technique will no longer be available. Be it that pollution requires a switch in technique (e.g. because more effort has to be put in the treatment of polluted water), or be it that a formerly chosen technique is outlawed because of the danger it poses to the environment. Thus, again, the factor price frontier shifts inward. All three paradigms predict that factor prices will be affected, although again the incidence differs.

Classical economics: As wages are given, the burden is borne by the rate of profit.

Neoclassical economics: The new factor price combination will lie somewhere below the former equilibrium point (triangle ACK). Again, both the wage rate and the rate profit will be affected.

Keynesian economics: As *r* is given, only the real wage rate will eventually be affected.

Table 4.2 Synopsis (comparative statics)

	Technological Progress	*Tax Incidence*	*Environment Affects*
Classical economics	rate of profit	rate of profit	rate of profit
Neoclassical economics	Both	both	both
Keynesian economics	wage rate	wage rate	wage rate

3 Income and employment (and money)

The market for goods and services and the factor markets (represented by the labour market) are linked by the production function. The market for goods and services is modelled along the lines of the income-expenditure model with demand on the vertical and the supply of goods and services (which by definition is equal to income Y) on the horizontal axis. For the market to be in equilibrium, (aggregate) supply has to be equal to (aggregate) demand. The 45° line therefore is not some sort of aggregate supply function but an equilibrium condition. As outlined in Keynes's treatise (Keynes 1930, chapters 9–12), at any point above the 45° curve demand outstrips supply, so that entrepreneurs will earn unexpected profits, which will induce them to expand supply (widow's cruse). Below the 45° line the reverse will be true (barrel of Danaïdes).

3.1 Money

Basic to Keynes's reasoning is that demand depends on income and that people may plan to spend less than their income at full employment, so that at full employment demand may fall short of supply and income has to contract in order to reach an equilibrium of supply and demand. The answer of supply-side economists to this is that either (classical economics: Say's law) people will always plan to spend all of their earnings: no one offers goods or services if not to purchase something in return (Say 1815 [1974], chapter 15). Or that relative prices will eventually equate supply and demand plans. While Say's argument is a behavioural assumption, which may or may not be correct,[7] both price mechanisms that neoclassical theory has to offer are flawed. Money is created by the extension of credit: banks create credit and deposits at the same time, when they write a credit contract and central bank money is created, when banks refinance themselves at the discount window of the central bank. So neither is money net wealth, nor is the quantity of money given exogenously. These properties of money render obsolete both the "Pigou effect" and the "Keynes effect".[8] The "Pigou effect" is obsolete, because (net) real money balances don't change when the price level changes (as zero divided by any number remains zero). And the "Keynes effect" does not work, because in comparative statics the nominal volume of credit (and therefore money) will be lower if prices are lower (and the nominal value of the purchases to be financed with credit is lower) – so money will contract along with prices. And in dynamics, falling prices induce losses which have to be refinanced, so that credit demand expands and the rate of interest won't fall. For this again see Keynes (1930).

So, in a nutshell, if demand depends on (effective) income and not on relative prices alone, then there is no market mechanism that will ensure that flexible prices will eventually draw the economy towards full employment.[9]

3.2 *Income and employment*

Classical economics: Labour supply is infinitely elastic at the reproduction wage. This determines the wage rate, the rate of profit and the technology described by the input coefficients (a, l). The capital stock K_t at the beginning of the period is given, being the result of past accumulation. Employment therefore is

$$L^* = (l/a) \cdot K_t.$$

Income is determined as employment times labour productivity,

$$Y^* = (1/l) \cdot L^*$$

(or K_t times capital productivity) while aggregate demand, thanks to Say's law, will always be equal to aggregate supply (i.e. income) (see Figure 4.3).

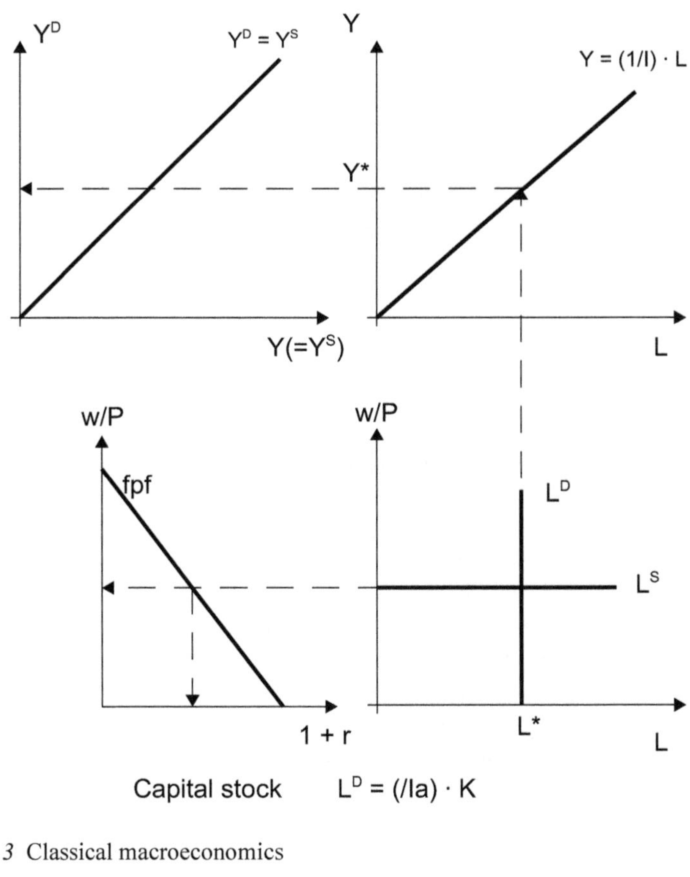

Figure 4.3 Classical macroeconomics

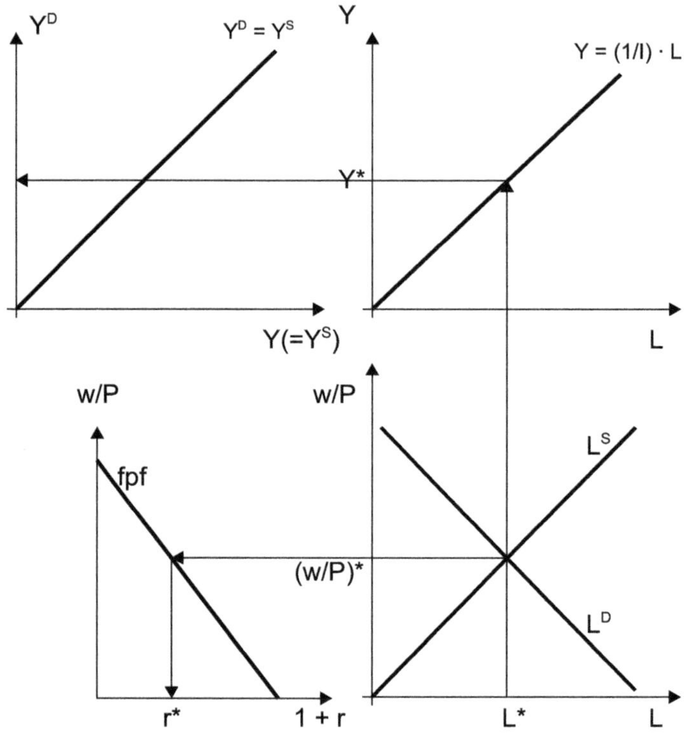

Figure 4.4 Neoclassical macroeconomics

Neoclassical economics: See Figure 4.4. Both labour supply and demand are elastic in the real wage rate. (Labour demand is a function of the real wage, because the rate of profit is a function of the real wage and therefore savings respond to changes in the real wage rate.) The factor markets thus decide on employment, the wage rate and the rate of profit.

Given full employment, the production function determines the level of output (Y). Flexible prices ensure that notional supply equals notional demand.[10] I assume that both the labour supply and demand curves are well behaved – even if this cannot be taken for granted – because I wish to stress the different logic of the underlying market model instead of discussing different assumptions about the properties of preference functions (which would remain in the same market framework). As changes in the real wage rate might induce a change in the chosen technique, input coefficients may change if labour supply or demand changes. So in the neoclassical case the production function may not be a straight line – but this is easier to draw and its slope is of no consequence to the arguments made here (as long as it is upward sloping).

Keynes: The two features of the Keynesian model are effective demand (which depends on income and, at full employment, may well fall short of supply) and the determination of the real rate of interest on the credit and asset markets. As the economy usually will not end up on the labour supply curve, its progression is not crucial to the argument; it is only referred to in order to determine the level of unemployment in equilibrium. For the sake of convenience I retain the neoclassical version, but any other supply function would do as well. The real rate of interest determines the real wage rate and it simultaneously influences effective demand.[11] Supply adjusts to effective demand, so that employment is determined as $L^* = Y^* \cdot l$ and the equilibrium capital stock is $K^* = Y^* \cdot a$. The limiting factor here is effective demand, which rations the use of inputs. While there is no unemployed capital, as capital goods which are not needed will not be produced, there is no unemployed capital;[12] people are too stubborn to cease to exist when their services are not in demand, so that the equilibrium level of unemployment is given by

$$U = L^S(w/P) - Y^* \cdot l$$

As discouraged workers may withdraw from the labour market, it is preferable to measure unemployment using the participation rate – say as the ratio of labour

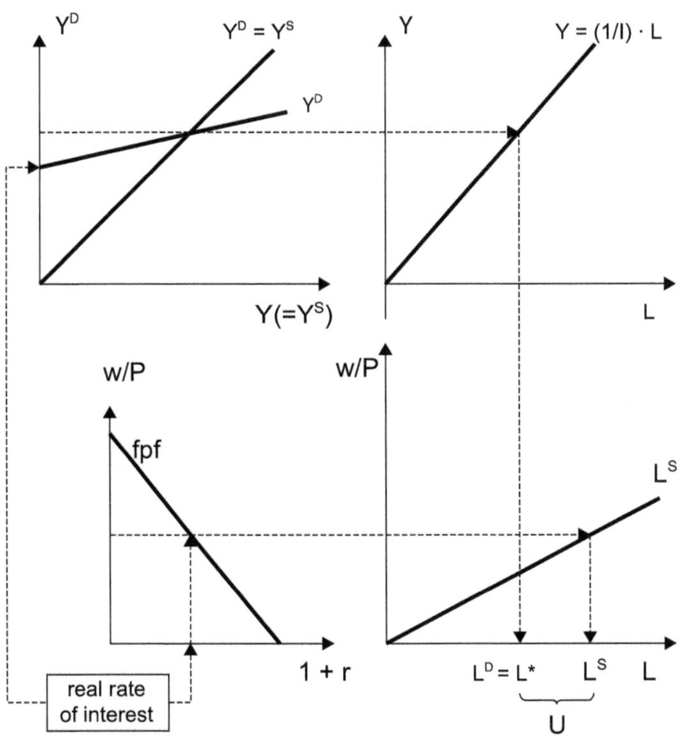

Figure 4.5 Keynesian macroeconomics

Table 4.3 Synopsis (income and employment)

	Limiting Factor	*Employment*
Classical economics	capital stock	full employment income (labour adjusts)
Neoclassical economics	labour supply curve capital supply curve	full employment income
Keynesian economics	effective demand	unemployment capital stock adjusts

volume to the adult population times the normal working hours. Please note that, while the level of wages is determined, the wage structure is not: while classical economists can explain different wages by differences in reproduction costs and neoclassical economists can explain it by the market clearing wages of heterogeneous labour services, here not all labour markets are cleared (possibly none), so that there is lots of room for wage discrimination and sociological factors which will have to be evoked to explain the wage structure.

Nevertheless, the profit-maximising condition of nominal wage rate equal to value of marginal product may still hold. As the wage structure influences relative prices and thereby (a) the choice of technology and (b) the output price, the value of the marginal product may adjust to the nominal wage.

3.2.1 Comparative statics

To compare the properties of the three models, the effect of two shocks are briefly discussed: technical progress and social policy.

3.3 Technical progress

Technical progress implies that the production function becomes steeper and that the fpf shifts outward, as already discussed.

Classical economics: Output increases and the rate of profit will increase. The impact on deployment however depends on the type of technological change. As $L = (l/a) \cdot K$, employment will increase if technical progress is capital saving, while it will decrease if it is labour saving. Ricardo therefore admitted that technological change may hurt the workers in the short run, as some of the formerly employed may become redundant. (Ricardo 1817, chapter 31: “On Machinery”).

Neoclassical economics: As the marginal product of labour increases, labour demand will increase. So output, employment and the real wage rate will go up.

Keynesian economics: As long as technical progress doesn’t affect demand (which it might, in case of product innovation or if it affects depreciation), the steeper production function implies a reduction of employment while real wages will increase.

3.4 *Social policy*

Social policy implies a redistribution of income. In classical economics this is discussed under the heading of poor laws. Classical economists were sceptical about those, because they basically meant that the state provided a subsistence wage (i.e. it demanded people whose labour services were not needed) – or, given the horizontal labour supply curve, the poor laws implied the production of unemployed. So social policy leads to the creation of unemployment – and it usually was recommended that these redundant workers should be kept in conditions under which they could not procreate (workhouses). There however is no effect on real wages, employment and income (at least as long as this policy is paid for with taxes on rent).

3.4.1 Neoclassical economics

The labour supply curve shifts inwards as (a) the opportunity cost of employment is raised and (b) the net real wage is reduced, as a part of the taxes needed to finance social policy is borne by labour. In consequence income and employment is reduced, the gross real wage increases while the net real wage decreases. The rate of profit decreases.

3.4.2 Keynesian economics

As the marginal rate of consumption is higher for lower income groups, it increases for the economy as a whole, so that the demand curve becomes steeper. Output and employment therefore will increase, the real wage rate will decrease, and

Table 4.4 Synopsis (comparative statics macro)

	Output	*Employment*	*Factor Income*
Technological Progress			
Classical economics	Increases	depends on type	rate of profit increases
Neoclassical economics	Increases	increases	r and w/p increase
Keynesian economics	Unaffected	reduced	wage rate increases
Social Policy			
Classical economics	Unaffected	Unaffected (but unemployment increases)	*r* reduced if not financed out of taxes on rents
Neoclassical economics	Decreases	decreases	*r* and *w/p* decrease
Keynesian economics	Increases	increases	*w/p* decreases

(involuntary) unemployment will be reduced because of (a) increased labour demand and, if one accepts the assumptions of the standard labour supply curve, (b) because a part of hitherto involuntary unemployment becomes voluntary.

4 Conclusion

Not to start with some special theory (neoclassical economics) but to give an overview over different economic paradigms allows the students to decide which approach is the most convincing for them. This can be done in a simple common framework, which allows to identify the differences between the classical, neoclassical and Keynesian approaches, which allows reconstruction of the arguments at the same (low) level of theoretical sophistication. The students are enabled to (a) discuss the consequences of shocks in the context of the different paradigms, (b) identify the different predictions which follow from the three models and (c) help them understand which policy prescriptions are motivated by which paradigm – why economists can differ in their suggestions for economic policy measures.

What becomes evident is, that the differences between classical, neoclassical and Keynesian economics are not due to different ways of formalisation. They yield different results and explanations within the same formal framework.

Acknowledgment

I would like to thank Martin Ehret and Wolfram Elsner for helpful suggestions (Karl Betz).

Notes

1 Karl Betz passed away on 28 July 2016. It was an honour for me to finish my colleague's last paper in his spirit (Martin Ehret).

2 At this point it is advisable to remark that the same would hold true in a more realistic model with zounds of commodities, where a would become $\mathbf{A}$ the (zounds × zounds) matrix of input coefficients, while l and p turn into $\mathbf{l}$ and $\mathbf{p}$ the vector of labour inputs and prices respectively. Still, to determine the zounds of relative prices, only r and w/p would be missing. Further complications, such as non-basics and joint production should be mentioned, but are relegated to a more specialised course.

3 Many classical economists sought ways to increase the reproduction price of labour. Malthus, for instance, suggested to allow weddings only at some threshold level of income. The ban on child labour and/or female labour may also be understood in this context.

4 For this approach to work, obviously the real interest rate has to be determined, so some modification of Keynes's version of liquidity preference theory is required.

5 Again, topics such as reswitching may be mentioned, but are relegated to more specialised courses.

6 Atkinson points out that it is important to distinguish wealth and capital. "Most of the wealth of the lower percentiles consists of housing wealth – which does not affect factor income distribution. . . . much of the wealth that people own conveys little or no control over the productive activities of the economy beyond their own front door. . . . It is

capital that is relevant, when we consider the macroeconomic distribution of income" (Atkinson 2015, 95). This goes along with Marx's distinction between property and private property, the latter being characterised by its functioning socially.

7 And there is a good chance for it to prove wrong: as the individual budget constraints imply that no one can plan to spend more than she earns, even a single agent who doesn't behave according to Say's assumption will negate Say's law.

8 The Pigou effect and the Keynes effect are so-called real-balance effects. They claim that a change of the price level affects aggregate demand. If the price level goes down, real wealth is rising and since consumers are getting richer, they tend to spend more (Pigou effect). Similarly, when prices are lower consumers need less money for their purchases, they demand more financial assets and interest rates go down. This leads to higher investments (Keynes effect).

9 While Clower's distinction between notional and effective plans is extremely helpful (Clower 1963), the new macroeconomics ended up in a full employment equilibrium because here too exogenous outside money was assumed.

10 In contrast to effective demand notional demand is not constrained by supply. For example, you plan to spend your spring break in Florida for a total cost of $800. Therefore you plan to work for two weeks in a food court for a salary of $400 per week. Your notional demand is $800 for your holiday trip. Since your notional supply is $800, your notional plans are in equilibrium. Unfortunately, when you go to the hamburger restaurant you realise that there is no job vacancy. No job, no holiday trip, and your effective demand is zero. Besides, since your effective supply is equal to zero too, your effective plans are in equilibrium as well.

11 This can be more elegantly discussed in an extended IS-MP-framework (see Betz 2015). But I usually don't manage to cram this in a one-semester course. So I don't deal with it here.

12 Therefore it is not convincing to measure the "output gap" by the degree of capital utilisation.

References

Atkinson, A. B. (2015): *Inequality: What Can Be Done?* Cambridge and London: Harvard University Press.

Betz, K. (2015): *The IS-MP-Model and the Difference between Neoclassical and Keynesian Economics*, www.boeckler.de/pdf/v_2012_10_25_betz.pdf, accessed 16 July 2018.

Clower, R. (1963 [1965]): "The Keynesian Counter-Revolution: A Theoretical Appraisal", in Hahn, F. H. and Brechling, F.P.R. (eds.), *The Theory of Interest Rates*. Basingstoke, UK: Palgrave Macmillan, 103–125.

Economist (2015): "George Osborne's Sad Triumph", Print Edition Britain, 9 July, www.economist.com/britain/2015/07/09/george-osbornes-sad-triumph, accessed 3 September 2018.

Gechert, S., Rietzler, K. and Tober, S. (2015 [2014]): "The European Commission's New NAIRU: Does It Deliver?", *IMK Working Paper* 142(12).

Hahn, F. (1982): "The Neo-Ricardians", *Cambridge Journal of Economics* (6), 352–374.

Keen, S. (2011): *Debunking Economics*. London and New York: Zed Books.

Keynes, J. M. (1930): *Vom Gelde (Treatise on Money)*. Berlin: Duncker & Humblot.

Keynes, J. M. (1936): "The General Theory of Employment, Interest and Money", in Johnson, E. and Moggridge, D. (eds.), *The Collected Writings of John Maynard Keynes*. Vol. 7. Cambridge: Royal Economic Society.

Marx, K. (1859 [1974]): *Zur Kritik der politischen Ökonomie. MEW 13*. Berlin: Dietz Verlag.

Marx, K. (1867 [1974]): *Das Kapital. Bd. 1 MEW 23*. Berlin: Dietz Verlag.
OECD (2015): *In It Together: Why Less Inequality Benefits All*. Paris: OECD Publishing.
Piketty, T. (2014): *Capital in the Twenty-First Century*. Cambridge and London: Harvard University Press.
Ricardo, D. (1817 [2004]): *On the Principles of Political Economy and Taxation*. New York: Dover Publications.
Say, J.-B. (1815 [1974]): *Traite d'economie politique*. Paris: Calmann-Lévy.

5 It needs two eyes to see in perspective

Teaching economics through the confrontation of dissenting views

Michael Derrer

Referring to Karl Betz's text, I will treat the confrontation of conflicting theories as a didactic method. Karl Betz's approach has the particular merit of allowing for the comparison of paradigms which at first sight appear to be caught in a specific worldview.

My professional experience[1] brought me to the conviction that knowledge generally progresses through the confrontation of different views – be it opposing paradigms, theories or models. This aligns with constructivist teaching, as it makes the relativity of any theorization attempt palpable. In the constructivist perspective, a learning process can be considered successful if one's own opinions and judgments are reflected, verified or falsified. Not only does this train the students' power of judgment, it also incites them to generate new positions of synthesis – and to develop a sense for the changeability of economic and social environments: what can and what should change, and how? In economics, the confrontation of the claims of different schools of thought furthermore aims to counter their mutual blindness – for most schools exist in their own world and communicate little with the outside.

Engarnter and Krisanthan (2013) rightly state that "not economic theories themselves are the core of economic education, but their transformation into categories relevant for education". The confrontation does indeed have a didactic value in itself, independently of the transmitted contents. Nevertheless, I want to suggest some possible topics for confrontational teaching.

One option would be to use Marx's analysis of 19th-century capitalism as a means to discern what today's society looks like (and where Marx went wrong). But today, the starting point of the "neoliberal" worldview appears to me as particularly fruitful; it can serve as one of the poles for a comparison. Depending on the specific topic, this position can be confronted with "critical", "social" or "interventionist" stances.

1 Manuals for the confrontational approach

Standard economics textbooks read like a linear story in which neoclassical concepts are laid out, one element building on another. There is hardly any confrontation in those textbooks (the exception confirming the rule usually being a superficial comparison of planned and market economies, and an incomplete comparison of Keynesian and monetarist conceptions and recommendations in economic policy).

As much as this lopsidedness is deplorable, we can put such a one-sided textbook to use by confronting it with a critical text. In my (heterodox) introductory class to economics at Lucerne University for Applied Sciences and Arts, we used the wordy 800-pager of Taylor and Mankiw (2014) for the part of mainstream economics, but I now prefer using the version "reduced to the max" of Andrew Gillespie's *Economics through Diagrams* (2009). This mainstream textbook can be compared to a critical book, such as Hill and Myatt's *Anti-Textbook* (2010) or to critical texts on individual topics. In their reports and class presentations, the students evaluate the pertinence of the critique and arrive at a personal conclusion about the use and limitations of mainstream economics.

There exist some newer textbooks which already contain a confrontational approach, such as van Staveren (2014), who compares four economic paradigms for every topic. Another approach is taken by Harvey (2016), who presents the essence of eight economic paradigms and critically appreciates them. Our own ongoing project, "Wirtschaft im Widerspruch" (German for "contradictory economic views") is a collection of opposing views on a choice of topics, intended for adult non-specialists, among which are the following:

- The neoclassical world of "platonic" models vs. real world economics;
- Economic institutional arrangements in different countries (e.g. Anglo-Saxon vs. Central European ("Rhenan") capitalism);[2]
- Real existing capitalism vs. utopias of the past and present;
- Market-oriented positions vs. its communitarian critique;[3]
- Arguments for and against minimum wages;
- How regulation of a new phenomenon is regulated in different countries (e.g. Uber, Airbnb);
- Public vs. private ownership in different sectors and its effects;
- The tension between the performance principle and wealth through heritage;
- Present money creation, in which 90% of the money is created by banks vs. "positive money" (in German, "Vollgeld")[4] vs. private currencies;[5]
- Diverging interpretations of historic events, such as the financial crisis of 2008 (e.g. was it a lack of state intervention in the financial sector that caused it, or [as authors of the Austrian school claim] central banks influencing the economy too much by keeping interest rates too low?);
- Benefits of globalized international trade and its negative effects.

2 Risks and how to address them

Should mainstream economics be given a prominent place in confrontational teaching? Heterodox economists might argue against it. I do believe, however, that the dominance of the neoclassical paradigm makes it an inevitable stepping-stone for many topics, as it is a major source shaping the public discourse, so students should discuss it in class. Through comparison, students get to see the cool seduction of the smoothness and calculability of neoclassical economics, but also develop a sense of its purely logical nature and (too) high abstraction level.

In a confrontational approach, teachers and authors can be tempted to reveal their own convictions from the start. I recommend resisting this temptation when presenting conflicting viewpoints on a topic. Instead, the contradictory discourses ought to be presented with the same care and conviction. Only in this way the students will be able to assume a role similar to that of judges in a courtroom who have to make up their minds when confronted with the lawyers' arguments.[6]

Of course, there often exist more than two positions on a certain topic. However, the reduction to two fundamentally differing standpoints avoids getting lost in aspects of minor importance and lets the controversy appear clear-cut. This is why I usually limit myself to presenting the most conflicting or most prominent positions about a certain topic. Compromises, shades of gray and nuances are to form in students' heads – and through their pens.

An economics course based on the confrontation of discourses becomes more student-driven. The teacher can indicate the cardinal points, but the students have to discover the paths themselves. Furthermore, a traditional lecturer might perceive a risk that the audience leaves without a clearly defined and circumscribed body of knowledge. However, in a constructivist perspective, this is not a drawback – to the contrary: as student must build their knowledge themselves, by extending bits of knowledge that preexist in their heads, learning is a highly personal process of the individual mind. Obviously, exams have to adapt to this, and questions have to allow for the manifestation of individual knowledge.

Notes

1 I mention the study of the socio-economic environment in Russia as compared to Western Europe; my teaching experience at institutions with a "left-leaning" or a "right-leaning" worldview (faculty of social work vs. business schools); and my side function as an elected layman judge in Switzerland.
2 As in Michel Albert, *Capitalism against Capitalism* (1993) and further literature on the varieties of capitalism.
3 E.g., Stephen Marglin, *The Dismal Science: How Thinking Like an Economist Undermines Community* (2008) and so forth.
4 As proposed by Joseph Huber and James Robertson, *Creating New Money. A Monetary Reform for the Information Age* (2000).
5 As championed by Friedrich Hayek, *The Denationalization of Money* (1976).
6 A difficult exercise for a judge, for lawyers can be very convincing in creating their narration.

References

Albert, M. (1993): *Capitalism Against Capitalism*. London: Whurr.

Engartner, T. and Krisanthan, B. (2013): "Ökonomische Bildung im sozialwissenschaftlichen Kontext – oder: Aspekte eines Konzepts sozio-ökonomischer Bildung", *Gesellschaft, Wirtschaft, Politik (GWP)* 2, 243–256.

Gillespie, B. A. (2009): *AS and A Level Economics through Diagrams: Oxford Revision Guides*. Oxford: Oxford University Press.

Harvey, J. T. (2016): *Contending Perspectives in Economics: A Guide to Contemporary Schools of Thought*. Cheltenham, UK and Northampton, MA: Edward Elgar.

Hayek, F. A. (1976): *The Denationalization of Money*. London: Institute of Economic Affairs.

Hill, R. and Myatt, T. (2010): *Economics Anti-Textbook*. Halifax: Zed Books.

Huber, J. and Robertson, J. (2000): *Creating New Money. A Monetary Reform for the Information age*. London: New Economics Foundation.

Marglin, S. A. (2008): *The Dismal Science: How Thinking Like an Economist Undermines Community*. Cambridge, MA and London, England: Harvard University Press.

Staveren, I. V. (2014): *Economics after the Crisis*. London and New York: Routledge.

Taylor, M. P. and Mankiw, G. N. (2014): *Economics*. Boston: Cengage Learning.

6 Economic competence, economic understanding, and reflexive judgment

A social theory of teaching teachers of economics

Alexander Lenger, Yvette Keipke and Nils Goldschmidt

1 Introduction

Great things have been accomplished in the teaching of economics in recent years: Besides the continued development of a system of didactics that examines both actions and problems, substantial findings and insights have been made with regard to individual economic competences and their measurement. It has essentially been proven that *individual* economic competence is dependent in particular on four factors: the learner's stage of cognitive development (Berti and Bombi 1988; Furnham and Lewis 1986; Leiser and Halachmi 2006), their educational level (Gleason and Scyoc 1995; Blendon et al. 1997; Zappalá 2001), their gender (Hirschfeld et al. 1995; Gleason and Scyoc 1995), and their parents' socio-economic status (Furnham and Kirkcaldy 2000).

However, to date, less attention has been paid to the question of how economic competence is integrated into real life. Of particular importance is the way in which economic competence is understood in different *societal* contexts and how it is related to normative judgments regarding financial matters. An individual's private, professional, social, and political life is mutually interlinked with the actual economy itself, and consequently the necessity arises for a comprehensive economic education to foster a better understanding of the complexity of and distinctions between economic and social processes. Such a broad approach to teaching economics should not just be practiced in teaching in schools, but should also be applied early on educating student teachers at university.

In this chapter, we shall argue that the primary goal in the university instruction of teachers of economics should be to enable these prospective teachers to shape their pupils into informed and considered participants in active civil society, instilling in them high levels of ability in economic decision-making, action, and judgment. The best way to put into place the conditions under which a sustainable discourse on a society's economic circumstances can develop is a form of economic education in universities and schools which is oriented not just towards competences, but also towards a *reflective and reflexive* (i.e. a considered and self-aware) understanding of economic processes; in order to become mature members of a modern market society, pupils must be able to fundamentally *understand* and *evaluate* these processes and how they are embedded in the societal context as a whole.

In approaching such a broad concept of economic education, it is helpful to differentiate analytically between economic competence and economic understanding. Economic competences can be thought of as the ability to act functionally, appropriately, and (ideally) with real responsibility in financial situations. All these competence definitions in line with Franz Weinert (2001) share the idea that pupils must gain a functional capacity to act in economic situations. Such a definition, however, only focuses on the ability to perform not the capability of decision-making and responsibility. Economic understanding is a more fundamental concept: it requires a meaningful understanding and evaluation of the substance of common economic situations and societal processes. One example might be the question whether inequality is a legitimate consequence of economic processes, what role political policy plays in assessing this question, and how concepts of justice can usefully be applied here.

This notion of economic understanding (*Sinnverstehen*) follows the tradition set by the interpretative sociology of Max Weber (Weber 1978 [1922]) and Alfred Schütz (1967 [1932]), referring to a hermeneutic process of cognition in which subjective interrelations of meaning, patterns of interpretation, and frameworks of action are constructed and thus determine the actions of social actors. It is a *meaningful reflection upon systematic comprehension.* Reflection is understood here to be the conscious deliberation or contemplation which takes place before, during, or after a specific situation or action (Wyss 2008, 3). The motivation behind the expansion of the existing process of teaching economic competence lies in the fact that although a pupil may be able to act appropriately (and thus competently) in multiple situations of an economic nature, he or she need not necessarily have understood or reflected upon the situation in question, or the structures and dynamics which underlie it.

Our objective of differentiating between economic competence and economic understanding is made more difficult by the fact that a number of synonyms are used in the literature as conceptual designations for the outcomes of education in economics. The terms 'economic intelligence', 'economic competence', 'economic comprehension', 'understanding the economy', or 'economic understanding' are all functionally equivalent (Seeber and Remmele 2009). Also, the concept of 'financial literacy', currently a focal point for academic discussion (Lusardi and Mitchell 2011, 2014), is generally split into two dimensions of economic education: knowledge and application (Huston 2010). Whereas in a great deal of the German literature regarding the measurement of economic competence the use of the term 'economic competence' itself is largely operative, referring to the measurement of various situative abilities, in the English-speaking world the term's use is predominantly conceptual. Only if economic concepts are understood fundamentally can actors make their own economic decisions and critically examine them (Remund 2010). A conceptual notion of competence, if understood in such a way, would correspond to a great degree with what we understand socio-economic education to mean.

Nevertheless, some limitations must be expressed here, too: the term 'economic understanding' is usually understood to be a dimension of financial literacy, and is limited to an applied form of comprehension.[1] For example, since the 1960s, the Test of Understanding of College Economics (TUCE) has taken quantitative measurements of the ability to communicate economic concepts such as 'market' or 'price' (Walstad 1998; Walstad et al. 2007).[2] The same thing could be said of the construct 'economic literacy': "Students attain economic literacy if they can apply basic economic concepts years later, in situations relevant to their lives and different from those encountered in the classroom" (Salemi 2005, 47). Here, too, the functional aspect of learned economic literacy is of greatest importance for pupils; economic concepts should be applicable to future real-life situations. To sum up, it seems that the positioning of economic understanding within the field of economic or financial education differs widely in the international and German-language literature on the subject. Common to both is the fact that the term 'economic understanding' is not clearly defined.

As we see it, economic understanding (*Sinnverstehen*) – alongside the concept of economic competency – focuses on the *interplay* between economic *and* societal processes and their evaluation. In the following chapter, we intend to expand upon this definition: we argue for the necessity of this interpretative and comprehensive construct on the grounds that an economically active person is always part of society, and socialized via the process of ontogenesis into a specific society (Section 2). In Section 3, the idea of economic competence is discussed in terms of the concept of economic understanding, oriented more towards a systemic construction of the economic system. Only this kind of comprehensive understanding of economic processes can form the foundations for reflective and reflexive conclusions regarding the financial system within which people live. The chapter closes with a brief conclusion (Section 4).

2 Enculturation and the comprehension of meaning

The goal of economic education is to turn school learners into informed and reflective members of an active civil society. School pupils should be empowered to actively and critically understand and evaluate economic processes as part of the society as a whole. This is challenging, as modern societies are systemically constructed and functionally differentiated societies (Luhmann 1995 [1984]). In order to fully and systematically understand modern societies, it is absolutely imperative that the interdependencies – that is, the structural linkages – between the different sub-systems be understood (Luhmann 1977). In other words, learners have to be equipped with an integrated and systemic knowledge of modern (market) societies so that they may be able to formulate considered judgements regarding the organization of society, and to constructively participate in this organization. Underlying this conclusion is the assumption that economies always exist within a political and legal framework (Buchanan 1984 [1975]), and that simultaneously, each individual is socialized or encultured in these specific political, legal, and economic conditional fields. For example, take the issue of environmental pollution and external effects. While a neoclassical approach would consider all external effects simply as a market failure, a comprehensive and reflected economic knowledge would take all dimensions of the problem into account. The political issue of collective action and free riding, the social and humanitarian perspective of environmental pollution and living conditions, the economic perspective of market failure and efficiency, and so forth. The central point is that there hardly can be identified a pure win-win solution so informed citizens must be able to make an informed decision in favor of the economic, the political, or the social dimension. An integrated and dynamic approach to economic education has to adequately reflect these receptive and constructive processes of human development.

Developing economic understanding is not an immutable anthropological constant in human development; it passes through new stages of development during the process of socialization and enculturation (Piaget 1997 [1932]). Economic learning, like human learning in general, is always about learning cultural contexts. Each member of a society learns, throughout their development (ontogenesis), the abilities they need as a member of that society – namely by way of interaction with that society and the culture which it has developed. Such a process is certainly not limited to primary socialization but also occurs as a result of school education. If the cultural understanding of economic education is defined in this way from an evolutionary and socio-constructivist perspective, then modern society may be described as ‘cumulative cultural evolution’ (Tomasello 2009). The cultural parameters and functional conditions of the society are constantly being relearned by every new member of modern market societies, necessarily so, as part of the individual process of socialization. The process of enculturation, consequently, does not mean a form of structuralist ‘programming’ within existing structures, but instead the constructive and evaluative interaction with one’s individual experiences and learning processes, as well as ultimately the flexibility to be able to innovate via the reflexive examination of meaningful relationships.

If we accept this analysis of societal relationships, economic education can be understood as part of a comprehensive global set of knowledge concerning social interactions and structural connections. This realization is accompanied by the rejection of categorical models of social roles and the acceptance of an integrative approach to explaining different learning environments. There is an opposition between the idea of the activation of different social roles in specific contexts, on the one hand, and a model of action that is integrative, consistent, and characteristic for each individual regardless of context on the other. This has been a point of discussion in sociology for some time, emerging from the incompatibility of the theories of habitus and social role (Krais and Gebauer 2002, 63–64; Lenger et al. 2013, 22, 27). The coherence of the subject and its behavior is ensured by the so-called habitus, which is to say certain social practices are linked to the human body itself, and thus inseparably bound to that person. Conversely, the concept of the social role is more strongly focused on what society expects of a person, be it in their career, in politics, or in family life (Krais and Gebauer 2002, 67). Equally, however, habitus explains how students – independent of situation – behave in their different roles and how they understand meaning, and how reflexive thinking can diverge from social expectations (Krais and Gebauer 2002, 69–70). For whereas social roles and the assessment of economic competence both tend to divide pupils into a number of functional categories, Bourdieu's concept of habitus in particular focuses on the coherence of an individual, which in our opinion is ultimately indispensable for integrated and habitualized economic understanding (*Sinnverstehen*) (Bourdieu 1987 [1980], 1982 [1979]).

In accordance with these preliminary observations, the teaching of economics at university level must aim to equip prospective teachers with the knowledge and applicable teaching competences so that, ultimately, their pupils are able to infer from their understanding of individual (economic) aspects the broader context of a functionally differentiated society, and are thus consequently able to critically reflect upon said society. This idea can be put more clearly as follows: prospective teachers must not be satisfied with merely transmitting various forms of economic information to their pupils so that they may apply them competently (e.g. knowing about the different forms of credit, or what to be aware of when signing a lease agreement). Instead, teachers must also consider the more fundamental form of economic understanding, for example the social or structural roles played by credit in modern societies (investment function, intertemporal allocation, etc.), and how these functions are to be evaluated in the context of societal processes as a whole. A university education which trains teachers of economics is only legitimate, in our opinion, if it successfully imparts an integrative understanding of the economy and other social systems to the participants, and thus an awareness of the problems involved in establishing modern societies. The goal of economic education, at every level, must be to enable school pupils to understand and indeed shape the economy and society as it affects their everyday lives. This is the paradox of the notion of a functionalistic assessment of economic competence: competences are tested for in pupils even if it is unclear whether or not they have learned to 'understand' their substance beforehand.

Pursuing a systemic perspective, economic education must be considered a compulsory element of general education. Consequently, we argue that those whose job it is to communicate this knowledge – prospective teachers of economics – must have a grasp of economics which is both pluralistic and grounded in the social sciences, and that they must be in a position to convey a comprehensive, reflexive, and integrated socio-economic understanding – this is what we mean when we use Weber's term *Sinnverstehen.*

3 Economic understanding and the capacity to form judgments: the goals of a reflexive didactics of economics

When Bloom and his colleagues set out their taxonomy of learning goals, it soon became a widely utilized system for classifying potential cognitive categories (Bloom 1956; Anderson and Krathwohl 2001; Marzano and Kendall 2007). The six categories of Bloom's taxonomy are organized hierarchically, and comprise the cognitive stages 'Knowledge', 'Comprehension', 'Application', 'Analysis', 'Synthesis', and 'Evaluation'. Economic understanding as we define it would involve all six stages of Bloom's taxonomy, and would thus go far beyond the definition of 'Comprehension' (stage 2) in Bloom's taxonomy of learning goals; the taxonomy defines 'Comprehension' solely as the student's ability to identify information he or she has learned in a potentially new context and then either formulate an example of their own or recognize an existing example. Our concept of reflexive economic understanding would also include evaluation, and thus encompass all six stages of learning, because alongside the processing of information, part of the inherent nature of economic understanding is an awareness of the problems themselves and reflexive consideration of the results of one's own actions within the economic system.

From the perspective of cognitive psychology, processes of understanding are characterized by the way each subject approaches the act of comprehension with prior knowledge and a set of values, and each object possesses an intrinsic structure and exists within a specific context (Reusser and Reusser-Weyeneth 1994, 9–15). Understanding here thus means a form of cognitive performance defined by the acquisition of meaning (Zwenger 2003, 655) and the 'comprehension of knowledge' (*verstehendes Wissen*) (Rehm 2006, 27–30). Consequently, one key aspect of processes of comprehension is the identification of associations and relationships and the semantic correlation between them. In this context, a process of reflexive understanding will be particularly successful if the process is of subjective interest, and if this comprehension can be associated with concepts deriving from everyday experience (Straßer 2008). Research in the field of educational psychology has shown that, at the preliminary level of abstraction, associations of sense and meaning are actively linked to prior knowledge and are subsequently consolidated in such a way that identifiable analogies emerge. The logical consequence of this is that learners are bound to develop a metacognitive appreciation of their own processes of comprehension (Reusser and Reusser-Weyeneth 1994, 26).

What, then, does *Sinnverstehen* mean? In the course of the acquisition of knowledge, new elements of knowledge are combined with pre-existing representations – that is, the existing structures of knowledge are extended (assimilation) or restructured (accommodation) (Weißeno 2006). School pupils already possess a level of financial general knowledge, which can be developed further in class by way of 'mental models'. From a cognitive psychology perspective, mental models are representations of reality that people use to understand specific phenomena. Donald A. Norman (1983, 7) describes them as follows:

> In interacting with the environment, with others, and with the artifacts of technology, people form internal, mental models of themselves and of the things with which they are interacting. These models provide predictive and explanatory power for understanding the interaction.

The generation of these mental models occurs as an individual's knowledge base concerning a topic is restructured (accommodation). If more complex subject matter is learned, the familiar schemes are no longer sufficient, and new mental models become necessary in order to develop strategies for solving problems in specific applications. These schemes are used to create conceptual notions (e.g. thought experiments) which can be helpful in solving problems. Mental models can be categorized either as prior conceptions, precursors to the understanding of a scientific subject, or as key conceptions, which represent the specialist scientific knowledge relevant to that subject. Prior conceptions, which are determined by everyday observations, are grounded in a subjective plausibility which often leads to faulty conceptions or misinterpretations. For instance, price increases are generally attributed to an increase in the intrinsic value of a product and not to market scarcities. In order to better support pupils in the formation and restructuration of their incorporated mental models, the teaching of economics as realistic problem-solving would seem to require an inquiring and reflexive form of learning, one which enables associations to be established between everyday observations and economic concepts. The conceptual change of existing mental models is only possible if economic concepts are linked to subjective prior knowledge (Carey 1986). Restructurations thus indicate, in cognitive psychology, the crossing of a learning threshold or reaching a certain tier of cognition.

From a didactic perspective, then, processes of comprehension proceed in the form of tiered cognitive processes or as a series of learning thresholds (Davies and Mangan 2007; Davies 2011). Davies's threshold concept demarcates novice from expert understanding by way of three levels (basic concepts, discipline threshold concepts, and modeling concepts), with different conceptual expectations on each level which are dependent on the way in which new information is transformed and integrated into cognitive schemes (Davies 2011, 4). At the basic level of comprehension, everyday experiences can be explained using the basic concepts of a discipline: for example, students will be able to distinguish investments from savings. At the disciplinary level, a discipline's concepts can be understood from a theoretical perspective: for example, market interaction is understood as being subject to supply and demand. At the procedural level, specific economic modes of thought and technical models are developed so that, for example, economic concepts such as price elasticity – especially that of everyday necessities such as fuel – may be understood (Kricks et al. 2013). At all stages, learners are to consider both the content and the processes of their learning reflexively: the goal of this reflexive form of economic understanding should be that school pupils reach the threshold of the disciplinary level, and students (i.e. prospective teachers) the procedural level. However, this approach does not stipulate any kind of systematization intended to measure levels or methods of comprehension; instead, specific economic ideas and concepts are developed, changing modes of thinking in such a way that a tiered process of comprehension may be assumed (Kricks et al. 2013).[3] Consequently – and this is key to our reflexive conception of the teaching of economics – the concept of thresholds is more than a perspective defined solely by the thematic categories of a discipline, and is extended to constitute a reflexive theory of society which includes an integrative approach to economic understanding. On the basic level, this reflexivity means, for example, that school pupils understand that they participate in the market society via their actions and actually help shape societal processes; on the procedural level, they learn about the influence exerted on the construction of a market society by institutions. On the modeling level, they will be capable of comprehending wide-reaching societal associations which may be composed of economic, political, and legal concepts – consequently, they will also be able to form their own critical, reflexive judgments.

This reflexive approach to economic understanding is corroborated by findings from developmental psychology regarding the tiered nature of cognitive development, and focuses on establishing which factors are associated with the ability to form normative judgments about societal processes. Following Piaget's (1997 [1932]) and Kohlberg's (1984) theories of the stages of moral development, we assume the existence of a structural-genetic process of development in economic learning as well, inferring that the development of pupils' economic competences also proceeds in stages. The logical conclusion of this assumption would be that processes of economic understanding and moral judgments may potentially correspond to pupils' cognitive development status – a correlation which has hitherto received no attention in research.

There is disagreement in the literature regarding "the number of stages, the points of transition and the exact understanding in each stage" (Furnham and Lewis 1986, 44). For example, children between the ages of four and five often imagine that the price of an item is dependent on its size; a tiny diamond cannot be of any great monetary value, as it is simply too small, whereas a book must be more expensive than a wristwatch. Only at the age of seven or eight do children begin to determine value from a consumer perspective, and thus the price of an item by its usefulness. At this stage, the durability of a product and the fun associated with its use play an important role. Finally, between the ages of 10 and 12, children move towards a producer's perspective, and the effort involved in a product's manufacture becomes the decisive factor in determining its price (Lea et al. 1987, 375).

To summarize, if economic understanding is a structural-genetic process of reflexive comprehension, then the university education of prospective teachers must equip them with a wide-ranging appreciation of social interactions and structural correlations. Economic understanding develops as young people grow up, dependent on their level of cognitive development, which itself can be seen as developing parallel to the ability to formulate moral judgments. If pupils are to be taught a comprehensive and profound appreciation for economic correlations, not only in order that they might act competently, but also be able to formulate reflexive judgments concerning the configuration of their own societies, then the study of this structural-genetic process of economic understanding must be the objective of future research into the teaching of economics.

Of proportionate importance is thus the orientation of teacher education towards the reconstruction and reproduction of pupils' economic understanding. Research must examine the ways in which this ability to form judgments reflexively is associated with existing patterns of thought, or 'shared mental models' (Denzau and North 1995), and how it can be better oriented towards a deeper understanding of aggregate economic and societal correlations. Establishing a link between economic competence and a more reflective and reflexive form of economic understanding leads, in our opinion, to the conclusion that the teaching of economic subject matter in schools requires a science of economics which is pluralistic and inspired by the social sciences (for further information, see Dow 2018; Kapeller 2018; Beckenbach 2018).[4] A pluralistic approach to economics drawing widely on the social sciences is necessary since a hermeneutic understanding of economic processes can only be achieved from different points of view on the individual as well on the paradigmatic level (see for example the chapters by Betz and Ehret or Derrer in this volume). Indeed, pluralism can be seen as an 'auto-correction' of scientific procedures and a competition to gain new economic insights and understanding of economic processes (Beckenbach 2018). Since modern economics fail to integrate such a multiple perspective, the need is for a pluralistic approach to teaching economics. In order to allow pupils to develop into reflective, considered individuals, their understanding, or *Sinnverstehen*, as it pertains to economic processes must occur by way of the intellectual observation and critical, considered analysis of modern market societies. Economic correlations can only be taught comprehensively, however, where the processes of market societies are analyzed and critically considered from different perspectives, utilizing different theories and methods.

Empowering teachers with a subject-specific didactic ability of this kind could be referred to as *integral empowerment*, creating a connection between the field's fundamental subject matter and both didactic elementarization and classroom teaching competences. For teacher training in the field of economics as a whole, and in order to develop a comprehensive and well-founded ability to form reflexive judgements – or 'critical reflexivity' (Moldaschl 2015, 343) – a concept of 'paradigmatic teaching and learning' seems especially promising in the context described here. A didactic perspective of this kind is explicitly opposed to a one-sided and monotheoretical approach to the subject matter. If we want to mold pupils into competent citizens, then a system of didactics which addresses the various economic paradigms both from a reconstructive and a reflexive perspective must be implemented more rigorously when educating prospective teachers of economics, instead of teaching them a form of didactics which models itself on the mainstream of the field. A one-sided focus on the 'neo-classical' perspective is insufficient for a comprehensive, socially oriented economic education and for demonstrating the complex problems of modern market societies.

Here, we might refer to the processes of change at work in the discipline itself: demands for a more pluralistic way of thinking are growing in economics (Fullbrook 2009; Reardon 2009; Garnett et al. 2010). This optimism has, for the most part, yet to materialize in the field of teacher education (for exemptions, see Groenewegen 2007; Freeman 2010; Stilwell 2011). We thus suggest that university teacher training in economics be thought of as a systematic encounter between the learners and their socio-economic requirements, life circumstances, and learning situations – an encounter which mirrors variously a cognitive conflict (Festinger 1957), the structure of a moral dilemma (Hardin 1968; Ostrom 1990), or a societal problem (Spector and Kitsuse 1973) which requires analysis from the perspectives of multiple approaches to economics.

We would like to point out here that, in principle, it will most likely be necessary to educate prospective economists and teachers of economics almost entirely separately. The measures required to educate economists and teachers differ fundamentally, so that it would make little sense to integrate teacher training into the study of economics itself – regardless of whether a more traditional or more pluralistically oriented economics is being taught.

The reflexive approach to socio-economic education discussed here can be made more concrete in three ways, valid both for the training of prospective teachers and for teaching economic understanding to pupils themselves: first, by exploring both societal problems and individual situations of an economic nature; second, by way of an orientation towards scientific, political, and ideological pluralism; and third, by understanding the performativity of economic research and its influence on social and economic reality. This subject-specific didactic appeal to the connectedness of social domains thus enables a thoroughly interdependent understanding of the economic correlations within the social environment as a whole. This reflexive approach to didactics – oriented towards actions and real life, but also guided by knowledge – derives an ideal jumping-off point for a communicative approach to learning and teaching from individual reflection upon our own everyday experiences with the market economy. By implementing a teaching method which revolves around the position of the individual – that is, the localization of and reflection upon the individual's own social position and their involvement in the fabric of society – an awareness of socially problematic situations can be generated while simultaneously fostering social responsibility. At the same time, this problem-oriented way of thinking in the context of the social sciences enables a substantive and profound appreciation of specific economic topics and problematic issues. Economic understanding is generated by a profound comprehension of economic correlations if they are 'decoded' using familiar structures of meaning, such as the fundamental principles of economic thought (top-down process of analysis), or if they are assessed reflexively, via the synthesis of old and new structures of meaning (bottom-up process of synthesis).

This reflexive didactics of economics – which simultaneously aims to promote economic *Sinnverstehen* in a school setting – is from a curricular perspective a pluralistic economics and, from a procedural perspective, a form of learning as a reflexive research project. Research as a form of learning is by definition reflexive, because as the learners attempt to understand their object, they examine both the object and themselves, thus gaining a greater understanding of themselves and their world. If this reflexive approach is to be implemented in the context of university didactics, then unconventional learning methods such as project-based learning might be appropriate.

4 Conclusion

It was our goal in this chapter to show that the concept of economic understanding is necessary in order to make any relevant claims about the state of contemporary teacher education in economics. Economic understanding is defined as the ability to properly recognize, examine, and assess economic problems both in the societal dimension and in their systemic construction. Whereas traditional models of competence revolve around the kind of knowledge which drives and explains behavior, the concept of economic understanding focuses on the analysis of knowledge deriving from reflection upon one's own behavior (Rauner et al. 2009). For example, many people do not understand the concept of sunk costs. In traditional microeconomic theory, only prospective (future) costs are relevant to an investment decision (i.e. economic actors should not let sunk costs determine prospective decisions). It is the goal of economic understanding to enable learners to first adjust their assumptions about sunk costs and then to modify their behavior accordingly.

In the future of the teaching of economics, the dynamics and construction of meaningful correlations for students should be monitored over multiple levels of development, reconstructed qualitatively, and made utilizable for further quantitative research. This will be a challenging task for the next years. This addition – namely the analysis of economic understanding – to traditional research on economic competence has three benefits, as we see it. First, it creates a new frame of reference for research into the teaching of economics by concentrating on the integrative understanding of economic systems. It is essential to life in a market economy that the underlying financial categories and mechanisms are, in their respective societal contexts, understood and given sufficient consideration. It is only in this way that prospective teachers can be empowered to orient their teaching towards more than an demonstration of financial categories, demanding instead of their pupils normative assessments and a profound understanding of economic processes so that they, the pupils, might be led to make well-reasoned contributions to the construction of the social order. Second, such a perspective broadens the scope of the existing literature on the traditional assessment of economic competence, adding to it the subjectively constructed and reflexively considered economic influence of the pupils themselves, which enables a more detailed examination of the pupils' knowledge of the subject matter and of their competences with regard to economic matters. Third, reconstructive procedures of the kind described here supplement existing research on competence with more differentiated models, thus enabling both the triangulation of empirical data and the generation of hypotheses for further quantitative research. In conclusion, our goal is to move the analytical focus away from the analysis of partial or situative problem-solving competence and closer to an analysis of structural problem awareness, of systematic thinking, and to anchor the goal of reflexive economic understanding in the curricula for prospective teachers of economics.

Notes

1 The Organisation for Economic Co-operation and Development (OECD 2005) defines "financial education" as "the process by which financial consumers/investors improve their understanding of financial products and concepts and, through information, instruction, and/or objective advice, develop the skills and confidence to become more aware

of financial risks and opportunities to make informed choices, to know where to go for help, and to take other effective actions to improve their financial well-being".

2 Paper-and-pencil tests targeted at students were first formulated as part of the TUCE in 1967. (originally Fels [1967]; 2nd version Fels and Welsh [1981]; 3rd version Saunders [1991]; 4th and current version Walstad et al. [2007]). The test has two primary goals: (1) the development of a reliable instrument to evaluate students participating in economics courses, and (2) to provide standardized data for a large, national sample of students in foundational subjects to allow lecturers to compare the performance of their classes with that of the classes in the national sample (Walstad et al. 2007, 1). The motivation behind TUCE is thus the goal of optimal comparative measurement on a large scale, intended to enable university teaching staff in introductory economics courses, in both micro- and macroeconomics, to measure learning progress relative to other locations and cohorts. The term 'economic understanding' is, however, not the focus of the analysis, but functions instead as a rather unconsidered general term for economic knowledge.

3 It is difficult to empirically establish whether a learning threshold has been crossed. Although learning outcomes can be assigned to the various stages by applying the SOLO taxonomy (Structure of Observed Learning Outcome), the instrument does not enable conclusions regarding when a learning threshold is reached.

4 In some federal states in Germany (e.g. North Rhine-Westphalia), economic education at schools is taught in an integrative social-scientific subject. However, it must be noted that only the pupils are trained in an integrative mode. The teachers, however, are still trained in the different disciplines separately (economics, sociology, and politics). Consequently, prospective economic teachers do not have an integrative and pluralistic economic education but are educated in line with modern mainstream economics.

References

Anderson, L. W. and Krathwohl, D. A. (eds.) (2001): *A Taxonomy for Learning, Teaching, and Assessing: A Revision of Bloom's Taxonomy of Educational Objectives*. New York: Longman.

Beckenbach, F. (2018): "Monism in Modern Science: The Case of Economics", in Decker, S., Elsner, W. and Flechtner, S. (eds.), *Advancing Pluralism in Teaching Economics: International Perspectives on a Textbook Science*. Abingdon and New York: Routledge, 31–54.

Berti, A. E. and Bombi, A. S. (1988): *The Child's Construction of Economics*. Cambridge: Cambridge University Press.

Blendon, R. J., Benson, J. M., Brodie, M., Morin, R., Altman, D. E., Gitterman, D., Brossard, M. and James, M. (1997): "Bridging the Gap between the Public's and Economists' Views of the Economy", *Journal of Economic Perspectives* 11(3), 105–118.

Bloom, B. S. (ed.) (1956): *Taxonomy of Educational Objectives, Book I: Cognitive Domain*. New York: Longmans, Green.

Bourdieu, P. (1982 [1979]): *Die feinen Unterschiede. Kritik der gesellschaftlichen Urteilskraft*. Frankfurt am Main: Suhrkamp.

Bourdieu, P. (1987 [1980]): *Sozialer Sinn. Kritik der theoretischen Vernunft*. Frankfurt am Main: Suhrkamp.

Buchanan, J. M. (1984 [1975]): *Die Grenzen der Freiheit. Zwischen Anarchie und Leviathan*. Tübingen: Mohr Siebeck.

Carey, S. (1986): "Cognitive Science and Science Education", *American Psychologist* 41(10), 1123–1130.

Davies, P. (2011): "Threshold Concepts in Economics", in Hoyt, G. M. and McGoldrick, K. M. (eds.), *The International Handbook on Teaching and Learning Economics*. Aldershot, UK: Edward Elgar, 250–256.

Davies, P. and Mangan, J. (2007): "Threshold Concepts and the Integration of Understanding in Economics", *Studies in Higher Education* 32(6), 711–726.

Denzau, A. T. and North, D. C. (1995): "Shared Mental Models: Ideologies and Institutions", *Kyklos* 47(1), 3–31.

Dow, S. (2018): "Pluralist Economics: Is It Scientific?", in Decker, S., Elsner, W. and Flechtner, S. (eds.), *Advancing Pluralism in Teaching Economics: International Perspectives on a Textbook Science*. Abingdon and New York: Routledge, 13–30.

Fels, R. (1967): "A New Test of Understanding in College Economics", *American Economic Review, Papers and Proceedings* 57(2), 660–666.

Festinger, L. (1957): *A Theory of Cognitive Dissonance*. Stanford: Stanford University Press.

Freeman, A. (2010): "The Economists of Tomorrow: The Case for Assertive Pluralism in Economics Education", *American Journal of Economics and Sociology* 69(5), 1591–1613.

Fullbrook, E. (ed.) (2009): *Pluralist Economics*. New York: Zed Books.

Furnham, A. and Kirkcaldy, B. (2000): "Economic Socialization: German Parents' Perceptions and Implementation of Allowances to Educate Children", *European Psychologist* 5(3), 202–215.

Furnham, A. and Lewis, A. (1986): *The Economic Mind: The Social Psychology of Economic Behavior*. New York: St. Martin's Press.

Garnett, R., Olson, E. K. and Starr, M. A. (eds.) (2010): *Economic Pluralism*. London: Routledge.

Gleason, J. and van Scyoc, L. J. (1995): "A Report on the Economic Literacy of Adults", *Journal of Economic Education* 26(3), 203–210.

Groenewegen, J. (ed.) (2007): *Teaching Pluralism in Economics*. Cheltenham, UK: Edward Elgar.

Hardin, G. (1968): "The Tragedy of the Commons", *Science* 162(3859), 1243–1248.

Hirschfeld, M., Moore, R. and Brown, E. (1995): "Exploring the Gender Gap on the GRE Subject Test in Economics", *Journal of Economic Education* 26(4), 3–16.

Huston, S. J. (2010): "Measuring Financial Literacy", *Journal of Consumer Affairs* 44(2), 296–316.

Kapeller, J. (2018): "Pluralism in Economics: Epistemological Rationales and Pedagogical Implementation", in Decker, S., Elsner, W. and Flechtner, S. (eds.), *Advancing Pluralism in Teaching Economics: International Perspectives on a Textbook Science*. Abingdon and New York: Routledge, 55–77.

Kohlberg, L. (1984): *Essays on Moral Development*. San Francisco: Harper & Row.

Krais, B. and Gebauer, G. (2002): *Habitus*. Bielefeld: Transcript Verlag.

Kricks, K., Mittelstädt, E. and Liening, A. (2013): "Schwellenkonzepte und Phänomenografie. Explorative Studie zur Messung von Unterschieden im ökonomischen Verstehen", *Zeitschrift für ökonomische Bildung* (2), 17–41.

Lea, S. E. G., Tarpy, R. M. and Webley, P. (1987): *The Individual in the Economy: A Textbook of Economic Psychology*. Cambridge: Cambridge University Press.

Leiser, D. and Halachmi, R. B. (2006): "Children's Understanding of Marker Forces", *Journal of Economic Psychology* 27(1), 6–19.

Lenger, A., Schneickert, C. and Schumacher, F. (2013): "Pierre Bourdieus Konzeption des Habitus", in Lenger, A., Schneickert, C. and Schumacher, F. (eds.), *Pierre Bourdieus*

Konzeption des Habitus. Grundlagen, Zugänge, Forschungsperspektiven. Wiesbaden: Springer VS, 3–41.

Luhmann, N. (1977): "Differentiation of Society", *Canadian Journal of Sociology* 2(1), 29–53.

Luhmann, N. (1995 [1984]): *Social Systems*. Stanford: Stanford University Press.

Lusardi, A. and Mitchell, O. S. (2011): "Financial Literacy around the World", *Journal of Pension Economics and Finance* 10(4), 497–508.

Lusardi, A. and Mitchell, O. S. (2014): "The Economic Importance of Financial Literacy: Theory and Evidence", *Journal of Economic Literature* 52(1), 5–44.

Marzano, R. J. and Kendall, J. S. (2007): *The New Taxonomy of Educational Objectives*. Thousand Oaks, CA: Corwin Press.

Moldaschl, M. (2015): "Paradigmatisches Lernen. Oder: Wie lehrt man Sozioökonomik", in Hedtke, R. (ed.), *Was ist und wozu Sozioökonomie?* Wiesbaden: Springer VS, 339–369.

Norman, D. A. (1983): "Some Observations on Mental Models", in Gentner, D. and Stevens, A. L. (eds.), *Mental Models*. New York: Taylor & Francis, 7–14.

OECD (2005): *Improving Financial Literacy: Analysis of Issues and Policies*. Paris: OECD Publishing.

Ostrom, E. (1990): *Governing the Commons: The Evolution of Institutions for Collective Action*. Cambridge: Cambridge University Press.

Piaget, J. (1997 [1932]): *The Moral Judgement of the Child*. New York: Simon & Schuster.

Rauner, F., Haasler, B., Heinemann, F. and Grollmann, P. (2009): *Messen beruflicher Kompetenzen. Band I: Grundlagen und Konzeption des KOMET-Projektes*. Berlin and Münster: LIT Verlag.

Reardon, J. (ed.) (2009): *The Handbook of Pluralist Economics Education*. London and New York: Routledge.

Rehm, M. (2006): "Allgemeine Naturwissenschaftliche Bildung – Entwicklung eines vom Begriff 'Verstehen' ausgehenden Kompetenzmodells", *Zeitschrift für Didaktik der Naturwissenschaften* 12, 23–44.

Remund, D. L. (2010): "Financial Literacy Explicated: The Case for a Clearer Definition in an Increasingly Complex Economy", *Journal of Consumer Affairs* 44(2), 276–295.

Reusser, K. and Reusser-Weyeneth, M. (1994): "Verstehen als psychologischer Prozess und als didaktische Aufgabe: Einführung und Überblick", in Reusser, K. and Reusser-Weyeneth, M. (eds.), *Verstehen. Psychologischer Prozess und didaktische Aufgabe*. Bern: Hans Huber, 9–35.

Salemi, M. K. (2005): "Teaching Economic Literacy: Why, What and How", *International Review of Economics Education* 4(2), 46–57.

Saunders, Philipp (1991): "The Third Edition of the Test of Understanding of College Economics", *American Economic Review, Papers and Proceedings*, 81(2), 32–37.

Schütz, A. (1967 [1932]): *The Phenomenology of the Social World*. Evanston: Northwestern University Press.

Seeber, G. and Remmele, B. (2009): "Ökonomische Kompetenz bedingt Einstellungen zur Marktwirtschaft – Entwurf eines Wirkmodells zur empirischen Analyse", in Seeber, G. (ed.): *Befähigung zur Partizipation. Gesellschaftliche Teilhabe durch ökonomische Bildung*. Schwalbach: Wochenschau Verlag, 27–40.

Spector, M. and Kitsuse, J. I. (1973): "Social Problems: A Re-Formulation", *Social Problems* 21(2), 145–159.

Stilwell, F. (2011): "Teaching a Pluralist Course in Economics: The University of Sydney Experience", *International Journal of Pluralism and Economics Education* 2(1), 39–56.

Straßer, P. (2008): *Können erkennen – reflexives Lehren und Lernen in der beruflichen Benachteiligtenförderung. Entwicklung, Erprobung und Evaluation eines reflexiven Lehr-Lerntrainings*. Bielefeld: Bertelsmann.

Tomasello, M. (2009): *Why We Cooperate*. Cambridge: MIT Press.

Walstad, W. B. (1998): "Why It's Important to Understand Economics", www.minneapolisfed.org/publications/the-region/why-its-important-to-understand-economics, accessed 4 February 2017.

Walstad, W. B., Watts, M. W. and Rebeck, K. (2007): *Test of Understanding in College Economics*. Examiner's Manual. 4th edition. New York: National Council on Economic Education.

Weber, M. (1978 [1922]): *Economy and Society: An Outline of Interpretive Sociology*. Berkeley: University of California Press.

Weinert, F. E. (2001): "Vergleichende Leistungsmessung in Schulen – eine umstrittene Selbstverständlichkeit", in Weinert, F. E. (ed.), *Leistungsmessungen in Schulen*. Weinheim: Beltz, 17–31.

Weißeno, G. (ed.) (2006): *Politik und Wirtschaft unterrichten*. Wiesbaden: VS Verlag für Sozialwissenschaften.

Wyss, C. (2008): "Zur Reflexionsfähigkeit und -praxis der Lehrperson", *Bildungsforschung* 5(2), 1–15, www.bildungsforschung.org/Archiv/2008-02/lehrperson/, accessed 2 November 2016.

Zappalá, S. (2001): "Social Representations of Economics across Cultures", in Roland-Lévy, C., Kirchler, E. and Penz, E. (eds.), *Everyday Representations of the Economy*. Wien: WUV, Universitätsverlag, 183–203.

Zwenger, T. (2003): "Verstehen", in Rehfus, W. D. (ed.), *Handwörterbuch Philosophie*. Göttingen: Vandenhoeck & Ruprecht, 655–656.

Part II

Approaches and building blocks

7 Introduction to critical political economy in a multi-paradigmatic setting

Johannes Jäger

1 Introduction

Contrary to mainstream introductions to economics, which in general consist of a common core of knowledge, a homogenous and generally accepted approach to critical political economy is missing. There are several reasons for this. First, critical political economy is interdisciplinary by its nature, as it opposes the historically produced disciplinary divisions. It rather considers itself as a pre-disciplinary approach which sees itself in the tradition of political economy, which was dedicated to integrated analyses of economic, political and societal developments. Transcending and neglecting the boundaries of today's disciplines also implies that critical political economy can be considered a post-disciplinary perspective (Jessop and Sum 2001). Second, related to this, research and teaching of critical political economy are located within or related to different disciplines. This means that authors within this paradigm do not just work in the field of economics but also in political science, sociology, geography, history and so forth. An introduction to critical political economy often addresses students within a certain discipline. For the discipline of economics, Bowles et al. (2005) provide an introduction to a critical political economy perspective which very much reflects the US tradition of radical economics. Sherman et al. (2008) go beyond that and present post-Keynesian and neoclassical perspectives alongside selected Marxist economic perspectives. Ben Fine and Saad-Filho (2012), in an edited volume, give an overview of a series of Marxist concepts and terms in alphabetical order. General introductions to critical political economy often represent interpretations of Marx's central works such as *Das Kapital* (Harvey 2010; Heinrich 2004). In political science there are several textbooks, such as Cafruny et al. (2016), which introduce international politics from a critical political economy perspective.

What is missing in the English-speaking literature is a book similar to Jäger and Springler (2012). This provides an overview of critical political economy for a reader interested in an economic discussion which goes beyond a narrow tradition of Marxist economics and includes a broader interdisciplinary perspective and methodology. In addition, this broad critical political economy perspective is systematically compared to neoclassical economics and the post-Keynesian tradition, and specific examples illustrating the differences between the different paradigms are provided. Thereby the common division into macroeconomics and microeconomics, which is usually followed in introductory textbooks, is abandoned. This is because this distinction puts a straitjacket on critical political economy and neither reflects its ontology nor its methodology.

This chapter briefly sketches out how one can introduce critical political economy along these lines. It is attempted to avoid limiting or narrowing down a critical political economy perspective to isolated economic issues. On the contrary, in the tradition of Marx and following his methodology, it is attempted to provide an integrative analysis of the economic and the political spheres. This is done by drawing on classical texts by Marx and other historical authors as well as contemporary literature and academic debates. Thereby the focus is on critical but not on post-critical approaches to political economy (Browning and Kilmister 2006). The structure of this chapter mirrors the structure of Jäger and Springler (2012). Section 2 creates an awareness of the existence of different paradigms in economics and different ontological and methodological approaches. This is followed by a brief overview of the key categories of critical political economy. Based on this, at lower levels of abstraction, the chapter presents the different ways in which critical political economy addresses central economic issues. Due to the lack of space in this chapter, this critical approach is only briefly contrasted with neoclassical economics and post-Keynesian perspectives. It is shown how critical political economy suggests different perspectives and alternative responses to key economic questions. Finally, conclusions are drawn and presented.

2 Methodological and ontological considerations

When introducing economics, it is important to raise awareness of the existence of different paradigms. This is a term which was introduced to the philosophy of science by Kuhn (2012 [1962]). A brief overview of the history of economic thought generally allows the reader to understand the emergence and the propagation of different paradigms of economics against the background of the specific economic and social history (Screpanti and Zamagni 2005; Milonakis and Fine 2009). In addition to ontological assumptions (starting points), the methodology and the purpose of a certain paradigm, it is important to present the core elements or key categories of the paradigm.

This practice is very different to mainstream introductions to economics, which tend to marginalise or not even mention the existence of alternatives such as critical political economy approaches to economics. Frequently, methodological individualism is introduced as "the" methodology in economics. In line with this approach, neoclassical economics is presented as the preliminary endpoint and highest level of the development of economic thought (Milonakis and Fine 2009). However, despite attempts to marginalise and annihilate alternative approaches in economics, their parallel existence is a fact. This might be difficult to understand for those who work on the grounds of a positivist philosophy of science and who might suppose that the process of scientific research will sort out theories in a process of falsification, as Critical Rationalism suggests. However, the existence of different approaches in scientific research is by no means surprising against the background of sociology of science (Kuhn 2012 [1962]). The prevalence of competing approaches is even more understandable against the background of modern alternative approaches in the philosophy of science, such as Critical Realism (Bhaskar 1998). A significant reason for the differences between the two approaches in philosophy of science is the different ontological assumptions on which they are based. Critical Rationalism assumes that the researcher can objectively analyse a given reality. In contrast, according to Critical Realism people have no "direct access" to reality but need "theoretical glasses" or perspectives in order to obtain access to empirical reality. As the world is assumed to be complex there is an infinite number of possible perspectives. Given the limits of the human brain, one has no choice but to adopt a (or various) selected perspective(s) to obtain access to reality. In so doing, one inevitably has to make a choice and leave out alternative perspectives. According to Critical Realism the researcher is, therefore, forced to choose a perspective. This choice should be made consciously (i.e. the researcher should reflect on what drives his/her choice and what are the implications of adopting specific paradigms). Critical Realism suggests an ethical ground on which this decision should take place: the researcher should ask how, by using a certain paradigm, one contributes to emancipatory processes and acts in a transformative way in this regard. In order to be able to make such a choice, one important precondition is that the researcher knows that they have a choice and that different paradigms exist (Jäger et al. 2016).

Perspectives such as economic paradigms do not simply exist. They are a historical product of society. According to Critical Realism the production of (scientific) knowledge is always embedded into societal processes. This is an argument which has its roots in the tradition of dialectical historical materialism (Van der Pijl 2007). With regard to the thinking about economic phenomena – which deals with the questions of how nature is transformed via human labour, who organises, who fulfils which tasks and who gets what – it is not surprising that there exist different and competing perspectives as there are different (economic) interests related to those questions. In the tradition of dialectical historical materialism it is argued that the dominant way of thinking about the economy is related to the existing organisation of the economy. As Marx and Engels (2011 [1845]) put it in *The German Ideology*:

> The ideas of the ruling class are in every epoch the ruling ideas, i.e. the class which is the ruling material force of society, is at the same time its ruling intellectual force. The class which has the means of material production at its disposal, has control at the same time over the means of mental production, so that thereby, generally speaking, the ideas of those who lack the means of mental production are subject to it. The ruling ideas are nothing more than the ideal expression of the dominant material relationships, the dominant material relationships grasped as ideas.

With the development of liberal capitalism and its increasing dominance in the UK during the 18th century, liberal economic thought emerged. Adam Smith (1991 [1776]) undoubtedly is the most prominent economist who for the first time in history tried to show how liberal capitalism could work and how such an economic system could be morally justified. His ideas were warmly welcomed by the rising bourgeoisie as they provided a legitimisation for their own economic and political strategies and helped them to argue against traditional feudal powers. David Ricardo (1997 [1817]) argued in a more systematic way, and with his land rent theory he directly opposed the interests of landed classes. In opposition to common mainstream interpretations of Adam Smith and David Ricardo, who emphasise the free market approach and the role of individuals, classical political economy was based on an integrative analysis of economics and politics and economic classes was a central element of their analysis. Classical economists were interested in the dynamics of capitalist development and the related societal implications. Talking about economic classes, Smith and Ricardo mainly argued against the traditional landowners and in favour of the emerging bourgeoisie and supported their desire for a liberal capitalism. In so doing, they provided a theoretical approach which helped to push back the interests of traditional landed classes.

Critical political economy has its roots in classical political economy of the late 18th and the 19th centuries. It is based on the works of Karl Marx. Marx (1992 [1867]) engaged with the classical political economists but provided a critique of their approach. The subtitle of his central work, *Capital* (*A Critique of Political Economy*), underlines this. Despite a common ground, there are important distinctions between Marx and liberal classical political economists. Above all, the motivation or overall goal is different. While Smith and Ricardo developed their approach in order to show the viability of and provide a moral justification for liberal capitalism and related economic interests, Marx analysed the economy from the point of view of the workers and marginalised social groups. Using Ricardo's formulation of the labour theory of value, he pointed to the fact that – given the reserve army of the unemployed – wages were pushed to subsistence levels. Hence, those who benefited from economic development were not the masses but capitalists and landlords because their profits and rents grew with the progress of capitalism while wages stagnated. This, however, was not considered a problem by Smith or Ricardo. Marx, by contrast, problematised this and called it exploitation.

In addition, there are important methodological distinctions. Marx, building on Hegel, introduced dialectical reasoning as a central methodology. His methodological tradition is mirrored in current perspectives of Dialectical Critical Realism (Bhaskar 1998). Marx outlined his methodology in the *Grundrisse* (Marx 1857 [2012]), but did not write extensively on this. Marx's dialectical approach can rather be discovered by following his practice of research. His dialectical approach focusses on processes and the split of apparent unities into parts. He leaves behind the Cartesian separations between mind and matter, consciousness and materiality. David Harvey (1996, 48) puts it in a nutshell by stating that a dialectical mode of argumentation is "a debate over how to abstract from the phenomena we encounter in everyday life". As Marx (1857) argues in the *Grundrisse*, the starting point of inquiry is concrete phenomena:

> The concrete is concrete because it is the concentration of many determinations, hence unity of the diverse. It appears in the process of thinking, therefore, as a process of concentration, as a result, not as a point of departure, even though it is the point of departure in reality and hence also the point of departure for observation and conception.

This implies that a scientific approach based on the dialectics of the abstract and the concrete always requires abstract-theoretical and concrete-empirical knowledge and investigation. In order to analyse a specific historical concrete reality or situation, therefore, one cannot rely merely on abstract categories. Concepts at a lower level of abstraction are necessary in order to adequately grasp reality. As the world is conceived as a complex and permanently changing reality, it is necessary to constantly adapt and redevelop more concrete abstractions to understand our reality by relating them to the analysis of reality. Hence, in order to analyse a specific historic situation it does not suffice to use fixed categories with content, but an intellectual effort is required which implies a reconfiguration of abstractions at a lower level or at the middle range (Heinrich 2004). However, on the very highest level of abstraction, critical political economy proposes to use certain concepts, respectively abstractions, which generally are helpful for understanding the interaction of human societies and nature in general and capitalism in particular. Those general abstractions are presented below.

3 Core elements of critical political economy

A general starting point for critical political economy is the interaction of human society and nature and the transhistorical fact that human beings can (re)produce only if they have enough to eat, adequate shelter and so forth. This is also the precondition for enabling other human activities, such as the production of art or scientific knowledge (Sayer 1992; Bruff 2011). The specific form of interaction between a human society and nature which helps a society to reproduce is grasped by the abstract concept of mode of production. A *mode of production* is based on productive forces and social relations of production. Those abstract categories are dialectically related. The term *productive forces* refers to the technologies and the equipment available which allows a society to transform nature for its own purposes. The abstract concept *social relations of production* describes the societal organisation of the transformation of nature, and hence, the labour process. In complex societies ruling and subaltern classes are usually distinguished. In the case of a feudal mode of production, serf labour may represent a social relation of production. Also slavery is a social relation of production. Thereby masters tend to belong to the ruling class, fulfil certain economic functions and appropriate the product of slave labour based on the fact that they own slaves and other means of production. Those different groups, masters and slaves, are called *economic classes*. It is obvious that classes are a relational concept: without a master there is no slave; without a slave there is no master.

According to critical political economy capitalism, the currently prevailing mode of production, is similarly based on a class-based society characterised by asymmetrical power relations. On a very abstract level capitalists and workers can be distinguished. While capitalists are characterised by the ownership of the means of production, workers are free in a double sense: on the one hand, they are free to sell their labour power (they are not owned as slaves are); on the other hand, they are free of the means of production. This means that they do not have their own means (land, machines, etc.) to produce for their needs. Capitalists who own the means of production are entitled to appropriate the *surplus value*. While production takes place within the social context of the firm and the society which provides educated human labour force, infrastructure and so forth, the surplus product is appropriated privately. This is expressed by the *labour theory of value*, which argues that the production of economic wealth is based on labour power. Capital goods are considered constant capital or dead labour power as they are the product of labour in previous periods. Labour power is called variable capital. Using this terminology, it is possible to calculate a surplus rate, which compares surplus value to variable capital, and the profit rate, which is calculated by dividing the surplus value by the sum of variable and constant capital.

A key characteristic of capitalism is that, compared to previous modes of production, it is very dynamic and constantly revolutionises production and reproduction and produces an increasing number of commodities. The social relations between people are commodified and, on the surface, social relations appear to be relations between things. Commodifying social relations, including the labour relation, is a central feature of capitalism (Marx 1993 [1894]). It is also a precondition for its dynamic development which is explained by the *accumulation imperative*. This term refers to the fact that due to competition between different capitalists or firms, the firms are forced to accumulate capital in order to reinvest it. In addition, they constantly have to implement innovative technologies and new forms of labour organisation in order to increase their productivity and stay competitive. As competition reduces profits for capitalists, they tend to seek ways to reduce competition by forming monopolies (Baran and Sweezy 1989 [1966]) and constantly seek a higher rate of accumulation relative to others, an attitude which was called differential accumulation (Nitzan and Bichler 2009). However, because of inherent contradictions of the capitalist mode of production and class struggle, capitalism is not just dynamic but also a system which suffers frequent crises. Each mode of production is temporarily stabilised by institutions. In the case of capitalism, these are the state, norms and ideologies or discourses, which argue that the present mode of production is the only possible or best way to organise the economy.

Critical political economy helps to understand the structural background for class struggles. Against the background of a dialectical perspective on structure and agency, it is argued that class struggles are fought about the specific configuration of a mode of production. Hence economic and societal practices do not just reproduce a mode of production, but class struggle also transforms it. As Marx (1973 [1852]) expressed it: “Men make their own history, but they do not make it as they please; they do not make it under self-selected circumstances, but under circumstances existing already, given and transmitted from the past”. Critical political economy uses the above abstractions to understand the underlying structures and dynamics of a specific mode of production.

4 Economic key issues

Related to highly abstract concepts presented above, more concrete concepts which help to shed light on the specificities of historical capitalist modes of production and important economic issues are presented in this section. As the specific capitalist modes of production have changed since the days of Marx, and in addition there are important differences between modes of production in different places, it was and is necessary to constantly further develop abstract categories at these lower levels of abstraction. However, all spheres and issues are interrelated and one tries to keep an eye on the entire mode of production, its dynamics and the important power relations and class struggles within it. In the following subsections, concepts are presented that are relevant for the analysis of (1) the state, society and politics and its relevance for the economic sphere; (2) economic dynamics, growth and crisis; (3) the distribution of wealth and income; (4) money and the financial sector; and (5) the geography of the global economy. For each of these fields, (economic) policy implications are discussed. While in Jäger and Springler (2012) this is done extensively and in similar length for all three paradigms (neoclassical economics, post-Keynesianism and critical political economy), this is different here. Given the lack of space, this section focusses on critical political economy and does not provide an extensive comparison, although this would be desirable. However, some differences to the other paradigms are highlighted at least briefly. This is based on the assumption that most readers are familiar with neoclassical perspectives and that post-Keynesian views are presented in other chapters of this book.

4.1 The state, society and politics

In a critical political economy perspective, the state, society and politics are not analysed separately from the economy but are considered to be intrinsic to the economic realm. As outlined above, the state, discourses, ideologies and political practices can be understood against the background of specific relations of production and the available productive forces. Hence power is not to be found only or mainly in the political arena as such, but political power is based on economic power structures characterised by dominating and dominated classes and (antagonistic) class interests. In the political sphere, a capitalist mode of production is usually reflected by a capitalist state and capitalist power relations. However, these relations and structures adopt different forms, and there is certain autonomy of political structures and processes from the economic sphere. In the field of critical political economy, several concepts at a lower level of abstraction were developed to deal with the question of political processes within capitalist modes of production. While during the 19th century political power in Europe was still concentrated in the hands of dominant classes given the absence of formal liberal democracy and free elections, it was obvious that the economically powerful classes also dominated the political arena. Hence the state was considered an instrument in the hands of dominant classes. It was the working class which struggled for democratic participation and free elections against the resistance of dominant classes.

With the rise of formal liberal democracy and the fascist backlash in the 1920s and 1930s, Antonio Gramsci (1999 [1971]) tried to further develop categories to better understand class struggles and the political dynamics of modern capitalism. He argued that not just the state but also struggles within the sphere of civil society have to be analysed in order to adequately address struggles and changes. Political power of dominant classes, hence, cannot rely only on coercion but needs also active or at least passive support by the subordinated classes. Civil society is the arena where those struggles for predominant ideas about the proper way of organising the economy – or as Gramsci called it, struggles for hegemony – take place. Related to this, he developed the idea of organic intellectuals and everyday knowledge, which are both important for understanding those struggles. Today critical political economists also point to the crucial role of mass media (Hardy 2014). Building on Gramsci, Nicos Poulantzas (1978 [1968]) provided a conceptualisation to analyse the specific structure of states and their implications for struggles over the mode of production. Based on those concepts, critical political economists have distinguished different types of states and civil society configurations which they relate to specific historical modes of production. They show, for example, how a Fordist welfare state, which was predominant in Western societies after World War II till the 1980s, is different from a post-1980 neoliberal workfare state and what this means for social struggles.

In order to analyse a specific historical situation, it is proposed to conduct a conjunctural analysis (Jessop 2008). This means that one tries to compile an integrative analysis of the totality of developments with the aim of understanding ongoing processes and guiding emancipatory strategies in relation with the dominated, oppressed, exploited and marginalised groups in society in a given point of time. Not only class relations but also related inequalities alongside gender and race have to be addressed (Fischer and Tepe 2011). In order to obtain such a broad and deep overview for a sound conjunctural analysis, it is obvious that a collective undertaking is required as it goes beyond the capacity of single researchers. This means that researchers focussing on different aspects and using different abstractions at the more concrete level and adequate methodologies together can undertake such a task.

The ultimate goal, therefore, is not to understand reality but to transform it in an emancipatory way. As Marx puts it in his 11th thesis on Feuerbach: “The philosophers have hitherto only interpreted the world in various ways; the point is to change it". (Marx and Engels 2011 [1845]). In line with this, Cox (1981) called for a critical approach in the practice of research trying to transform and overcome power structures instead of just "problem-solving" within given power structures. In addition to a conjunctural analysis, an important contribution of critical political economy is to critique an existing capitalist mode of production and unveil its power structure, contradictions and oppressive and exploitative nature. This implies an adequate use of language which explicitly relies on emancipatory ethical perspectives (Sayer 2005).

With regard to the state, it is important for the reader to think about how and why a critical political economy perspective is different from mainstream neoclassical economics and also from other frequently used heterodox economic perspectives, such as a post-Keynesian view. Reflection on this and thinking about the implications of using these different approaches and about which groups in society might benefit more from which approaches may raise the awareness regarding the implications of different paradigms in economics. If one compares a critical political economy approach to a neoclassical perspective, the differences become very clear. In neoclassical mainstream economics there is a space for the state only in case of market failure and in order to provide necessary infrastructure including property laws and in the case of so-called public goods. In the neoclassical new political economy tradition, the state is analysed using methodological individualism and by focussing on activities of individuals, such as lobbying and rent-seeking. Critical political economy's perspective on the state, society and politics is also very different from a post-Keynesian view. In the latter, the state is often conceived as an impartial institution which is expected to conduct adequate (Keynesian) policies and to ensure the existence of adequate economic institutions. This technocratic understanding is very different from a critical political economy view (Jäger and Springler 2012).

4.2 Economic development, growth and crisis

Economic development, growth and crisis have traditionally been a central focus of critical political economy perspectives. The reason for the dynamic development of capitalism which constantly revolutionises production and consumption were explained by pointing to the *imperative to accumulate*. As already indicated, in the market individual capitalists are forced to compete against one another. In order to survive competition it is necessary to make a profit (i.e. to accumulate capital), to reinvest it and to improve production techniques. This includes keeping costs of production and therefore wages low. In addition, obtaining a profit in capitalism is always uncertain because it is not perfectly foreseeable whether, given the undertaken investments, commodities can be sold profitably. This and many other *contradictions* of capitalism may lead to different types of crises (Heinrich 2004). *Small crises* or the business cycle downturns are mainly explained by the dynamics of the investment cycle. Big or *structural crises* are related to the central contradictions of capitalism between societal production and private appropriation of surplus value.

The *social structure of accumulation approach* was developed in order to analyse long-term growth trends and crises of the global economy (Kotz, McDonough and Reich 1994; McDonough et al. 2010). In a similar vein, the *regulation approach* (Aglietta 2000 [1979]; Jessop and Sum 2006) deals with the question of how, given the inherent instability of capitalism, longer periods of high and stable economic growth are possible. Central concepts of this approach are the mode of regulation and the regime of accumulation. A mode of regulation refers to a coherent set of institutions which deal with central contradictions in capitalism such as capital-labour relations, the relation of competition between capitalists, and the organisation of money including the financial sector and the use of nature. Potentially a mode of regulation at least temporarily offsets the contradictions and allows for a longer period of stable capitalist expansion. The regulation approach distinguishes different types of growth characterised as regimes of accumulation. They are classified with regard to the predominant type of surplus production (extensive or intensive), the dominance of productive or financialised accumulation and whether they are outward or inward oriented. Historically, periods of crises and different regimes of accumulation and different modes of regulation are distinguished. However, such a stable regime of growth is rather not the result of design but the outcome of social struggles between different classes and class fractions within a specific setting which can be analysed by using a Gramscian perspective. Hence economic growth is therefore the result of the interaction of complex economic dynamics, institutional configurations and political struggles (see also Jäger and Springler in this volume).

In a traditional neoclassical perspective, economic growth is described by a production function and external technological progress. It is assumed that markets use resources efficiently and output is rather stable. In case of short-term deviations from the equilibrium output, it is supposed that market processes bring the economy back to the equilibrium soon. However, newer versions of neoclassical economics, such as the new growth theory or the endogenous growth theory, relax some assumptions and see therefore the possibilities for market intervention. Post-Keynesians very much reject the idea of a neoclassical production function and consider output to be determined by effective demand. Effective demand is inherently instable and tends to be insufficient. Hence, in a post-Keynesian view it is necessary that the state actively stabilises the economy and thereby ensures economic growth and full employment.

In addition, by contrast to neoclassical perspectives as well as to post-Keynesian views, in critical political economy economic growth is not considered positive per se. Economic growth does not necessarily mean that the living conditions for (all) workers improve. It is a question of growth for whom. This is because an expansion of capitalist production may go along with increasing exploitation and the depletion of the environment and tends to destroy non-capitalist modes of production and lifestyles. A critical political economy perspective, therefore, does not ask how growth can be brought about but rather which type of economic transformations and patterns of consumption should be achieved. This includes the question of how nature is used for economic activities (David Harvey 1996) and links to recent developments of degrowth literature.

4.3 Inequality and the distribution of income and wealth

Critical political economy conceives inequality as an expression of social relations and therefore specific modes of production. A capitalist society which is divided into classes shows large differences in terms of distribution of wealth and income because the ownership of the means of production is highly concentrated. This allows capitalists to earn profits while the large majority of people mainly depend on income based on their work. As outlined earlier, labour is the only productive force which produces value, while owners of capital appropriate the surplus value. However, the distribution of income and therefore the share of wages and profits are not fixed but subject to social struggles. Those struggles take place not only over the primary distribution of income (the wages, the length of the working day, etc.) but also over the secondary distribution of income. This is about the distribution of the tax burden and the use of state revenues including the social wage (pensions, health insurance, etc.), which have a significant importance given the substantial share of government revenues in the economy.

Historically, different capitalist modes of production show different specific patterns of distribution of income and wealth. This is related to relative class power and class compromises. While in the post-WWII era the class compromise in Western Europe and North America was relatively favourable for labour in historical terms, this has changed with neoliberalism since the 1980s. Neoliberalism has favoured capital in general and financial capital in particular, and its income share has risen (Harvey 2005; Duménil and Lévy 2011).

Beyond the distribution of income and wealth within countries, critical political economy points to the international and the material dimensions of inequality. For instance, extremely low wages in peripheral countries may allow for a transfer of surplus value from the periphery to the core countries of the world economy. In the core countries this allows for either higher profit, because wage goods become cheaper and lower wages can be paid, or for higher real wages. The foreign ownership of natural resources allows the appropriation of rent, which then is often transferred to core countries. Against this background, Ehrlich Reifer (2011, 73) points to the global differences in the per capita use of natural resources and proposes to distinguish between oligarchic and democratic well-being. While oligarchic well-being is based on huge international inequality in terms of quantity of natural resources used, democratic well-being implies a lifestyle which is possible and sustainable for the whole global population. Moreover, other multiple dimensions of inequality going along with capitalist modes of production are critiqued. This includes gender inequality, differences in access to education and culture and inequality in terms of working conditions. Equality in terms of a classless society, solidarity and balanced job complexes is the ultimate goal (Hahnel and Albert 1991).

A critical political economy perspective on inequality and the distribution of income and wealth stands in sharp contrast to the neoclassical view of marginal productivity determining income. This neoclassical view is also criticised by post-Keynesians, who point to the so-called Cambridge controversy on capital. Critical political economists criticise the ideological dimension of the neoclassical approach, which hides the fact that values are only produced by workers, and surplus value in form of profits, rents and interest are appropriated by others thanks to their privileged position in capitalism. The neoclassical assumption that well-being cannot be compared between different individuals – this view is at the core of neoclassical welfare economics – and the idea of a Pareto optimum fades out any discussion of inequality by definition. In critical political economy, a desired world is not a Pareto optimal one which does not take inequality in account but a world which is characterised by equity and solidarity. Such an alternative world should be the outcome of democratic processes which explicitly deal with the alternative organisation of the mode of production. However, in practice a more equal and just world is the outcome of (class) struggles. The emancipatory goal of these different struggles is to reduce multiple dimensions of inequality in the short and medium terms and to contribute to overcoming capitalism in the longer term because this mode of production is characterised by inherently high inequality.

4.4 Money and the financial sector

In a critical political economy perspective, money is essential for capitalism. It is both the starting point and the end point of the accumulation process. Capitalists use money to produce and sell commodities with the ultimate goal of obtaining more money. Modern money has no intrinsic value. It is rather a symbol which allows access to commodities. As labour power is a commodity in capitalism, money also directly provides social power to its owner. Alongside these general characteristics of money in capitalism, its historically specific configuration is of crucial importance (Nelson 1999). Today, money and its use are genuinely based on central banking and a modern banking and financial system. It commonly pays interest to its owners which entitles them to appropriate a share of the surplus value. According to critical political economy, the specific configuration of money and the financial system are subject to struggles between different classes and class fractions. Hence the specific form of money and the structure of the financial system undergo important changes (Guttmann 1994). Certain configurations of money and finance favour different groups over others. For example, they favour financial capital over productive capital, debtors over creditors and capital over workers. In times of financial crisis, those struggles tend to become more intense as the question arises who suffers the burden and who is protected.

National monetary and financial systems are different and embedded into the international financial regime. Beginning with the emergence of the Bretton Woods system, US capitalism and US global monetary rules have dominated internationally. Since the end of the 1970s the international monetary non-system, called Dollar-Wall Street Regime by Peter Gowan (1999), has favoured US (financial) interests even more than the previous Bretton Woods regime and contributed to sustained US hegemony (Panitch and Gindin 2012). This neoliberal global monetary regime has made monetary policy in the rest of the world more difficult to manage effectively and contributed to numerous financial crises. Peripheral countries were among those most affected. This is explained not just by their inferior status in the global hierarchy but also by the fact that they tend to suffer from dependent forms of financialisation (Becker et al. 2010).

The treatment of money and the financial sector in the neoclassical paradigm is characterised by the idea of the "neutrality" of money and the efficiency of financial markets. A monetary policy which stabilises the amount of money (or the inflation rate) together with measures which ensure transparent and non-restricted financial markets are considered to be an adequate answer to ensure economic stability and efficiency. Obviously, the critical political economy approach to money and the financial sector is very different from a neoclassical perspective. It argues that money and a financial sector are essential for capitalism and at the same time socially contested. Different monetary policies and financial system configurations favour certain interests over others, and moreover, they have important implications for accumulation processes and may cause financial and economic crisis. In this regard it is similar to post-Keynesian perspectives which consider money and finance as a key issue in the economy (Evans 2004). Money is, therefore, neither a veil nor is the structure of the financial system neutral but rather subject to struggles between different classes and class fractions. Hence, neoclassical policy suggestions with regard to monetary policy and the structure of the financial system should be evaluated critically against their effects on different class fractions. In addition, critical political economy points to the highly uneven effects of the global monetary regime and its negative effects on subaltern classes in peripheral countries and seeks ways to overcome them.

4.5 The geography of the global economy

According to critical political economy, capitalism produces an uneven and constantly changing geography. Space is considered to be not a fixed natural constant but a product of historical modes of production. As Smith (2008, 6) puts it:

> The logic of uneven development derives specifically from the opposed tendencies, inherent to capital, toward the differentiation but simultaneously equalization of the levels and conditions of production. Capital is continually invested in the built environment so that it can move elsewhere and take advantage of higher profit rates. The spatial immobilization of productive capital in its material form is no more or less a necessity than the perpetual circulation of capital as value. Thus it is possible to see the uneven development of capitalism as the geographical expression of the more fundamental contradiction between use-value and exchange-value. The pattern which results in the landscape is well known: development at one pole and underdevelopment at the other.

On a more concrete level, different concepts were developed in the tradition of critical political economy to deal with the uneven and asymmetric nature of capitalist development. The theory of imperialism dates back to Lenin as well as Luxemburg (1970 [1913]). It is argued that crises to realise surplus value contribute to a geographic expansion of capitalism and the inclusion of other (colonial) spaces. The expansion of capital from the core of the world economy and the penetration of other spaces in peripheral areas is still an ongoing phenomenon. The term *neo-imperialism* is used to refer to those developments today which often have a violent character and are secured by military strategies (Petras and Veltmeyer 2005; Van der Pijl 2006). Another concept to explain the dynamics of the global economy is provided by the world systems approach (Wallerstein 2004; Arrighi 1994). This explains the relationship between the core, the semi-periphery and the periphery in the world economy and long-run changes. While the world systems approach tends to emphasise the structural unevenness of capitalist development, neo-Gramscian conceptualisations point to the related political dimensions and the role of global US hegemony and international institutions (Cox 1981; Gill 1998). Moreover, under the heading of dependency theories, political economy scholars focus on the possibilities of emancipatory strategies in (semi-)peripheral countries (Cardoso and Faletto 1979 [1971]).

In a traditional neoclassical perspective, markets are supposed to tend to equilibrium and spread economic well-being over the world. However, in the new economic geography there are models which show that due to externalities the concentration of economic activity in certain spaces or countries is possible and therefore uneven economic patterns may arise. Often "bad" institutions are considered the reason for "underdevelopment". What is neglected is that those institutions are to an important extent a result of colonialism and contemporary global economic governance structures which are an expression of imperialist structures and strategies. Contrary to neoclassical perspectives, critical political economy points to the fact that capitalism produces a very uneven geography and a division between core and periphery, which is characterised by an asymmetric relationship and by the exploitation of the latter. Hence there is a struggle between the economic core and the periphery. Although these structural asymmetries are very strong, critical political economy also searches for strategies to overcome dependency and to contribute to emancipatory developments in peripheral countries and regions.

5 Conclusion

It can be concluded that an introduction to critical political economy should reject the neoclassical distinction between microeconomics and macroeconomics. Instead, it should unveil the ontological assumptions and methodological approaches of neoclassical and relatively widespread post-Keynesian approaches and compare them to perspectives in the tradition of critical political economy. An introduction to economics which shows how and why these different paradigms are different and how they differ in their historical background and their general goals is expected to be very insightful to the reader. Based on this, it is important to show how each of these paradigms approaches economic key issues and which (economic) policy conclusions are respectively drawn. Due to the lack of space, this chapter focussed mainly on presenting the critical political economy perspective and only briefly undertook comparisons with other paradigms. It is important to underline in the conclusions that critical political economy is not a narrow economistic approach but a paradigm which provides an integrative perspective on the economy, politics and society. This is also the reason for using the broader term "critical political economy" rather than "Marxian economics". Critical political economy represents a historical dialectical methodology which combines concepts at different levels of abstraction and relates them to concrete reality. However, the ultimate goal is not just to understand reality but to change it in favour of the oppressed and the exploited. Hence, it is a highly valuable approach for all those who want to overcome inequality, poverty, exploitation and dominance by contributing to emancipatory perspectives and pushing for respective transformations in and of economy and society.

References

Aglietta, M. (2000 [1979]): *A Theory of Capitalist Regulation: The US Experience*. London: Verso.

Arrighi, G. (1994): *The Long Twentieth Century: Money, Power and the Origins of Our Times*. London: Verso.

Baran, P. A. and Sweezy, P. M. (1989 [1966]): *Monopoly Capital: An Essay on the American Economic and Social Order*. New York: Monthly Review Press.

Becker, J., Jäger, J., Leubolt, B. and Weissenbacher, R. (2010): "Peripheral Financialization and Vulnerability to Crisis: A Regulationist Perspective", *Competition & Change* 14(3–4), 225–247.

Bhaskar, R. (1998): "Critical Realism and Dialectic", in Margaret, A. et al. (eds.), *Critical Realism: Essential Readings*. London: Routledge, 575–640.

Bowles, S., Edwards, R. and Roosevelt, F. (2005): *Understanding Capitalism: Competition, Command and Change*. 3rd edition. Oxford: Oxford University Press.

Browning, G. and Kilmister, A. (2006): *Critical and Post-Critical Political Economy*. Houndmills: Palgrave Macmillan.

Bruff, I. (2011): "The Case for a Foundational Materialism: Going Beyond Historical Materialist IPE in Order to Strengthen It", *Journal of International Relations and Development* 14, 391–399.

Cafruny, A., Talani, L. S. and Pozo, G. (2016): *The Palgrave Handbook of Critical International Political Economy*. London: Palgrave Macmillan.

Cardoso, F. H. and Faletto, E. (1979 [1971]): *Dependency and Development in Latin America*. Berkeley: University of California Press.

Cox, R. (1981): "Social Forces, States, and World Orders", *Millennium: Journal of International Studies* 10(2), 126–155.

Duménil, G. and Lévy, D. (2011): *The Crisis of Neoliberalism*. Cambridge, MA: Harvard University Press.

Ehrlich, R. T. (2011): "Global Inequalities, Alternative Regionalisms and the Future of Socialism", *Journal für Entwicklungspolitik* 27(1), 72–94.

Evans, T. (2004): "Marxian and Post-Keynesian Theories of Finance and the Business Cycle", *Capital & Class* 83, 47–100.

Fine, B. and Saad-Filho, A. (2012): *The Elgar Companion to Marxist Economics*. Cheltenham, UK: Edward Elgar.

Fischer, A. and Tepe, D. (2011): "What's Critical about Critical Theory: Feminist Materialism, Intersectionality and the Social Totality of the Frankfurt School", in Shields, S., Bruff, I. and Macartney, H. (eds.), *Critical International Political Economy: Dialogue, Debate and Dissensus*. London: Palgrave Macmillan, 132–148.

Gill, S. (1998): "New Constitutionalism, Democratisation & Global Political Economy", *Pacifica Review* 10(1), 23–38.

Gowan, P. (1999): *The Global Gamble: Washington's Faustian Bid for World Dominance*. London: Verso.

Gramsci, A. (1999 [1971]): *Selections from the Prison Notebooks*. London: ElecBook.

Guttmann, R. (1994): *How Credit Money Shapes the Economy: The United States in a Global System*. Armonk, NY: M. E. Sharpe.

Hahnel, R. and Albert, M. (1991): *Political Economy of Participatory Economics*. Princeton, NJ: Princeton University Press.

Hardy, J. (2014): *Critical Political Economy of the Media: An Introduction*. London: Routledge.

Harvey, D. (1996): *Justice, Nature & the Geography of Difference*. Oxford: Blackwell.

Harvey, D. (2005): *A Brief History of Neoliberalism*. Oxford: Oxford University Press.

Harvey, D. (2010): *A Companion to Marx's Capital*. London: Verso.

Heinrich, M. (2004): *An Introduction to the Three Volumes of Karl Marx's Capital*. New York: Monthly Review Press.

Jäger, J., Horn, L. and Becker, J. (2016): "Critical International Political Economy and Method", in Cafruny, A., Talani, L. S. and Pozo, G. (eds.), *The Palgrave Handbook of Critical International Political Economy*. London: Palgrave Macmillan, 101–118.

Jäger, J. and Springler, E. (2012): *Ökonomie der internationalen Entwicklung. Eine kritische Einführung in die Volkswirtschaftslehre*. Wien: Mandelbaum Verlag.

Jessop, B. (2008): *State Power*. Cambridge: Polity Press.

Jessop, B. and Sum, N.-L. (2001): "Pre-Disciplinary and Post-Disciplinary Perspectives in Political Economy", *New Political Economy* 6(1), 89–101.

Jessop, B. and Sum, N.-L. (2006): *Beyond the Regulation Approach: Putting Capitalist Economies in Their Place*. Cheltenham, UK: Edward Elgar.

Kotz, D. M., McDonough, T. and Reich, M. (1994): *Social Structures of Accumulation: The Political Economy of Growth and Crisis*. Cambridge, MA: Cambridge University Press.

Kuhn, T. S. (2012 [1962]): *The Structure of Scientific Revolutions*. Chicago: University of Chicago Press.

Luxemburg, R. (1970 [1913]): *Die Akkumulation des Kapitals. Ein Beitrag zur ökonomischen Erklärung des Imperialismus*. Berlin: Verlag Neue Kritik.

Marx, K. (1973 [1852]): "The Eighteenth Brumaire of Louis Bonaparte", in *Surveys from Exile*. London: Penguin Books.

Marx, K. (1992 [1867]): *Capital: A Critique of Political Economy*. Vol. 1. London: Penguin Books.

Marx, K. (1993 [1894]): *Capital: A Critique of Political Economy*. Vol. 3. London: Penguin Books.

Marx, K. (2012 [1857]): *Grundrisse: Foundations of the Critique of Political Economy*. London: Penguin Classics.

Marx, K. and Engels, F. (2011 [1845]): *The German Ideology*. Eastford: Martino Publishing.

McDonough, T., Reich, M. and Kotz, D. M. (2010): *Contemporary Capitalism and Its Crises: Social Structure of Accumulation Theory for the 21st Century*. Cambridge, MA: Cambridge University Press.

Milonakis, D. and Fine, B. (2009): *From Political Economy to Economics: Method, the Social and the Historical Evolution of Economic Theory*. London: Routledge.

Nelson, A. (1999): *Marx's Concept of Money: The God of Commodities*. London: Routledge.

Nitzan, J. and Bichler, S. (2009): *Capital as Power: A Study of Order and Creorder*. London: Routledge.

Panitch, L. and Gindin, S. (2012): *The Making of Global Capitalism: The Political Economy of American Empire*. London: Verso.

Petras, J. and Veltmeyer, H. (2005): *Empire with Imperialism: The Globalizing Dynamics of Neo-Liberal Capitalism*. London: Zed Books.

Poulantzas, N. (1978 [1968]): *Political Power and Social Classes*. London: New Left Books.

Ricardo, D. (1997 [1817]): *Principles of Political Economy and Taxation*. Amherst: Prometheus Books.

Sayer, A. (1992): *Method in Social Science: A Realist Approach*. 2nd edition. London: Routledge.

Sayer, A. (2005): *The Moral Significance of Class*. Cambridge: Cambridge University Press.

Screpanti, E. and Zamagni, S. (2005): *An Outline of the History of Economic Thought*. 2nd edition. Oxford: Oxford University Press.

Sherman, H. J., Hunt, E. K., Fesiba, R. F., O'Hara, P. A. and Wiens-Tuers, B. (2008): *Economics: An Introduction to Traditional and Progressive Views*. 7th edition. Armonk, NY: M. E. Sharpe.

Smith, A. (1991 [1776]): *Wealth of Nations*. Amherst: Prometheus Books.

Smith, N. (2008): *Uneven Development: Nature, Capital, and the Production of Space*. 3rd edition. Athens and Georgia: The University of Georgia Press.

Van der Pijl, K. (2006): *Global Rivalries: From the Cold War to Iraq*. London: Pluto Press.

Van der Pijl, K. (2007): *Nomades, Empires, States: Modes of Foreign Relations and Political Economy*. Vol. 1. London: Pluto Press.

Wallerstein, I. (2004): *World-Systems Analysis: An Introduction*. Durham, NC: Duke University Press.

8 Heterodox perspectives in teaching the European integration and crisis

Critical political economy and post-Keynesianism[1]

Johannes Jäger and Elisabeth Springler

1 Introduction

For decades mainstream approaches to teaching European integration have been based on a neoclassical understanding of reality (e.g. Hitiris 2003). Reducing restrictions on the free movement of capital, labour, goods and services were considered to be welfare enhancing. This included the idea that some regulation and coordination at the level of the European Union, such as common rules for competition, were necessary and functional to promote market forces and economic development. While mainstream economics was concerned with highlighting the merits of the free market, mainstream political sciences focussed on institutional settings and the functionality of different policy fields within the EU, assuming that a neoliberal approach was the only possible way of organizing European integration (Bieling et al. 2016). Since the 1970s European integration has increasingly adopted a neoliberal form which was justified by neoclassical economic theory. However, it has suffered from constantly declining growth rates since the 1970s (Cafruny and Ryner 2007). Even in its own terms, namely with regards to economic growth, neoliberal European integration has been no success. In addition, the decades before the crisis were already characterized by a tendency towards a declining share of labour income and a rising share of profits, contributing to increasing inequality (OECD 2011).

In the ideal world of neoliberalism, a crisis in Europe should not have happened. When the crisis broke out in Europe, mainstream economists and mainstream political scientists struggled to explain this (Ryner 2015). The lacking success of neoliberal austerity policy as a response to the crisis in Europe remains an unresolved puzzle in neoclassical economics. The problems and shortcomings of neoclassical theory to explain the European integration and crisis have been analyzed in detail (see e.g. EuroMemogroup (2017). Even prominent economists at the margin of the mainstream, like Stiglitz (2016), criticised the anti-Keynesian nature of European economic policies and the problematic institutional structures of the Eurozone. In addition, flaws of mainstream literature on European integration and its crisis are well documented (Van Apeldoorn et al. 2009; Nousios et al. 2012a).

Alternative and more illustrating ways of understanding European integration and its crisis are therefore required. Traditionally, post-Keynesian and critical political economy perspectives have offered strong alternative views to mainstream approaches to European integration. However, critical political economy and post-Keynesianism hitherto have presented usually separated strands and were often not related to each other. In Jäger and Springler (2015), we brought together critical political economists and post-Keynesian economists in an edited volume and argued that both approaches and can and should be combined in order to have a more complete understanding of European integration and of the crisis. In our view, this is also crucial for teaching European integration and studying its crisis because it allows for students to get a systematic access to two highly relevant heterodox theoretical perspectives and their explanatory power.

Given the fact that the European crisis is all but over and the struggle about the future of European integration is ongoing, it is important to understand those developments based on an adequate and sound theoretical perspective. In this chapter we mainly follow the argument in the introductory chapter and the concluding chapter of Jäger and Springler (2015). First, we argue how those two approaches speak to each other and how they can be combined. Second, we show how they explain and evaluate the European crisis and anti-crisis policies. Based on this we briefly discuss some scenarios for the future development in Europe. Finally, conclusions are drawn.

2 Critical political economy and post-Keynesianism

With regards to its philosophical roots, critical political economy (CPE) relies on Critical Realism or philosophies which are relatively close to it, such as historical materialism (Jäger et al. 2016), and post-Keynesian (PK) work is often based on Critical Realism, too (Lawson 1999). Hence, CPE and PK perspectives do stand on a similar philosophical ground. The concept of financialization (Epstein 2005; Erturk et al. 2008; Lapavitsas 2013) and also the regulation approach (Clévenot 2011) turned out to provide important links which combined insights from PK and CPE. Financialized, finance-led, or finance-dominated capitalism were terms used to describe pre-crisis modes of development (Stockhammer 2008; Stockhammer and Köhler 2015). Also, both approaches point to the importance of the global economic and financial structures and the euro in explaining dynamics of European integration (Cafruny and Ryner 2007; Lapavitsas and Flassbeck 2015). The analysis of the role of money, the financial sector and central banking tend to be less developed in CPE, but there are important links and both perspectives are complementary in this regard (Evans 2004). From a CPE position, PK contributions can be seen as a more concrete approach to the analysis of economic processes at the surface or price level while CPE often deals with economic issues in a more abstract way and often focusses on the political dimension.

However, there are important differences between both approaches. In the following we briefly show the differences with regards to the general focus, the

Table 8.1 PK and CPE approaches compared

	Post-Keynesianism	*Critical Political Economy*
General focus	Focus on specific economic mechanisms and causal relations and macroeconomic aggregates	Integrative analysis of economy, society and politics
Ultimate goal and source of policy change	Establish full employment and welfare state	Radical reformism as a step to overcome capitalism in the long run
	Benevolent politicians establish adequate institutions and implement the correct PK economic policy	Configuration of social forces and class struggles determine who is able decide on economic structures and policies

Source: Own compilation.

ultimate goal, the understanding of crisis and the source of policy change (for an overview, see Table 8.1).

2.1 General focus

CPE stands in the tradition of political economy, includes the insights of Marx, and analyzes the society as a whole by providing an integrated framework for the analysis of economy, society and the state which overcomes today's prevailing disciplinary divisions. At the core of CPE is the abstract concept of social relations of production. In general, CPE tries to understand, explain and critique given societal structures and developments. It focusses on the inherent instability of the capital-labour relation and the transformation of capitalism. There are long-standing traditions in CPE, such as the social structures of accumulation approach or the regulation approach which explicitly focusses on the dynamics of capitalist development and its crisis (Kotz 1994). CPE analyzes how power in capitalism is organized and tries to contribute to emancipatory struggles in order to overcome exploitation and power relations (Cox 1981) . Thereby CPE does not only focus on class-based power relations and forms of exploitation but also includes inequalities related to questions of gender and race (Fischer and Tepe 2011). CPE searches for conditions that allow for alternative developments which overcome specific historical forms of domination and exploitation and hence modes of capitalism such as neoliberalism. However, against the background of the multiple contradictions of capitalism, ultimately CPE seeks to overcome a capitalist mode of production. Within CPE there are numerous more specific theories, approaches and methodologies which address different aspects of capitalist developments (for a more detailed overview, see Jäger in this volume).

PK approaches stand in the tradition of Keynes but also combine elements of classical political economy, Marx and institutionalist approaches and often explicitly criticize neoclassical approaches. This historical view is imperative to understand the characteristics of post-Keynesian economics, as the time framework for economic policy analysis is in the centre of the analysis. The main drivers for the development were the continuous struggles with mainstream economists, which shaped the theoretical and policy approaches of this economic alternative. The first post-Keynesians, though not named as such but joined in their economic beliefs, emerged with the publication of the General Theory in 1936 and framed the opposition to the equilibrium modelling of Hicks (1937) in his interpretation of the General Theory (see e.g. Snowdon and Vane 2005, chapter 2). Therefore the general focus of PK can be stated as *Focus on specific economic mechanisms and causal relations and macroeconomic aggregates*. The hierarchical order of markets follows Keynes and leads to the PK priority on increasing employment and boosting economic development via a demand-driven view on the economy. Early post-Keynesians were united in their opposition to the existing economic mainstream, which also manifested in the Cambridge Controversies (e.g. King 2002, chapter 4), and it becomes evident that their economic thinking was also influenced by their own economic experiences.

While the focus of CPE tends to be based on an integrative perspective of the dynamics of capitalism, PK offers different strands of causal arguments to overcome specific macroeconomic problems.

2.2 *Ultimate goal and source of policy change*

Building on the hierarchical structure mentioned earlier, which puts full employment and therefore the goods market on the top of macroeconomic goals, PK aims at better living conditions for workers within a reformed capitalism. In order to rescue capitalism as a social mode of production, a specific configuration of economic institutions and policies is considered indispensable. To avoid or to quickly overcome economic crisis is considered crucial. The key addressee of PK work is 'the state', which is expected to implement adequate institutions and policies to ensure growth and full employment. Besides government spending, a more equal income distribution (including a strong welfare state) and an adequate monetary policy and regulation of the financial sector are considered crucial to ensure stable and high economic growth and full employment. With this causal argumentation, again opposition is built against the understanding of mainstream analysis and its critical view towards the role of the state. The impact of this opposing view of PK economics towards neoliberal policies becomes especially evident when focussing on issues of European integration, as presented in the following section.

CPE aspires to radical reformism in the short run and the overcoming of capitalism and the implementation of solidary and rational society (Demirovic 2005) in the long run. Hence, with regards to the ultimate goal there is an important difference between CPE and PK perspectives. CPE understands the economy as part of society, which means that economics and politics are intrinsically linked and the 'economic' is considered to be part of a broader social relation and hence the result of class struggle. In general, CPE approaches tend to be less optimistic than PK that the 'correct' policies and institutions – and not the wrong neoclassical policies – can be implemented by benevolent politicians and economic policy makers. CPE approaches therefore tend to argue that it is not a question of the correct economic ideas and policies but of the configuration of social forces which have the power to implement desired structures, hence economic policy and economic development in the end are political questions.

3 European integration and its crisis

At the surface, the economic crisis appeared in Europe in 2008. It was not just a crisis of the Eurozone but a crisis which affected the European Union as a whole. Recovery has been very weak, and unemployment in the Eurozone was still close to 10% in 2015 (Eurostat 2016). The fact that interest rates are still at historically low record levels shows that this is a serious crisis. Low interest rates and measures by the European Central Bank (ECB) to buy bonds did not boost investment significantly. On the contrary, new structural weaknesses become evident (e.g. the side effects of low interest rates for the eligibility of treasury bonds to participate in the third pillar of the European quantitative easing structure). In 2015 Europe was still lagging behind in a global perspective (IMF 2016). Moreover, the crisis has exacerbated the split between the core and the periphery in Europe. It is evident that the European crisis management in 2009–2010 was inspired by rescuing the financial sector and by Keynesian 'deficit spending' in the core countries of the EU which were first hit by the crisis. Although those efforts were much weaker compared to the United States, for example, they helped to avoid a complete meltdown. When the crisis later hit the peripheral countries (Portugal, Italy, Greece and Spain, the so-called PIGS), the reaction was completely different. Given the fact that the ECB does not act as a lender of last resort for governments, financial speculation against peripheral EU countries had set in and it became increasingly difficult and costly for them refinance their debts. The European reaction were different so-called rescue measures which were bound to anti-Keynesian policies. Later on, this conditionality provided the blueprint for reforming EU economic governance alongside even stricter neoliberal rules. The implementation of these rules in part was not an element of established formal procedures within the EU. This was called a deepening of authoritarian neoliberalism at the level of the EU because of the content of the new economic governance rules, the way how were implemented and the reduction of democratic policy space that went along with this (cf. Bruff 2014a; Oberndorfer 2015). Although several years of European crisis management have helped to prevent a total economic and political collapse, it has been far from successful – even in its own terms – namely in restoring solid economic growth. In addition, centrifugal forces which hitherto became manifest in the Brexit underline the crisis of European integration.

Post-Keynesians have provided an opposing view to neoliberal approaches to European integration by mainly critiquing restrictive fiscal and monetary policy frameworks at the level of the EU, such as the Maastricht treaty or the monetary policy framework of the ECB because of their negative impact on growth and employment. The European crisis and the restrictive polices applied showed dramatically the negative consequence of austerity-oriented policies leading to a drop in gross domestic product (GDP) in Greece by more than 25% and a stagnation in Europe as a whole, which only in 2015 returned on the average to the pre-crisis level of GDP (EuroMemogroup 2014; Eurostat 2016).

Critical political economists have traditionally pointed to the class dimension of the European integration project. They argued that a neoliberal form of integration in Europe took place against the background of the transformation of capitalism in Europe and the crisis of Fordist development models and the welfare state in the 1970s and 1980s (Bieling et al. 2016). Critical political economy also showed that the neoliberal transition of European integration was an expression of a weakening working class and promoted actively by capital in general and by transnational corporations in particular (Van Apeldoorn 2013). With regard to the crisis, critical political economists continued to focus on specific contradictions and problems of capitalist development in Europe and the role of different class agents to deal with the crisis (Bieling 2015).

With regards to crises in general and the crisis of EU integration in particular CPE and PK offer different and in part complementary perspectives. In the following subsections we briefly demonstrate the key aspects of both approaches. Thereby we focus on (1) crises in general, (2) the spatial dimension, (3) the EU crisis in particular, and (4) ways to overcome it (for an overview, see Table 8.2).

Table 8.2 Combining post-Keynesianism and critical political economy on the European crisis

	Post-Keynesianism	*Critical Political Economy*
Explaining crisis	Low economic growth due to economic policies which do not promote effective demand adequately	Structural crisis resulting from systemic contradictions and leading to a multiple crisis
Spatial considerations	Nation-states and regional analysis with their specific institutional structure; view on unequal developments	Integrated multilevel analysis; focus on asymmetric relations and structures of dependency
Focus on EU crisis	What are the problems in economic policy? How could the structure/setting be changed to improve the situation?	What are the economic structures and class strategies at different spatial levels which lead to neoliberal integration and crisis?
Dealing with the crisis	The institutional setting of the EU/Eurozone has to be improved: the implementation of proper structural setting is imperative.	Emancipatory (class) agents have to be sufficiently powerful to push for progressive changes in Europe.

Source: Own compilation.

3.1 Explaining crisis

Post-Keynesians usually refer to an economic crisis in terms of the lack of economic growth. In general, growth is considered to be endogenous, path-dependent and mainly driven by investment as a substantial factor of aggregate demand (Setterfield 2001). When explaining crisis, PK scholars point to falling investment, a development which may have different origins. One important cause is the inherent instability of financial structures (Minsky 1992). The outbreak of the global economic crisis in the financial sector underlines the importance of this aspect and drew again more attention towards Minsky, who focussed on increasing financial fragility in boom phases and pointed out that the financial structures of developed economies were unstable even in these times, for example in the 1960s (Minsky 1982). However, a lack of aggregate demand may also be caused by defective institutional configurations which lead to economic imbalances such as those from which Europe is suffering. Hence, PK analysis provides a very specific account of the concrete 'mechanisms' of economic crisis. In addition, it provides instruments for analyzing the medium-term implications of overall economic policy measures such as increasing wages, government expenditure, taxes or interest rates. Parts of these economic policy recommendations are directly influenced by Minsky (2008, chapter 13), such as the discussion of the importance of the state as employer or the argument for strong and stable institutional settings in the financial markets that offset overly strong economic upswings and downturns (e.g. Palley 2003; Auerback et al. 2010). Other PK proposals reflect on the underlying theoretical incapabilities of mainstream economics and provide more general propositions such as a Keynesian new deal, which in turn should lead to a shift in overall economic policy adjustment from neoliberal proposals to Keynesian policies (e.g. Hein and Truger 2013 [2012]). Strong institutional settings are manifested in the demand for international macroeconomic coordination, combined with a re-regulation of financial markets and stronger Keynesian macroeconomic policies. More concretely, the latter part cumulates into a third strand of proposals focussing on the inadequacy of austerity measures in times of economic crisis (e.g. Kitromilides 2011). At the centre of their attention are the effects of austerity measures in times of economic distress.

When it comes to teaching PK economics, step-by-step alternative arguments for the financial crisis in opposition to mainstream economics can be given. The efficient market hypothesis can be compared with the Minsky instability hypothesis, for example, which clearly shows the inherent instability of the capitalistic system driven by boom phases. Different policy proposals can be derived and compared, for example, the importance of strong institutional settings and the regulation of financial markets.

In CPE, the term *crisis* is used more broadly. First, it refers to an economic crisis in the sense of the absence of dynamic economic accumulation. This is very similar to the PK view although the mode of analysis differs substantially. CPE does not aim to manifest step by step the explanatory weaknesses of mainstream economics and to offer an alternative view on each causal argument, but views economic crisis as a structural problem of the capitalist system. The lack of accumulation of capital and economic growth is addressed in particular by the regulation school (Jessop and Sum 2006), which represents an important strand in CPE. The regulation school traditionally focuses on the national level while also seeking to address accumulation and regulation at different interrelated spatial scales. The starting point for the regulation approach was the question why in capitalism, despite its multiple contradictions, stable periods of economic growth can be observed. This is explained by the coherence of a regime of accumulation with a specific mode of regulation based on structurally stable institutional forms. Cyclical and structural crises are distinguished. While cyclical crises are solved within a given mode of regulation, in order to overcome a structural crisis a new regime of accumulation and a substantial change in the mode of regulation is required. The European crisis is considered a big or structural crisis in this perspective (Bieling et al. 2016). Second, the term crisis is used to refer to other related types of crisis such as political crisis, ideological crisis, social crisis, ecological crisis and so forth. CPE scholars point to multiple crises in the current conjuncture and to the interconnectedness of different types of crises (Heinrich and Jessop 2013). Hence, in a CPE tradition a broad variety of explanations for the crisis which focus on different and interconnected causalities exists, and complexity is reduced in different ways (Overbeek 2012).

3.2 Spatial considerations

The spatial dimension within the question of European integration is considered crucial for CPE and PK scholars. In PK approaches, the analysis of national states and regions with their specific institutional setting is at the core of analysis. The distinctive, historically embedded structural features and potentially institutionally weaknesses ask for detailed nation-state and regionally clustered comparative analysis (see e.g. Chick and Dow 1988; Chick 1992). The spatial dimension of the crisis is mainly discussed when referring to economic imbalances within Europe, and this analysis mainly applies to Thirlwall's (e.g. 2003, 41) work stating that growth might be restrained by the balance of payments (e.g. Soukiazis et al. 2014 [2013]). Permanent current account deficits serve as the crucial factor for growth repression, and surpluses in the European north have mirrored the current account deficits in the European south. The flow of funds from the European north to the European south had led to substantial imbalances, and diverging unit labour costs are emphasized when searching for the reason for persisting imbalances (see Niechoj 2015; Lapavitsas and Flassbeck 2015). The importance of reshaping labour costs, increasing wage levels in the European north and strengthening wage bargaining coordination across Europe becomes even more important when taking the results from empirical studies on a European level into account (Ederer and Reschenhofer 2013).

CPE has a long-standing tradition of dealing with uneven development. It often focuses on the globally uneven dimensions of capitalist development and the perspectives for less developed or dependent countries and regions (see Jäger in this volume). However, uneven development in Europe has also been addressed (Becker and Jäger 2012; Drahokoupil and Myant 2012). The concepts of core and periphery are crucial for the understanding of uneven development. Generally speaking, core and periphery interact in an asymmetric way. This leads to the emergence of different economic and political structures in the core and periphery. According to critical political economy, developments in the core should not be understood without including the analysis of the periphery and vice versa. Core and periphery are not just concepts to be applied to the global scale but are also useful for discussing inner-European developments because of the huge disparities, structural differences and very asymmetrical links between different European political economies. Previously to the crisis the asymmetries were expressed by asymmetrically linked growth regimes, namely dominant neomercantilist export regimes in the core of the EU and dependent financialized or debt led growth models in the periphery (Becker et al. 2015; Stockhammer and Köhler 2015).

3.3 Focus on the crisis

While in general PK work shows 'what is wrong' with Europe's economy and what should be done in order to return to stable economic growth (Springler 2013), CPE explains why this does not happen but under which conditions it could happen (Bieling et al. 2016). Within the PK perspective especially, the strand with a strong focus on Kalecki (1943) is very useful for understanding why the crisis was managed after 2010 in an anti-Keynesian way. The policies led to further increasing unemployment and thereby favoured capital over labour.

Complementary to this, CPE insists that an abstract class interest does not transform itself automatically into class agency but is always mediated. Moreover, CPE points to some additional economic aspects, such as the material dimension of economic growth or the role of industry and productivity growth in development. A European development model also has to deal with the question of how productivity can be increased in the periphery, as for large parts of the periphery neoliberal strategies have failed (Becker et al. 2015). Contrary to PK approaches, CPE argues that growth is not an ultimate goal but is at best a means for emancipatory strategies which aim at the reduction of power asymmetries.

However, from a PK perspective, income policies in favour of workers and lower income groups are considered to be beneficial for economic growth and for counteracting measures such as strong austerity programmes which might account for even deeper recessions (see e.g. Ederer and Reschenhofer 2013; Stockhammer and Köhler 2015).

3.4 Dealing with the crisis

There is another important difference between the way CPE and PK perspectives understand the crisis. While PK approaches mainly focus on the economic dimension of the crisis, that is, economic recession or stagnation, CPE points to the multiple dimensions of the European crisis, including a political crisis and a crisis of integration (Bieling 2015). While neoliberalism has been the guiding principle for European integration since the 1980s, and the existence of finance-dominated regimes of accumulation alongside neomercantilist export orientation were the outcome of the crisis of Fordism, those neoliberal accumulation strategies are in crisis now. This has triggered a political crisis at the level of the EU. However, since 2010 neoliberal regulation has deepened further, and a partial transfer of regulations from the national to the EU level has taken place (Becker et al. 2015; Stockhammer and Köhler 2015). In this understanding, PK and CPE perspectives formulate similar points of view. CPE, however, pins the argumentation down and understands this process as a politics of scale (Gough 2004) and of changing class relations (i.e. it sees the shift of regulations to the EU level as a consequence of capitalist class strategies). The new economic arrangements at the level of the EU particularly affects the relation between capital and labour and tends to have negative implications for national welfare regimes (Oberndorfer 2015; Bieling et al. 2016).

Both CPE and PK scholars claim that economic coordination and adequate wage policies are necessary, but the latter refrain from a class analysis and from an acknowledgement of the power relations within the wage bargaining process. However, while a totally chaotic crisis has been avoided, stagnation and uneven development of the crisis multiplied contradictions and centrifugal processes within the European Union. So-called anti-crisis polices aimed at restoring the pre-crisis status quo, and traditional power blocs and ruling classes have not changed significantly (Van Apeldoorn 2013; Heinrich and Jessop 2013). Moreover, increasing dominance by these dominant groups and countries (Cafruny 2015) was used to compensate for a drastically diminishing hegemony. The central contradictions of European integration, which led to a crisis of over-accumulation from a CPE perspective or which cause a lack of effective demand and huge imbalances within the Eurozone from a PK perspective, have not been tackled yet. On the contrary, the development of wages in the context of record levels of unemployment and the overall European strategy to 'increase competitiveness' (Wigger 2015) point to the opposite direction.

The uneven nature of European development and thus the crisis, and the fragmented and asymmetrically linked national/regional modes of production, make a coherent and forceful response by organized labour very difficult (Clua-Losada and Horn 2015). The weakness of labour, despite numerous but uneven (nationally) fragmented protests, the surge of new social movements, and the absence of a set of coherent national and/or regional regimes of accumulation for large parts of Europe, still represent important obstacles to progressive/emancipatory solutions to the crisis. However, the unfolding contradictions and a strengthening power of subaltern classes give hope that, despite the authoritarian constitutionalism in the European Union and authoritarian and right-wing tendencies in large parts of Europe, emancipatory forces at the national and the European scale may become more influential in the medium and long terms.

4 Scenarios of European integration

In order to better understand the respective contributions of PK and CPE and to show how an analysis combining both approaches helps to discuss systematically possible and likely futures, in the following subsections we discuss different scenarios of European integration. We analyze the conditions in which they may materialize and which structural changes and the strategies of which agents will be required for this. Thereby we distinguish four future outcomes: three that are possible (scenario 1–3) and one that is very likely (scenario 4).

Scenario 1: Total meltdown into the unknown

A scenario such as the total 'meltdown into the unknown' (Duménil and Lévy 2004) does not seem to be very likely. It can be argued that a very deep crisis such as in Greece might happen in other countries, but is not very likely for the European Union as a whole. In 2008–2009 a general and extremely deep recession in the EU was avoided by rescuing the financial sector with public money and by adopting Keynesian policies to stabilize the economy. Although public debts due to those measures are higher now, there is still the possibility of encountering another drastic collapse of economic activity. An even stronger focus on competition (Wigger 2015) and the new European economic governance show a very strong anti-Keynesian bias (Stockhammer and Köhler 2015). This tends to promote stagnation. This new authoritarian and neoliberal governance which has been institutionalized at the level of the EU can be understood as a 'new constitutionalism' (Gill 1998). However, one may expect those rules to be violated and pragmatic heterodox Keynesian measures in fiscal and monetary policy to be implemented when necessary in order to prevent a total collapse of the system. Obviously, the ruling classes are interested in avoiding chaotic episodes which might not just drastically reduce their legitimacy but also end up in unforeseeable social upheavals and their own defeat. And it is the safeguarding of class power which is the ultimate goal of capitalist ruling classes. At least in the financial crisis of 2008–2009, but also during the eruption of the Eurozone crisis in 2011–2012, they have proven to be capable of this. However, due to the uneven nature of development and the resultant complexity and divergence of European capitalist fractions and interests (Heinrich and Jessop 2013, 30), it is not certain that the ruling classes will be successful again. Hence, a total economic meltdown is not a very likely but still a possible European future.

Scenario 2: Social democratic (green) Europe

In a post-Keynesian perspective, at least at a very high level of abstraction, the scenario of a social democratic (green) Europe is shared as a common vision of a desired European solution to the crisis. Most clearly this is summarized by Niechoj (2015). The desired scenario he describes is based on the implementation of Keynesian institutions and policies at the EU level. At its core is a coordinated fiscal policy with strong European fiscal statehood. Complementary to this, Lapavitsas and Flassbeck (2015) argue that wage coordination based on productivity increases is necessary to stabilize demand and therefore wage-led growth. In addition, in order to combat imbalances within the Eurozone, nominal wages should temporarily increase much stronger in surplus countries such as Germany until imbalances disappear. Moreover, unsustainable public debts in the periphery should be reduced in order to open up possibilities for fiscal policy, and also an exit from the Eurozone might be a necessary step for peripheral countries (Lapavitsas 2011). As Grahl (2014) argues, the implementation of a progressive European social welfare system would be desirable and could be part of this scenario. In addition, adequate regulation of the financial sector is a necessary element of the PK agenda to stabilize the economy, but it cannot be the only one (see Toporowski 2015). Besides such demand-oriented post-Keynesian perspectives, a strategy which allows for a reconstruction of productive sectors, in particular of industry, is also essential for economic development in the periphery (Becker et al. 2015). Already before the crisis, large parts of the European periphery had been characterized by dramatic deindustrialization (Becker and Jäger 2010). These aspects are barely touched in a PK scenario. Hence, from a CPE perspective a European framework which allows for development of the periphery would be another essential element of this scenario.

This vision of a social democratic Europe and a further step of progressive integration have the Fordist national welfare states and the corresponding incomes policies as a reference. However, CPE perspectives point to the fact that Fordist (or at least peripheral) welfare states and respective income policies were implemented in most parts of Western Europe within a very specific historical and geopolitical context. The basis for this was a social democratic class compromise between capital and labour after the Second World War and within the context of US hegemony and the Soviet challenge.

The situation has completely changed. The power of capital vis-à-vis labour has increased and the national class compromises have eroded. In addition, finance-dominated capitalism tends inherently to instability and poses severe constraints on progressive developments (Petit 2012). Against this background it seems very unlikely that something similar to a Fordist class compromise can be institutionalized at the level of the European Union within the near future. Although in the 1980s and 1990s there was an attempt to implement a social democratic project at the level of the EU, this by and large failed and neoliberal and neomercantilist interests succeeded. This has been manifested in the Maastricht criteria and the Lisbon Agenda, and also during the recent crisis (Van Apeldoorn et al. 2009). Today, labour is even weaker and more fragmented. Although it is argued that there is a transnational European capitalist class (Van Apeldoorn 2013), we should not underestimate the importance of national capitalist classes (see Cafruny 2015) within Europe and the existence of nationally fragmented working classes. Hence, from a CPE perspective it seems very unlikely that such a pro-European social democratic project (including some 'green' elements), which has a small and very weak social basis (see Buckel et al. 2012), can be implemented within the foreseeable future.

Scenario 3: Radical reformism to overcome capitalism

CPE scholars usually are in favour of overcoming capitalism or, as a first step, of much-undesired forms of capitalism such as neoliberalism. Conversely to this, PK approaches stick to the latter aspect. This scenario discusses the crisis in such a more fundamental way and promotes respective alternatives; therefore this is an important potential scenario which has to be dealt with. The crisis has opened up the space for more radical critique and visionary proposals which question the capitalist organization of the economy in general and its neoliberal type in particular. Hence, within the context of an erosion of neoliberal hegemony and a surge of public discontent, a fundamental critique and the discussion of alternative ideas are back on the agenda. Among them there is the questioning of economic growth as such and the reemergence of a broad development discourse.

In the tradition of critical political economy, the discussion should not be limited to the question of overcoming the crisis in terms of returning to economic growth based on the emergence of an ensemble of stable growth regimes in Europe.

While post-Keynesianism gives hints of how capitalism can be reorganized to overcome stagnation and turn back to economic growth (Davidson 2009), critical political economy provides a variety of more far-reaching alternatives to reduce exploitation, to eliminate power relations and to socialize production. Besides the questioning of economic growth, this does not just include the control of the financial sector and speculation but also a radically more equal income distribution, a shortening of working hours, the creation of decent jobs, investment in 'meaningful' areas, and strict public control in order to implement a new society and make the world a better place for all (Herrmann and Frangakis 2014, 192) In addition, the necessity of environmental sustainability means that new modes of production and of consumption are considered to be indispensable for providing a good life for all (Lipietz 2013; Novy 2013). Green capitalism is not progressive but may be a concrete solution to the current multiple crisis (Brand 2012).

Radical debates and visionary proposals are important for discursively expanding the room for possible alternatives. Hence, they may play their role for progressive long-term transformations towards post-capitalist societies. However, the agents promoting such a radical reformist approach are still very weak and fragmented, not least because of the uneven development of the crisis (Becker et al. 2015; Buckel et al. 2012). Today, the coming of a radical reformist future within the medium term is even less likely than a social democratic European Union. At the best, the latter could be a step towards more radical reforms because of shifting power relations implied by a social democratic Europe.

Scenario 4: Authoritarian neoliberalism and muddling through

The preliminary outcome of the crisis at the level of the European Union has been the implementation of an authoritarian neoliberalism which shows a strong anti-Keynesian bias. While with the exception of a Kaleckian tradition this is diffcult to explain from a PK perspective, CPE points to the fact that neoliberalism is less a strategy for growth but rather a mode to combat labour, and hence an expression of class struggle from above (Duménil and Lévy 2011; Stockhammer and Köhler 2015). During the crisis, powerful export-oriented German capitalists (Heinrich and Jessop 2013; Cafruny 2015) and well-organized transnational fractions of capital at the European level (Van Apeldoorn 2013) have pushed for a deepening of neoliberalism at the European level. This has not just caused problems for the European periphery but even for the German economic model itself, which has become more export-dependent (Bruff 2014b). Hence, as Bieling (2015) argues, these European developments can be called a passive revolution which is not yet completed but in trouble. However, capitalist fractions in the periphery have also supported neoliberal policies and a subordinate position because this at least secured their class position (Navarro 2011).

CPE points out not only the complexity of agents and process in particular but also the structural contradictions inherent to capitalism in general. While it was possible to stabilize dynamic capitalist accumulation during the post–Second World War Fordist era on a national scale and within a very specific framework (US hegemony, Bretton Woods system, an EU supportive of national Fordist regimes of accumulation), and on the basis of a class compromise relatively favourable to labour, this is different today. There is a strategic selectivity in favour of capital at the level of the European Union (Bieling 2013), and the crisis has led to a further shift of economic governance to this macro-regional level.

Neoliberal European economic governance tends to reproduce and consolidate a very heterogeneous European economic space. Transnational European firms (usually their headquarters are located in the centre) may take advantage of persistently different productivities and wage levels within Europe in organizing their production chains. In line with this, bilateral and multilateral trade and investment partnerships might be understood as another way forward for the promotion of exports from the Germany-centred productive system (Cafruny 2015) beyond Europe to the rest of the world. However, given Europe's economic size it is very unlikely if not impossible that such an outward-oriented strategy can provide the basis for European-wide growth.

Hence, the deepening of neoliberalism does not contribute to overcome capitalist contradictions, and the problem of realizing profits will be a constant feature in the future European trajectory. Contradictions are likely to continue to be most visible in the European periphery, because the given economic governance structure in Europe tends to support the powerful interests of the European core countries and to shift the problems onto the periphery. However, as Drahokoupil and Myant (2012) and Becker et al. (2015) insist, peripheral European countries are integrated into the core in different ways. Those who are part of the Germany-centred productive core are in a better position than those countries in which the dominant patterns of accumulation were based on financialization. Particularly for countries which have a very weak industrial basis and which are not integrated into the productive core, the outlook is rather gloomy.

This may promote the search for national development strategies and even imply a (partial) dissolution of the EU, because in many cases national development seems to be impossible within the EU's neoliberal competitive framework. However, as (Bohle 2013, 118) insists, despite common external structures it is necessary to assess the specific internal processes and struggles. Moreover, persistently high unemployment and increasing inequality may also cause centrifugal tendencies in less peripheral countries. The Brexit is the first example showing how contradictions within the EU may contribute to a (partial) dissolution of the EU. Overall, a long-run persistence of instability, no early end of the structural crisis and increasing rift between the core and the periphery seem to be very likely in the future. Despite the discourses which proclaim the end of the crisis, so-called anti-crisis policies continue to deepen polarization in Europe.

5 Conclusion

Combining PK and CPE perspectives helps to highlight aspects which usually are completely neglected by mainstream approaches in economics. Presenting those perspectives and applying them together sheds a different light on the European crisis and turns out to be highly illuminating, not just for students and scholars but also for emancipatory political agents and their strategies. For teaching purposes, the case of the European crisis is very useful to highlight the differences, weaknesses, strengths and complementarities of both approaches. In addition, the systematic discussion of different scenarios helps to illustrate how specific policy options and their conditions to be implemented may be analyzed.

While CPE and PK tend to share a common philosophical ground with Critical Realism, they tend to have important differences with regard to the overall goal. This becomes obvious in debating the European crises and possible scenarios. PK tends to prefer a social democratic solution to the European crisis, at the core of which is a return to stable economic growth and full employment. CPE is in favour of more radical emancipatory transformations of the mode of production in the short run and overcoming of capitalism in the long run. However, as the above analysis based on insights from CPE has shown, neither scenario is likely to materialize. On the contrary, given the prevalence of finance-dominated capitalism, uneven processes of economic development and the power relations at the level of the European Union it is very likely that the current period of authoritarian neoliberalism and muddling through is going to be continued. This implies a continuation of political crises in Europe and increasing centrifugal forces. The rise of right-wing populism and the Brexit are symptomatic for this.

As outlined above, CPE and PK focus on different aspects. While PK tends to show 'what is wrong' with Europe's economy and what should be done in order to return to stable economic growth and full employment, CPE explains why this does not happen but under which conditions it could happen. PK is therefore more concerned with growth and CPE deals more with questions of power. Hence, each perspective has its merits and depending on what students are interested in, they may choose among those two alternative views. However, CPE and PK complement each other and together provide a more comprehensive and complete understanding of economic and political processes. Hence, for those who have a PK perspective, it is very useful to engage with CPE literature and vice versa. This is a massage which not only addresses students but scholars more generally.

Note

1 This text is an amended, integrated and updated version of Jäger and Springler, "Debating the Future of Europe: Critical Political Economy and Post-Keynesian Perspectives", 1–14; and Jäger and Springler, "Conclusions and Possible Futures", 224–233. Both chapters were published in Jäger and Springler (2015) *Asymmetric Crisis in Europe and Possible Futures – Critical Political Economy and Post-Keynesian Perspectives*. They are reprinted with the kind permission of Routledge/Taylor and Francis.

References

Auerback, M., McCulley, P. and Parenteau, R. W. (2010): "What Would Minsky Do?", in Papadimitriou, D. and Wray, R. (eds.), *The Elgar Companion to Hyman Minsky*. Cheltenham and Northampton: Edward Elgar, 117–133.

Becker, J. and Jäger, J. (2010): "Development Trajectories in the Crisis in Europe", *Debatte: Journal of Contemporary Central and Eastern Europe* 18(1), 5–27.

Becker, J. and Jäger, J. (2012): "Integration in Crisis: A Regulationist Perspective on the Interaction of European Varieties of Capitalism", *Competition & Change* 16(3), 169–187.

Becker, J., Jäger, J. and Weissenbacher, R. (2015): "Uneven and Dependent Development in Europe: The Crisis and Its Implications", in Jäger, J. and Springler, E. (eds.), *Asymmetric Crisis in Europe and Possible Futures: Critical Political Economy and Post-Keynesian Perspectives*. Oxon: Routledge, 81–97.

Bieling, H.-J. (2013): "European Financial Capitalism and the Politics of (De-)financialization", *Competition & Change* 17(3), 283–298.

Bieling, H.-J. (2015): "Uneven Development and 'European Crisis Institutionalism', or: The Reasons and Conditions of a 'Passive Revolution in Trouble'", in Jäger, J. and Springler, E. (eds.), *Asymmetric Crisis in Europe and Possible Futures: Critical Political Economy and Post-Keynesian Perspectives*. Oxon: Routledge, 98–113.

Bieling, H.-J., Jäger, J. and Ryner, M. (2016): "Regulation Theory and the Political Economy of the European Union", *Journal of Common Market Studies* 54(1), 53–69.

Bohle, D. (2013): "Europas andere Peripherie: Osteuropa in der Krise", *Das Argument* 55(1/2), 118–129.

Brand, U. (2012): "Green Economy and Green Capitalism: Some Theoretical Considerations", *Journal für Entwicklungspolitik* 28(3), 118–137.

Bruff, I. (2014a): "The Rise of Authoritarian Neoliberalism", *Rethinking Marxism* 26(1), 113–129.

Bruff, I. (2014b): "Germany and the Crisis: Steady as She Goes?", in Westra, R., Badeen, D. and Albritton, R. (eds.), *The Future of Capitalism after the Financial Crisis: The Varieties of Capitalism Debate in the Age of Austerity*. Oxon: Routledge.

Buckel, S., Georgi, F., Kannankulam, J. and Wissel, J. 2012): "'. . . wenn das Alte nicht stirbt und das Neue nicht zur Welt kommen kann.' Kräfteverhältnisse in der Europäischen Krise", in Forschungsgruppe Staatsprojekt Europa (ed.), *Die EU in der Krise*. Münster: Westfälisches Dampfboot, 12–49.

Cafruny, A. W. (2015): "The European Question and the Rise of German Power", in Jäger, J. and Springler, E. (eds.), *Asymmetric Crisis in Europe and Possible Futures: Critical Political Economy and Post-Keynesian Perspectives*. Oxon: Routledge, 61–73.

Cafruny, A. W. and Ryner, J. M. (2007): *Europa at Bay: In the Shadow of US Hegemony*. London: Lynne Rienner Publishers.

Chick, V. (1992): "The Evolution of the Banking System and the Theory of Saving, Investment and Interest", in Arestis, P. and Dow, S. (eds.), *On Money, Method and Keynes*. New York: St. Martin's Press, 193–205.

Chick, V. and Dow, S. (1988): *Post-Keynesian Perspective on the Relations between Banking & Regional Development*. London: Thames Polytechnic, School of Social Sciences.

Clévenot, M. (2011): "Post-keynésianisme et théorie de la régulation: des perspectives communes", *Revue de la Régulation* 10(2).

Clua-Losada, M. and Horn, L. (2015): "Labour and the Crisis in Europe", in Jäger, J. and Springler, E. (eds.), *Asymmetric Crisis in Europe and Possible Futures: Critical Political Economy and Post-Keynesian Perspectives*. Oxon: Routledge, 208–223.

Cox, R. (1981): "Social Forces, States, and World Orders", *Millennium: Journal of International Studies* 10(2), 126–155.

Davidson, P. (2009): *The Keynes Solution: The Path to Global Economic Prosperity*. New York: Palgrave Macmillan.

Demirovic, A. (2005): "Die Perspektive der vernünftigen Gesellschaft", *PROKLA. Zeitschrift für Kritische Sozialwissenschaft* 35(4), 479–496.

Drahokoupil, J. and Myant, M. (2012): "The European Sub-Prime? Financial Crisis and the East-European Periphery", in Nousios, P., Overbeek, H. and Tsolakis, A. (eds.), *Globalisation and European Integration: Critical Approaches to Regional Order and International Relations*. Oxon: Routledge, 130–153.

Duménil, G. and Lévy, D. (2004): *Capital Resurgent: Roots of the Neoliberal Revolution*. Cambridge, MA: Harvard University Press.

Duménil, G. and Lévy, D. (2011): *The Crisis of Neoliberalism*. Cambridge, MA: Harvard University Press.

Ederer, St. and Reschenhofer, P. (2013): "Macroeconomic Imbalances in the EU: Working Paper No 42", *WWW for Europe*, www.foreurope.eu/fileadmin/documents/pdf/Workingpapers/WWWforEurope_WPS_no042_MS71.pdf, accessed 1 June 2014.

Epstein, G. A. (ed.) (2005): *Financialization and the World Economy*. Cheltenham, UK: Edward Elgar.

Erturk, I., Froud, J., Johal, S., Leaver, A. and Williams, K. (2008): *Financialization at Work*. London: Routledge.

EuroMemogroup (2014): *EuroMemorandum 2014: The Deepening Divisions in Europe and the Need for a Radical Alternative to EU Policies*, http://www2.euromemorandum.eu/uploads/euromemorandum_2014.pdf,accessed 1 June 2014.

EuroMemogroup (2017): *The European Union: The Threat of Disintegration*, http://www2.euromemorandum.eu/uploads/euromemorandum_2017.pdf, accessed 15 January 2017.

Eurostat (2016): *Database*, http://ec.europa.eu/eurostat/de/data/database, accessed 15 January 2017.

Evans, T. (2004): "Marxian and Post-Keynesian Theories of Finance and the Business Cycle", *Capital & Class* (83), 47–100.

Fischer, A. and Tepe, D. (2011): "What's Critical about Critical Theory: Feminist Materialism, Intersectionality and the Social Totality of the Frankfurt School", in Shields, S.,

Bruff, I. and Macartney, H. (eds.), *Critical International Political Economy: Dialogue, Debate and Dissensus*. London: Palgrave Macmillan.

Gill, S. (1998): "European Governance and New Constitutionalism: Economic and Monetary Union and Alternatives to Disciplinary Neoliberalism in Europe", *New Political Economy* 3(1), 5–26.

Gough, J. (2004): "Changing Scale as Changing Class Relations: Variety and Contradiction in the Politics of Scale", *Political Geography* 23, 185–211.

Grahl, J. (2014): "Social Europe and the Crisis of the European Union", in Jäger, J. and Springler, E. (eds.), *Asymmetric Crisis in Europe and Possible Futures: Critical Political Economy and Post-Keynesian Perspectives*. Oxon: Routledge, 168–185.

Hein, E. and Truger, A. (2013 [2012]): "Finance-Dominated Capitalism in Crisis: The Case for a Global Keynesian New Deal", *Journal of Post Keynesian Economics* 35(2), 187–213.

Heinrich, M. and Jessop, B. (2013): "Die EU-Krise aus Sicht der Kulturellen Politischen Ökonomie", *Das Argument* 55(1/2), 19–33.

Herrmann, P. and Frangakis, M. (2014): "The Need for a Radical 'Growth Policy' Agenda for Europe at a Time of Crisis", in Dymarski, W., Frangakis, M. and Leaman, J. (eds.), *The Deepening Crisis of the European Union: The Case for Radical Change*. Poznán: Poznán University of Economics Press, 179–194.

Hicks, J. R. (1937): "Mr. Keynes and the 'Classics': A Suggested Interpretation", *Econometrica* 5(2), 147–159.

Hitiris, T. (2003): *European Union Economics*. 5th edition. Harlow: Prentice Hall.

IMF (2016): *World Economic Outlook: Too Slow for Too Long*, www.imf.org/external/pubs/ft/weo/2016/01/pdf/text.pdf, accessed 1 February 2017.

Jäger, J., Horn, L. and Becker, J. (2016): "Critical International Political Economy and Method", in Cafruny, A., Simona, L. and Gonzalo Pozo, T. (eds.), *The Palgrave Handbook of Critical International Political Economy*. London: Palgrave Macmillan, 101–118.

Jäger, J. and Springler, E. (eds.) (2015): *Asymmetric Crisis in Europe and Possible Futures: Critical Political Economy and Post-Keynesian Perspectives*. Oxon: Routledge (RIPE Series in Global Political Economy).

Jessop, B. and Sum, N.-L. (2006): *Beyond the Regulation Approach: Putting Capitalist Economies in Their Place*. Cheltenham, UK: Edward Elgar.

Kalecki, M. (1943): "Political Aspects of Full Employment", *Political Quarterly* 14, 322–331.

King, J. E. (2002): *A History of Post Keynesian Economics Since 1936*. Cheltenham and Northampton: Edward Elgar.

Kitromilides, Y. (2011): "Deficit Reduction, the Age of Austerity, and the Paradox of Insolvency", *Journal of Post Keynesian Economics* 33(3), 517–535.

Kotz, D. M. (1994): "The Regulation Theory and the Social Structure of Accumulation Approach", in Kotz, D. M., McDonough, T. and Reich, M. (eds.), *Social Structures of Accumulation: The Political Economy of Growth and Crisis*. Cambridge, MA: Cambridge University Press, 85–98.

Lapavitsas, C. (ed.) (2013): *Financialization in Crisis*. Chicago: Haymarket Books.

Lapavitsas, C. et al. (2011): *Breaking Up? A Route Out of the Eurozone*. Occasional Report. RMF. London.

Lapavitsas, C. and Flassbeck, H. (2015): "Confronting the Failure of the European Monetary Union", in Jäger, J. and Springler, E. (eds.), *Asymmetric Crisis in Europe and*

Possible Futures: Critical Political Economy and Post-Keynesian Perspectives. Oxon: Routledge, 131–148.

Lawson, T. (1999): "What Has Realism Got to Do With It?", *Economics and Philosophy*, 15(2), 269.Lipietz, A. (2013): "Fears and Hopes: The Crisis of the Liberal-Productivist Model and Its Green Alternative", *Capital & Class* 37(1), 127–141.

Minsky, H. (1982): *Can "It" Happen Again? Essays on Instability and Finance*. New York: M. E. Sharpe, 3–13.

Minsky, H. (1992): *The Financial Instability Hypothesis*. Working Paper No. 74. The Jerome Levy Institute.

Minsky, H. (2008 [1986]): *Stabilizing an Unstable Economy*. New York: McGraw Hill.

Navarro, V. (2011): "Crisis and Class Struggle in the Eurozone: The Cases of Spain, Greece, Ireland and Portugal", *Counter Punch* (Weekend Edition), 19–21 August.

Niechoj, T. (2015): "Which Future for Europe? A Scenario Analysis of European Integration", in Jäger, J. and Springler, E. (eds.), *Asymmetric Crisis in Europe and Possible Futures: Critical Political Economy and Post-Keynesian Perspectives*. Oxon: Routledge, 151–167.

Nousios, P., Overbeek, H. and Tsolakis, A. (eds.) (2012a). *Globalization and European Integration: Critical Approaches to Regional Order and International Relations*. Oxon: Routledge.

Nousios, P., Overbeek, H. and Tsolakis, A. (2012b): "Globalisation and European Integration: The Nature of the Beast", in Nousios, P., Overbeek, H. and Tsolakis, A. (eds.), *Globalization and European Integration: Critical Approaches to Regional Order and International Relations*. Oxon: Routledge, 3–32.

Novy, A. (2013): "Ein gutes Leben für alle – ein europäisches Entwicklungsmodell", *Journal für Entwicklungspolitik* 29(3), 77–104.

Oberndorfer, L. (2015): "From New Constitutionalism to Authoritarian Constitutionalism: New Economic Governance and the State of European Democracy", in Jäger, J. and Springler, E. (eds.), *Asymmetric Crisis in Europe and Possible Futures: Critical Political Economy and Post-Keynesian Perspectives*. Oxon: Routledge, 186–207.

OECD (2011): *Divided We Stand: Why Inequality Keeps Rising*. Paris: OECD Publishing.

Overbeek, H. (2012): "Sovereign Debt Crisis in Euroland: Root, Causes and Implications for European Integration", *The International Spectator: Italian Journal of International Affairs* 47(1), 30–48.

Palley, T. (2003): "Asset Price Bubbles and the Case for Asset Based Reserve Requirements", *Challenge* 46(3), 53–72.

Petit, P. (2012): "In Search of Politically Sustainable Growth Regimes", *Capital & Class* 37(1), 25–35.

Ryner, M. (2015): "The Crisis of European Integration and Economic Reason: Orthodoxy vs. Heterodoxy", in Jäger, J. and Springler, E. (eds.), *Asymmetric Crisis in Europe and Possible Futures: Critical Political Economy and Post-Keynesian Perspectives*. Oxon: Routledge, 17–33.

Setterfield, M. (2001): "Macrodynamics", in Holt, R.P.F. and Pressman, S. (eds.), *A New Guide to Post Keynesian Economics*. London: Routledge.

Snowdon, B. and Vane, H. (2005): *Modern Macroeconomics, Its Origins, Development and Current State*. Cheltenham and Northampton: Edward Elgar.

Soukiazis, E., Cerqueira, P. A. and Antunes, M. (2014 [2013]): "Growth Rates Constrained by Internal and External Imbalances and the Role of Relative Prices: Empirical Evidence from Portugal", *Journal of Post Keynesian Economics* 36(2), 275–298.

Springler, E. (2013): "Postkeynesianische Alternativen in Wirtschaftstheorie und Wirtschaftspolitik: Lösungsvorschläge zur globalen Finanz- und Wirtschaftskrise", *Wirtschaft und Gesellschaft* 39(2), 125–151.

Stiglitz, J. (2016): *The Euro: How a Common Currency Threatens the Future of Europe*. New York: W. W. Norton & Company.

Stockhammer, E. (2008): "Some Stylized Facts on the Finance-Dominated Accumulation Regime", *Competition & Change* 12(2), 184–202.

Stockhammer, E. and Köhler, K. (2015): "Linking a Post-Keynesian Approach to Political Economy: Debt-Led Growth, Export-Led Growth and the Crisis in Europe", in Jäger, J. and Springler, E. (eds.), *Asymmetric Crisis in Europe and Possible Futures: Critical Political Economy and Post-Keynesian Perspectives*. Oxon: Routledge, 34–49.

Thirlwall, A. P. (2003): *Trade, the Balance of Payments and Exchange Rate Policy in Developing Countries*. Cheltenham and Northampton: Edward Elgar.

Toporowski, J. (2015): "Global Finance and Banking or Macroeconomic Regulation in the EU Crisis?", in Jäger, J. and Springler, E. (eds.), *Asymmetric Crisis in Europe and Possible Futures: Critical Political Economy and Post-Keynesian Perspectives*. Oxon: Routledge, 50–60.

Van Apeldoorn, B. (2013): "The European Capitalist Class and the Crisis of Its Hegemonic Project", in Panitch, L., Albo, G. and Chibber, V. (eds.), *Registering Class: Socialist Register 2014*. London: Merlin Press.

Van Apeldoorn, B., Drahokoupil, J. and Horn, L. (eds.) (2009): *Contradictions and Limits of Neoliberal European Governance: From Lisbon to Lisbon*. Houndmills: Palgrave Macmillan.

Wigger, A. (2015): "Enhancing 'Competitiveness' in Response to the Crisis: A Wrong and Dangerous Obsession", in Jäger, J. and Springler, E. (eds.), *Asymmetric Crisis in Europe and Possible Futures: Critical Political Economy and Post-Keynesian Perspectives*. Oxon: Routledge, 114–130.

9 Ecological economics in research and teaching

A matter of theoretical and ideological perspective

Peter Söderbaum

1 Introduction

It is not difficult to identify development trends that are unsustainable at local, national or global level. Uncertainties about climate change, pollution of soil and water and loss of biological diversity are some examples. Poverty and different kinds of inequality among people are other issues where a lot remains to be done to get closer to sustainability. Many politicians are aware of the problems and they may also be ready to discuss possible policies and actions. But they know that the present institutional framework and attitudes among influential actors are not easily changed and represent possible barriers to a constructive sustainability policy. Ideological orientations and power relationships are involved. In relation to this, politicians may act strategically and tactically, which too often means reluctance to act or a tendency to be content with only minor adjustments.

Politicians may turn to scientists for advice when dealing with climate change or other issues. Scientists have their own ideas about what needs to be done, however, and are often locked into specific views of good science with connected power relationships. Much like politicians, economists and other scholars are behaving strategically when considering their professional opportunities. We may for example limit attention to mainstream perspectives concerning conceptual framework (paradigm) and ideology. Behavior of this kind may imply personal advantages but can be costly to society.

The tendency to limit attention to one paradigm, such as neoclassical economics, goes back to traditional ideas that there is only one true paradigm at a time in each scientific field or discipline. It is admitted that the status of a paradigm may change – the so-called paradigm shift (Kuhn 1970), in the sense that one paradigm replaces another at some stage. The possibility of two or more co-existing paradigms is thereby denied. In this chapter it will be argued that "paradigm co-existence" and a degree of pluralism should be a normal state of affairs in economics and other social sciences (Söderbaum 2000, 29–30). Monopoly for one paradigm should then be regarded as an exception. But one paradigm may still be dominant among scholars and other actors.

One reason why we need to consider more than one paradigm in social sciences, such as economics, is that values and ideology are involved. Value neutrality is an illusion (von Egan-Krieger 2014). "Values are always with us" in economics and social science research and education, as argued by Gunnar Myrdal (1978). Rather than pretending that scientific approaches are neutral we should, as actors in a democratic society, openly discuss value issues. Sustainability problems are not only technical issues, and the actual situation in university departments of economics should not be excluded when the nature of sustainability problems is discussed. If paradigm and ideology is part of the problem, then we need to study options at this level of perspective.

2 Many kinds of potential failures

The issue of paradigms in economics should not be approached in either-or terms in the sense that one paradigm has the potential of solving all problems while another is without value. Mainstream neoclassical economic theory with its assumptions can contribute when the claims for monopoly have been abandoned. In relation to sustainability policy, environmental charges or taxes can play an important role. But beliefs in unregulated markets too often undermine attempts for such constructive sustainability policies.

The conceptual framework of neoclassical theory can also play an important role as a basis of comparison when alternative conceptual frameworks are proposed.[1] In the present chapter, such a comparative approach will be attempted. In neoclassical theory, the entities emphasized are "firms" and "consumers". They interact in markets for financial capital, labor and commodities. Such markets can be regulated by the government or state. In neoclassical environmental economics, it is admitted that there may be "market failure" in commodity markets and "government failure". In the former case, reference is made to negative "externalities", that is, the possibility that third parties may suffer from a transaction between seller and buyer and a "polluter pays principle" is invoked.[2] Governments may also fail by subsidizing activities with negative environmental impacts. Such financial support should be withdrawn, it is argued.

As I see it, the neoclassical ideas about potential failures while being relevant for sustainability policy are too restricted. In addition, there are possibilities of:

- Paradigm failure
- Ideological failure
- Institutional failure.

We need to openly discuss the limits to the neoclassical paradigm and what kind of alternatives exist or can be socially constructed. As part of this, the ideological orientation of neoclassical theory as well as ideologies more connected with political parties, such as neoliberalism (with its extreme beliefs in markets and privatization), need to be scrutinized in relation to sustainability politics. Thus dominant as well as alternative political ideologies should be considered as part of any serious effort to deal with environmental or inequality problems.

Related to paradigms and ideological orientations is the actual existing institutional framework. As long as unsustainable trends prevail, something is probably wrong with institutional arrangements. As an example, the orientation or focus of transnational corporations (or firms in neoclassical language) on monetary profits may not be appropriate in the present crisis situation. Attempts to deal with this through environmental standardization schemes (such as ISO 14001) or invitations to consider corporate social responsibility are probably not enough. A policy to facilitate establishment of other organizations than joint stock companies is then needed.

3 Redefining economics in relation to Sustainable Development Goals and democracy

One recurrent feature of neoclassical theory and analysis is its focus on the monetary dimension, the idea being that impacts should be quantified and that money is the natural measuring rod. Impacts of different kinds could then be traded against each other in attempts to find optimal solutions to specific problems.

Again, without denying that analysis of this kind can be relevant, this general feature of neoclassical analysis can be referred to as "monetary reductionism". Why should we, when considering issues at the societal level, reduce all kinds of impacts, even ecosystem services, to their alleged monetary equivalents?

The alternative here is multidimensional analysis, where each kind of impact is described and when possible measured in its own terms. The United Nations General Assembly has recently (United Nations 2015, 35) sanctioned 17 Sustainable Development Goals (SDGs). They are:

1. End poverty in all its forms everywhere.
2. End hunger, achieve food security and improved nutrition and promote sustainable agriculture.
3. Ensure healthy lives and promote well-being for all at all ages.
4. Ensure inclusive and equitable quality education and promote lifelong learning opportunities for all.
5. Achieve gender equality and empower all women and girls.
6. Ensure availability and sustainable management of water and sanitation for all.
7. Ensure access to affordable, reliable, sustainable and modern energy for all.
8. Promote sustained, inclusive and sustainable economic growth, full and productive employment and decent work for all.
9. Build resilient infrastructure, promote inclusive and sustainable industrialization and foster innovation.
10. Reduce inequality within and among countries.
11. Make cities and human settlements inclusive, safe, resilient and sustainable.
12. Ensure sustainable consumption and production patterns.
13. Take urgent action to combat climate change and its impacts.

14 Conserve and sustainably use the oceans, seas and marine resources for sustainable development.
15 Protect, restore and promote sustainable use of terrestrial ecosystems, sustainably manage forests, combat desertification and halt and reverse land degradation and halt biodiversity loss.
16 Promote peaceful and inclusive societies for sustainable development, provide access to justice for all and build effective, accountable and inclusive institutions at all levels.
17 Strengthen the means of implementation and revitalize the Global Partnership for Sustainable Development.

Any attempt to reduce this multidimensional view to a single figure in monetary or other terms must be described as heroic. Assigning prices to each impact can only be done with reference to a specific market (or other) ideology. Why that particular ideology? In democratic societies we claim to be ready to listen to different voices. Individuals as actors and citizens differ with respect to ideological orientation, and the economist as analyst has no right to reduce all ideological orientations to one with reference to science.

Economics as part of neoclassical theory is often described as “allocation of scarce resources”. An alternative definition follows from the previous reasoning: “Economics is multidimensional management of (limited) resources in a democratic society” (Söderbaum 2018, 13).

The two words “multidimensional” and “democracy” are emphasized when compared with a neoclassical definition of economics. Reference to “multidimensional” suggests that aspects connected with all 17 SDGs are part of economic considerations and included in the “economy”. The economy is no longer limited to markets but includes society and ecosystems at various levels. It is no longer possible to claim that “economic growth” in terms of gross domestic product (GDP) is enough as measure of progress in societies. The use of neoclassical cost-benefit analysis (CBA) has to be abandoned, furthermore, since it is not compatible with the new definition of economics. CBA is one-dimensional monetary analysis and builds on an idea of correct market prices for each impact and therefore a specific ideological orientation among all possibilities. This is not compatible with democracy but rather an extremely technocratic approach (where experts claim expertise in values and ideology). Ezra Mishan, himself a textbook writer in CBA (1971) has later admitted that CBA is built on an assumption of a consensus in society about how to value impacts. The nonexistence of such a consensus, for example in relation to environmental issues, has become clear (Mishan 1980).

4 Implications for economics education

A definition of economics in terms of multidimensional analysis and democracy has profound implications for education of students in economics and management science. With democracy the political aspect enters the scene. It is no longer possible to regard democracy and politics as a responsibility for other disciplines, such as political science. Values and ideology are present in all parts of the research and education process.

Each research program or project is based upon a series of decisions concerning how problems are perceived and described (or research questions), conceptual framework, methods to be applied, ways of presenting results and conclusions. There are established ways of approaching an issue or measuring things but also less established approaches and always a potential role for the subjectivity and engagement of the scholar:

> Valuations are always with us. Disinterested research there has never been and can never be. Prior to answers there must be questions. There can be no view except from a viewpoint. In the questions raised and the viewpoint chosen, valuations are implied.
>
> (Myrdal 1978, 778)

It is then not possible to hide behind arguments about value neutrality. Also, ideology and political elements are present even when the scholar refers to a specific theory of science. Scholars should in principle be held responsible and accountable for their decisions and work in a broader sense.

When planning economics education or single courses in a university context, a number of decisions are similarly taken. In the case of a course, for example an introductory economics course, there is a choice of responsible persons, lecturers, textbooks, forms of examination and so forth. The persons involved are not expected to act as programmed machines (pointing to the same textbook as last year, for example). Should the history of economic thought be part of the course (or educational program)? Should critical thinking be avoided or encouraged? Can new challenges in society be taken care of within the scope of the existing mainstream paradigm, or should new scientific and ideological perspectives be encouraged? How can students contribute to the content of the course?

4.1 Political economic person and political economic organization assumptions

The necessary presence of ideological and political elements tells us that there is no single paradigm in economics that can claim monopoly. There may be a dominant paradigm supported for scientific and ideological reasons, but this paradigm should always be looked upon as part of a pluralist philosophy. There are always competing theoretical-ideological perspectives.

Our emphasis on value, ethical, ideological and political aspects suggests that the view of individuals and organizations need to depart from neoclassical *Homo oeconomicus* (or Economic Man) and profit-maximizing firm. While there are research situations where some average idea of consumer or firm (goals and behavior), a so-called representative agent may be relevant as part of modeling efforts, in relation to more recent challenges such as sustainable development, it seems more constructive to think in terms of case studies (as is common in business management literature). Each individual in all her different roles and each firm (or other organization) is specified and can be approached and scrutinized with respect to ideological orientation and behavior or action.

For this reason, a "political economic person" (PEP) is proposed, that is, an individual as actor guided by her "ideological orientation" rather than the Economic Man of neoclassical theory (Söderbaum 1998). Similarly, a "political economic organization" (PEO), that is, an organization as actor guided by its ideological orientation or "mission" replaces the profit-maximizing firm of neoclassical theory. Again, ideological orientation (or mission) is something to be investigated in each case rather than assumed to be given. There will be cases of business leaders as actors who think only in monetary terms (considering the single-minded education that many economists have gone through) but there will also (hopefully) be those that have internalized some version of sustainable development or corporate social responsibility (CSR) where non-monetary impacts are taken seriously.

4.2 Ideological orientation and mission as key concepts

A "political economic person" was described as an individual guided by her "ideological orientation". What is the meaning of "ideological orientation"? To start with, it differs from the neoclassical idea that analysis should be limited to that which can be quantified. Qualitative and visual aspects are essential. Ideological orientation is about who you are, your view of the world and how you want to act on your own and with others.

Among economists, Douglass North has attempted to clarify the meaning of "ideology" as follows:

> By ideology, I mean the subjective perceptions (models, theories) all people possess to explain the world around them. Whether at the microlevel of individual relationships or at the macrolevel of organized ideologies providing integrated explanations of the past and the present, such as communism or religions, the *theories* individuals construct are *colored* by normative views of how the world should be organized.
>
> (North 1990, 23, emphasis in original)

In contemporary political dialogue, "ideology" is often connected with specific political parties, such as social democracy, green party, liberals and conservatives. To become elected, politicians turn to us as citizens with their ideologies. And as citizens we respond in one way or other to their arguments, suggesting that also we are guided by ideologies or ideological orientations.

"Ideology" and "ideological orientation" are so-called contested concepts (Connolly 1993), in the sense that they can be defined or interpreted in more ways than one.[3] For a social or political science to be relevant, one has to live with contested concepts such as ideology, power, institution and even "sustainable development", which are the focus in this chapter because they play a role in contemporary political dialogue.

Ideological orientation is here understood as a means-ends relationship. It is about where you are (present position), where you want to go (future positions) and how to get there (strategy). A person's ideological orientation is fragmentary and uncertain rather than complete and certain. It changes with social, cultural and physical context. A person's ideological orientation may furthermore change systematically over time, for example in the sense of more (or less) concern about climate change or other sustainability issues.

Decision-making is understood as a compatibility test or matching process between a person's ideological orientation (or an organization's mission) and the expected multidimensional impact profile of each alternative considered. Sometimes there is a good fit between ideological orientation and the impact profile of an alternative, while in other cases no alternative is perceived as appropriate or good enough.

Neoclassical economics can be understood as an attempt to avoid ethical and ideological issues (or perhaps rather taking a stand for a specific market ideology). Our conceptual frame of reference with political economic person and political economic organization instead opens the door for competing ideas about ethics and ideology. Multidimensional thinking, together with ideas such as "fair trade", corporate social responsibility, environmental management systems (e.g. ISO 14001) and our focus in this chapter on sustainable development or sustainability is compatible with the new frame of reference. In this manner democracy can be strengthened. It does not mean, however, that the mentioned concepts are enough to guide us toward a well-functioning society. But in my view, they are pointing in the right direction.

To summarize this part, the idea with PEP and PEO assumptions is to encourage dialogue between actually existing researchers or analysts and various actors about how they understand sustainable development and how this understanding influences their professional and private life. The idea is not to present an alternative standardized or "representative actor" for mathematical modeling purposes to that of neoclassical theory. An additional different and equally interesting challenge is to use social science literature to discuss features of a person who is ideally equipped with capabilities to deal with sustainability issues. In his book *Homo Sustinens* (2001), Bend Siebenhüner discusses such an ideal person.

4.3 Markets understood in terms of PEPs and PEOs

In neoclassical theory the individual is a self-interested person related to markets, for example, markets for commodities. Among organizations, only the firm or business organization is considered, and it is similarly assumed that only narrow interests in the form of monetary profits are relevant. When other aspects are considered, they should support the monetary motive in a win-win relationship.

Sustainable development is a challenge for individuals as well as organizations. Focus on self-interest and monetary profits should not be excluded but appears a bit dysfunctional. And we know that present development is unsustainable. To deal with climate change, for example, it is clear for most people that we need changes in institutional framework as well as in the behavior of individuals and organizations. Individuals as well as organizations should be encouraged to broaden their perspectives. Contrary to this, neoclassical theory tends to encourage narrow motives. Neoclassical economists may counter that the mentioned assumptions are just that – assumptions – and they have some relevance in the real world. But when these assumptions are repeated for millions of students in economics globally then it probably has some impact. It becomes legitimate for economists as professionals to refer to a narrow ideological orientation. Fortunately, one can consult business management literature where the possibility that market actors are "concerned" for broader issues (Geiger et al. 2014) is discussed. Individuals and organizations can cooperate in networks, and concern for other parts of the networks (Ford et al. 1998; Håkansson et al. 2009) often makes assumptions of simple profit maximization less relevant.

4.4 Sustainability assessment – a political issue

When preparing decisions concerning investments in infrastructure, neoclassical economists advocate cost-benefit analysis. As previously indicated, this monetary approach is extremely technocratic (see also Self 1975; Earle et al. 2017). Our present emphasis on democracy suggests that other approaches should be used.

Democracy is about listening to many voices. As argued by Ezra Mishan (1980), it is not realistic to assume that all citizens, or even political parties, can agree about the specific market ideology built into CBA. While there are exceptional decision situations where decision makers can refer to a consensus about how to value alternatives of choice, in the normal case their opinions will differ. As an example, many non-monetary environmental impacts are irreversible. How do we value them in relation to other impacts? Should we refer to an infinite negative value? Can money be used as a measuring rod, or would that be a mistake? How do we value CO_2 emissions or exploitation of agricultural land for housing or transportation purposes?

The alternative here is to accept some complexity by considering more than one ideological orientation. The task of the analyst becomes one of identifying three or four ideological orientations that appear to be relevant among decision makers and other concerned actors. The neoclassical CBA ideology may be embraced by a segment of decision makers. Other decision makers may emphasize reduced inequality and some may argue for a specific interpretation of sustainable development.

Positional Analysis (PA) is built upon such an idea of illuminating ideological orientations and alternatives with respect to expected impacts in a many-sided way. Assuming a specific set of alternatives, the ranking of them will presumably differ depending upon ideological orientation. Instead of one optimal solution, we get conditional conclusions. Ideological orientation A suggests a ranking of three or four alternatives in one way, while ideological orientation B may suggest a different ranking.

Two comments will be made here. When it is recommended that only three or four ideological orientations and a similar number of alternatives are considered, this is done for practical reasons. Decision makers with an ideological orientation that differs from those directly considered in analysis will probably still find the analysis useful for them in some respects.

A second point is that "sustainability assessment" as used in the subtitle of this section is necessarily about applying an ideology where a specific interpretation of sustainable development is among the ideological options. In the case of PA, the analyst should articulate one idea of sustainable development but not limit herself to this viewpoint. Single nations as well as regional entities, such as EU, and the United Nations (with the 17 SDGs, for example) have declared their intentions to transform society in the direction of sustainable development. The actual ideological orientation of specific decision makers should certainly be considered. But it is the responsibility of the analyst to see to it that all decision makers are faced with sustainable development as one among several ideological options. This will hopefully in some cases lead to debate and new thinking. Those who advocate a conventional GDP and market ideology will be respected as participants in the dialogue but may get into difficulties if the alternative that they advocate in fact is part of an unsustainable development.

Positional Analysis has been presented at other places with scheme of analysis and so forth (Söderbaum 2000, 2008; Brown et al. 2017). PA is compatible with the way economics has been defined above. It is multidimensional in the sense that "costs" and "benefits" are understood in monetary as well as non-monetary terms. Development, sustainable or unsustainable, is similarly understood in monetary and non-monetary terms. Expected impacts can be expressed per time period as flows or for points in time as states or "positions". PA is largely a recommendation to focus on non-monetary positions if we are interested in a more sustainable development. And non-monetary flows and positions are as "economic" as monetary ones. Sustainable development is largely about non-degradation of natural resources, health status and social positions of a population. Such positional changes can be discussed in terms of inertia, such as irreversibility, and can be illustrated with specific kinds of decision trees (Söderbaum 2000, 93–97).

Political debate sometimes leads to consensus about what to do. But democracy is perhaps primarily about accepting the existence of conflicts of interest between stakeholders or for one stakeholder between her interests. Again, the idea is to illuminate such conflicts (rather than hide them behind technocratic approaches to alleged optimal solutions). There are conflicts between the ideological orientations of different persons or groups but also in the concrete decision situation, where different activities of different categories of stakeholders and of single stakeholders are expected to be affected. For each activity affected, the analyst may assume a specific goal which makes ranking of alternatives possible in relation to that activity. It should finally be added that not all aspects of complexity need to be part of a PA study. It is possible to cover some of the essential features of PA in partial studies. And PA is as much an approach to thinking about planning and decision-making as a way of producing documents.

4.5 *Ten years of ecological economics at Mälardalen University: some experiences*

Many books have been written about the need for pluralism rather than monism (or monopoly) in university departments of economics. Pluralism is needed for research as well as education in economics. Some part of the literature focuses on economics education, for example, *The Economics Curriculum: Towards a Radical Reformulation* (Madi and Reardon 2014), *40 Critical Pointers for Students of Economics* (Birks 2016) and *The Econocracy: The Perils of Leaving Economics to the Experts* (Earle et al. 2017). There is also the *International Journal of Pluralism and Economics Education*.

Among those being critical to the present state of affairs in departments of economics there appear to be some agreement about what is needed. The neoclassical monopoly has to be abandoned; the history of economic doctrines has to enter the curriculum. Interdisciplinary or transdisciplinary openings are recommended. I will not here try to summarize the criticism but rather point to two examples based on my own experiences about how things can be reorganized.

Ecological economics became a hot topic in the early 1990s. The International Society for Ecological Economics (ISEE) was formed 1990 with the journal *Ecological Economics*. Regional societies such as the European Society for Ecological Economics (ESEE) followed in 1992. I was employed at the Department of Economics, Swedish University of Agricultural Sciences, and wrote a book in Swedish on ecological economics (Söderbaum 1993). A five-week course was arranged, attracting students also from Uppsala University and universities in Stockholm. The course program in the section of Land Economics was rearranged somewhat. In an introductory course, students had a chance to listen to lecturers with different preferences with respect to theoretical perspective or paradigm. They then had to make a choice between neoclassical environmental economics and institutional ecological economics in the next course. This was followed by writing a thesis, where students again could look for supervisors according to their own preferences.

This way of organizing education worked well for two or three years (too well perhaps) but was abandoned in 1995. I will not here go into details about what happened, but I was approached by Mälardalen University where there was a demand for new initiatives and courses relevant in relation to challenges in the larger society. Mälardalen University has campuses in Västerås and Eskilstuna, and in both cities the challenge of sustainable development was taken seriously by some politicians and civil servants. A three-year bachelor program in ecological economics was arranged beginning in 1994 with 60 students, and was later on extended by one year to a master program. Courses in ecological economics were given each year in the program, and there was also an emphasis on existing courses in business management such as organization theory and accounting. An attempt was made to compare conventional approaches with what was more promising in relation to the sustainability challenge. Students could add courses in neoclassical economics on a voluntary basis and the neoclassical economics program continued unaffected with their own program.

A large part of the students was successful in terms of employment, and some became politicians at the local or national level. There were even cases of a career in the European Union administration and in the United Nations. Things came to an end, at least partially, when I retired in 2005 and my successor declared that his interests were limited to business management issues.

Why did we succeed, at least in part? I think three kinds of partnerships could be mentioned:

- Partnership with the local and regional community, as previously mentioned
- Partnership within the university with actors connected with business management
- Partnership with natural scientists and engineers engaged in sustainability issues.

I will here only further comment upon the latter two partnerships. Some business management courses can certainly be criticized in relation to what is needed for sustainable development. Analysis of investment decisions in business tends to be limited to the monetary, financial aspect, and accounting courses seldom depart from monetary principles of profit and loss statements and balance sheets. But courses in organization theory and marketing represent a more dynamic and interdisciplinary part of the business studies literature. My experience from teaching marketing courses at Uppsala University and its Department of Business Management is that actors in this department are ready to learn from other social science disciplines. To understand consumer behavior neoclassical demand curves may be of some help, but something essential is added if you bring in parts of the conceptual framework of social psychology (role, relationship, trust, network, motive, perception, cognition, learning theory, attitude, dissonance, etc.). Business management actors are of interest also, since the popularity among students tends to move in favor of business management studies. Economics departments are losing ground these days and certainly need a change.

One argument in the present chapter is that ideology is involved in attempts to understand the behavior of different actors. In relation to sustainable development positivistic thinking at a distance is seldom enough. We need engaged economists, engineers and representatives of natural sciences, such as ecologists. University lecturers and professors are actors in political arenas whether they admit it or not.[4]

5 Concluding comments

When arguing in favor of new thinking, heterodox economists often point to specific events, such as the 2008 financial crisis and the fact that few, if any neoclassical economists were able to predict this crisis. This failure should certainly be taken seriously in attempts to reconsider economics. But for me unsustainable trends in relation to climate change and other environmental issues are even more important as sign of the failure of mainstream economics. Neoclassical economics with its limitations has made the present system of governance legitimate and this system is not performing well in relation to sustainable development. Indeed, I look upon the present monopoly for neoclassical economics as a sustainability problem in its own right.

A different economics is needed, and the proposed definition in terms of multidimensional analysis and democracy is hopefully a way forward. As a first step, a conceptual framework that is useful in understanding what is going on in the economy (in a broad sense) and how to deal with various problems is called for. We need alternative ideas of human beings, organizations, markets, decision-making, institutional change processes and so forth. And comparing different paradigms is not only a technocratic project. It is also a matter of subjective engagement and ideology. Neither I nor any other economist can claim value neutrality. But we can act based on the acceptance of normal principles of democracy, such as openness and acceptance of more than one point of view.

As an example, the so-called Nobel Prize in Economics is not only a scientific prize in a technical sense. It at the same time plays an ideological role in contemporary political debate. In the book *The Nobel Factor: The Prize in Economics, Social Democracy, and the Market Turn* (2016), Avner Offer and Gabriel Söderberg discuss the role of the award in relation to politics in Sweden and elsewhere. Again, it should be noted that this book is not written by neoclassical economists but by economic historians. It could then be suggested that heterodox economists will benefit further by cooperation in networks with sociologists, philosophers, economic historians and students of organizations, business organizations included.

My final remark is then that pluralism is very much needed in education as well as research. University departments of economics have to become open in relation to other social sciences and to other ideological orientations than those built into neoclassical theory. Considering present challenges of climate change, biodiversity loss, environmental pollution as well as inequality, educational programs have to be framed in new ways. And if mainstream economists continue to protect their paradigm and ideology, then new partnerships and organizations are needed. Today there exist a considerable number of professional organizations, journals and publishers that look for new thinking.

Notes

1 It can even be argued that neoclassical theory can only understood when compared with alternative theories. Neoclassical economists who understand this can therefore be expected to "demand" a more pluralistic economics.

2 Among institutional economists K. William Kapp, argued at an early stage (1950) that it is not meaningful to suggest an analysis for one externality at a time. Externalities are ubiquitous and exemplify failure at a systems level. In order to improve profits (reduce costs), business corporations systematically carry over negative impacts upon taxpayers, other stakeholders and the economy at large.

3 For a more complete study of the concept of "ideology" in relation to mainstream economics, see Helgesson (2002).

4 It is true that some economists in their ideological orientation emphasize mathematical modeling and the alleged beauty of equations. For a criticism of this predilection for mathematical modeling among neoclassical economists, see Lawson (2015).

References

Birks, S. (2016): *40 Critical Pointers for Students of Economics*. World Economics Association Books, www.worldeconomicsassociation.org

Brown, J., Dereniowska, M. and Söderbaum, P. (2017): *Positional Analysis for Sustainable Development: Reconsidering Policy, Economics and Accounting*. London: Routledge.

Connolly, W. E. (1993): *The Terms of Political Discourse*. 3rd edition. Oxford: Blackwell.

Earle, J., Moran, C. and Ward-Perkins, Z. (2017): *The Econocracy: The Perils of Leaving Economics to the Experts*. Manchester: Manchester University Press.

Ford, D., Gadde, L.-E., Håkansson, H., Lundgren, A., Snehota, I., Turnbult, P. and Wilson, D. (1998): *Managing Business Relationships*. Chichester: Wiley-Blackwell.

Geiger, S., Harrison, D., Kjellberg, H. and Mallard, A. (2014): *Concerned Markets: Economic Ordering for Multiple Values*. Cheltenham, UK: Edward Elgar.

Håkansson, H., Ford, D., Gadde, L.-E., Snehota, I. and Waluszewski, A. (2009): *Business in Networks*. Chichester: Wiley-Blackwell.

Helgesson, G. (2002): *Values, Norms & Ideology in Mainstream Economics*. PhD-Dissertation, Department of Philosophy. Uppsala: Uppsala University.

Kapp, K. W. (1971 [1950]): *The Social Costs of Private Enterprise*. New York: Schocken Books.

Kuhn, T. S. (1970): *The Structure of Scientific Revolutions*. Chicago: University of Chicago Press.

Lawson, T. (2015): *Essays on the Nature and State of Modern Economics*. Abingdon: Routledge.

Madi, M. A. and Reardon, J. (eds.) (2014): *The Economics Curriculum: Towards a Radical Reformulation*. World Economics Association Books, www.worldeconomicsassociation.org

Mishan, E. J. (1971): *Cost-Benefit Analysis*. London: Allen & Unwin.

Mishan, E. J. (1980): "How Valid Are Economic Valuations of Allocative Changes?", *Journal of Economic Issues* 14(1), 143–161.

Myrdal, G. (1978): "Institutional Economics", *Journal of Economic Issues* 12(4), 771–783.

North, D. C. (1990): *Institutions, Institutional Change and Economic Performance*. Cambridge: Cambridge University Press.

Offer, A. and Söderberg, G. (2016): *The Nobel Factor: The Prize in Economics, Social Democracy, and the Market Turn*. Princeton, NJ: Princeton University Press.

Self, P. (1975): *Econocrats and the Policy Process*. London: Palgrave Macmillan.

Siebenhüner, B. (2001): *Homo sustinens. Auf dem Weg zu einem Menschenbild der Nachhaltigkeit*. Marburg: Metropolis.

Söderbaum, P. (1993): *Ekologisk ekonomi. Miljö och utveckling i ny belysning*. Lund: Studentlitteratur.

Söderbaum, P. (1998): "Stakeholders as Political Economic Persons: On Participation, Responsibility and Democracy", in Biesecker, A., Elsner, W. and Grenzdörfer, K. (eds.), *Ökonomie der Betroffenen und Mitwirkenden: Erweiterte Stakeholder-Prozesse*. Pfaffenweiler: Centaurus-Verlagsgesellschaft, 241–260.

Söderbaum, P. (2000): *Ecological Economics: A Political Economics Approach to Environment and Development*. London: Earthscan.

Söderbaum, P. (2008): *Understanding Sustainability Economics: Towards Pluralism in Economics*. London: Earthscan.

Söderbaum, P. (2018): *Economics, Ideological Orientation and Democracy for Sustainable Development*. Bristol: World Economics Association Books.

United Nations (2015): *General Assembly, Resolution Adopted on 25 September 2015: Transforming Our World: The 2030 Agenda for Sustainable Development*. New York: United Nations.

von Egan-Krieger, T. (2014): *Die Illusion wertfreier Ökonomie. Eine Untersuchung der Normativität heterodoxer Theorien*. Frankfurt am Main: Campus Verlag.

10 Suggestions for incorporating sustainability into the macroeconomics course

Jack Reardon and Maria Alejandra Madi

1 Introduction

Despite the dysfunctional disconnect at the national level, today's students are very much interested in climate change, with most recognizing (at least from our perspective) that climate change is caused by humans. There is no need to read arcane scientific journals to learn about climate change, for it is happening all around us: record temperatures, rising ocean levels, increasing drought, more severe storms and so forth.

The New York Times (2015) recently editorialized:

> Children today stand to inherit a climate severely changed by the actions of previous generations. They need to understand how those changes came about, how to mitigate them and how to prevent more damage to the planet. Schools can start by adopting science standards that deal extensively with human-caused climate change and that accurately reflect the scientific consensus.

It is hard to argue with this; after all, isn't this the purpose of education? But worrisome is the lack of concern with climate change at the university level, specifically within the discipline of economics, and specifically neoclassical economics which still dominates university teaching. Students concerned about the future and the effects of climate change are excited to take courses in economics, but are unfortunately quickly disappointed to find instead "a branch of applied mathematics, where the aim is not to explain real process and outcomes in the economic world [giving] economics the perception as a technical and rarefied discipline, of questionable relevance and limited practical use" (Hodgson 1999, 6, 9). If we are to adequately prepare students for the challenges of climate change, economics must play a role not as a silo-based discipline but as a holistic, open-minded, pluralist discipline that teaches our students how to think like social scientists. Easier said than done!

The purpose of this chapter is to suggest how to incorporate sustainability into the economics curriculum. As will be discussed below, since sustainability is ipso facto pluralist at all levels (ontological, methodological, epistemological), incorporating sustainability into the curriculum will (at least hopefully) make economics more pluralistic pedagogically. The focus will be macroeconomics, specifically at the principles level – the port of entry for economics majors, and for many undergraduates perhaps their only exposure to economics. Section 2 will address the absence of sustainability in neoclassical economics; section 3 will discuss the definition of sustainability; section 4 will offer specific ways to include sustainability into the curriculum; while section 5 concludes.

2 Why the absence of sustainability in neoclassical economics?

Alfred Marshall, in the eighth edition of his *Principles of Economics*, wrote that "economic conditions are constantly changing, and each generation looks at its own problems in its own way" (Marshall 1946 [1890], v). Our generation is beset with many problems including climate change, a global financial crisis, a palpable disparity in income and wealth and a health care crisis. These problems are mutually reinforcing and will only worsen.

One explanation for our subtitle question is that neoclassical economics "was conceived in the 19th century during an era of unlimited boundaries . . . in a world with empty land, shoals of undisturbed fish, vast forests, and a robust ozone shield" (McNeil 2000, 236). Rather than expand, diversify and engage with other social sciences, neoclassical economics turned inward, focusing on method rather than content, ignoring advances in other disciplines, especially math and physics. Steve Keen notes:

> Think of the many revolutions in our understanding of the physical world which have occurred in the twentieth century: from Newtonian to Einsteinian physics; from Mendelian genetics to DNA and the human genome; from determinism to chaos theory. Any scientist from the nineteenth century would be bewildered by what is commonplace today in his [*sic*] discipline – save an economist.
>
> (Keen 2011, 169)

Alfred Marshall's perceptive criticism of narrow-minded specialists is doubly true today in the context of sustainability. Such specialists who

> never look beyond their own domain are apt to see things out of true proportion; much of the knowledge they get together is of comparatively little use; they work away at the details of the old problems which have lost most of their significance and have been supplanted by new questions rising out of new points of view; and they fail to gain that large illumination which the progress of every science throws by comparison and analogy on those around it.
>
> (Marshall 1946, 770–771)

In addition to the subject matter, neoclassical economics still stubbornly clings to the Newtonian linear, deterministic, mechanistic modus operandi, bypassing the richer, more realistic viewpoints of modern science, especially chaos theory and quantum physics. Ironically (and sadly) as neoclassical economics stubbornly emulates 19th-century science, modern science has pulled light-years away:

> we social scientists strain for respectability, using the methodologies and thought patterns of 17th century science, while the scientists, traveling away from us faster than the speed of light, are moving into a universe that calls for entirely new ways of understanding.
>
> (Wheatley 1999, 160)

Perhaps then, it should not be surprising that discussion of sustainability in any form is absent from neoclassical economics. Why discuss sustainability when 19th-century Newtonian physics has imbued us with a confident ability to deterministically affect our economic objectives with little effect on the environment?

In a comprehensive study of the principles of economics textbooks, the author found very little coverage on environmental issues, climate change and global warming, writing:

> From a sustainability perspective, restricting the domain of economics as the science of choice under scarcity while using a framework of methodological individualism, is problematic. The lens of choice results in the textbook's content and the students' attention being heavily weighted towards issues of market exchange, price formation and to exploring the implications of marginal changes. It limits attention to environment-economy linkages, the sources of natural resources, how resources are utilised and where waste products go.
>
> (Green 2012, 215)

Isn't this bothersome? That one of the most pressing problems of our generation is ignored by economics textbooks? Contemporary economics not only gives students the wrong message but leaves them ill-prepared to conceptualize the problem of climate change and its solutions.

A quick glance at three leading macroeconomics textbooks reveals that little has changed. In Mankiw's *Principles of Economics* (2018), the book index contains no sustainability entries and only one entry on climate change associated with carbon taxes and externalities. In the chapter on economic growth, Mankiw asks a loaded (19th-century) question, "Are natural resources a limit to growth?" (2018, 532) and concludes "market prices give no reason to believe that natural resources are a limit to economic growth" (2018, 532). In Robert Gordon's *Macroeconomics* (2012), a popular text at the intermediate level, sustainability, energy, and the environment is completely absent. The same can be said for Carlin and Soskice's *Macroeconomics – Institutions, Instability and the Financial System* (2015). It is as if the problem doesn't exist. In not one model introduced in any of these textbooks is energy, the environment, climate change or sustainability mentioned in anything but a tangential and trivial manner. No wonder Tim Jackson wrote that "economics – and macroeconomics in particular – is ecologically illiterate" (2011, 123).

While some might argue that in any given course the teacher has recourse to ancillary materials, nevertheless the textbook, regardless of other materials used, is of paramount importance, especially in economics, and especially at the principles level:

> The importance of economics' introductory level textbooks tends to be underappreciated. In the United States alone more than a million young minds annually take a year-long introductory course. For over 90 percent of them this experience is dominated by a textbook little changed from Paul Samuelson's 1948 text *Economics*. With few exceptions, their textbook fundamentally shapes how they think about economics and economic issues for the rest of their lives. As such, these books are a powerful and long-lasting cultural and political force. And of course their influence extends to the economics profession itself, because these textbooks also serve as the formative introduction to economics of that small minority of students who go on to become economists.
>
> (Fullbrook 2010)

And needless to say, such textbooks are highly ideological, as Hill and Myatt write:

> We see the standard textbooks as part of a broader system of persuasion (or 'propaganda') that permeates our culture and that has the effect of shaping or influencing people's view of the world, or at least trying to do so.
>
> (2010, 5)

Indeed, the ideological content of neoclassical economics – pro-market, antigovernment, with its utopia in the early 19th century (Diesing 1982, 325) – prevents students from apprehending today's climate change challenges.

The author of the previously discussed sustainability study exhorted that "students would be better served if authors of standard textbooks would improve the sophistication with which their texts address environment-economy interactions" (Green 2012, 219). It is the purpose of this chapter to do so. Economics must modernize into the 21st century by becoming less arrogant and more humble, more pluralist within its borders and in turn opening its own borders to other disciplines. The key to doing so is addressing sustainability, for sustainability ipso facto is multidisciplinary, open and pluralist; thus focus on sustainability is efficacious to reconceptualize and hence modernize economics.

3 What is sustainability?

Sustainability is a multifaceted word (like freedom, democracy and pluralism) meaning different things to different people. Even among supporters of sustainability, significant disagreement exists over exactly what it means and how to implement it. While several definitions of sustainability exist, the most widely used is from the 1987 Brundtland Commission Report (chaired by Norwegian

Prime Minister Gro Harlem Brundtland): "development that meets the needs of the present without compromising the ability of future generations to meet their own needs" (1987, 16). A key element of sustainable development is ethical concern for others as well as non-humans, and concern for future generations and especially the poor:

> Meeting essential needs requires not only a new era of economic growth for nations in which the majority are poor, but an assurance that those poor get their fair share of the resources required to sustain that growth. Such equity would be aided by political systems that secure effective citizen participation in decision making and by greater democracy in international decision making.
>
> (Bruntland Commission 1987, 16)

Jahnke and Nutzinger (2003) note that *sustainability* is a regulative idea while *sustainable development* is a more concrete concept leading to practical actions. Thus, although ostensibly dissimilar, these two words are flip sides of the same coin.

One widely used interpretation of sustainable development is that it consists of three intersecting pillars: economic development, social development and environmental protection. Different societies weight each pillar differently, giving precedence to one over another, and quite often economic development wins. While this helps to visualize the intersection of the social, economic and environmental, and is a step forward, nevertheless it represents 19th-century linear thinking (which still pervades economics) that we can successfully decompose an entity into its constituent components, find out what is wrong, then put the pieces back together. It is more accurate to view the economy as a system and an integrated whole. Adding a level of complexity, sustainability can be either weak or strong: weak sustainability accepts depletion of natural resources such as coal, oil, fisheries and forests if replaced with other types of capital; whereas strong sustainability argues that natures' resources must be preserved and passed on to future generations, while human-made resources are not substitutable for nature's.

Widespread disagreement exists over how to interpret and thus to implement sustainability ranging from superficial (lip-service) support to a radical change in lifestyle. Peter Söderbaum (2008, 14–15) elaborates three different interpretations of how sustainability should be practiced:

- *Business as usual*: The language of sustainability is adopted without changing underlying values and ideology. Reports about ecological and social problems are considered to be exaggerated, and any future problems can be handled within the traditional paradigm of economic growth and reliance on technology.
- *Social and ecological moderation*: Environmental and social problems are acknowledged, but they can be solved within the current economic system. Specific policies are urged to attenuate the worst behavior and nudge consumers, firms and workers in the "correct" direction.

- *Radical change*: Our way of life is on a collision course with the environment; business-as-usual policies will result in ecological disaster. We need a major change and rethinking in our values. We must rethink the heretofore acceptance of continued economic growth.

While weak sustainability is compatible with either of Söderbaum's first two approaches, strong sustainability is compatible only with the third.

Considering that significant difference in understanding and practicing sustainability exists (even among the committed), it is important to move forward: doing nothing is not an option, for our window of opportunity to affect change is narrowing.

In this light the United Nations promulgated (after countless hours of debate and talking with myriad individuals and groups) its 17 Sustainable Development Goals (17 UN SDGs; see Box 10.1), which taken together can and will provide us with a recipe for sustainable living.

Box 10.1 UN Sustainable Development Goals

1 End poverty in all its forms.
2 End hunger, achieve food security and improved nutrition and promote sustainable agriculture.
3 Ensure healthy lives and improve well-being of all.
4 Ensure inclusive and equitable quality education and promote lifelong earning opportunities for all.
5 Achieve gender equality and empower all women and girls.
6 Clean water and sanitation.
7 Affordable and clean energy. Ensure access to modern, affordable, reliable energy for all.
8 Promote inclusive and sustainable economic growth, employment and decent work for all.
9 Build resilient infrastructure, promote sustainable industrialization and foster innovation.
10 Reduce innovation within and among countries.
11 Make cities inclusive, safe, resilient and sustainable.
12 Ensure sustainable consumption and production.
13 Take urgent action to combat climate change and its actions.
14 Conserve and sustainably use the oceans, seas and marine resources.
15 Sustainably manage forests, combat desertification, halt and reverse land degradation and halt biodiversity loss.
16 Promote just, peaceful and inclusive societies.
17 Revitalize the global partnership for sustainable development.

The 17 UN SDGs underscore that sustainability involves a lot more than concern with the environment. Notice the wording ("all," "inclusive," "urgent") and the use of active verbs (end, ensure, achieve, promote, reduce, conserve, revitalize). This is the language of the 17 UN SDGs, and this should become the language of economics. These goals are also interrelated, so that by tackling one, we tackle others. One example is charcoal. It is cheaper and easier to use than firewood or natural gas, and the gathering and selling of charcoal has become one of the biggest drivers of Africa, enabling people to earn money in order to survive. But obviously charcoal comes from wood and wood comes from trees, so that the more trees cut down, the greater the forest loss and the greater the loss of biodiversity. And given that women in developing countries are the preponderant gatherers of firewood (spending an additional 2 to 20 hours per week) as more trees are cut down, they spend more time looking for wood – time which could have been devoted to other issues.

But by providing clean renewable energy to Africa (Goal #7), then we don't have to de-forest, increasing biodiversity (meeting Goal #15), which in turn can be used to increase the quality education of girls (Goal #4), which will help achieve gender equality and empower all women and girls (Goal #5), which would help make cities more inclusive (Goal #11) and reduce climate change (Goal #13), which will promote just, peaceful and inclusive societies (Goal #16). Of course, whether and how these goals are achieved is a function of Goal #17: revitalize the global partnership for sustainable development.

4 How to incorporate sustainability into the curriculum

The easiest way to incorporate sustainability into the undergraduate curriculum is to append it as a later chapter, treating it as just another unit in the course syllabus, devoting maybe a couple of lectures to it, while not connecting it to the rest of the course. This underscores the lack of centrality of the topic and sends a clear message that it is of little concern, that sustainability is a mere afterthought, nothing more than an appendage.

A second method is to make it a major theme of the book and a core issue of every chapter. Make every economics concept, issue and theory begin with sustainability, which becomes the lens to teach economics. This is a far more difficult task, and at least from our perspective necessitates a complete rewriting of the textbook and the undergraduate curriculum.

A criticism of the second approach is that given the inherent disagreement over sustainability, the course content could significantly differ among teachers and between locales, especially since the instructor can reframe selected topics in terms of sustainability in the context of pluralist and interdisciplinary learning. And furthermore, this approach could augment an already encyclopedic principles text with a high opportunity cost for inclusion. Nonsense. As discussed later in this section, this need not happen.

We believe the first approach is inconsistent with the overall goal of implementing sustainability; thus the remainder of this chapter will be primarily concerned with the second approach.

Three changes in the economics curriculum must be implemented immediately: incorporating pluralism, incorporating justice and changing the definition of economics. Each will now be discussed.

4.1 Incorporating pluralism

A simple definition of pluralism that captures its essence is, "Pluralism is the acceptance of the legitimization of diverse views." Pluralism doesn't mean that anything goes, or that all viewpoints are correct, only that there is more than one way to define reality, and no one single way is correct.[1] Teaching our students how to be pluralist doesn't mean that they must become master experts in every ideology; rather to become pluralists means they must learn to listen, how to dialogue, and how to learn from each other. Once again, easier said than done. Pluralism is a modus vivendi and not a measure of a repository of knowledge.

Thankfully, a global movement to reconceptualize economics has made pluralism a central objective, and a plethora of resources exists to help both students and teachers.

Similar to sustainability, pluralism exists on many different levels. The focus in this chapter is on pedagogical pluralism.

4.2 Economics must be concerned with justice

Justice is another multifaceted term like sustainability and pluralism (and democracy and freedom), meaning different things to different people. Joan Robinson exhorted that economists should "speak up on the side of humanity" (1980, xiii). At its core is concern with the welfare and well-being of others, although a long-standing debate has occurred over what exactly is justice.

Failure to agree on a specific definition of justice does not mean that we jettison its discussion. Rather, Amartya Sen, a Nobel laureate in economics, suggested that rather than searching for a universal (yet elusive) definition of justice, it might be easier to search for instances of injustice, since "what moves us, reasonably enough, is not the realization that the world falls short of being completely just – which few of us expect – but that there are clearly remediable injustices around us which we want to eliminate" (Sen 2009, vii). Thus we agree with Sen that a fundamental objective of economics and economics education is "identification of redressable injustice" (Sen 2009, xiii).

Focus on sustainability and justice also means that discussion of power – completely ignored in the neoclassical curriculum – must occur.

4.3 Change the definition of economics

The definition of any subject not only shapes the course but also informs about the methodology, ideology, course boundaries and even possible topics. The (mainstream) definition found in most textbooks is the means/end: "economics is the study of how scarce resources are allocated between unlimited wants." This definition constricts the scope and purview of economics to rationalizing individuals content on optimizing; and furthermore it only describes the methodology while ignoring the subject matter.

A better definition of economics, one that more efficaciously captures its quintessence and its purview, is "economics is provisioning, or how societies organize themselves to sustain life and enhance its quality" (Nelson 2009, 61). Since such a definition "does not focus on individual rational choice, [it] can encompass social and economic institutions, real human psychology, and the actual unfolding of historical events" (Nelson 2009, 61). This multidimensional definition is amenable to a focus on sustainability and the achievement of the 17 UN SDGs, while the means/end definition is clearly not.

4.4 Adopt the values, ideas and modus operandi of modern science

While the founding fathers of neoclassical economics readily embraced and incorporated elements of 19th-century physics, physics envy stopped at the late 19th century, failing to incorporate and even recognize the radical advances of relativity and quantum physics. Science provides us with both lenses and metaphors to understand our lives. Why should we adopt the lens of an earlier age that restricts and distorts rather than enables and illuminates? The values of Newtonian physics, which underlie every textbook, assume that reality is linear, deterministic and mechanical, with reality explained by linear cause and effect, and that an observer can separate from the observed. The revolution of quantum physics, however, disproved this and has empirically argued that reality is probabilistic, that relationships matter (there is no such thing as an isolated individual); indeed the individual is only defined in relational to others (uncertainty is pervasive, as is change); and that the activities of the researcher actively influenced the subject of study.

This approach to sustainability by incorporating pluralism and justice, changing the definition of economics, and adapting the insights of modern physics science naturally lends itself to cooperation across the disciplines. A helpful interdisciplinary tool is to use the following terms to link across disciplines, and thus effectuate and enable both interdisciplinary and transdisciplinary learning: diversity, community, equity, ethics, interdependence, resilience, well-being, systems thinking, limits/scale, change, and ecological health (Creative Change 2013, 8–12). These are mental constructs that are universal, abstract and broad, and thus transferable across disciplines, but at the same time they can be applied as a lens to explore specific topics such as unemployment, growth, poverty and energy (Ibid.).

Finally, in this section we list additional elements to incorporate sustainability in macroeconomics.

(A) REPLACE THE CIRCULAR FLOW DIAGRAM IN THE DISCUSSION ON THE ORGANIZATION AND DYNAMICS OF THE ECONOMY

Nothing turns off students attention more than this abstract simplified model, ostensibly designed to introduce scarcity and the interconnectedness of economic activity but suffused with 19th-century cause and effect and linear values, and it is largely anthropomorphic, ignoring our interconnection with ecology. This 19th-century diagram should be replaced (or expanded) with emphasis that an economy is part of society and the environment. Perhaps start the course with an introduction to an ecosystem, such as a barrier reef, and how human activity affects it; or even a physical visit. This leads quite naturally to class discussion on the purposes and effects of economic activity in a pluralist macroeconomic perspective.

(B) RETHINKING THE CONCEPT OF GROSS DOMESTIC PRODUCT

Gross domestic product (GDP), developed the 1930s as a crude aggregate of an economy's performance, served its purpose in categorizing an economy's production but is in need of a desperate makeover to align it with the goals of sustainability. Yes, it still remains the lingua franca, and the entire edifice of neoclassical economics has been structured around increased GDP, but it must be significantly revised. Numerous suggestions have been made to incorporate environmental depletion and each should be incorporated into the macroeconomics curriculum, exposing students to all of them.[2] The market value of a good or service to the national economy – the traditional metric of GDP – should be replaced by the carbon use content (and other global warming gases), setting the stage for a reconceptualization of how we produce, market, consume and measure goods and services, to be explained in the next section. This also suggests that in additional to the traditional variables that play such an important role in macroeconomics, such as consumption, savings, investment and so forth.

> new macroeconomic variables will need to be brought explicitly into play. These will almost certainly include variables to reflect the energy and resource dependency of the economy and the limits on carbon. They may also include variables to reflect the value of ecosystem services or stocks of natural capital.
>
> (Jackson 2011, 141)

Of course, such variables must comport with the conceptualization that the environment is a complex system, not easily quantified as neoclassical economists are wont to do.

(C) RECONCEPTUALIZING SUSTAINABLE ECONOMIC GROWTH

Sustainability doesn't necessary mean zero or negative rates of economic growth, but rather that economic growth is compatible with the boundaries and parameters of the environment.[3] This is an important point and needs to be addressed in public dialogue. Becoming sustainable as individuals and a society does not simply mean that we produce less and minimize, halt or limit the production of bads, but that we fundamentally reconceptualize (with a lot of imagination) how we produce, market and consume, and how we measure such activity (Braungart and McDonough

2009, 45). Instead of designing and producing goods with unintended and pernicious side effects, let's design, produce and consume with deliberate, positive sustainable effects, complementing rather than conquering nature (Braungart and McDonough 2009, 81). This requires that we understand and emulate nature, especially the role of waste:

> If humans are truly going to prosper, we will have to learn to imitate nature's highly effective cradle-to-cradle system of nutrient flow and metabolism, [rather than our highly environmentally destructive, cradle-to-grave system] in which the very concept of waste does not exist. To eliminate the concept of waste means to design things – products, packaging, and systems – from the very beginning on the understanding that waste does not exist. It means that the valuable nutrients contained in the materials shape and determine the design: form follows evolution, not just function.
>
> (Braungart and McDonough 2009, 103–104)

Not only is this necessary for survival and sustainability, but simply producing less bads won't cut it. To do so requires a fundamental reconceptualization of how we produce and how we measure, necessitating an in-depth, pluralist, multidisciplinary immersion in sustainability. To help set the table, so to speak, we recommend Braungart and McDonough's book *Cradle to Cradle: Remaking the Way We Make Things* (2009) as required reading for all undergraduates.

(D) INTRODUCING CLIMATE CHANGE OUTCOMES TO ILLUSTRATE ECONOMIC POLICY

If the current production and consumption pattern is maintained, further economic growth will increase extraction levels and humanity's ecological footprint while doing little or nothing to improve overall human well-being. Indeed, many people have warned of impending water shortages caused by climate change and aquifer depletion in the context of current growth models. Impending water shortages can be used frequently in the macroeconomics curriculum to illustrate the concept of free goods, satisfying basic needs, pricing of scarce resources and allocating scarce resources in the context of public policies.

(E) EXPLORING THE BOTTOM LINES IN OPEN MACROECONOMICS DYNAMICS

Every aspect of macroeconomics should be reexamined for its effect on energy and environmental effects. So for example, how does the call for open markets affect energy use and hence climate change? How do flexible exchange rates affect the environment? How do consumption and investment affect the environment, and how can we remodel consumption and investment theory to incorporate environmental affects? Is a single global currency compatible with sustainability?

(F) RETHINKING THE MACROECONOMIC OUTCOMES OF RURAL SUSTAINABILITY IN DEVELOPING COUNTRIES

Underdeveloped economies cannot be understood in isolation but only in relation to the global system, since development and underdevelopment are part of the same process of global capital expansion. Since the 1990s, agriculture modernization in underdeveloped countries has increased crop productivity; moreover, from 2000 to 2008 the world experienced one of the greatest commodity and credit booms in history, stimulated by the US expansionary monetary policy, flooding the world with cheap financing, but especially benefiting some developing countries. After a decade, growth rates have fallen and current account balances have somewhat deteriorated. Brazil and Russia, for example, have been adversely affected by declining commodity prices.

Peasants and others working in rural areas are currently regarded as among the most marginalized of groups in the context of the rapidly globalizing world, confronted with increasing competition for resources from much larger businesses, corporations and traders. Indeed, 80% of the world's hungry people live and work in rural areas: around half of those subsist in marginal farming areas and are unable to achieve self-sufficiency because they are denied adequate access to land, water and seeds. For instance, the majority of people in Africa live in rural areas and make a living from agriculture, but many suffer from hunger and malnutrition and are excluded from basic social services, including health, education and social security. People working in rural areas, including small-scale farmers and fishers, for example, directly confront the outcomes of climate change, environmental degradation and loss of biodiversity.

Concerns about food security result from high food prices. Indeed, high food prices have increased the hungry population in underdeveloped countries since the 1990s. As the poor in developing countries spend most of their income on food, the increase in food prices disproportionately impacts them. Two factors exerting strong pressure on demand (and high food prices, ceteris paribus) for food in coming years contribute to these high prices include:

- The growth of the world's population by 2.24 billion (or 32%) by the year 2050 (UN forecast).
- The growth of the Chinese GDP and the urbanization of China with millions of people migrating from rural areas and from subsistence agriculture to exert greater pressure on the food supply in urban areas.

Indeed, reports from the UN Food and Agriculture Organization (FAO) and the Organisation for Economic Co-operation and Development (OECD) predict high food prices in the near future that will certainly pose a challenge to conventional macroeconomic issues such as inflation, monetary policy and income distribution. Thus it is important to account for the macroeconomic interrelationships between food prices, inflation and environmental sustainability.

(G) INTRODUCING URBANIZATION CHALLENGES TO ILLUSTRATE FINANCIAL SUSTAINABLE MACROECONOMIC POLICIES IN DEVELOPING COUNTRIES

Composed of regional leaders, the BRICS (Brazil, Russia, India, China and South Africa) represent almost half of the world's population and about a fifth of the earth's surface, with a combined GDP comparable to the EU or the United States. The BRICS have diversified economies with an abundance of natural resources. Despite similarities there are significant political, cultural and social differences. The evolution of their economies will certainly impact global consumption, investment and the environment.

In the BRICS, urban workers face increasing challenges. It is worth remembering that in the period between 2000 and 2025, the urban population in developing countries is expected to nearly double from almost 2 billion to more than 3.5 billion, surpassing the rural population by 2020. Thus after 2025, about 90% of the world's population growth is expected to occur in the urban areas of developing countries.

Within developing countries such as the BRICS, intense urbanization has increased real estate prices in city centers that has forced low-income populations into urban peripheries characterized by lack of infrastructure (water, sewer, light, public transport). As urban concentration aggravates environmental problems (due primarily to the lack of restricted public budgets and the lack of urban investment planning), financial macroeconomic policies oriented to infrastructure investments in urban areas require new solutions acknowledging the macroeconomic links between finance and environment.

(H) EXPLORE THE LINKS BETWEEN ENTREPRENEURSHIP AND ENVIRONMENTAL SUSTAINABILITY IN A MACROECONOMIC PERSPECTIVE

Following the guidelines of the Global Entrepreneurship Monitor research on entrepreneurship, we can say that the entrepreneurial startup environment in developing economies has been decisively affected by the role of public policies. The specifics of entrepreneurship among developing countries reveal the importance of public policies that could coordinate financial resources and stimuli for innovation (investments, processes and products). However, the resilience of entrepreneurship requires the consolidation of specific competitive advantages to support growth, profitable performance and the preservation of the environment. As a result, a macroeconomic approach to entrepreneurship should rethink the links between finance, innovation and environmental sustainability in order to enhance firms' higher resilience.

(I) CONNECTING ANTI-AUSTERITY AND SUSTAINABILITY IN DEVELOPING COUNTRIES

Austerity programs require fiscal measures regarding surplus, tax increases and expenditure cuts. However, austerity could become a risky long-term strategy as a tighter fiscal policy would certainly result in even weaker economic growth rates and higher public debt/GDP rates. Moreover, under high uncertain expectations, the expansion of productive capacity would be postponed. Consequently, austerity programs certainly affect day-to-day lives of citizens, and indeed subordinate the whole policy decision process not only to a realignment of relative prices (mainly real wages) but also to further structural reforms (mainly in the public sector and the labor market). In this context, many environmental regulations are being removed.

As Keynes noted, there are conflicts between public and private interests in the organization of economic life (1923). He also argued that austerity programs influence the relationship between money, markets and wealth distribution, and cogently argued against deflation:

> Deflation is not desirable because it affects, what is always harmful, a change in the existing Standard of Value, and redistributes wealth in a manner injurious, at the same time, to business and to social stability. Deflation, as we have already seen, involves transference of wealth from the rest of the community to the rentier class and to all holders of titles to money; just as inflation involves the opposite. In particular, it involves a transference from all borrowers, that is to say from traders, manufacturers, and farmers, to lenders, from the active to the inactive. But whilst the oppression of the taxpayer for the enrichment of *the rentier* is the chief lasting result, there is another, more violent, disturbance during the period of transition. . . . Modern business being carried on largely with borrowed money, must necessarily be brought to a standstill by such a process. It will be to the interest of everyone in business to go out of business for the time being; and of everyone who is contemplating expenditure to postpone his orders as long as he can. The wise man will be he who turns his assets into cash, withdraws from the risks and the exertions of activity, and awaits in country retirement the steady appreciation promised him in the value of his cash. A probable expectation of Deflation is bad enough; a certain expectation is disastrous.
>
> (Keynes 1923, 143–144)

Following austerity programs, developing countries undergo painful adjustments mainly through deflationary policies favoring the reduction of public expenditures to cope with climate change challenges; in this context, public expenditures are considered inefficient and wasteful. As a result, many governments have disappointed their citizens because of the increasing enhancing unsustainable patterns of growth. The anti-austerity struggle raises the defense of public utilities and democratic control on public goods. Indeed, macroeconomic policies against climate change and against austerity have to address concrete problems and solutions in people's daily life.

(J) RETHINKING GENDER ISSUES IN A MACROECONOMIC APPROACH IN DEVELOPING COUNTRIES

More than half the poor citizens of developing countries are women. Men and women experience poverty differently since gender inequalities and gender power relations interact with other inequalities and power relations. The roots of gender and poverty studies began with Pearce (1978), who coined the expression "feminization of poverty." Pearce considered female-headed families, excluding poor women who live in male-headed families, based on the argument that the proportion of families headed by women among the poor has been increasing since the 1950s. In her opinion, women have become poorer because of their gender. Infant mortality rate, for example, could elucidate how poverty affects women.

More recently, in the attempt to fight poverty, new principles and values have been associated with women's empowerment, recognizing diversity and pluralism. Building on the UN goals, gender equality is required for the eradication of the many dimensions of poverty and to promote sustainable human development.

Taking into account a macroeconomic approach, the "vicious circle" of impoverishment could be surmounted if policy makers (1) rethink the process of job creation in order to avoid poor women being concentrated in generally low-paying occupations and (2) shape infrastructure investments that directly address climate change challenges. Lack of infrastructure, water and sewage, among other factors, dampen human dignity. Indeed, there is a strong link between sustainability and gender issues.

5 Conclusion

Many commentators have written that we are living in some difficult times with challenging problems. Eva Kraus, for example, writes:

> presently we are living in a period of dramatic change – a period of chaos – where conventional structures, business and development outlooks and even the human role on earth are going through a period of controversy, questioning and change. Conventional assumptions or truths, based on conventional values are breaking down.
>
> (Kraus 2007, 47)

If economics is to help provide workable solutions to the challenges of climate change, it must embrace and incorporate sustainability, which in turn requires the cooperation of multiple disciplines. In addition, doing so will help us effectuate and implement the following goals of higher education: interdisciplinary knowledge, inquiry, communication, problem solving and collaborations; democratic practices of equity, inclusion and community engagement; and thinking critically and solving meaningful problems.

Tacking on a chapter on sustainability at the end of the course as an extra, superfluous lecture does not work; rather the entire macroeconomics curriculum must be redesigned in order to comport with sustainability and its requirements. Economics must radically change, and by incorporating the 17 UN SDGs it will be forced to. In this chapter we have offered some suggestions at the macro principles level.

Notes

1 For a top-to-bottom discussion/evaluation/critique of pluralism, see Heise (2017). For an interesting roundtable discussion of pluralism in all its dimensions, see Roundtable Dialogue on Pluralism (2015).
2 For a helpful discussion, see Harris and Roach (2013).
3 A good pedagogical exercise to illustrate the interrelationships between economic growth and sustainability is Van den Berg's extension of the Solow model (2012) to include environmental effects.

References

Braungart, M. and McDonough, W. (2009): *Cradle to Cradle: Remaking the Way We Make Things*. London: Vintage Books.

Brundtland Commission (1987): *Report of the World Commission on Environment and Development: Our Common Future*, www.un-documents.net/wced-ocf.htm, accessed 1 May 2012.

Carlin, W. and Soskice, D. (2015): *Macroeconomics: Institutions, Instability, and the Financial System*. Oxford: Oxford University Press.

Creative Change: Educational Solutions (2013): *Educating for Sustainability: A Framework of Essential Knowledge, Skills and Dispositions*, www.creativechange.net, accessed 12 April 2017.

Diesing, P. (1982): *Science & Ideology in the Policy Sciences*. Hawthorne and New York: Aldine Publishing.

Fullbrook, E. (2010): "How to Bring Economics into the 3rd Millennium by 2020", *Real-World Economics Review* (54), 89–102, www.paecon.net/PAEReview/issue54/Fullbrook54.pdf, accessed 1 May 2012.

Gordon, R. (2012): *Macroeconomics*. Boston: Addison Wesley.

Green, T. (2012): "Introductory Economics Textbooks: What Do They Teach about Sustainability?", *International Journal of Pluralism and Economics Education* 3(2), 189–223.

Harris, J. and Roach, B. (2013): *Environmental and Natural Resource Economics: A Contemporary Approach*. Armonk, NY: M. E. Sharpe.

Heise, A. (2017): "Defining Economic Pluralism as an Ethical Norm or Scientific Imperative", *International Journal of Pluralism and Economics Education* 8(1), 18–41.

Hill, R. and Myatt, T. (2010): *The Economics Anti-Textbook: A Critical Thinker's Guide to Microeconomics*. London: Zed Books.

Hodgson, G. (1999): *Evolution and Institutions*. Cheltenham, UK: Edward Elgar.

Jackson, T. (2011): *Prosperity without Growth: Economics for a Finite Planet*. London: Earthscan.

Jahnke, M. and Nutzinger, H. G. (2003): "Sustainability? A Theoretical Idea or a Practical Recipe?", *Poiesis and Praxis* 1(4), 275–294.

Keen, S. (2011): *Debunking Economics: The Naked Emperor Dethroned?* London: Zed Books.

Keynes, J. M. (1923): *A Tract on Monetary Reform*. London: Palgrave Macmillan.

Kraus, E. (2007): *The Blockage: Rethinking Organizational Principles for the 21st Century*. Baltimore, MD: American Literary Press.

Mankiw, N. G. (2018): *Principles of Economics*. Stamford, CT: Cengage Learning.

Marshall, A. (1946 [1890]): *Principles of Economics*. London: Palgrave Macmillan.

McNeil, J. R. (2000): *An Environmental History of the Twentieth-Century World-Something New Under the Sun*. New York: Norton.

Nelson, J. (2009): "The Principles Course", in Reardon, J. (ed.): *The Handbook for Pluralist Economics Education*. London: Routledge.

The New York Times (2015): "Teaching the Truth about Climate Change", Editorial, 11 October, 8.

Pearce, D. (1978): "The Feminization of Poverty: Women, Work, and Welfare", *Urban and Social Change Review, Special Issue: Women and Work* 11(1–2), 28–36.

Robinson, J. (1980): *What Are the Questions?* Armonk, NY: M. E. Sharpe.

Roundtable Dialogue on Pluralism (2015): *International Journal of Pluralism and Economics Education* 6(3), 272–308.

Sen, A. (2009): *The Idea of Justice*. London: Allen Lane.

Söderbaum, P. (2008): *Understanding Sustainability Economics: Towards Pluralism in Economics*. London: Earthscan.

Van den Berg, H. (2012): "Explaining Neoclassical Economists Pro-Growth Agenda: Does the Popular Solow Model Bias Economic Growth?", *International Journal of Pluralism and Economics Education* 3(1), 40–62.

Wheatley, M. (1999): *Leadership and the New Science: Discovering Order in a Chaotic World*. San Francisco: Berrett-Koehler.

11 Demand-driven ecological collapse

A stock-flow fund-service model of money, energy and ecological scale

Jonathan Barth and Oliver Richters

1 Introduction

One of the key issues faced by modern society is navigating the transformation towards a sustainable economy that respects 'planetary boundaries' (Rockström et al. 2009). However, most models in the line of neoclassical theory taught to students worldwide are neglecting environmental and physical variables. In addition, most general equilibrium models abstract from the monetary stocks and flows and base their reasoning on 'real' economic variables and exchange. The word 'real' does in no way mean that 'physical' variables such as energy or material flows are treated. This chapter highlights possible links between ecological and post-Keynesian economics and develops a simple toy model that can serve as a foundation for studying interrelations between the monetary economy and the physical environment. Its economy is modeled in discrete time using a balance sheet approach, and production is demand-driven. The source of production is the ecosystem that is affected by economic 'harvest,' and economic degradation can generate restrictions on supply. Both the monetary and physical economy are modeled in a stock-flow consistent way.

The chapter is structured as follows: in the next section, we give a short overview about the theoretical background. We outline important aspects of post-Keynesian monetary theory and ecological economics considering a possible synthesis. In section 3, we provide a comprehensive description of what we call the monetary-physical stock-flow fund-service model. First simulation results provide a first intuition of the model behavior. A stability analysis gives general insights into the parameter dependence of different model outcomes. The chapter ends with final remarks.

2 Theoretical background

2.1 Monetary theory of production

Most neoclassical theories tend to assume that money is neutral in the long term, a mere numeraire or means of exchange, without significant differences from circulating commodities. It improves efficiency of barter but plays a rather passive role in the economic process. Therefore, the impact of monetary issues on long-run economic processes such as economic growth or environmental issues is considered negligible. Those emphasizing the need for a monetary theory of production reject this assumption. One effort to explicitly represent the dynamics of debt, finance and other monetary factors has been the balance sheet approach (see the chapter by Dirk Ehnts in this volume), which tracks assets and liabilities and their interdependence in the economy. The central importance of attention to financial detail was illustrated by the failure of the macroeconomics profession to anticipate the 2007–2008 global financial crisis, which was predicted nearly exclusively by those who deployed implicit or explicit macro-accounting frameworks (Galbraith 2009; Bezemer 2010; Koo 2011).

In recent years, models based on these accounting relationships and a coherent study of monetary stocks and flows were advanced particularly by post-Keynesian authors using the term 'stock-flow consistent models' (SFC); see Godley and Lavoie (2012). This strand of theory argues with reference to Keynes (1936) that production adapts to demand. Keynesian macroeconomic theory places great emphasis on the determination of a level of effective demand commensurate with key economic policy goals, but the ecological implications of those economic policy goals have often been neglected (Berg et al. 2015).

2.2 Ecological economics

Ecological economists have criticized approaches such as SFC models on grounds that they focus on the circular flow of exchange value (i.e. money) rather than on the physical throughput of natural resources from which all goods and services are ultimately derived (Georgescu-Roegen 1971; Daly 1985). Sustainable economic activity that 'meets the needs of the present without compromising the ability of future generations to meet their own needs' (WCED 1987) has to stay within an environmentally sustainable scale: the ecosystem has to absorb waste and recycle the inputs which are required for physical production (Daly 1992). As capital is highly dependent on energy usage, the regeneration rate and the availability of renewable energy resources are the final constraints to the production process (Dale et al. 2012). However, the importance of energy and natural resources for economic production is systematically underestimated in many economic theories (Kümmel 2011). Thus, analyzing the physical and environmental sustainability requires studying the interdependencies between the ecosystem and the economy. Georgescu-Roegen (1971) has emphasized that models need to track the physical funds and flows of physical variables such as energy explicitly. Within ecological economics, monetary questions are studied only recently (Berg et al. 2015; Dafermos et al. 2017).

2.3 Common ground: ecological macroeconomics

From a philosophy of science perspective, synthesis of different economic paradigms seems possible, if these share similar ontological and methodological approaches (Dobusch and Kapeller 2012). Several authors have explicitly argued that post-Keynesian economics and ecological economics share substantial common ground and are ripe for a synthesis. Ontological similarities have been recognized in terms of consumption, production theory, cumulative causation (path dependency), uncertainty as opposed to computable probability, and the irreversibility of historical time (Gowdy 1991; Lavoie 2006; Holt et al. 2009; Kronenberg 2010). Post-Keynesians argue that this uncertainty and instability is inherent in economic processes, while ecological economists locate the reason within environmental risks. Therefore, intertemporal optimization with unlimited time horizon and rational expectations about the future seems unrealistic. Ecological economists arguing that consumption is a central driver of economic growth also seem to agree with the Keynesian argument that effective demand matters.

From a methodological point of view, there are similarities in looking at the world as composed of a complex system of stocks and flows, ecological economists mostly from a physical perspective and post-Keynesian authors from a monetary perspective. This lends itself to economic modeling and is therefore suitable for bridging the gap between ecological and post-Keynesian models. Models that integrate monetary and ecological issues may be helpful to study pressing problems such as climate change, which are neither purely economic, nor purely environmental, nor purely physical, but rather are all of the above. The recent development of 'ecological macroeconomics' has developed exploiting these similarities (Berg et al. 2015; Rezai and Stagl 2016), for example for studying the stability of a non-growing economy (Richters and Siemoneit 2017).

The only approach known to us to integrate the physical framework by Georgescu-Roegen and the monetary stock-flow consistent framework is Dafermos et al. (2017). Different to their very complex and interdependent model, we offer a simple toy model that may help to understand and combine the two paradigms. The model treats physical and monetary stocks and flows explicitly and is coupled to a minimal environmental model.

2.4 The stock-flow fund-service approach

Before we get to the description of the model, we want to outline the idea of the stock-flow fund-service approach (SFFS), which provides a common framework for model development.

Stocks represent an amount of energy, matter or money at a point of time given in joules (J), kilograms (kg) or euros (€), whereas flows represent a stream of matter, energy or money from one stock to another in a certain period of time, given or J/s, kg/s or €/s. The distinctive feature is that stocks can be instantaneously consumed or transferred as a whole (Georgescu-Roegen 1971). This concept is also used in post-Keynesian SFC models, where the balance sheets include the financial stocks and the transaction matrix the financial flows from one sector to another (Godley and Lavoie 2012), which we will describe below.

Besides the stock-flow approach, it is useful to introduce another concept, as proposed by Georgescu-Roegen (1971, 224 ff.) – the fund-service approach, which is not included in the post-Keynesian theory. A fund represents the counterpart to stock-flows. They cannot be instantaneously consumed, such as the service of the worker to assemble a good (Georgescu-Roegen 1971, 226) or the sun to provide high-energetic radiation. One square meter of land only receives a certain maximum amount of 'radiation service' at any moment in time. Therefore, the amount of funds includes the time dimension (*service time*), whereas the service is without a time dimension. Note that this is the other way around for stocks and flows.[1]

Stocks and funds are qualitatively different. So, one cannot be replaced by the other. If one needs a flow as energy (e.g. for production), one can have as much capital as she wants. If there is no energy left for consumption, there is no possibility to substitute it with something else. This is reflected in the concept of strong sustainability (Ott and Döring 2008), as counterpart to the weak formulation, which is mostly used by environmental economists such as Perman (2011). Its underlying assumption of perfect substitutability is criticized by ecological and post-Keynesian economists alike (Kronenberg 2010).

3 Description of the monetary-physical stock-flow fund-service model

In the following, we describe the SFFS model for a one-good economy which includes physical services as well as energy and monetary flows. The model represents a dynamical system in discrete time. Both monetary and physical flows are equally represented. Its monetary representation is based on the model The simplest model with government money (SIM) of Godley and Lavoie (2012), whereas money is replaced by government bills and interest payments are included in addition.[2]

For a better understanding, we differentiate physical flows with upper index p from monetary flows without an upper index. The former is measured in joules (J) per time step as measure for energy, the latter in € per time step as measure for money. The monetary flows are described in Table 11.1 and physical flows and

Table 11.1 Monetary transaction-flows matrix

Monetary transaction matrix				
	Households	*Production*	*Government*	Σ
Consumption	$-C$	$+C$		0
Government exp.	$+G$		$-G$	0
Wages	$+Y$	$-Y$		0
Taxes	$-T$		$+T$	0
Interest Payments	$+rM_{t-1}$		$-rM_{t-1}$	0
Change in bills	$-\Delta M_h$		$+\Delta M_g$	0
Σ	0	0	0	0

services in Table 11.2, while both are represented in Figure 11.1. In the tables, the direction of the flows is indicated by the signs. Positive values are uses of the stock and represent outflows, while negative values are sources and represent inflows accordingly. Time is indicated by the index t, whereas $t(t-1)$ indicates the stock-flow at the end of the current (previous) period. In the diagram, the different sectors described by their balance sheets are connected by monetary flows depicted with solid arrows. Flows of physical goods are dashed, while the transfer of energy is indicated by broad, filled arrows.

Table 11.2 Physical transaction flow-service matrix

	Households	*Production*	*Biomass Low entropy*	*Heat on Earth High entropy*	*Space*	Σ
Flows						
Household consumption	$-C^p$			$+H^p_{he}$		0
Product transfer	$+Y^p_{ph}$	$-Y^p_{ph}$				0
Energy consumption		$-Y^p_{pp}$		$+H^p_{pe}$		0
Harvest		$+E^p$	$-E^p$			0
Dissipation				$-H^p_{es}$	$+H^p_s$	0
Services						
Change in stock of Energy			$-\Delta S$ (biomass)	$-\Delta H^p_e$	$-\Delta H^p_s$	0
Radiation and absorption			$+R^p_{sb}$	$+H^p_{se}$	$-R^p_s$	0
Σ	0	0	0	0	0	0

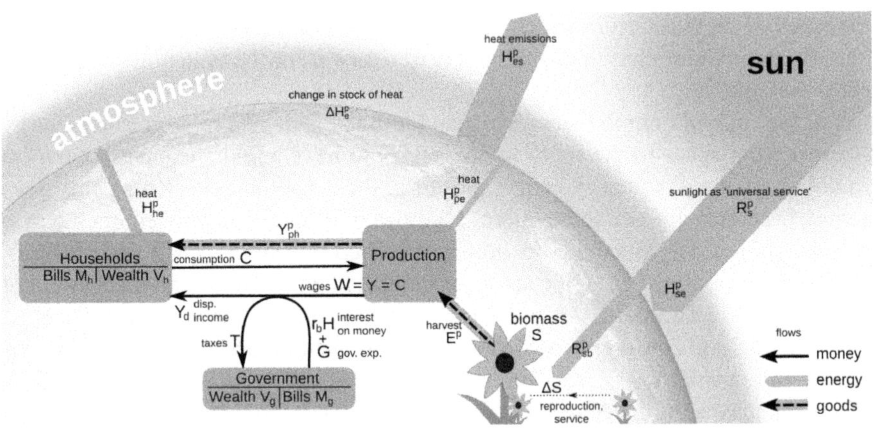

Figure 11.1 Monetary stocks-flows and physical funds-services of the model

The economy consists of households, one production sector and one government sector.[3] Consumption expenditures C flow from households to the production sector. In this sector, products are produced and the incoming monetary flows from consumption are fully paid as wages Y to the households.[4] For simplicity, government engages workers directly for governmental duties.

Besides of consumption, households use their income from wages, government expenditures and interest on government bills for paying taxes T to the government. All remaining income is accumulated as government bills, ΔM_h.[5] Accordingly, the government receives taxes, pays interest on government bills and expenditures to workers, and the amount of bills issued by the government increases by ΔM_g.

The system is closed 'in the sense that everything comes from somewhere and everything goes somewhere'; with this framework 'there are no black holes' (Godley and Lavoie 2012, 38). Also, the balance sheet (the stocks) as provided in Figure 11.1 cancel out, as the bills held by households M_h must always be equal to the bills issued by the government M_g.

The monetary economy is embedded into an ecological system, as shown in Table 11.2. The interaction between environment and economy occurs by harvesting biomass to provide low-entropy energy (exergy) input for the production of the economy E^p. Within the production sector, this biomass is transformed into an energy good, such as oil. The biomass can be thought of as sunflowers, corn, or similar plants which are suitable for transformation into energy inputs for production and for consumption likewise and are renewable.

The good created is used for production itself Y^p_{pp} or transferred to the household Y^p_{ph}. There, it is finally consumed (C^p) and ends up as heat (anergy) on planet Earth H^p_{pe}. The same is true for the consumption within the production process H^p_{pe}. It becomes obvious that the economic subsystem is fully dependent on harvest, without which no production is possible. However, the reproduction of biomass ΔS is an environmental service and not a flow and therefore does not happen instantaneously but needs time, as shown in section 3.2. The service increases the stock of biomass, from which harvest is subtracted. Consequently, the rate of harvest at maximum has to equal the rate of renewal for the system to be ecologically sustainable.

For the sake of completeness, we also included low- and high-entropy energy streams from space to the Earth in Table 11.2 to have a realistic energy balance. In doing so, the physical system is closed in the sense that everything that goes somewhere comes from somewhere. A constant inflow of exergy enters the system as sunlight ($\boldsymbol{R^p_s}$), some parts are transformed to biomass ($\boldsymbol{R^p_{sp}}$) and changes, together with harvest ($\boldsymbol{E^p}$), the stock of biomass ($\boldsymbol{\Delta S}$). The radiation that is not metabolized is dissipated on the Earth's surface and in the atmosphere ($\boldsymbol{H^p_{se}}$). Harvest ($\boldsymbol{E^p}$) and consumption of biomass by households and firms turn the stored energy into anergy ($\boldsymbol{H^p_{pe}}, \boldsymbol{H^p_{he}}$) and reduce the stock of biomass. A constant flow of anergy leaves the Earth as radiation to space ($\boldsymbol{H^p_{es}}$). To determine the distribution of energy changes to space and Earth ($\Delta \mathbf{H^p_e}, \Delta \mathbf{H^p_s}$), a climate model would be needed.

One can easily see the irreversibility of the energy consumption process here. As Georgescu-Roegen (1971, 281) puts it:

> [The economic process] is not circular, but unidirectional. As far as this facet alone is concerned, the economic process consists of a continuous transformation of low entropy into high entropy, that is, into irrevocable waste or, with topical term, into pollution.

Pollution, also referred as heat emissions or anergy, can neither be used for the reproduction of biomass nor the production process. Rather, all exergy consumed finally ends up as heat in on Earth. For climate models, these anthropogenic heat emissions are estimated to be about 0.0025 Wm^{-2} (Stocker et al. 2013, 14). Besides of the ecological constraints given by the reproduction of biomass, we face another hidden constraint here. If the amount of heat emissions increases to exceed 3.10^{14} W, the economy crosses the so-called heat barrier (Buttlar 1975), where global climate changes will occur even without the anthropogenic greenhouse effect (Kümmel 2011, 179). This could be included using, for example, a simple climate model as provided in Berg et al. (2015).

For the sake of simplicity, we will refer to the left-hand part of Table 11.2 (framed in black) in the remainder of this chapter and leave the rest open for further research. In the following, we will describe the balance equations and the behavior of the system.

3.1 Monetary behavioral equations

The model is consumption-driven, meaning that the level of consumption of households C_t determines the level of production $Y_{ph,t}$:

$$Y_{ph,t} = C_t. \tag{11.1}$$

To simplify the model, we assume that government expenditures $G_t = G$ are constant over time and go directly to the households. All earnings by the production sector C_t are paid to households as wages. Capital is not included in the model.

In addition to wages, households receive income by interest payments with interest rate r on bills M_t from the government sector. r is assumed to be exogenously given and constant. Taxes with rate θ are paid on income, so disposable income $Y_{D,t}$ and taxes T_t are given by

$$Y_{D,t} = (1-\theta)(C_t + G_t + rM_t), \tag{11.2}$$

$$T_t = \theta(C_t + G_t + rM_t). \tag{11.3}$$

The discrete equation of motion for the stock of bills (M_h and M_g, that are identical) is given by

$$M_t = M_{t-1} + Y_{D,t} - C_t. \tag{11.4}$$

Bills of the previous period M_{t-1} are increased by disposable income less realized consumption C_t. Note that households have a consumption target C_t^T, which is different from realized consumption C_t. It is determined by the propensity to consume out of disposable income of the last period (the first term) and out of wealth (the second term):[6]

$$C_t^T = c_y(1-\theta)(C_{t-1} + G_{t-1} + rM_{t-1}) + c_M M_{t-1}. \tag{11.5}$$

We differentiate between targeted and realized consumption C_t because targeted consumption may be decreased due to ecological constraints, which will be the focus of the physical equations (see Equation [11.11]). For targeted production, it follows that

$$Y_{ph,t}^T = C_t^T. \tag{11.6}$$

3.2 Physical flow equations

Before producers can produce anything, there must be a stock of biomass. We differ here from Heyes (2000) and Lawn (2003) and assume that biomass is not growing exponentially if undisturbed, but as logistic growth. These growth functions are very common in environmental modeling (Wainwright and Mulligan 2013).

$$S_t = S_{t-1} + S_{t-1}a\left(1 - \frac{S_{t-1}}{S_{max}}\right) - E_t \text{ with } 0 < a < 2.6. \tag{11.7}$$

The growth function can be thought of as an *S*-curve, whereas the stock is limited to S_{max}. Only for small S_{t-1}, the stock of the next period S_t increases exponentially, for $S_{t-1} = \frac{1}{2}S_{max}$ absolute growth is maximum with $\Delta S = \frac{1}{4}aS_{max}$ to decline as S_{t-1} approaches S_{max}, as shown in Figure 11.2. Thus the relation between the radiation turned into biomass $R_{sb}^p = S_{t-1}a\left(1 - \frac{S_{t-1}}{S_{max}}\right)$ and the dissipation to heat on Earth H_{se}^p is altered depending on the biomass already available: in the desert, all radiation is turned to heat, as no radiation is transformed into biomass. The maximum absolute growth corresponds to the optimal use of radiation input, thus $\frac{1}{4}aS_{max} = \mu R_s^p$ with $\mu < 1$ because of sunlight reflection and efficiency of photosynthesis.

Physical and monetary flows are linked by the fixed parameter price $p \in \frac{€}{J}$ to physical flows.

$$C_t = p \cdot C_t^p;\ C_t^T = p \cdot C_t^{T,p};\ Y_{ph,t}^T = p \cdot Y_{ph,t}^{T,p} \tag{11.8}$$

Price adaptations play a crucial role in many dynamic models. Nevertheless, we chose to treat prices as constant parameters in our model to avoid a detailed discussion of the strategic determination of prices and the conception of the firm in post-Keynesian theory, and because the added dimension would have made the stringent stability analysis less comprehensible. The inclusion of price adaptation may significantly alter the results.

Total targeted production is determined by consumption and resulting own energy requirements of the production sector $Y^{p}_{pp,t}$. We assume the requirements of energy being proportional to production with $0 < \epsilon < 1$:

$$Y_t^{T,p} = Y^{p}_{pp,t} + Y^{T,p}_{ph,t} = (1+\epsilon)C_t^{T,p}. \tag{11.9}$$

The stock of biomass is decreased by harvest E_t in kg, which satisfies the need for biomass of production for total production Y_t^p. To account for different units, $\gamma\left[\frac{kg}{J}\right]$ is introduced to transfer the stock of biomass, given in kg, to energy units:

$$E_t = \gamma Y_t^p. \tag{11.10}$$

To include the ecological limits on harvest which are given by the stock of biomass S_t at period t, the following equation constrains total targeted harvest $E_t^T = Y_t^{T,p}$ including energy requirements by the production sector to realized production E_t^p:

$$E_t = \frac{E_t^T}{1 + E_t^T / S_{t-1}} = \frac{\gamma(1+\epsilon)C_t^T}{p\left(1+\gamma(1+\epsilon)C_t^T/(p\cdot S_{t-1})\right)}. \tag{11.11}$$

The rationale behind Equation (11.11) is that if harvest is small compared to the stock of biomass (as is for example the case for forestry in most countries), the

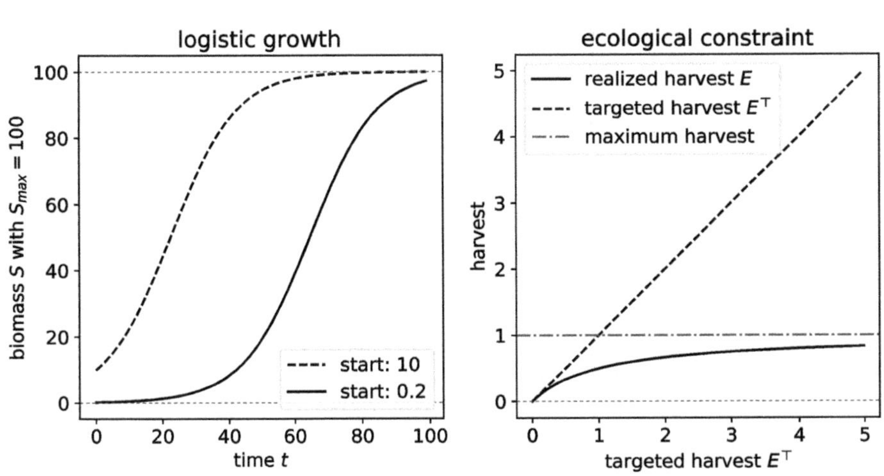

Figure 11.2 Example of logistic growth for different initial values and maximum growth rate a = 0.1 (left) and constrained production (right) following Equation (11.11) with $S(t-1) = 1$

realized harvest is close to identical to the desired one, to demand. On the other hand, if targeted harvest is very high, the dynamical system has to guarantee that the harvest does not exceed the available stock, which would be impossible. This equation is an example how such a 'smooth rationing' in the case of ecological scarcity can be implemented. Compared to a piecewise linear function, it avoids discontinuities which would make the stability analysis much more challenging. It follows that the realized physical consumption of households is given by:

$$C_t^P = \frac{Y_t^P}{1+\epsilon}. \tag{11.12}$$

3.3 System of equations

Accordingly, we can derive the equations that determine the behavior of the system. To simplify the notation, we use the relation $\gamma_\epsilon = (1+\epsilon)\gamma$ and $Y_t^P = \frac{Y_{t,\epsilon}^P}{1+\epsilon}$. Y_t^P differs from $Y_{t,\epsilon}^P$ by not including internal energy consumption of production. The three equations are:

$$Y_t^P = \frac{C_t^T}{p + \gamma_\epsilon C_t^T / S_{t-1}}, \tag{11.13}$$

$$S_t = S_{t-1} + S_{t-1} a \left(1 - \frac{S_{t-1}}{S_{max}}\right) - \gamma_\varepsilon Y_t^P \text{ with } 0 < a < 2.6, \tag{11.14}$$

$$M_t = M_{t-1} + (1-\theta)(G_0 + rM_{t-1}) - \theta Y_t^P p, \tag{11.15}$$

with

$$C_t^T = c_y (1-\theta)\left(pY_{t-1}^P + G_0 + rM_{t-1}\right) + c_M M_{t-1}, \tag{11.16}$$

$$Y_{t,\epsilon}^P = Y_t^P (1+\epsilon). \tag{11.17}$$

It is a three-dimensional system dependent on M_t, Y_t^P and S_t that determines the behavior of the system. Equations (11.16) and (11.17) are only substitutes for the values of C_t^T and $Y_{t,\epsilon}^P$, so the system remains three-dimensional. For the simulation, one has to know the initial values of Y_0^P, M_0 and S_0. With these initial conditions, we can calculate C_t^T according to Equation (11.16) by using values known from the previous period C_{t-1} and M_{t-1}. The result is substituted into Y_t^P from Equation (11.13) which goes into S_t via Equation (11.14) and M_t via Equation (11.15). This procedure is repeated for as many time steps as preferred.

4 Simulation results of the model

To give a first intuition of the model behavior, we obtained simulation results for the model with Python. From these, we can derive three different kinds of model behavior, represented in Figure 11.3. The left graph shows an ecologically and

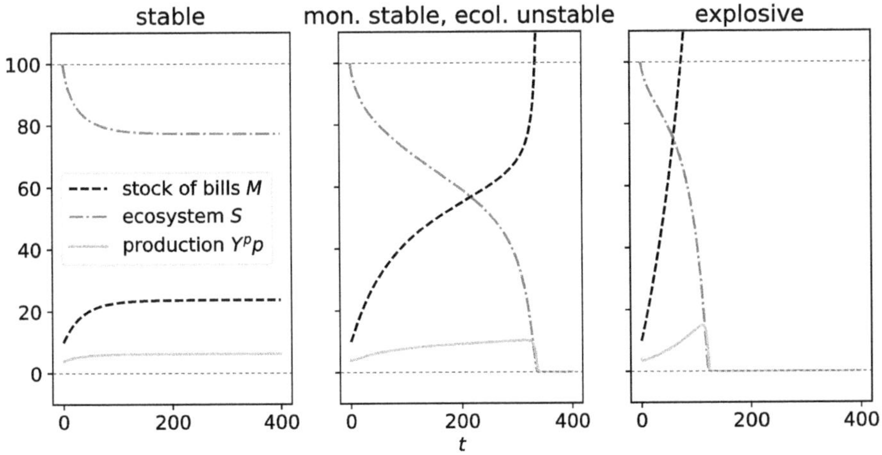

Figure 11.3 Time evolution of the system for different propensities to consume out of wealth. Parameters $\theta = 0.5, c_y = 0.8, a = 0.1, p = 4, \gamma = 1.1, S_{\max} = 100, G = 4, r = 0.1$ and initial values $S_0 = 100$, $Y_0^P = 1, Y_0 = pY_0^P = 4, M_0 = 10$. Left graph: monetarily and ecologically stable system with $c_m = 0.06$. Center: monetarily stable, but ecologically unstable economy with $c_m = 0.04$. Right graph: monetarily and ecologically unstable 'explosive' system with $c_m = 0.01$.

monetarily stable system that converges towards a stationary state for *M*, *S* and *Y*. In this case, economically driven harvest and ecologically driven reproduction are equal, leading to an ecological stability. Furthermore, the system is monetarily stable, due to high levels of consumption out of wealth compared to the interest rate. We will give a detailed explanation of this behavior in section 5. In the middle graph, the system tends to a monetarily stable stationary state, indicated by the concave shape of *M* and *Y*. However, as one can see from the monotonically declining course of *S*, the ecological system is continuously overused leading to an ecological collapse at $t = 360$, causing an immediate economic collapse. However, since the government continues to pay interests on bills, the monetary stock continuously increases. A more drastic result is obtained in the 'explosive' right graph of Figure 11.3. Due to high interest rates compared to consumption out of wealth, the system is monetarily unstable and grows out of bound, indicated by the convex shape of *M*. As the economy cannot grow forever due to ecological constraints, it collapses at $t = 150$ – just like in the middle graph – because it continuously overuses the ecology. Note that in this scenario, the government debt to gross domestic product (GDP) ratio increases unlimitedly even before the ecological collapse – thus we don't see stable growth but rather a debt spiral where the consumptive government expenditures become negligible compared to debt services, not indicating economic stability. Furthermore, the model abstracts from expectations that might cause negative output effects due to high debt to GDP ratios.

5 Stability analysis of the model

To analyze the model, explain the differences pictured in Figure 11.3 and derive more insights in its general behavior, we conducted a stability analysis of the three-dimensional system.[7] For the calculation of fixed points, where no change in either variable occurs, we must state that

$$S_t = S_{t-1};\; M_t = M_{t-1};\; Y_t^p = Y_{t-1}^p. \tag{11.18}$$

In doing so, we can derive the coordinates of the fixed points (see Appendix C). The stationary state for the biomass stock S^* is the closed form solution of the cubic equation

$$\frac{a}{\gamma_\epsilon} S^* \left(1 - \frac{S^*}{S_{max}}\right) \underbrace{\left(\frac{1}{1 - a\left(1 - \frac{S^*}{S_{max}}\right)} - c_y - \frac{c_m \theta}{(1-\theta) r} \right)}_{F(S)} = \frac{-c_m}{rp} G. \tag{11.19}$$

Reasonable results can be obtained for $S^* \in [0, S_{max}]$, whereby the equation is solvable for $r \neq 0;\ \theta \neq 1;\ p \neq 0;\ a \neq 1;\ \gamma_\varepsilon \neq 0$.

Knowing S^*, we can calculate the stationary states of production Y^{p*} and the stock of bills M^* with

$$Y^{p*} = \frac{a}{\gamma_\varepsilon} S^* \left(1 - \frac{S^*}{S_{max}}\right), \tag{11.20}$$

$$M^* = \frac{\theta p Y^{p*} - (1-\theta) G}{1 - \theta r}. \tag{11.21}$$

From Equations (11.19) to (11.21) we can conclude, that the number of fixed points depends solely on the number of solutions for Equation (11.19). Since by definition $S^* \in [0, S_{max}]$, we can state further that no solution exists and accordingly, there will be no stationary state within this domain, if $F(S^*) > 0$. In this case, the stock of biomass $S^* < 0$ or $S^* > S_{max}$. We can interpret this result as a global instability, which leads to over-depletion of the biomass stock and consequently to the collapse of the ecological system. As shown in Appendix B, $F(S^*) > 0$ for any $S^* \in [0, S_{max}]$ if

$$c_r = \frac{c_m}{r} < \frac{(1 - c_y)(1 - \theta)}{\theta}. \tag{11.22}$$

This result is equal to the relation derived for the SIM model of Godley and Lavoie (2012) by Richters and Siemoneit (2017). However, in contrast to this paper, they do not consider ecological variables. Note that this relation is independent of the biomass growth rate a. Therefore, it can be interpreted as the *monetary stability condition*. If Equation (11.22) is fulfilled, consumption and production will increase unboundedly, which necessarily leads to an ecological collapse at some point in time in our model, even for very high ecological regeneration. However, it is possible to have positive interest rates within a monetarily stable economy. In this case, positive interest rates have a positive effect on the stock of government bills of the economy, as they determine the speed of the accumulation of bills. If the dampening effect by consumption out of wealth c_m is high compared to the interest rate r, the economy becomes stable (compare Figure 11.1).

To analyze the conditions for stability dependent on changes on certain parameters, as for example the ratio c_y of c_m and r, we can convert Equation (11.19) to an implicit function as follows:

$$K\left(S^*,c_r\right)=\frac{a}{\gamma_\epsilon}S^*\left(1-\frac{S^*}{S_{max}}\right)\left(\frac{1}{1-a\left(1-\frac{S^*}{S_{max}}\right)}-c_y-\frac{c_r\theta}{(1-\theta)}\right)+\frac{c_r}{p}G=0. \quad (11.23)$$

We can now picture the solutions for Equation (11.19) for different values of c_y by plotting the implicit function of Equation (11.47), as shown in the bifurcation diagram in Figure 11.4.

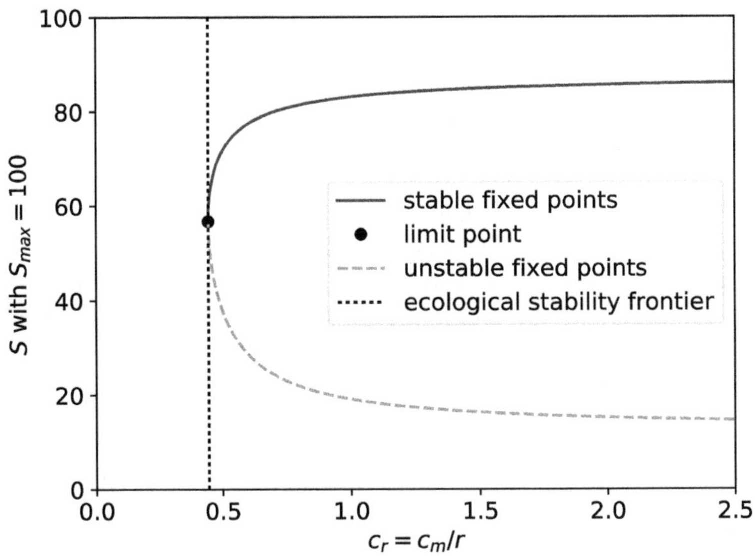

Figure 11.4 Bifurcation diagram for the stationary state of the biomass stock S and the consumption out of wealth – interest rate ratio c_r. Parameter values: $\theta = 0.5$, $c_y = 0.8$, $a = 0.1$, $G/p = 1$, $\gamma_\epsilon = 1.1$, $S_{max} = 100$.

On the x-axis, we see $c_r = \frac{c_m}{r}$ and on the y-axis the solutions S^*, which are the fixed points for any value of c_r with $\theta, a, p, G, \gamma_\epsilon, S_{max}$ and c_y as fixed parameters. For $c_y < 0.44$, no fixed point exists and the system becomes unstable. We can calculate this value by solving Equation (11.47) for $c_r = H\left(S^*\right)$ (see Appendix B) and deriving the minimum value for c_r from $H'\left(S^*\right) = \frac{dH\left(S^*\right)}{dS^*} = 0$ in the domain $S^* \in \left[0, S_{max}\right]$. In general, we can derive the ecological stability condition

$$\nexists S^* \in \left[0, S_{max}\right] \; if \; c_r < min\left(H\left(S^*_{min}\right)\right). \tag{11.24}$$

For $c_r > 0.44$, the lower fixed point is unstable. Consequently, if the initial value for S_0 is below the bottom line in Figure 11.4, the system will not converge towards the stable fixed point, but collapse. If the initial condition is above the bottom line, the system will converge towards the stable fixed point (blue line). Another way to obtain these conditions is by solving the Jacobian matrix at a fixed point S^*, which is derived and presented in Appendix C, and calculating the eigenvalues of the matrix. For $c_r = 1$, the eigenvalues are derived for the fixed point below the limit point ($S^*_L = 19.1$) in Figure 11.4, and for the fixed point above the limit point ($S^*_H = 83.1$):

$$\lambda_{S^*_L} = \left(0.37 \quad 0.95 \quad 1.06\right), \lambda_{S^*_H} = \left(0.43 \quad 0.93 \quad 0.94\right).$$

Since one of the eigenvalues of S^*_L is greater than 1, this fixed point is unstable. For S^*_H all eigenvalues are less than 1, consequently this fixed point is stable and the system will converge to it.

From the conditions in Equation (11.22) and (11.24), we can now plot a stability diagram (Figure 11.5), which shows the existence of stationary states at different values of c_m and r.

This result adds further insights to the results derived by Richters and Siemoneit (2017) by adding an ecological dimension. If the ratio of c_m and r is above (below) the monetary stability condition (dashed line), the system is monetarily stable (unstable). This is equivalent to the results of the middle and right graphs in Figure 11.3. Without ecological constraints, the stock of bills and the level of production would converge towards stationary states M and Y^p. However, if we add ecological constraints, the level of harvest associated with the production in the monetary stationary state might exceed what is regenerated by the biomass stock. Therefore, the system still collapses if the ratio of c_m and r is between the two stability frontiers. If the stationary state level of harvest is equal to what is regenerated by the ecology, the system reaches an ecologically and monetarily stable stationary state (see left graph of Figure 11.3). Consequently, if we assume that consumption out of wealth is exogenously given and below 0.44, which is the value for which instability may occur, interest rates must be low for the overall economy to be within ecological boundaries and work at a sustainable level of production.

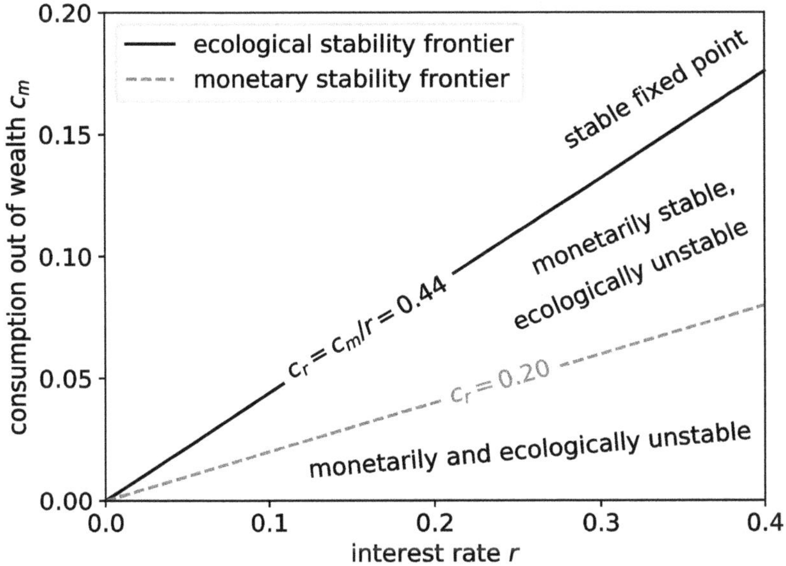

Figure 11.5 Stability diagram for the ecological stability condition and the monetary stability condition for different values of consumption out of wealth c_m and interest rates r with $\theta = 0.5$, $c_y = 0.8$, $a = 0.1$, $\gamma_\epsilon = 1.1$, $S_{max} = 100$, $G / p = 1$

6 Conclusion

Using a simple baseline model, this chapter examines the interactions of financial assets, real physical goods and services and the physical environment. It shows that post-Keynesian stock-flow consistent models can successfully be integrated with the study of physical stocks, flow and funds as suggested by Georgescu-Roegen. The model consistently integrates a demand-driven monetary economy with ecological constraints. Ecological scale introduces a non-linearity into the model, leading to rich dynamics. Depending on parameters such as interest rates or government expenditures, we can observe three different states of the model. The first state is a stable, non-growing economy compatible with ecological stability. In the second state, the economy approaches a monetary stationary state while constantly degrading its ecological environment, causing an ecological and economic collapse. In the third state, exponential accumulation of monetary assets through interest income leads to ever-increasing demand, ecological degradation and finally breakdown. One major factor driving these differences is the parameter ratio of consumption out of wealth and interest rate. If consumption out of wealth is low, low interest rates are needed for the model to converge towards a sustainable stationary state of production. The (relative) simplicity of the model makes it tractable and easier to analyze, while obviously neglecting several important aspects such as multiple goods, pricing, fixed capital, income distribution, complex financial assets or portfolio choice. Restricting our depiction to energy, even a treatment of physical mass, waste or carbon emissions is missing, as provided by Taylor et al. (2016) or Dafermos et al. (2017). The integration of these concepts can profit from a growing literature in post-Keynesian and ecological economics. Combining both approaches and integrating monetary and ecological issues may be helpful to determine the conditions under which a sustainable economy is possible, a problem that is neither purely economic, nor purely environmental, nor purely physical, but rather are all of the above.

Acknowledgments

Special thanks go to Ulrike Feudel, who contributed with her expertise in theoretical physics to a better understanding of the model dynamics. Furthermore, we thank the participants of the session on stock-flow consistent modeling at the Ecological Economics Conference 2017 for their constructive feedback.

Appendix

A. Derivation of stability conditions

We have the following system of equations:

$$Y_t^p = \frac{C_t^T}{p+\gamma_\varepsilon C_t^T / S_{t-1}} \Leftrightarrow Y_t^p = \left(\frac{p}{C_t^T} + \frac{\gamma_\varepsilon}{S_{t-1}}\right)^{-1}, \tag{11.25}$$

$$S_t = S_{t-1} + S_{t-1} a \left(1 - \frac{S_{t-1}}{S_{max}}\right) - \gamma_\varepsilon Y_t^p \text{ with } 0 < a < 2.6, \tag{11.26}$$

$$M_t = M_{t-1} + (1-\theta)(G + rM_{t-1}) - \theta Y_t^p p, \tag{11.27}$$

with

$$C_t^T = c_y (1-\theta)(p Y_{t-1}^p + G + rM_{t-1}) + c_M M_{t-1},$$
$$Y_{t,\epsilon}^p = Y_t^p (1+\epsilon). \tag{11.28}$$

With $M_t = M_{t-1} = M^*$ we can derive from (11.27)

$$M^* = \frac{\theta Y^{p^*} p - (1-\theta) G}{(1-\theta) r}. \tag{11.29}$$

Accordingly, we can derive from (11.26)

$$Y^{p^*} = \frac{a}{\gamma} S^* \left(1 - \frac{S^*}{S_{max}}\right) \Leftrightarrow \frac{\gamma_\epsilon}{S^*} = \frac{a}{Y^{p^*}} \left(1 - \frac{S^*}{S_{max}}\right). \tag{11.30}$$

From (11.25) we can derive

$$\frac{1}{Y^{p^*}} = \frac{p}{C^T} + \frac{\gamma_\epsilon}{S^*}. \tag{11.31}$$

Substitute (11.29) in (11.28) to obtain

$$C^T = Y^{p^*} p \left(c_y + \frac{c_m \theta}{(1-\theta) r}\right) - \frac{c_m}{r} G. \tag{11.32}$$

Substitute (11.30) and (11.32) in (11.31) and extract Y^* to obtain

$$Y^{p*}\left(\frac{1}{1-a\left(1-\frac{S^*}{S_{max}}\right)}-c_y-\frac{c_m\theta}{(1-\theta)r}\right)=-\frac{c_m}{rp}G,$$

$$\Leftrightarrow\frac{a}{\gamma_\epsilon}S^*\left(1-\frac{S^*}{S_{max}}\right)\left(\frac{1}{1-a\left(1-\frac{S^*}{S_{max}}\right)}-c_y-\frac{c_m\theta}{(1-\theta)r}\right)=-\frac{c_m}{rp}G. \quad (11.33)$$

B. Derivation of the global instability

The model is unstable for $F\left(S^*\right)=\frac{1}{1-a\left(1-\frac{S^*}{S_{max}}\right)}-c_y-\frac{c_m\theta}{(1-\theta)r}>0$ if $S^*\in\left[0,S_{max}\right]$.

With $c_r=\frac{c_m}{r}$ we can derive that this condition is fulfilled for

$$c_r<\left(\frac{1}{1-a\left(1-\frac{S^*}{S_{max}}\right)}-c_y\right)\frac{1-\theta}{\theta}.$$

Derive $\min\left(\left(\frac{1}{1-a\left(1-\frac{S^*}{S_{max}}\right)}-c_y\right)\frac{1-\theta}{\theta}\right)$ if $S^*\in\left[0,S_{max}\right]$ to obtain the minimum possible value of $\left(\frac{1}{1-a\left(1-\frac{S^*}{S_{max}}\right)}-c_y\right)\frac{1-\theta}{\theta}$. This is the case for $S^*=S_{max}$. After substitution we can state

$$\text{if } c_r\left\langle\frac{(1-c_y)(1-\theta)}{\theta}\Rightarrow F\left(S^*\right)\right\rangle 0\,\forall S\in\left[0,S_{max}\right]. \quad (11.34)$$

C. Derivation of the Jacobian

Deriving the partial derivatives of each variable of the system of equations given by Equations (11.25) to (11.27) and using the following condition for the stationary state value, we can derive the Jacobian matrix. For Y_t we know[8]

$$Y_t = \left(\frac{p}{C_t^T \left(Y_{t-1}, M_{t-1} \right)} + \frac{\gamma_\epsilon}{S_{t-1}} \right)^{-1}. \tag{11.35}$$

At the fixed point we know from Equations (11.30), (11.31) and (11.32):

$$\begin{aligned} \left(C^{T*} \right)^{-1} &= \left[c_y (1-\theta) \left(p Y^{p*} + G \right) + \left(c_m + c_y (1-\theta) r \right) M^* \right]^{-1} \\ &= \frac{1}{Y^{p*} p} \left(1 - a + a \frac{S^*}{S_{max}} \right), \end{aligned} \tag{11.36}$$

$$\frac{Y^{p*}}{S^*} = \frac{a}{\gamma_\epsilon} \left(1 - \frac{S^*}{S_{max}} \right). \tag{11.37}$$

Using these relations, we can simplify the partial derivatives at the fixed point dependent on S^*:

$$\frac{dY_t}{dY_{t-1}} = \left(Y^{p*} \right)^2 p^2 c_y (1-\theta) \left(C^T \right)^{-2} = c_y (1-\theta) \left(1 - a + a \frac{S^*}{S_{max}} \right)^2, \tag{11.38}$$

$$\begin{aligned} \frac{dY_t}{dM_{t-1}} &= \left(Y^{p*} \right)^2 p \left(c_m + c_y (1-\theta) r \right) \left(C^T \right)^{-2} \\ &= \frac{1}{p} \left(c_m + c_y (1-\theta) r \right) \left(1 - a + a \frac{S^*}{S_{max}} \right)^2, \end{aligned} \tag{11.39}$$

$$\frac{dY_t}{dS_{t-1}} = \gamma_\varepsilon \left(\frac{Y^{p*}}{S^*} \right)^2 = \frac{a^2}{\gamma_\varepsilon} \left(1 - \frac{S^*}{S_{max}} \right)^2, \tag{11.40}$$

$$\frac{dM_t}{dY_{t-1}} = -\theta p c_y (1-\theta) \left(1 - a + a \frac{S^*}{S_{max}} \right)^2, \tag{11.41}$$

$$\frac{dM_t}{dM_{t-1}} = \left(1 + (1-\theta) r \right) - \theta \left(c_m + c_y (1-\theta) r \right) \left(1 - a + a \frac{S^*}{S_{max}} \right)^2, \tag{11.42}$$

$$\frac{dM_t}{dS_{t-1}} = -\theta p \gamma_\varepsilon \left(\frac{Y^{p*}}{S^*} \right)^2 = -\theta p \frac{a^2}{\gamma_\varepsilon} \left(1 - \frac{S^*}{S_{max}} \right)^2, \tag{11.43}$$

$$\frac{dS_t}{dY_{t-1}} = -\gamma_\varepsilon c_y (1-\theta)\left(1-a+a\frac{S^*}{S_{max}}\right)^2, \tag{11.44}$$

$$\frac{dS_t}{dM_{t-1}} = -\frac{\gamma_\varepsilon}{p}\left(c_m + c_y(1-\theta)r\right)\left(1-a+a\frac{S^*}{S_{max}}\right)^2, \tag{11.45}$$

$$\frac{dS_t}{dS_{t-1}} = 1+a-2a\frac{S^*}{S_{max}} - \gamma_\varepsilon^2\left(\frac{Y^{P*}}{S^*}\right)^2 = 1+a-2a\frac{S^*}{S_{max}} - a^2\left(1-\frac{S^*}{S_{max}}\right)^2. \tag{11.46}$$

With $Z_A = \left(1-a+a\frac{S^*}{S_{max}}\right)^2$ *and* $Z_B = \left(1-\frac{S^*}{S_{max}}\right)^2$ this yields the Jacobian

$$J = \begin{pmatrix} c_y(1-\theta)Z_A & \frac{1}{p}\left(c_v + c_m(1-\theta)r\right)Z_A & \frac{1}{\gamma}a^2 Z_B \\ -\theta p c_y(1-\theta)Z_A & \left(1+(1-\theta)r\right) - \theta\left(c_v + c_m(1-\theta)r\right)Z_A & -\frac{\theta p}{\gamma}a^2 Z_B \\ -\gamma c_y(1-\theta)Z_A & -\frac{\gamma}{p}\left(c_v + c_y(1-\theta)r\right)Z_A & 1+a-2a\frac{S^*}{S_{max}} - aZ_B \end{pmatrix}. \tag{11.47}$$

D. Derivation of $c_r = H(S^*)$

We can convert (11.33) $< I >$) to

$$H(S^*) = c_r = \frac{a S^*\left(S_{max} - S^*\right)\left(\left(S_{max} - S^*\right)a c_y + S_{max}\left(1-c_y\right)\right)(1-\theta)p}{\left(\left(a\theta p S^*\left(S_{max} - S^*\right) + G\gamma(1-\theta)S_{max}\right)\right)\left(S_{max} - a\left(S_{max} - S^*\right)\right)}. \tag{11.48}$$

Notes

1 In the theory of monetary economics, the term fund is used in the label 'flow of funds.' However, this represents financial transfers. Note that the meaning used here differs from this definition.

2 Bills are a short-term debt obligation backed by the government with a maturity of less than one year, here: in one period. Scripts and a spreadsheet version of this model are available at www.oliver-richters.de/sfc-models/.

3 SFC model with various sectors, banks and different financial assets can be found in Godley and Lavoie (2012) or Berg et al. (2015).

4 For the sake of simplicity, we neglect the differentiation between profits and wages.

5 It is often noted that sign for the change in financial assets is counterintuitive, because the acquisition of government bills seems to be an incoming flow, resulting in a positive sign. However, this must be interpreted as households paying from the money they earn into their stock of government bills. Even if this is an action happening within the household it is a use of money, which consequently carries a negative sign (Godley and Lavoie 2012, S. 40).

6 Consumption out of interest payments is neglected to simplify the model.

7 For general information on stability analysis, see Argyris et al. (2015). An application to stock-flow consistent models is provided by Richters and Siemoneit (2017).

8 All variables used here are in joules per time step, except of M with is in € per time step. Therefore, we leave aside p in the upper index of the variables to simplify the variable names.

References

Argyris, J. H., Faust, G. and Haase, M. (2015): *An Exploration of Dynamical Systems and Chaos: Completely Revised and Enlarged Second Edition.* Berlin and Heidelberg: Springer Fachmedien.

Berg, M., Hartley, B. and Richters, O. (2015): "A Stock-Flow Consistent Input-Output Model with Applications to Energy Price Shocks, Interest Rates, and Heat Emissions", *New Journal of Physics* 17(1), 015011.

Bezemer, D. J. (2010): "Understanding Financial Crisis through Accounting Models", *Accounting, Organizations and Society* 35(7), 676–688.

Buttlar, H. V. (1975): "Umweltprobleme", *Physikalische Blätter* 31(4), 145–155.

Dafermos, Y., Nikolaidi, M. and Galanis, G. (2017): "A Stock-Flow-Fund Ecological Macroeconomic Model", *Ecological Economics* 131, 191–207.

Dale, M., Krumdieck, S. and Bodger, P. S. (2012): "Global Energy Modelling: A Biophysical Approach (GEMBA) Part 1: An Overview of Biophysical Economics", *Ecological Economics* 73, 152–157.

Daly, H. E. (1985): "The Circular Flow of Exchange Value and the Linear Throughput of Matter-Energy: A Case of Misplaced Concreteness", *Review of Social Economy* 43(3), 279–297.

Daly, H. E. (1992): "Allocation, Distribution, and Scale: Towards an Economics That Is Efficient, Just, and Sustainable", *Ecological Economics* 6(3), 185–193.

Dobusch, L. and Kapeller, J. (2012): "Heterodox United vs. Mainstream City? Sketching a Framework for Interested Pluralism in Economics", *Journal of Economic Issues* 46(4), 1035–1058.

Galbraith, J. K. (2009): "Who Are These Economists, Anyway?", *Thought & Action* Fall, 85–97.

Georgescu-Roegen, N. (1971): *The Entropy Law and the Economic Process.* Cambridge, MA: Harvard University Press.

Godley, W. and Lavoie, M. (2012): *Monetary Economics: An Integrated Approach to Credit, Money, Income, Production and Wealth.* New York: Palgrave Macmillan.

Gowdy, J. M. (1991): "Bioeconomics and Post Keynesian Economics: A Search for Common Ground", *Ecological Economics* 3(1), 77–87.

Heyes, A. (2000): "A Proposal for the Greening of Textbook Macro: 'IS-LM-EE'", *Ecological Economics* 32(1), 1–7.

Holt, R.P.F., Pressman, S. and Spash, C. (eds.) (2009): *Post Keynesian and Ecological Economics: Confronting Environmental Issues.* Cheltenham, UK: Edward Elgar.

Keynes, J. M. (1936): *The General Theory of Employment, Interest and Money.* New York: Harcourt.

Koo, R. (2011): "The World in Balance Sheet Recession: Causes, Cure, and Politics", *Real-World Economics Review* 58(12), 19–37.

Kronenberg, T. (2010): "Finding Common Ground between Ecological Economics and Post-Keynesian Economics", *Ecological Economics* 69(7), 1488–1494.

Kümmel, R. (2011): *The Second Law of Economics: Energy, Entropy, and the Origins of Wealth.* New York, Dordrecht, Heidelberg, and London: Springer Fachmedien.

Lavoie, M. (2006): "Do Heterodox Theories Have Anything in Common? A Post-Keynesian Point of View", *European Journal of Economics and Economic Policies: Intervention* 3(1), 87–112.

Lawn, P. A. (2003): "On Heyes' IS-LM-EE Proposal to Establish an Environmental Macroeconomics", *Environment and Development Economics* 8(1), 31–56.

Ott, K. and Döring, R. (2008): *Theorie und Praxis starker Nachhaltigkeit, Beiträge zur Theorie und Praxis starker Nachhaltigkeit*. Metropolis and Marburg: Metropolis.

Perman, R. (2011): *Natural Resource and Environmental Economics*. Harlow and Munich: Pearson Education Limited.

Rezai, A. and Stagl, S. (2016): "Ecological Macroeconomics: Introduction and Review", *Ecological Economics* 121, 181–185.

Richters, O. and Siemoneit, A. (2017): "Consistency and Stability Analysis of Models of a Monetary Growth Imperative", *Ecological Economics* 136, 114–125.

Rockström, J., Steffen, W., Noone, K., Persson, Å., Chapin, F. S., Lambin, E. F., Lenton, T. M., Scheffer, M., Folke, C., Schellnhuber, H. J., Nykvist, B., Wit, C. A. de, Hughes, T., van der Leeuw, S., Rodhe, H., Sörlin, S., Snyder, P. K., Costanza, R., Svedin, U., Falkenmark, M., Karlberg, L., Corell, R. W., Fabry, V. J., Hansen, J., Walker, B., Liverman, D., Richardson, K., Crutzen, P. and Foley, J. A. (2009): "A Safe Operating Space for Humanity", *Nature* 461, 472–475.

Stocker, T. F., Qin, D., Plattner, G. K., Tignor, M., Allen, S. K., Boschung, J., Nauels, A., Xia, Y., Bex, V. and Midgley, P. M. (eds.) (2013): *Climate Change 2013: The Physical Science Basis: Contribution of Working Group I to the Fifth Assessment Report of the Intergovernmental Panel on Climate Change*. Cambridge, UK: Cambridge University Press.

Taylor, L., Rezai, A. and Foley, D. K. (2016): "An Integrated Approach to Climate Change, Income Distribution, Employment, and Economic Growth", *Ecological Economics* 121, 196–205.

Wainwright, J. and Mulligan, M. (2013): *Environmental Modelling: Finding Simplicity in Complexity*. Chichester: Wiley-Blackwell.

WCED (1987): *Our Common Future*. Oxford and New York: Oxford University Press.

12 Teaching feminist economics through student-written diaries[1]

Genna R. Miller

1 Introduction

Feminist economists range in their views of what actually constitutes 'feminist economics' and what the exact definition is (Robeyns 2000). However, there is general agreement that feminist economics commonly involves efforts towards understanding and improving women's economic status and/or towards reducing the androcentric bias in the mainstream economics discipline (Ferber and Nelson 2003). Thus, the subject content of courses focusing on feminist economics is heterodox in nature and does not conform to the course material in mainstream economics. However, while feminist economics courses[2] may introduce different material to students, a variety of pedagogies are also required for teaching students in a more inclusive manner commensurate with the subject of feminist economics. In particular, this chapter argues that student-written diaries are an especially appropriate and meaningful pedagogical tool for teaching feminist economics.

The chapter begins with a background on feminist economics and the types of subjects covered in courses devoted to a feminist economics perspective. Pedagogical practices related to teaching feminist economics are then discussed. An argument is then made for the use of student-written diaries and journals as an important tool for teaching feminist economics in addition to the traditional lecture-based teaching. Lastly, a case study is presented from a 'Women in the Economy' course that focused on feminist economics.

2 The subject of feminist economics

As a heterodox, non-neoclassical paradigm, feminist economics tends to focus on economic issues and methodologies that have previously been excluded or marginalized within the mainstream economics discipline. Although feminist economists vary in their specific definitions of 'feminist economics' (Robeyns 2000), feminist economics usually involves some aspects of striving to improve women's economic status and/or reducing the androcentric bias in mainstream economics (Ferber and Nelson 2003). The first of these goals, to formally analyze women's economic status, is often believed to have been spurred on by the second-wave, radical feminist[3] movement of the 1960s (Strober 2003). Many feminist economists whose aim is to analyze and elevate women's status have done so by embracing a 'feminist empiricist' approach in which traditional economic tools and methods are used, but they are used to analyze topics that have traditionally[4] been associated more with women (Harding 1986), and that have previously been excluded from orthodox economic analysis. A main aspect of second wave feminism is the argument that the traditional, gendered division of household labor is an important site of women's oppression. Thus, heterodox economists engaging with second-wave feminism initiate more formal economic analyses of household and care work as well as women's labor force participation rates and the gender wage gap and occupational segregation. As such, many of these topics form the basis of material for courses designed around feminist economics.

In analyzing these topics, feminist economists point out that not only have these topics been previously ignored by mainstream economists, but there has also been a lack of attention paid to social inequalities, whether they be based on gender or on/with other social categories such as race, ethnicity, sexual orientation, and many other social categories. Within neoclassical economics, the focus on efficiency in markets often obscures and minimizes issues of social inequalities. Thus when feminist economics courses highlight the importance of analyzing the household, labor market outcomes, and care work, this also pinpoints major sites and activities through which gender-based social inequalities are constructed. By drawing attention to social inequalities in this way, feminist economics courses may assist in elevating women's economic status.

In addition to the emphasis on improving women's economic status, Strober (2003) notes that more recent focus within feminist economics involves reducing the androcentric bias in economics. Much of this interest began in the 1970s and 1980s with the rise of postmodernism as a framework for Critical Theory. As postmodernism rejects the notion of universal and objective truths in favor of subjectivity and situated knowledge, there is an emphasis on the ways in which language and discourse construct social meanings. Of particular interest for feminist economists has been the discursive ways in which 'gender' becomes a socially meaningful category. Although there may be differences among people based on biological sex,[5] postmodern feminists point out that social meaning has become attached to these differences. As such, stereotypical notions of what it means to be a 'man' or to be a 'woman' emerge and are maintained, often with much essentializing occurring such that it is assumed that all females act as 'women' and all males act as 'men.'[6] Thus, these assumed traits and characteristics and labels of 'man' and 'woman' are social in nature, generating social categories of 'gender.'[7] In addition, this gender dichotomy has been constructed in ways that form a hierarchy among social categories, with 'women' and traits traditionally associated as 'feminine' often being denigrated and placed in a lower status relative to 'men' and 'masculinity.'

The postmodern notion of gender is meaningful to many feminist economists as they note that there has been and continues to be a dearth of women economists (Fraumeni 2011). In terms of material conditions, this tells us about women's economic status in terms of there being occupational segregation and a glass ceiling, as women appear to be excluded from the prestigious and often well-paying professional jobs as economists. In addition, though, as gender relations are often constructed in ways that result in 'women' and 'men' having different life experiences, the exclusion of women from the economics field has meant that topics and traits traditionally associated more with women's experiences have been ignored, while men's experiences have been glorified within mainstream economics. In this way, the discipline of economics displays an androcentric, or masculinist, bias in which the field centers around men's experiences as *men*.

This androcentric bias manifests itself in terms of the topics that are examined in mainstream economics. As feminist empiricist economists point out, less attention has been paid to households, care work, and other topics traditionally associated more with women's experiences than with men's.[8] In addition, the androcentric bias also plays out in terms of epistemological and methodological aspects and in the assumptions about human behavior in the field of economics. For example, Nelson (1993) argues that the neoclassical paradigm implicitly adheres to a Cartesian, epistemological framework that favors quantitative and mathematical reasoning over intuitive and emotive instincts, where the former has been traditionally associated with masculinity and the latter with femininity. Furthermore, Nelson invokes a non-essentializing analysis and suggests that all of these methods and epistemologies should be used within economics as they are all human traits.

Similarly, Harding (1995) suggests that the mainstream economics community espouses a concept of (scientific) 'objectivity' that emphasizes detachment from research subjects and colleagues. As such, this notion of 'objectivity' glorifies separation and independence from others, where these traits have traditionally been associated with masculinity. This concept of 'objectivity' simultaneously devalues aspects of subjectivity and connections with other economists and with the community that is being researched, where these are traits that have traditionally been associated with femininity. Instead, Harding espouses a concept of 'strong objectivity' that utilizes all types of traits and characteristics including notions of community and connections that have traditionally been coded as feminine. As Harding explains, this would improve 'objectivity' by enabling researchers to make analyses independently but to simultaneously come together as a community to come up with ideas and critiques while also coming together with the subject of one's research to get their ideas and viewpoints. In this way, a more diverse group of viewpoints will bring about 'strong objectivity.'[9] In Harding's (1995) analysis, both traditionally 'masculine' and 'feminine' traits get valued and utilized in the concept of objectivity rather than submitting to a gendered dichotomy of 'this or that.'

In a similar vein, England (1993, 2003) argues that mainstream economics bases its assumptions of human behavior on a rational economic agent who displays the characteristics of what she calls the 'separative self,' who is autonomous, devoid of social connections, lacks empathy, and does not consider issues of equality so that the individual may easily maximize their well-being. England concludes that these traits have traditionally been coded as 'masculine' and are exalted within mainstream economic models. At the same time, traits traditionally associated with femininity are marginalized from the assumptions made about human behavior. Instead, England argues for consideration of all human traits and actions in our analyses of economic behaviors.

As can be seen through the cases of Nelson (1993), Harding (1995), and England (1993, 2003), many feminist economics courses focus on revealing and dismantling the androcentric biases that persist within the discipline of economics. In doing so, feminist economists often emphasize a non-essentializing view of the economy, stressing that traits that have been socially coded as 'masculine' or 'feminine' are actually just human traits that everyone possesses to some degree, and so all human traits are valuable for conducting economic enquiries (Nelson 1993). Thus gender dualisms are challenged by exploring non-essentializing discourses, thereby enabling hierarchical ranking of gender relations to be challenged. In this way, strict binaries are dismantled so that all human traits can be examined and valued within the field of economics.

I argue that this concept of de-linking gender and value systems can be applied to notions of appropriate pedagogies for teaching economics in general, and feminist economics in particular. This chapter explores this aspect, stressing the need for more inclusive pedagogies that go beyond traditional lecture-based teaching to also include less orthodox methods of teaching including diary writing. This would enable the de-linking of gender and value systems in terms of the types of teaching that occur, allowing all types of valuable teaching techniques to be used. Rather than conceptualizing lectures and diary writing as distinct, gendered, oppositional pedagogies that get coded as masculine or feminine, these pedagogies may be viewed from a non-essentializing lens in which all types of pedagogies may be used by humans and may complement one another within the economics classroom in general and the feminist economics class in particular.[10]

In addition to these aspects of feminist economics in de-linking gender and value, many feminist economists also note the ways in which women's economic status and the androcentric bias in economics are intertwined and impact one another.[11] For example, if the percentage of women in the economics field increases, this may indicate an improvement in women's economic status, as they are now able to break through some of the occupational segregation and glass ceiling. In addition, the increased presence of women in economics may[12] result in an expansion of the types of topics explored and traits used and valued within economics. As the range of 'valid' economic topics expands and traditionally 'feminine' traits are revalorized, this may improve women's economic status as issues and characteristics traditionally associated with women and femininity gain legitimacy. Overall, the two main aspects of feminist economics are a focus on improving women's status and an emphasis on reducing the androcentric bias in the discipline. These two goals may also be intertwined and impact one another.

3 Teaching feminist economics

Mainstream economics focuses on a narrow range of topics, methods, and epistemological frameworks that have excluded and marginalized the experiences of many women. Similarly, there is a very limited range of pedagogical techniques used in teaching economics courses. Becker and Watts (2001a, 2001b) find that economics instructors continue to use the 'chalk and talk' method of teaching 83% of the time, while other disciplines have become more diverse and inclusive in their use of different pedagogies. That is, most economics teachers in college courses lecture as the 'sage on the stage,' writing notes and drawing graphs on the chalkboard (or whiteboard) while students take notes. Becker and Watts's findings suggest the need for expanding pedagogies to be more inclusive within the field of economics. Furthermore, Aerni et al. (1999) call for a combined increase in inclusiveness in economics in terms of both pedagogy and subject matter, arguing that both course content and pedagogy must be simultaneously changed in order to bring about greater inclusiveness in the field of economics. In particular, they suggest that feminist economics courses must expand on the material covered in mainstream economics courses in order to provide a richer and more extensive range of topics for students to explore and to connect with. However, they argue that this must be accompanied by an expansion in the types of teaching techniques used, as the 'chalk and talk' method is viewed as just one, rather limited, method of teaching and learning. Thus, Aerni et al (1999) explain that 'feminist teaching methods might serve economists well in transforming the economics classroom to one that is more hospitable to wider audiences.' In this way, diary writing may be a useful pedagogy to use in conjunction with traditional lecture-based teaching.

4 Diaries in a feminist economics course

Despite the calls for more inclusive teaching styles to be used in the field of economics, little attention has been paid to the use of student-written diaries as a specifically feminist pedagogy. Therefore, in this paper I more fully investigate this aspect and argue that the use of the student-written diary[13] as an assignment serves as a feminist pedagogy and is especially appropriate for teaching feminist economics courses, in complement with traditional lecture-based teaching. As Barnhardt and O'Quinn (2003) suggest, 'The journal [diary] is a feminist form of writing that easily enhances a feminist pedagogy.' More specifically, I suggest that the diary assignment allows students to more fully connect with the two main goals of feminist economics. That is, students may engage with actions that are commensurate with elevating women's economic status and with critiquing the androcentric biases in mainstream economics. However, whereas Barnhardt and O'Quinn (2003) tend to essentialize about the feminist qualities of journal writing, I argue for a de-linking of gender connotations and value within economic pedagogy, insisting that both traditional lectures and journal writing both can be utilized within the feminist classroom and are simply human ways of teaching rather than being gendered ways of teaching.

With respect to writing assignments, in the 1990s, the Writing across the Disciplines/Curriculum movement within institutions of higher education sparked some interest in more experiential, constructivist, and student-centered approaches to teaching within universities and colleges (Brewer and Jozefowicz 2006; Dalton

2010; Hawtrey 2007), as writing became a more central component of college teaching. However, economics instructors continue to rely on the chalk-and-talk method of teaching (Becker and Watts 2001a). Writing assignments in particular have experienced little popularity among economics instructors (Hansen 1998), despite several findings that writing assignments are useful for teaching economics. For example, Frank (2006) argues for an 'economic naturalist' writing assignment, in which students write a journal of their daily observations from their lives in order to enable students to discover economic situations in their everyday existence. Similarly, Brewer and Jozefowicz (2006) recommend the use of student-written journals and reflection papers to try to make economics more relevant to students' lives. Here, students write what is personally meaningful to them rather than just a summary of a chapter or other less personal aspects. In students writing about what is specifically meaningful to them, Brewer and Jozefowicz note that this allows for gender differences in experiences and in what women and men may find meaningful to write about. However, the authors do not fully explore the feminist or gender-related implications of the student-written journal.

Furthermore, while some feminist economists have noted the benefits of writing assignments in making economics courses more inclusive, they also have not expanded on the precise ways in which journals and diaries function in conjunction with lectures as learning tools within the feminist economics classroom. For instance, Lage and Treglia (1998) argue that learning is a very personal experience, so that learning styles may differ based on social constructions of race, gender, and other social categories. As such, they suggest a multitude of active learning styles to be employed in teaching economics, including the use of writing assignments. However, the mechanism by which writing assignments become appropriated within a feminist pedagogy of inclusiveness is not discussed. Likewise, although Aerni et al. (1999) suggest the use of a variety of pedagogical approaches within the feminist economics classroom, including journal keeping, they do not fully explore the feminist orientation of student-written diaries for engaging students in feminist economics in terms of the two goals of feminist economics in improving women's status and reducing androcentric biases. Furthermore, Aerni et al. conceptualize lecture-based teaching and alternative types of teaching as being on opposite sides of the teaching spectrum, at odds with one another, polarized, and dichotomized, with lectures shoring up the mainstream economics classroom and all other teaching methods being emancipating. As such, they tend to essentialize about teaching methods rather than de-linking notions of gender, value, pedagogy, and economics. These aspects are discussed below.

5 Improving the economic status of women

There are several ways in which writing diaries allows students to assist in improving women's economic status. In particular, diary writing allows students to identify a larger range of topics in economics, including topics traditionally associated more with women and topics that address issues of social inequalities. In addition, diary writing allows students to challenge the legitimacy of social hierarchies by empowering students relative to their instructors with respect to the construction of knowledge. In tandem with traditional lecture-based teaching, this widens the scope of possible topics and aspects of social hierarchies to be both explored and maintained.

The traditional 'chalk and talk' method of teaching economics involves students being lectured to on a narrow range of (usually) mainstream economic topics that are chosen by the instructor. As has been previously mentioned, this has resulted in a lack of focus on topics and issues traditionally associated more with women, while social inequalities have also been normalized as part of a well-functioning market system. Thus, the 'chalk and talk' method often precludes any discussion of women's economic status and/or any discussion of how to elevate women's economic status (Aerni et al. 1999). However, writing diaries may assist students in accessing these topics more freely. According to Hyers et al. (2006), 'In common usage a "diary" is typically a *private . . . unstructured narrative* of the events an individual *chooses* as important to document' (emphasis in the original). In this way, McGuinness (2009) concludes that diaries and journals serve a feminist goal of expanding topics to be analyzed to include those that may have been ignored under traditional teaching methods. Similarly, Brewer and Jozefowicz (2006) find that as students continue with their journal assignments, they notice an increase in topics that they can make economic applications to. Thus, as students choose for themselves what to write about in their journals/diaries, they may be able to explore and inquire into the nature of household and care work, labor market experiences, and aspects of social inequality. In this way, students' diary writing assists in bringing these previously marginalized topics into the foreground, enabling students to actively participate in elevating women's economic status by noting these issues, analyzing these issues, and possibly becoming activists through these experiences.[14]

Although the feminist classroom aims to expand the topics of analysis, preservation of some degree of lecture-based teaching may also be useful, as instructors may help guide the course material in this way, rather than relying solely on students' discretion in choosing and identifying topics to explore. For example, even within the feminist classroom, it may be necessary for instructors to engage in lecturing in order to point out specific topics in relation to women's status and other marginalized groups' status that students may not have otherwise chosen to examine. For instance, I often find that students are completely unaware of the ways in which capitalist relations intersect with the construction and maintenance of gender oppression. In this case, it is useful to provide a brief lecture to students about capitalist relations and then let the students write journal entries about their experiences and observations of capitalism. In this way, rather than dichotomizing lectures and journals as preferred teaching methods, they may be complementary in striving to expand economic topics beyond traditional, mainstream topics. Thus, lecture-based teaching must be expanded to include journaling, but not at the expense of dismissing lectures altogether.

In addition to these uses of diaries, student diaries also help to break down the teacher-student hierarchy in a way that de-legitimizes the normalization of social hierarchies, so that students may challenge other social hierarchies which they encounter. The traditional 'chalk and talk' method assumes that the only valid knowledge comes from the instructor who must impart their knowledge to the students. This sets up a hierarchical relationship between the instructor and the students in regard to the construction of knowledge. As such, this further serves to normalize and legitimize notions of social hierarchies, as the classroom functions as a means by which to establish (or re-establish) social hierarchies. This is especially notable given that the majority of economics instructors continue to be white men (Becker and Watts 2001b). Thus, these white men continue to serve as the holders of economic knowledge to provide to their students within the 'chalk and talk' framework. This situation replicates the very hierarchies that feminist economics intends to challenge, in terms of gender hierarchies and hierarchies based on race and ethnicity.

Feminism, as a political movement, is interested in dismantling social hierarchies (Barnhardt and O'Quinn 2003), and feminist pedagogy is similarly interested in breaking down hierarchies within the classroom (Aerni et al. 1999; Barnhardt and O'Quinn 2003). Feminist pedagogy accomplishes this by encouraging more equal participation in knowledge construction between students and instructors, rather than instructors being the sole providers of knowledge. In this way, a less hierarchical and more democratic classroom is encouraged within feminist pedagogy (Hausman 2011). A democratic classroom may be one that is envisioned to involve knowledge construction that comes from *both the instructor and the students*. That is, within the democratic classroom, the instructor surrenders their role of 'expert' and converses with students as intellectual equals (Schneider 2010).

By breaking down hierarchies within the classroom, students are encouraged, then, to question the legitimacy of social hierarchies that they encounter elsewhere with respect to gender (and other social categories). The hierarchy within the classroom with respect to knowledge construction can be challenged through the use of student-written diaries. As students write in their own voices, choosing their own ideas and thoughts to explore, they are empowered to add to the construction of the knowledge base within their classroom. Students' ideas and writing are given status as 'knowledge,' empowering students to be active constructors of knowledge rather than the instructor remaining the only valid source of knowledge (Barnhardt and O'Quinn 2003; McGuinness 2009). In this way, diary and journal writing is one method through which to equalize the classroom, serving as a specifically feminist pedagogy. This technique meshes well with the goals of feminist economics courses in wanting to elevate women's economic status, as diary writing and the subsequent reduction in hierarchies in the classroom may motivate students to question and change social hierarchies that they observe around them.

However, as discussed earlier, the feminist classroom is interested in hearing all voices and all forms of knowledge. As such, this implies that lectures and journals need not be mutually exclusive, as this would suggest using only lectures at one end of the spectrum and only journals on the other end. Instead, I suggest the usefulness of both types of pedagogies, as knowledge and 'voice' may come from both students and instructors, as the class as a whole co-creates knowledge and hears one another. Thus, while students generate their own legitimate knowledge and get heard through their journals, instructors may also have legitimate knowledge of their own to 'voice.' For example, while students have their own ideas and experiences regarding a particular topic, they may not know all of the different ways to model or analyze the topics. Here the instructor may step in to offer alternative or additional ways of modeling and understanding, not as the *only* way of understanding but as one possible way. Additionally, the instructor is also a human being who has their own experiences and stories to relate to the students and the class, often via lectures, which may provide valuable knowledge within the classroom. For instance, within my own classroom I often share my 'stories' with my students in terms of my own unique experiences as being generally older and from a different generation than my students, as being in the labor force when most of the students are not, as being a parent when the majority of my students are not parents, and being a Jew in the South when many of my students are not. Thus, in many ways some degree of instruction and guidance may be necessary within the classroom to encourage many different styles of learning and teaching. In these ways, both lectures and diaries may be useful in elevating women's economic status by expanding the topics explored and examining issues of hierarchy and knowledge production.

6 Reducing the androcentric bias in economics

In tandem with lectures, diary writing may also help to bring about a reduction in the androcentric bias in economics in terms of the notions of epistemology and objectivity used in mainstream economics as well as the assumptions of human behavior that neoclassical economics is premised upon. Mainstream economics emphasizes knowledge gained through formal, mathematical modeling and quantitative reasoning, where these traits have traditionally been associated more with masculinity. At the same time, this marginalizes knowledge gained through intuition, emotion, and experiential aspects, where these traits have traditionally been associated with femininity. Diary writing, with its more personal, emotional, and experiential emphasis, is one way of valuing and validating knowledge that is gained in this way (Barnhardt and O'Quinn 2003; Gannett 1992). Indeed, journal writing defies traditional academic writing because it is viewed as being personal and expressive rather than purely scientific (Barnhardt and O'Quinn 2003). Journal writing requires students to use their instincts and emotions to observe their own experiences in the world and to then analyze them in relation to the course material. This enables students to determine for themselves the value of these ways of gaining knowledge as they participate in using these techniques. Students are then equipped to question the legitimacy of relying only on ways of knowing that involve quantitative aspects rather than also including ways of knowing that involve intuition and emotion within the field of economics.

However, rather than completely eschewing quantitative analyses and the lecture-based teaching that accompanies them, and posing such aspects as being in opposition to diaries and emotionality, this dichotomy can be de-linked and challenged. Here I argue that by utilizing both lectures and diary writing within the classroom, many different human styles of teaching and learning can be exhibited. This may serve to challenge the notion of lectures as masculine and superior and diaries as feminine and inferior. Instead all types of teaching can be valued and utilized without essentializing about pedagogical techniques. Thus both lectures and diaries can be useful for teaching economics, especially within the feminist economics classroom, which strives to hear all voices and to enjoy all types of teaching and learning methods. Thus, the expansion of lecture-based teaching towards the inclusion of diary usage assists in expanding economic concepts and methods beyond the mainstream focus on quantitative reasoning to include emotive reasoning as well, so that all human traits may be considered.

In addition, though, mainstream economics often relies on concepts of objectivity that posit the unbiased discovery of universal truths through independent research freed from the biases of connections with other researchers or with the subjects of research. It can be noted, though, that traits of separation and independence have been traditionally associated more with masculinity, while traits of connections with others and social aspects have been associated more traditionally with notions of femininity. Thus, this style of objectivity used in mainstream economics privileges a masculinist view of the world. However, diary writing encourages the questioning of this type of objectivity, generating the type of 'strong objectivity' suggested by Harding (1995). As students explore topics and experiences with their own voices and ideas, they note that there is not just one universal way of understanding the world. Rather, diary writing reveals that knowledge is situated based on social hierarchies and contexts (Hyers et al. 2006), making both diary writing and knowledge formation highly subjective. In this way, social contexts and stratifications become meaningful ways in which knowledge is generated, making social connections and connections with other researchers and with research subjects important aspects of the generation of ('strong') 'objective' knowledge.

Furthermore, McGuinness (2009) points out that student diary writing is extremely compatible with asking students to learn about the feminist standpoint theory. The feminist standpoint theory argues that knowledge is often based on one's position within society and social stratifications (Harding 2008). For example, those on the bottom of social hierarchies and who have been marginalized within society may have different knowledge of their own social situation than those at the top of the hierarchy. That is, many women may have a different way of understanding the world than most men, due to the types of activities or actions they engage in, such as cleaning toilets or constant childcare, where this knowledge is only gained through participating in this position in society (or possibly via strong empathy). Thus the feminist standpoint theory suggests that knowledge is situated based on one's place in society. Writing diaries helps to access this type of knowledge as well as allowing students to question notions of 'objectivity.' As McGuinness (2009) explains:

> I found that the subjective nature of the [diary assignment], asking students constantly to search their own lives and experiences, mapped well onto more

> sophisticated arguments about the nature of science and objectivity in Western science (Haraway 1991; Harding 1991).
>
> McGuinness (2009)

Mainstream economics also utilizes the rational choice model. According to England (1993, 2003), this model assumes a separative self model of human behavior that privileges traditionally masculine notions of separation, autonomy, and a lack of both social connections and empathy. The 'chalk and talk' method of teaching that most economists use serves to uphold these characteristics. As instructors lecture and students take notes, this teaching style precludes social relationships between the instructor and students and between students within the classroom, as students merely take notes and are unlikely to engage in social relationships with the teacher or other students under this format of teaching. However, the introduction of diary writing reduces this androcentric bias in economics and in the teaching style by revalorizing the traditionally feminine notions of empathy and social connections, so that all human traits can be valued within the field of economics.

More specifically, writing diaries enables students to be more empathetic and socially connected, allowing them to value these traits for themselves and therefore questioning the legitimacy of the rational choice model. As students write about what they see around them, the personal quality of these actions allows them to emotionally connect with themselves and with others who they observe and write about. For instance, Brewer and Jozefowicz (2006) found that when their students kept journals, the students reported that the journals helped them to increase their knowledge so that they were able to discuss issues with their friends and family outside of the class. In this way, their social relations and connections were deepened. Similarly, Barnhardt and O'Quinn (2003) explain that journal writing enables students to connect with their own lives and with the lives of others and to become more aware of these social connections. Aerni et al. (1999) argue that to learn effectively, many students want and need to be more connected to other students, to the instructor, to the course material, and to their communities. Diary writing is one way in which this can occur.

In particular, diary writing enables students to experience emotional connections to themselves, to the instructor, to society, and to other students. As explained above, journal writing enables self-awareness through a connection between the diary writer and themselves. Furthermore, as the instructor collects and grades journals, there is an additional connection between the student and the instructor, as the student shares their own 'stories' with the instructor. In addition, in making observations about their own lives, about which to write for their diaries, students often observe their relationships with others and with society as a whole. Students become more aware of their surroundings and interactions with others, yielding an additional connection between the students and society. Diary writing also often fosters deeper relationships between students in the class, as I use the assignment to help initiate class discussions among students in relation to the topics they feel are important enough to write about. This aspect of journal writing is explored more fully below in the case study.

In addition to the emotional connections generated through diary writing, the diary approach also allows students to notice and reflect on the social contexts in which they live and interact. For example, if students notice the ways in which an individual's social context often impacts an individual's status with respect to economic inequalities, they may be less likely to consider only the ways that an individual's choices impact their status as in the rational choice model, and may, instead, become more aware of how social structures of patriarchy and within-sex altruism may serve to disadvantage women and other marginalized groups (England 1993). In this way, students may be more likely to challenge the legitimacy of relying only on the rational choice model, and this may lead students to look at models of human behavior that also recognize the social contexts and social connections within which humans interact. Thus diary writing allows students themselves to act more emotionally connected and also allows students to notice the importance of these connections and social contexts within economic analyses. Then, in combination with lecture-based teaching, the diary writing may enable the de-linking of gender-based pedagogical dualisms. Lecture-based teaching may uphold the rational choice model along with notions of individualism and separation that enable students to appreciate their own individuality and uniqueness and particular concepts of rationality that some people do espouse. Expanding the pedagogies used in economics to include diary writing, though, allows students to also exercise their feelings of connectedness and emotionality. In this way, a range of human attributes and teaching styles can occur within the economics classroom, de-linking gendered pedagogical dualisms and becoming more inclusive. This is in line with the goals of the feminist classroom in becoming more inclusive.

7 Case study: 'Women in the Economy' class

In order to more fully consider the effects of student-written diaries on accomplishing the goals of a feminist economics course, I provide a case study of a 'Women in the Economy' course taught during the spring 2011 semester. The course material included analyses of women's economic status and discussions of the androcentric biases in economics. Students were required to keep a 'gender diary' throughout the semester, in which they were asked to record their own observations of their life experiences, relating these experiences to the current course material and providing a critical analysis of the situation based on what we had discussed in class. Students were instructed to write one journal entry per week of class. In order to get students to think more analytically when writing their journals, rather than merely descriptively, students were provided with an example of what type of journal entry was expected of them. The example that was handed out is provided in an abbreviated form in Appendix A. Furthermore, students were also guided in their writing by being instructed to consider why they felt a particular experience or observation in their life was significant to our work in the class. Students were also instructed that if they mentioned a situation that involved social inequalities and/or an androcentric bias, they should then explain why and how they thought the situation had resulted, what was causing it, and how to bring about social changes to the situation to be more equitable. In this way, students would be providing a critical analysis to the descriptions of their observations.

Students handed in their journals for grading periodically throughout the semester, with the journal assignment in total counting as 10% of students' final grades. In addition, students were provided with a grading rubric regarding the grade scale for each journal entry that was submitted. The grading rubric is shown in Appendix B. As shown in the rubric, journal entries were expected to be based on students' life experiences, to relate to the current topic in the course, and to be analytical/critical.

In addition to collecting and grading the diaries, the diaries were also used within the classroom as a teaching device. Specifically, there were two main pedagogical techniques that were used. First, after submitting their journals, students were asked if they wanted to share any of their stories with the class, and this often led to more in-depth and personalized discussions of material than would have been possible through a purely lecture-based format. Thus, students were empowered to bring up their own ideas and specific topics related to our class material and to discuss them as a class, which also provided students with an opportunity to connect with other students.

However, several students also appeared to be less comfortable about speaking up in class, even about their own journal entries. For this reason, I also used a second pedagogical approach in which, after reading and grading the students' diaries and handing them back to them, I would consider any recurrent themes or topics that the students, as a class, seemed to focus on. I would then introduce these topics and themes to the class for an open discussion time. For example, towards the beginning of the semester when many of the fraternities and sororities had their 'rush' events, students had written about gendered aspects of this process. When I explored this topic further with the students during class, they expanded on this subject, and many argued that fraternities construct many more work-related networking opportunities for men in comparison to the networking opportunities that women get from being in sororities. In this way, many of the students felt there was an 'old boys' network' established through the fraternities and other aspects of 'Greek' life on campus. Such a conversation may have been less likely if pure lecture-based teaching was used.

Similarly, at one point in the semester, the university's marketing club held an event at the university library titled 'Mad Men, Mad Women,' which was meant to explore the television show *Mad Men*. Attendees were invited to dress in retro style and to discuss the implications of the show. Several posters for the event were up around campus, including one that had a woman's silhouette and stated 'You don't kiss boys, they kiss you.' Many of the students had written about the event, the television show, and the posters. When I mentioned this in class, it sparked a long conversation by the students in terms of occupational segregation in the advertising industry both in the past and present. We also analyzed the posters that were up around campus, with specific emphasis on the one mentioned above. Together, as a class, we pointed out that the poster reinforced notions of women being in passive roles (being kissed) and men being in active roles (doing the kissing).[15] Not only do such notions play out in terms of sexuality, but many students pointed out that these passive/active gender roles may also play out in the workplace, as women may be expected to be passive, and therefore not to take on leadership roles and never to ask for raises in salaries.

Other topics that were explored through the students' journals included Super Bowl commercials, Valentine's Day rituals, the ABC television show *Modern Family*, job interviews and recruitment, the division of labor for couples, experiences with gender that differed based on cultures and nationality (the class had a diverse range of demographics and had many international students and many students who had studied abroad), and many other topics. Thus, I took cues for topics from the students, but I also connected with the students themselves via their journals. I then showed the students that many of them shared similar themes in their diaries as a group. Even when students had different views and topics, by using the journals to start conversations in the classroom I was able to illuminate not just the ways the students may have had similar situations and experiences, but also to highlight different ways that students might feel about and experience life, allowing students to connect with each other and to learn about each other and about themselves. I do not think this depth of connection would be possible if only lecture-based teaching were to be used.

In terms of the class's demographics, there were 30 students in the class, mainly juniors and seniors. The course was sponsored by the economics department but was also cross-listed through the women's studies program. Twenty-five of the students were registered for the course under economics and five students were registered through women's studies. Although many of the students had kept diaries before, none of them had written one for an economics course.

In order to more fully understand students' feelings about keeping a diary, an email survey was conducted after students' grades had been submitted. Out of 30 students, 13 responded, giving a response rate of 43%.[16] The survey questions are listed in Appendix C. Survey participants were also asked to provide any thoughts or comments they had about the diary assignment. Ten of the 13 respondents provided written comments.

Throughout the semester, students were extremely enthusiastic about the journal entries and many of them often submitted more entries than the assignment called for. There were many times when students included clippings from magazines and newspapers with their journal entries, or included pictures from websites they had seen. Students also often emailed me additional articles and incidents that they had come across. At the conclusion of the semester, several students explained that after writing their diaries they now saw 'gender issues' all over the place! For example, one respondent from the survey explained:

> I think the journal was very helpful and relevant for this course. I found so many examples of what we talked about in class in magazines, TV, conversations, etc. I would say I had too much to write about in my journals!

Another student told me that his friends now called him a feminist. Still other students spoke with me and told me that they were now conversing more with their friends about issues such as 'Who pays for dinner?' if a heterosexual couple goes out on a date, or 'Are there certain jobs that are male dominated? Does this prevent college women from trying to get into these jobs?'

The majority of students found it enjoyable to keep the gender diary, as 77% of respondents reported that they either 'somewhat agree' or 'strongly agree' that keeping a diary is enjoyable. Furthermore, the majority of respondents felt that keeping a journal helped them to learn. In particular, 85% of respondents either 'somewhat agree' or 'strongly agree' that keeping a journal helped them to learn 'basic theories concerning the economics of gender.' For example, one of the respondents explained:

> Diaries are useful in [t]he field of economics especially because so much of it is about describing the behavior of people and their everyday transactions, and keeping a diary is important for all kinds of academics just in terms of coming up with new ideas etc.

Ninety-two percent of respondents reported that they either 'somewhat agree' or 'strongly agree' that writing a diary helped them 'to apply concepts in the economics of gender to real life.' As one respondent stated:

> I thought the journal was one of the best elements of [this course]. After taking this class, I feel like I see the world in a way I did not before, question things in a way I did not before, and desire to know more in a way I did not before. I think part of this owes to the fact that the journal encouraged us to relate weekly lessons or economic/feminist theories learned in class to events going on in the real world. The journal entries were not intended to exceed a page, but I often found myself writing three or four! Economics, in relation to other areas of learning at [the University], tends to fall into the trap of abstract models and mathematical equations which is definitely a good base for reading, analyzing and understanding economic statistics and systems but Economics give[s] an unnecessary prestige to models and to math. Economics, like every area of learning, is inevitably learned by doing. Economics is ultimately about applying the models and the equations that we learn to real events in the current economy. While we had the opportunity to incorporate philosophy and psychology into our journals in Women [in] the Economy, which made them especially fun and though[t]-provoking.

Students were also asked if they would recommend the diary assignment for continued use in the 'Women in the Economy' course, for use in other economics courses, and for use in non-economics courses. The majority of respondents (92%) either 'somewhat recommend' or 'strongly recommend' continued use of the diary assignment for the 'Women in the Economy' course, while only 46% of respondents either 'somewhat recommend' or 'strongly recommend' using the diary assignment in other economics courses. As one respondent explained, 'I'm not sure how relevant it would be to keep a journal in a more traditional economics course.' Interestingly, a higher percentage of respondents (69%) either 'somewhat recommend' or 'strongly recommend' using the diary assignment for non-economics courses. Overall, the findings and anecdotal evidence from students' conversations with me suggest that the student diary method of teaching is an important feminist pedagogical tool to use, in conjunction with traditional lectures, specifically for courses that involve feminist economics.

8 Conclusion

Teaching feminist economics involves course material and content that differs significantly from mainstream economics courses. In particular, such courses often focus on improving women's economic status and/or addressing the androcentric bias in economics. Although feminist economists have recognized that more inclusive teaching methods must be used to teach heterodox economic paradigms, little attention has been paid to the use of student-written diaries to challenge pedagogical dualisms within economics teaching. I argue that student-written diaries are a useful pedagogical tool for teaching feminist economics. Diary writing allows students to address issues of social hierarchies more fully, thereby helping to improve women's economic status. Writing diaries also helps students to access and valorize traditionally feminine traits of emotionality and social connections, thereby valuing the use of such traits within economic enquiry. In conjunction with traditional lecture-based teaching, the inclusion of the diary approach to teaching serves to de-link notions of a gendered pedagogical dualism, enabling the establishment of a more inclusive classroom. This is concomitant with the goals of feminist classrooms. Furthermore, a case study of a 'Women in the Economy' course suggests that students find diary writing to be both enjoyable and useful for learning feminist economics, and that they recommend continued usage of this teaching method for feminist economics courses.

Acknowledgments

I appreciate the participation of the students in my 'Women in the Economy' class, and I thank them for sharing their stories with me.

Appendix A

Diary/journal assignment

Gender diary/journal assignment

Throughout the semester, each student is expected to keep a gender diary or journal. This can be handwritten in a notebook or may be typed on the computer. The diaries/journals will be collected periodically throughout the semester and will be graded.

The purpose of this assignment is to allow students to relate the course material to situations and experiences in their own lives. These may be experiences that the students have themselves in their daily lives, or this may relate to situations which students observe among other people, in the media, in the news, in books, and so forth. Students are expected to record one entry in their diary/journal each week. Each entry should relate to the current course material being discussed at that time. Journal/diary entries must be analytical in nature. That is, it is not sufficient to merely describe a situation that you observe or experience. You must also analyze the situation and give a critical perspective based on course material.

Example of journal/diary entry:

Unacceptable: Today I noticed that the majority of the housekeeping workers at the university are women – women of color. I wondered about the social significance of this. It brought up ideas about gender and race/ethnicity.

Acceptable: Today I noticed that the majority of the housekeeping workers at the university are women – women of color. I wondered about the social significance of this. It brought up ideas about gender and race/ethnicity. In particular, I noticed the ways in which the social meaning of gender and race and ethnicity get constructed, often intersecting and interacting. Notions of what it means to be a 'woman,' to be a 'person of color,' or to be a 'woman of color' (although being a 'woman of color' is by no means simply additive of being a woman and being a person of color, it is more complex than that), and how these roles and notions get enacted.

This also brought to notion the concepts developed by third-wave, transnational feminism, in noticing that not all women share the same experiences. Women's situations and perceptions vary by race, ethnicity, class, age, religion, sexual orientation . . . thus, we cannot universalize about what it means to be a woman. However, we might note that in considering the role and social construction of 'housekeeping women of color at [our] University,' there seem to be many ways in which this social category gets constructed and maintained in opposition to other categories (such as white women on campus? Or white, professional men on campus?) . . .

Furthermore, women in particular are often essentialized as being skilled in housework and as preferring/enjoying this type of work, validating women's position in this job. By essentializing, people in society assume that characteristics associated with housekeeping are somehow inherent in females, and that the entire social category of 'women' hold these traits. Indeed, this becomes part of the social definition of 'womanhood' in many cultural contexts. This association also seems to mimic the notion that within the private, household sphere women are viewed as naturally being responsible for housekeeping tasks. Here, then, within the public sphere of jobs in the labor force (at the university), the implication is, again, that housekeeping is 'women's work.' In addition, these jobs as hired, domestic workers have historically been associated with women of color. White, privileged, middle class women and families have often employed women of color to perform household tasks within the home . . . Thus, the further implication is that women of color, in particular, are somehow well-suited to such jobs, where these are often jobs with relatively low levels of prestige given. There is often the notion that cleaning up after other people is seen as less rewarding and demeaning. Yet, housekeeping work is much more complex than that, as it may be both tedious and rewarding, and much social meaning gets attached to who does this type of work and for whom (i.e. who cleans up after whom?). However, there may also be much agency and collective action among housekeeping workers to organize and resist stereotypes and to construct their own social meanings. Overall, there are many aspects of the social category of housekeeping women of color at [our] University which are complex. In addition, there is a diversity of experiences that occur.

Appendix B
Diary/journal grading rubric

Journals/diaries grading rubric

Criteria: On current topic and analytical, based on observations in your own life.

Grade scale

100 On topic and highly analytical
95 On topic and somewhat analytical, but needs more analysis
90 Either on topic but lacking analysis OR not on topic but analytical
85 Neither on topic nor analytical
0 Failure to hand in the assignment

Appendix C
Questionnaire

Please mark the box that best fits your answers to the following questions:

1 To what degree do you agree or disagree with this statement: 'A variety of teaching methods should be used in college courses.'

- □ Strongly agree
- □ Somewhat agree
- □ Neither agree nor disagree
- □ Somewhat disagree
- □ Strongly disagree
- □ No opinion

2 Prior to taking the course 'Women in the Economy' during the spring 2011 semester, had you ever kept a diary or journal for any reason?

□ Yes □ No (Skip to question 4.)

3 Which of the following best indicates your reasons for keeping a diary/journal in the past?

- □ Personal reasons
- □ For a course in high school or college
- □ Both for personal reasons and for a course
- □ Other (Please explain____________________________)

4 During the course 'Women in the Economy' you were assigned to keep a gender journal/diary. To what extent do you agree or disagree with this statement: 'Keeping a journal or diary is enjoyable.'

- □ Strongly agree
- □ Somewhat agree
- □ Neither agree nor disagree
- □ Somewhat disagree
- □ Strongly disagree
- □ No opinion

5 To what degree do you agree or disagree with this statement: 'Keeping a journal helped me to learn basic theories concerning the economics of gender.'

- □ Strongly agree
- □ Somewhat agree
- □ Neither agree nor disagree
- □ Somewhat disagree
- □ Strongly disagree
- □ No opinion

6 To what degree do you agree or disagree with this statement: 'Keeping a journal helped me to apply concepts in the economics of gender to real life.'

- □ Strongly agree
- □ Somewhat agree
- □ Neither agree nor disagree
- □ Somewhat disagree
- □ Strongly disagree
- □ No opinion

7 To what degree would you recommend or oppose the use of the diary/journal assignment in each of these situations:

	Strongly recommend	*Somewhat recommend*	*Neither recommend nor oppose*	*Somewhat oppose*	*Strongly oppose*	*No opinion*
Continued use in 'Women in the Economy'	□	□	□	□	□	□
For use in other economics courses	□	□	□	□	□	□
For use in non-economics courses	□	□	□	□	□	□

8 Are you interested in volunteering to donate your diary or journal for use in this study? (If Yes or Unsure/Maybe, you may be contacted by email for further questions/instructions.)

□ Yes, definitely □ No, definitely □ Unsure/Maybe

9 Please take a few moments to give any of your own comments on the usefulness and/or limitations of the diary method for learning in the field of economics. It is important for us to hear your ideas and opinions since you are a student who has actually completed a diary/journal for an economics course:

Notes

1 This chapter is a reprint from G. Miller (2012), *Forum for Social Economics* 42(1), 88–112. Reprinted with permission by Taylor & Francis Ltd.
2 Such courses are often titled Women in the Economy, Women and the Economy, Gender and the Economy, or similar titles, although not all such courses necessarily have a feminist bent.
3 Note that not all women are feminists and not all feminists are women.
4 Note that to avoid essentializing and universalizing about gender relations, gender stereotypes and traits are discussed in terms of 'traditional' notions of masculinity and femininity, although such traditional notions may not hold for all individuals and/or groups and societies.
5 Although some postmodernists argue that the concept of biological 'sex' is also socially constructed (see Bryson's (2003) discussion of the literature on this subject in her chapter titled 'Black and Postmodern Feminisms').
6 Note that little attention is given in the literature to those who are intersexed or transgendered and who might therefore disrupt the male/female and man/woman dichotomies.
7 Note, though, that gender categories are neither universal nor stable. They may vary over time, across place and context, and based on other social categories that intersect with gender, including age, race, ethnicity, class, sexual orientation, and other social categories.
8 For example, note that within mainstream economics there is great primacy placed on analyzing paid employment and other activities that are traditionally associated more with men's experiences.
9 This concept of 'strong objectivity' has similarities to McCloskey's (1993) notion of 'conjectivity.'
10 I am thankful to an anonymous reviewer for pointing out this conceptual aspect.
11 These ideas have also been put forth by feminists who argue that material and discursive/ideological conditions are intertwined in determining women's status. For example, see Walby (1991).
12 Since not all women are feminists, nor do all women have the same life experiences, there is some possibility that women's increased numbers and percentages in economics may not have varying effects on making the field of economics more inclusive.
13 Some instructors have referred to a similar diary assignment as a journal, a reflection paper, or a reflective diary (McGuinness 2009).
14 Or, at the very least, this may enable students to break down previous stereotypes and the status quo regarding women's status with respect to cultural and social notions of 'women's place.'
15 The poster also upheld heteronormativity, which we then discussed in class.
16 There may be some non-response bias to be aware of, as those students who did not respond to the survey may not have found diary writing to be useful to them.

References

Aerni, A., Bartlett, R., Lewis, M., McGoldrick, K. and Shackelford, J. (1999): "Toward a Feminist Pedagogy in Economics", *Feminist Economics* 5(1), 29–44.

Barnhardt, K. D. and O'Quinn, E. (2003): "Making a Space for Girls: Feminism, Journal Writing, and the English Classroom", *WILLA* 12, 10–17.

Becker, W. and Watts, M. (2001a): "Teaching Economics at the Start of the 21st Century: Still Chalk-and-Talk", *American Economic Review* 91(2), 446–451.

Becker, W. and Watts, M. (2001b): "Teaching Methods in U.S. Undergraduate Economics Courses", *Journal of Economic Education* 32(3), 269–279.

Brewer, S. and Jozefowicz, J. (2006): "Making Economic Principles Personal: Student Journals and Reflection Papers", *Journal of Economic Education*, 202–216.

Bryson, V. (2003): *Feminist Political Theory*. New York, NY: Palgrave Macmillan.

Dalton, P. (2010): "The Use of Narrative Interview in Teaching Principles of Macroeconomics", *Journal of Economics Education* 41(3), 252–258.

England, P. (1993): "The Separative Self: Androcentric Bias in Neoclassical Assumptions", in Ferber, M. and Nelson, J. (eds.), *Beyond Economic Man: Feminist Theory and Economics*. Chicago: University of Chicago Press, 37–53.

England, P. (2003): "Separative and Soluble Selves: Dichotomous Thinking in Economics", in Ferber, M. and Nelson, J. (eds.), *Feminist Economics Today: Beyond Economic Man*. Chicago: University of Chicago Press, 33–60.

Ferber, M. and Nelson, J. (12003): "Introduction: The Social Construction of Economics and the Social Construction of Gender", in Ferber, M. and Nelson, J. (eds.), *Beyond Economic Man: Feminist Theory and Economics*. Chicago: University of Chicago Press, 1–22.

Frank, R. (2006): "The Economic Naturalist Writing Assignment", *Journal of Economic Education* 37(1), 58–67.

Fraumeni, B. (2011): "From the Chasair", *Newsletter of the Committee on the Status of Women in the Economics Profession* Winter, 2.

Gannett, C. (1992): *Gender and the Journal: Diaries and Academic Discourse*. Albany, NY: State University of New York.

Hansen, W. L. (1998): "Integrating the Practice of Writing into Economics Instruction", in Becker, W. and Watts, M. (eds.), *Teaching Economics to Undergraduates: Alternatives to Chalk and Talk*. Northampton, MA: Edward Elgar.

Harding, S. (1986): *The Science Question in Feminism*. Ithaca, NY: Cornell University Press.

Harding, S. (1995): "Can Feminist Thought Make Economics More Objective?", *Feminist Economics* 1(1), 7–32.

Harding, S. (2008): *Sciences from Below: Feminisms, Postcolonialities, and Modernities*. Durham, NC: Duke University Press.

Hausman, B. (2011): http://filebox.vt.edu/users/bhausman.information/femped.html, accessed 16 May 2011.

Hawtrey, K. (2007): "Using Experiential Learning Techniques", *Journal of Economic Education* Spring, 143–152.

Hyers, L., Swim, J. and Mallett, R. (2006): "The Personal Is Political: Using Daily Diaries to Examine Everyday Prejudice-Related Experiences", in Nagy Hesse-Biber, S. and Leavy, P. (eds.), *Emergent Methods in Social Research*. Thousand Oaks, CA: Sage.

Lage, M. and Treglia, M. (1998): "Gender and Active Learning", in Becker, W. and Watts, M. (eds.), *Teaching Economics to Undergraduates: Alternatives to Chalk and Talk*. Northampton, MA: Edward Elgar.

McCloskey, D. N. (1993): "Some consequences of a Conjective Economics", in Ferber, M. and Nelson, J. (eds.), *Beyond Economic Man: Feminist Theory and Economics*. Chicago: University of Chicago Press, 23–36.

McGuinness, M. (2009): "Putting Themselves in the Picture: Using Reflective Diaries in the Teaching of Feminist Geography", *Journal of Geography in Higher Education* 33(3), 339–349.

Nelson, J. (1993): "The Study of Choice or the Study of Provisioning? Gender and the Definition of Economics", in Ferber, M. and Nelson, J. (eds.), *Beyond Economic Man: Feminist Theory and Economics*. Chicago: University of Chicago Press, 23–36.

Robeyns, I. (2000): *Is There a Feminist Economic Methodology?* Cambridge, UK: Wolfson College, www.ingridrobeyns.nl/content/articles/Robeyns_2000_Is%20there%20a%20Feminist%20Economic%20Methodology.pdf, accessed 16 May 2011.
Schneider, G. (2010): "Democratizing the Classroom: Sequencing Discussions and Assignments to Promote Student Ownership of the Course", *Review of Radical Political Economics* 42(1), 101–107.
Strober, M. (2003): "Rethinking Economics through a Feminist Lens", in Mutari, E. and Figart, D. (eds.), *Women and the Economy: A Reader*. Armonk, NY: M. E. Sharpe, 5–12.
Walby, S. (1991): *Theorizing Patriarchy*. Cambridge, MA: Blackwell.

13 Undermining the microeconomic textbook approach

Steps towards competitive pluralism

Frank Beckenbach

1 Introduction

Due to a dubious division of activities in economics, microeconomics is a limited field of research and teaching. It has been marked as a special area of scientific activities in economics by being separated from macroeconomics (Machlup 1960). This separation still holds, although there is an ongoing debate about synthesizing these different realms of economics either by generalizing the (market) activities of agents or by giving macroeconomics a sound microfoundation (King 2012).

Whereas the modern research in microeconomics can be assessed as being ambiguous in terms of pluralism in microeconomic instruction and teaching, a crude monism still dominates. Starting from the latter, first, a suggestion is made how the requirement of pluralism can be realized on an introductory level by picking up the tensions in the 'protective belt' in the modern neoclassical research programme and transform it into a comparative introductory course. Second, a more comprehensive and competing heterodox microeconomic alternative on the advanced level is sketched, thereby radicalizing the difference to conventional neoclassical axioms.

2 A pluralist introductory course in microeconomics

Learning and applying conceptual consistency are essential features of scientific education. This necessitates a selection of theories/concepts as well as a selective focus on the subject matter under investigation. But there is no need to consider only one concept – quite the contrary: what methodological consistency (instead of blind faith) is can best be learned by comparing (at least two) different approaches.[1] Especially on an introductory level, establishing such a comparison and thereby training self-reflectivity is an essential feature if the goals of scientific education are taken into account.[2] Hence, in this case the desiderata of 'competitive pluralism' are realized in one and the same course.

According to its role in the economic education as a whole, the starting point in this course is a condensed but consistent presentation of the subject matter, of the assumptions and of the methods of modern neoclassical microeconomics.[3] For the sake of neat comparability with the corresponding heterodox part of this course, the assumptions and methods of the neoclassical fundamentals are changed only in a parsimonious but nevertheless far-reaching way: (1) there is no complete information anymore about the agent's possibilities to act and therefore no maximization; instead, (2) there is a kind of adaptation in that agents explore the state space (which is in a first step still the stylized neoclassical one)[4] and process the information about their experience in a simple learning algorithm. As a consequence, a new level of explanation is introduced and postulating equilibrium becomes arbitrary. Hence, essential features of the mainstream concept (like the separation of constraints on the one hand and goal-related sorting of alternatives on the other hand, or the isomorphic treatment of households and firms) remain untouched by this modification. Already at this elementary level, such a modification implies a broader spectrum of possible results. Even in a partial analytic framework, effects of changing prices and/or budgets are influenced by the adaptation procedure. Hence, whereas the results are not that unique as in the neoclassical counterpart, this modification is nevertheless more 'plausible' and includes the neoclassical results as a special case. Hence, the trade-off between elegance and plausibility can be illustrated by such a procedure.

How consistency and comparability are linked in this case can be deduced from the syllabus (Figure 13.1): not only can the orthodox and heterodox view

I. Basics (2)
I.0 Introduction
I.1 Historical conditions for the separation of economics
I.2 Economics in the system of science
I.3 Topics of microeconomics
I.4 Embeddednes of microeconomics
I.5 Views and strands of microeconomics
I.6 Concepts and methods of microeconomics

II. Households (3)
II.1 Definitions and empirical findings
II.2 Orthodox household analysis
II.2.1 Perfect rationality and utility maximization
II.2.2 Internal household equilibrium
II.3 Heterodox household analysis
II.3.1 Imperfect rationality and utility sufficiency
II.3.2 Learning in households
II.4 Comparison of orthodox and heterodox view
II.5 Broadening the perspective

III. Firms (3)
III.1 Definitions and empirical findings
III.2 Orthodox firm analysis
III.2.1 Perfect rationality and profit maximization
III.2.2 Internal firm equilibrium
III.3 Heterodox firm analysis
III.3.1 Imperfect rationality and profit sufficiency
III.3.2 Learning in firms
III.4 Comparison of orthodox and heterodox view
III.5 Broadening the perspective

IV. Markets (2)
IV.1 Definitions and empirical finding
IV.2 Orthodox market analysis: features of equilibrium
IV.3 Heterodox market analysis: features of evolution
IV.4 Comparison of orthodox and heterodox view
IV.5 Broadening the perspective

Figure 13.1 Syllabus of an introductory course in microeconomics

each be composed in a systematic manner, but also the comparison between the approaches is enacted in each chapter. Furthermore, the methodological isomorphism between the way households and firms are dealt with (as well as its limits) becomes transparent.

The modelling architecture of the heterodox part has some features which will be explained in more detail for showing exemplarily how the neoclassical framework can be partially abandoned.

First, in mainstream microeconomics the agent's architecture consists only of one layer (relation between cause and effect in the form of 'dominant dependence')[5] and has the same basic structure for households and firms (Figure 13.2). Contrary to that, there is a two-layer structure in the architecture of agents supposed in the heterodox part of the introductory course with the aspiration level as the intermediary variable for adaption (whereas the similarities for households and firms are still given). This variable links limited information and learning as mentioned above. Hence, the attribute of hierarchy (in the sense of modern complexity theory) is introduced in an elementary fashion (Figure 13.3).

Second, an essential feature of the heterodox part is the adaptation algorithm ascribed to the agents for exploring and exploiting the state space. To illustrate the way this algorithm works, a very simple starting point is chosen: the case of partial factor variation in firms with a traditional Cobb-Douglas-production function. The profit function for the factors *a* and *m* and their given respective prices (p_a, p_m) can

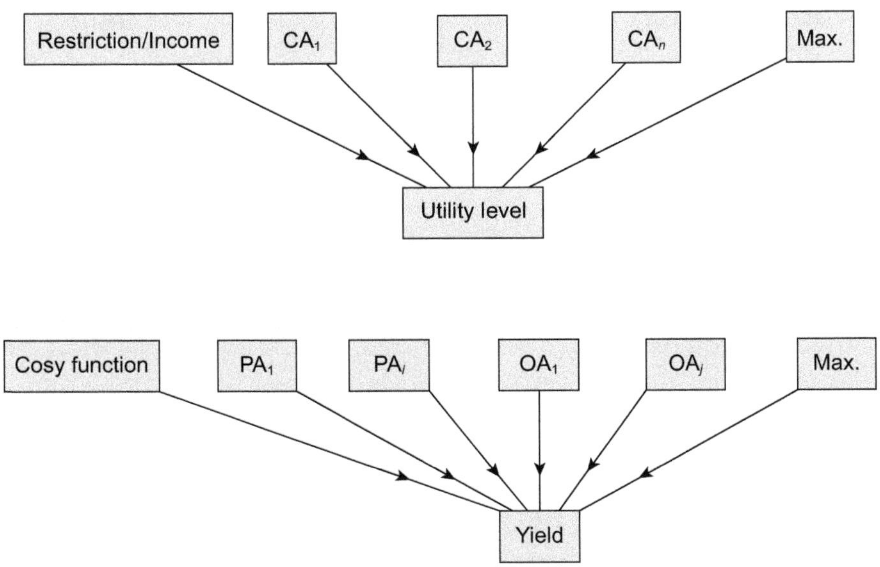

Figure 13.2 Basic architecture of microeconomic agents in the mainstream (left: household with CA_i for the possible consumption activities; right: firms with PA_i and OA_i for the possible production and organization activities, respectively)

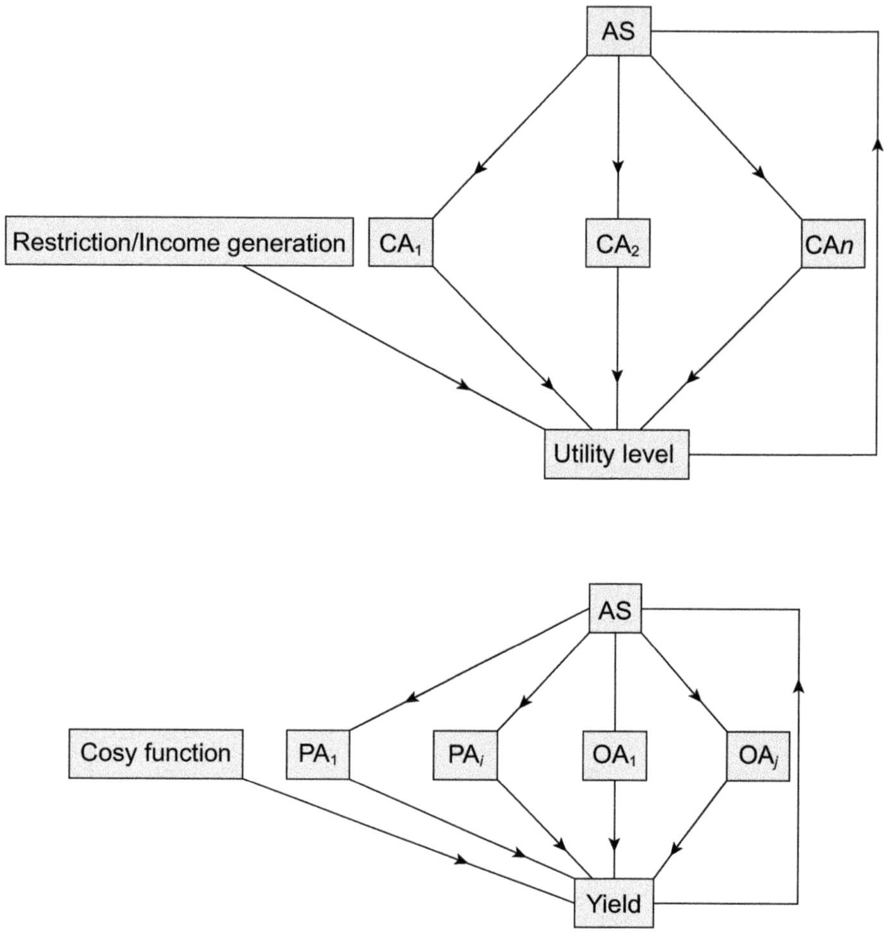

Figure 13.3 Basic architecture of microeconomic agents in elementary heterodox microeconomics (left: household with CA_i for the possible consumption activities and *AS* for the aspiration level; right: firms with PA_i and OA_i for the possible production and organization activities, respectively, and *AS* for the aspiration level)

be noted as follows (*p* being the given product price and *a* being the variable factor which is controlled by the firm):

$$G(a) = pa^{0.5}(m)^{0.5} - (ap_a + mp_m).$$

This is depicted in Figure 13.4.

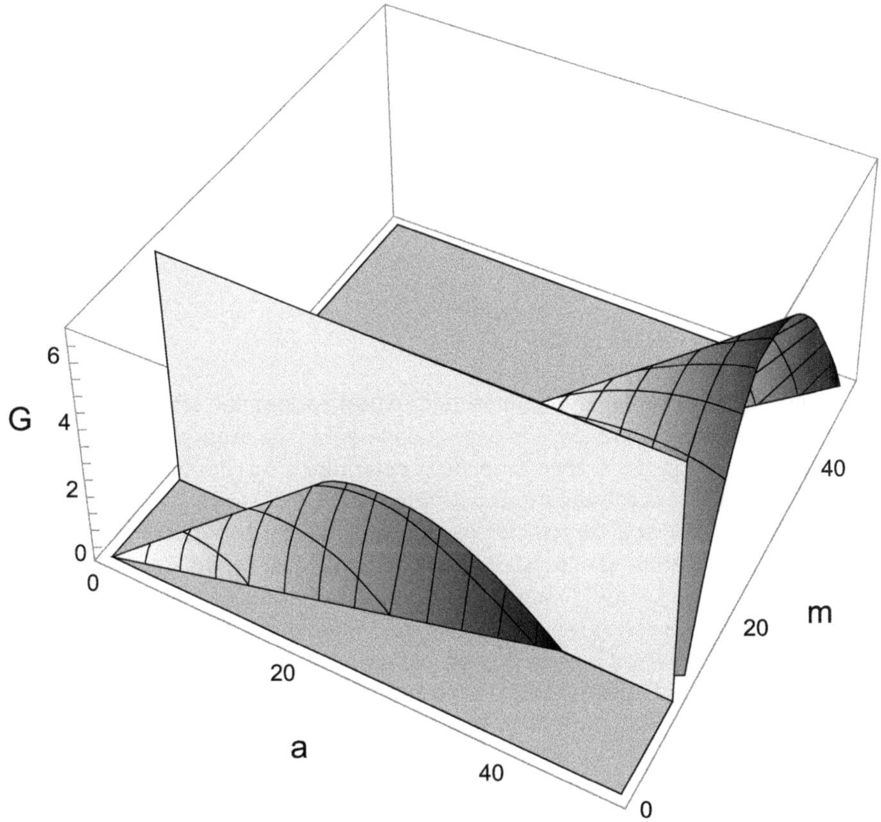

Figure 13.4 Profit function for partial factor variation

Assuming that – according to the assumption of limited information – the production function is not known to the firm, this boils down to the following (Q being the amount of output):

$$G(a) = pQ - (ap_a + mp_m).$$

Hence, third, there is a need that the firm explores its technological state space by varying the amount of a. A simple search algorithm for such exploration (and a possible switch to exploitation) can now be conceptualized by using the information that the agent can acquire by his/her own activity in different time steps t (i.e. $a(t)$ as observable input and $G(t)$ as observable profit for different t). Starting from an initial amount of a, $a(0)$, the agent has the alternative to apply the same a in the next time step, to reduce it or to increase it. If the last two cases are given, it has to be determined to what amount *a* should be changed. This is captured by the following difference equation (Wall 1993):

$$a(t) = a(t-1) + \frac{AS(t) - G(t-1)}{\dfrac{G(t-1) - G(t-2)}{a(t-1) - a(t-2)}}, \text{ where}$$

$$AS(t) = (1-\varphi)\,AS(t-1) + \varphi\left[(1-\lambda)\sum_{i=1}^{mem}\frac{G(t-i)}{mem} + \lambda G(t-1)\right] + \gamma\left[(1-\omega)\sum_{i=1}^{mem-1}\frac{G(t-i) - G(t-i-1)}{mem-1} + \omega(G(t-1) - G(t-2))\right].$$

A crucial role in this adaptation algorithm plays the aspiration level (*AS*) synthesizing the past profit experience in terms of averaging the profit and of averaging profit differences in proximate time steps determined by the memory capacity (*mem*) of the agent. According to the insights about the working of the memory in cognitive psychology, the last step has a special weight in both components for processing information about past profit experience. Hence, bounded rationality is depicted in a very simple manner by stipulating limited knowledge, memory constraints and, as a measuring rod for the individual performance, the aspiration level. Figure 13.5 shows how in this simple case (for a given numerical specification) the exploring agent is even approaching the profit optimum by using the search algorithm above.[6]

Fourth, a feedback from the agent's experience to the state space itself can be integrated in such an adaptation framework: the more the firm is getting experienced in applying factor *a*, the more the production function can change in that the productivity of *a* is increasing.[7] Hence, the corresponding learning effect is not simply given but generated by the exploration of the state space. To depict that, the background production function (still unknown to the agent) is defined as:

$$G(a) = pa^{\beta}(\mathrm{m})^{(1-\beta)} - (ap_a + mp_m), \text{ where}$$
$$\beta = f(t, a), \text{ and } \Delta\beta > 0, \text{ if } \Delta a > 0.$$

This is a simple way to integrate the idea of path dependency (in terms of production or organization) in this framework. The changing state space as well as the exploration trajectory (which is scanning only a small part of this state space) are depicted (again with a given numerical specification) in Figure 13.6.

The advantage of such a heterodox complement to the standard approach in microeconomics is obvious: a direct explanatory competition between both views is possible without requiring much research for figuring out the heterodox element. But there still remains an antithetic fixation on the neoclassical starting point. Furthermore, the potential of heterodox ideas as regards the core of microeconomics is not fully exploited.

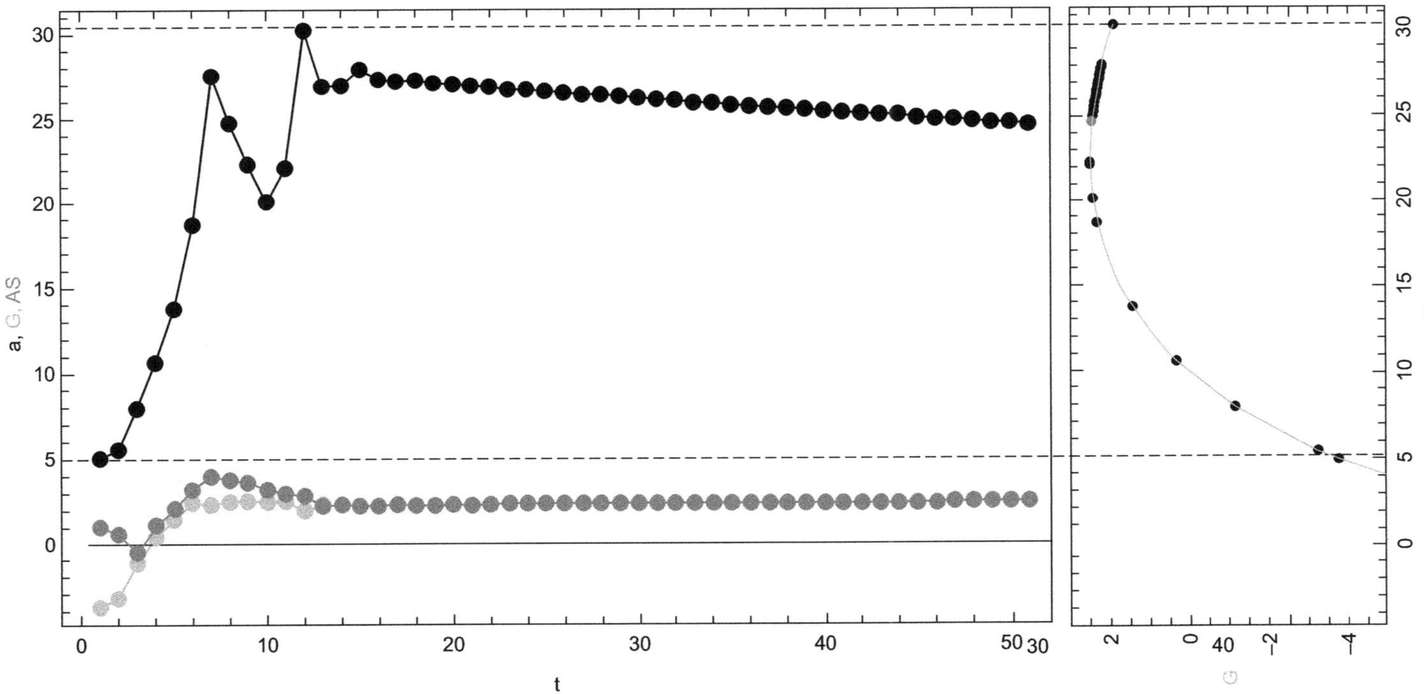

Figure 13.5 Simulating exploration/adaptation for partial factor variation of a firm. Time diagram (left) for different variables and corresponding state space diagram (right), with light grey point in the optimum

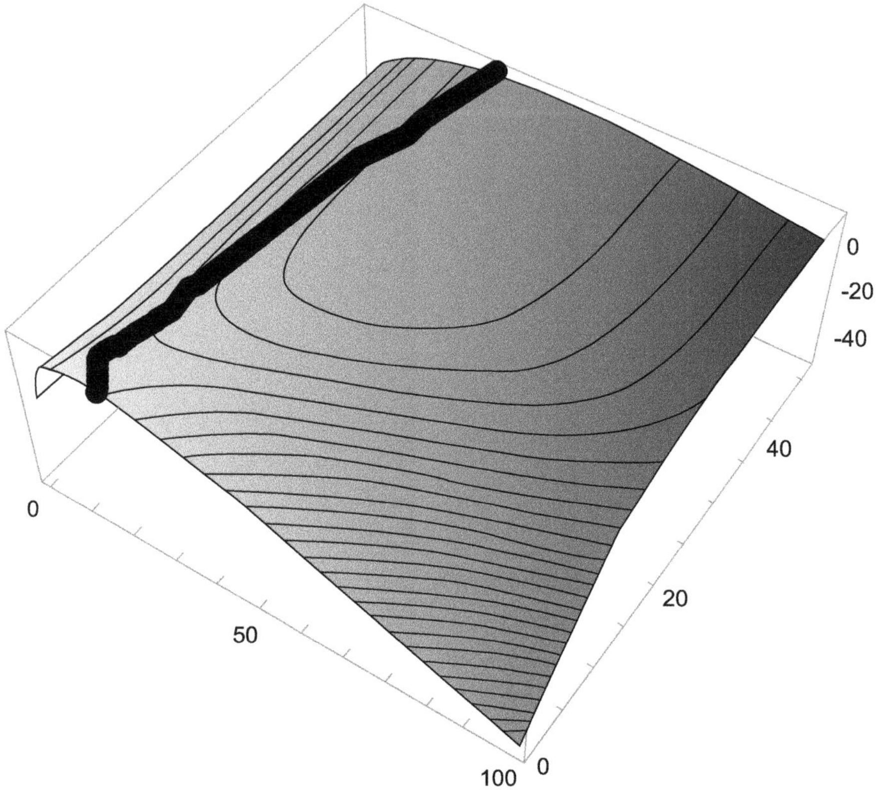

Figure 13.6 Exploration path, and dynamic state space for partial factor variation of a firm

3 Perspectives: a heterodox advanced course in microeconomics

In this course, an attempt is made to synthesize various heterodox ideas to a template for modelling the agents which are typically considered in microeconomics. As a background, it is assumed that the modern economy can be conceptualized as an operationally closed subsystem in the society as a whole. In the same way as the subsystem of science it is oriented toward a central 'Leitdifferenz' (a central, leading or indicating difference). In the case of the economy, the basic operations are payments which create new payments (Luhmann 1988). Hence, the main feature of the economy is to organize comparability of heterogeneous activities and products by mapping them into payment aspirations and to proceed with this comparability in terms of market operations.[8] The operations required in such a context are pursued by agents. Focussing on the way the agents are conditioning this context as well as on the way this context is recursively conditioning the agents is tantamount to an agent-based foundation of economic operations.[9] The idea of 'near decomposability' (Simon 1977, 1996, 2002) is not only the backbone for differentiating operationally closed subsystems as a means for complexity reduction in the society as a whole, but is also a useful heuristic for analyzing what is going on within these subsystems in terms of agent's activities. Hence, it can also be stipulated for the economy that complexity reduction on the agent level can be depicted by activity clusters being loosely linked to each other but consisting of strongly related elements inside. This distinction is not only useful if the coupling between agents shall be distinguished from what is going on within agents (or agencies); it is also a useful heuristic for characterizing the internal architecture of agents themselves (below).[10] This multilevel architecture is a feature of maintaining the ability to act in a complex state space and runs strictly counter to the two-level architecture of the mainstream concept of agents (see section 2).

Such a heterodox approach dispenses with all essential features of mainstream economics. As can be deduced from the previous paragraph, it is not 'scarcity' by which economic operations are founded, but rather social dependence and comparability. Contrary to the usual ideological supra-historic background of the neoclassical standard approach, a modern capitalist and market dominated economy is assumed to be at stake here. Hence households and firms are considered as 'social forms' (Marx), being shaped by money and commodity relations as well as unequal abilities in their way to act. All agents are subject to a precarious process of acceptance and integration in economic terms (for which the aforementioned comparability is an essential precondition). The activities of the microeconomic agents have macroeconomic preconditions (e.g. division of labour and structure of industries, organization of money and credit) as well as macroeconomic outcomes (e.g. patterns of overall activities in the course of time like the economic cycle) which cannot be deduced by considering the agents alone.[11] Hence, there are substantial limits to methodological individualism in the heterodox view of microeconomic affairs.[12] Common features for the heterodox portrayal of the internal architecture of agents can be emphasized: (1) the hierarchical clustering of different types of activities, (2) a recursive control and adaptation, (3) multiple modes of action (like deliberate decision, routines, search in an unknown state space) as well as (4) a 'multiple self'-nature (like having contradicting goals or following different operational procedures) of these agents.

Rare attempts have been made to figure out households, firms and their market operations from a heterodox point of view (for exceptions, see Lavoie 2014; Hill and Myatt 2010; Goodwin et al. 2005; Himmelweit et al. 2001; Elsner et al. 2015). The suggestions offered in this contribution are inspired by complexity economics and evolutionary economics and take into account the requirements of 'competitive pluralism' mentioned above.

Households in a capitalist economy can be ascribed the basic property to combine elementary reproduction with figuring out a social role on a low level of internal differentiation (in terms of division of labour, etc.). The background for both levels (clusters) of activity is the assumption of a hierarchy of needs (Lavoie 2014; Georgescu-Roegen 1966, 193ff.; Maslow 1954). This concept is specified for the given context by synthesizing the classical distinction between necessary und luxury consumption (Schefold 1986, 206ff.; Smith ([1776] 1979, 869ff.) and Veblen's elaboration of the social role of consumption (Ramstad 1994; Veblen [1899] 1949). Hence the hierarchically ordered levels of household activities are related to essential reproduction, variable reproduction (including 'defensive consumption') and the social role consumption (including 'keeping up consumption' and 'positional consumption').[13] The corresponding activities are shaped by the precarious process of social acceptance and integration in terms of market participation. This is implemented by a feedback between social role consumption and the corresponding aspiration level. In case of a persistent divergence from this aspiration level the efforts to gain income are varied (Figure 13.7, left).

Contrary to that, it is assumed that *firms* have the essential property to maintain/increase capital by realizing a surplus on the market. The internal structure of their activities is based on a high level of internal differentiation. This structure is shaped by market conditions (buying and selling) and by internal power relations. To capture these features, a synthesis of Marx's ideas and the modelling attempts of Nelson and Winter (1982) is proposed.[14] Again there is a hierarchy of activity levels: the management defining market/firm strategy as well as aspiration levels, the strategic operational level (research and development [R&D] leading eventually to innovation options, finance and investment) and the tactical operational level (procurement, organization/production and turnover). The dynamics is constituted by a recursive binding of operational activities to management decisions (Figure 13.7, right).

Based on these conceptualizations of agents, a heterodox market process can be figured out. At the core of such a market process is an endogenously generated supply of commodities and labour power, each in terms of posted prices in different sectors on the one side and the sectoral differentiated demand for commodities and labour power on the other side. Because there is no hidden construction guaranteeing the accordance between these two market sides, not only money plays an essential role (in terms of accounting and credit) but furthermore adaptation in terms of prices as well as quantities is required (including heterogeneity of prices, inventories and varying capacity utilization). This is intertwined with a market- and power-induced exploration of the technology state space (Figure 13.8).[15] Based on given macroeconomic prerequisites, prices, quantities and (un)employment emerge – possibly even in a cyclical manner.

In such a concept, the antithetic binding to the mainstream approach is abandoned and the full range of heterodox ideas can be scanned for their appropriateness. Especially as regards the selection of relevant conceptual ideas as well as their compatibility, a lot of research has to be done in the future. Furthermore, it has to be investigated in what sense (i.e. according to which criteria) comparability with advanced mainstream economics can be established and operationalized. In what sense is such an approach 'more plausible'? In what sense can there be a better explaining of 'stylized facts'? Can it be demonstrated in such a heterodox framework that mainstream microeconomics is dealing only with special cases?

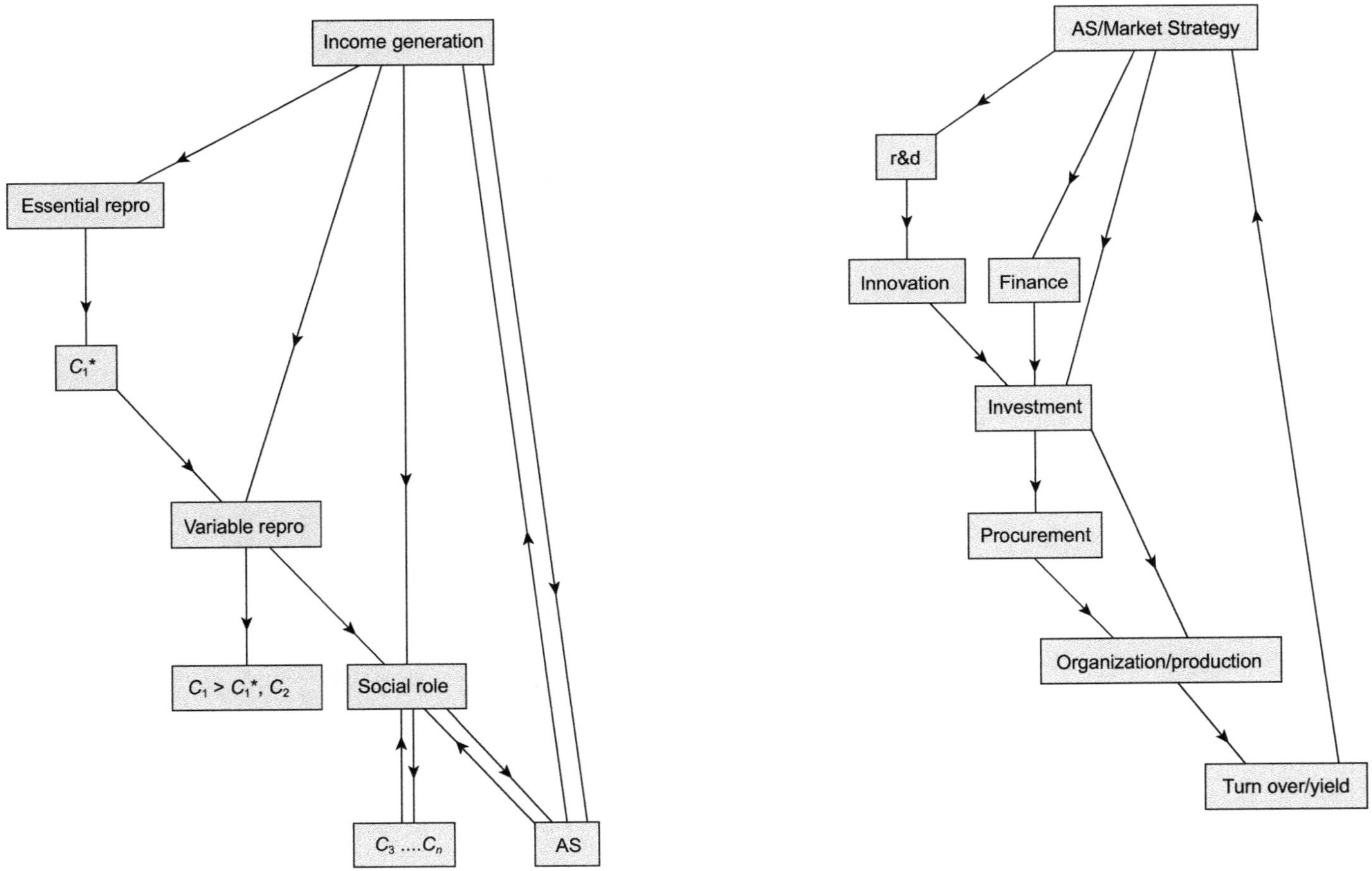

Figure 13.7 Basic architecture of microeconomic agents in advanced heterodox microeconomics (left: household with C_i consumption activities on different levels; right: firms)

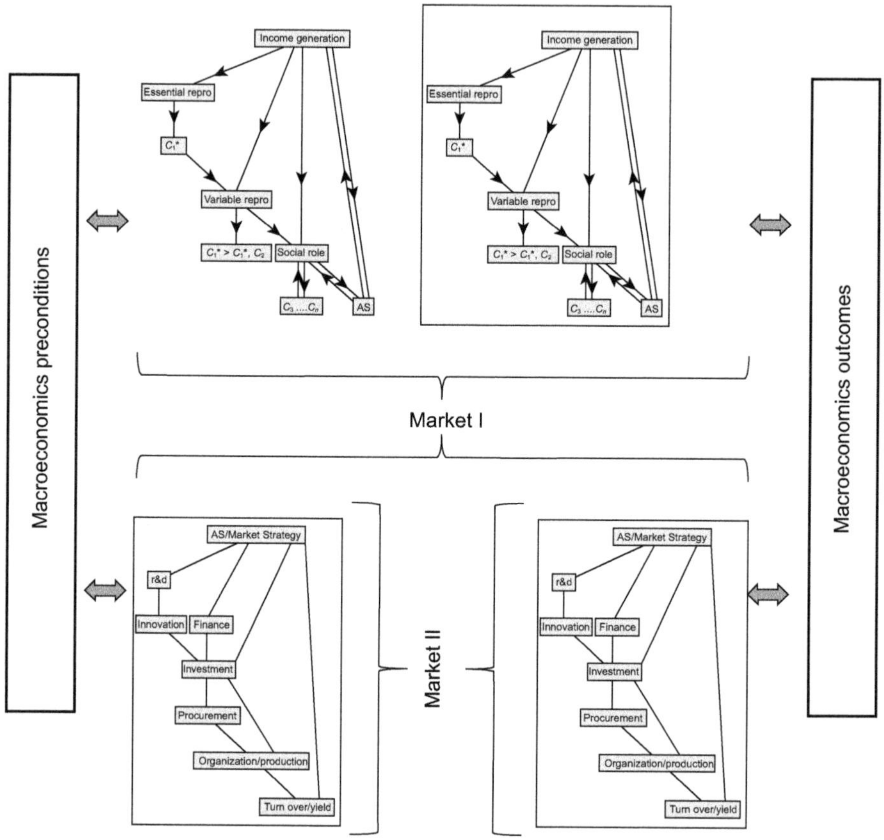

Figure 13.8 Market interaction between firms and households and complementarity to macroeconomics

4 Conclusion

This contribution tries to show that on the elementary as well as on the intermediary/advanced level of economic education a heterodox microeconomic alternative can be implemented. The common denominator of the suggestions made is that the static equilibrium orientation is substituted by a dynamic and adaptive evolutionary orientation. To be aware of this difference is not only crucial for understanding the controversies in many fields of economics but also for the student's ability to solve problems in economic practice.

Acknowledgments

Recommendations of an anonymous referee are gratefully acknowledged without sharing the responsibility for what is written here.

Notes

1 Identifying pluralism with considering all given concepts/theories as well as all aspects of a topic under consideration ('excessive pluralism', Vromen 2007, 72f.) is a strawman. Nevertheless, Vromen uses this strawman for legitimizing a monistic education in economics: 'I believe that it is better that students get a solid training in a particular school, tradition, and approach than that they only touch upon, in a rather facile way, various schools and approaches. And it seems obvious to me that this particular school, tradition and approach should be the one that is dominating the discipline' (ibid., 73). It is not explained on what criteria a 'solid training' is assessed as being 'better' than 'touching upon . . . various schools and approaches' (letting the suggestive wording apart). In the present contribution, it is shown that the implied trade-off between 'deepness' and 'broadness' can be solved in a way that learning consistency can persist as a feature of education even if pluralism is allowed for.

2 Of course there is a trade-off between guaranteeing self-reflectivity and completeness, but given the time constraints, a reasonable compromise seems possible.

3 It is assumed here that the reader is familiar with the basic topics, assumptions and methods in standard microeconomics.

4 This is done only for didactical reasons. Neither nice functions nor functions at all are required for the working of the heterodox modification.

5 See Georgescu-Roegen (1966, 103ff.) for an early criticism of this view.

6 This quasi-optimal result is by no means necessary. It is the more improbable, the more complicated the state space is and/or the less appropriate the calibration of the search algorithm is in terms of γ, λ, ω and φ. Finding the appropriate calibration for a given state space can then be modelled as a second-order learning process.

7 Hence, the state space is not given but has to be explored; nevertheless it remains stylized in formal terms by using a 'nice' production function.

8 In such a perspective, it is clear that institutions enabling this comparability like money and its organization play a central role for constituting the modern economy.

9 This is an essential difference to Luhmann's approach, who wants to get rid of actor concepts by separating communication processes from their social environment.

10 In very broad terms, there is a self-similarity on the different levels of analysis.

11 This does not exclude that an overall approach is possible in which a large part of the macroeconomic prerequisites as well as outcomes can be explained by referring to agents and their interaction in different sectors. But this is beyond the usual limits of microeconomics.

12 Correspondingly, methodological holism in macroeconomics has substantial limits in that meaningful microeconomic requirements – beyond the usual ad hoc constructions under the headline of 'microfoundation' – have to be postulated in a heterodox macroeconomics.

13 The distinction between these levels is an analytical device to classify empirically observable household behaviour.

14 Beckenbach (2017).

15 This is tantamount to an agent-based explanation of technical change and transcends the usual aggregative post-Keynesian approach (e.g. in Lavoie 2014, 428ff.).

References

Beckenbach, F. (2017): *Marx Evolving*. Marburg: Metropolis.

Elsner, W., Heinrich, T. and Schwardt, H. (2015): *The Microeconomics of Complex Economies: Evolutionary, Institutional, Neoclassical, and Complexity Perspectives*. San Diego, New York, Oxford and Amsterdam: Elsevier and Academic Press.

Georgescu-Roegen, N. (1966): *Analytical Economics: Issues and Problems*. Cambridge, MA: Harvard University Press.
Goodwin, N. et al. (2005): *Microeconomics in Context*. Boston: Houghton Mifflin.
Hill, R. and Myatt, T. (2010): *The Economics Anti-Textbook: A Critical Thinkers Guide to Macroeconomics*. London: Zed Books.
Himmelweit, S. et al. (2001): *Microeconomics: Neoclassical and Institutionalist Perspectives on Economic Behavior*. London: Thomson Learning.
King, J. E. (2012): *The Microfoundation Delusion: Metaphor and Dogma in the History of Macroeconomics*. Cheltenham, UK: Edward Elgar.
Lavoie, M. (2014): *Post-Keynesian Economics: New Foundations*. Cheltenham, UK: Edward Elgar.
Luhmann, N. (1988): *Die Wirtschaft der Gesellschaft*. Frankfurt am Main: Suhrkamp.
Machlup, F. (1960): *Der Wettstreit zwischen Mikro- und Makrotheorien in der Nationalökonomie*. Tubingen: J.C.B. Mohr.
Maslow, A. H. (1954): *Motivation and Personality*. New York: Harper & Row.
Nelson, R. R. and Winter, S. G. (1982): *An Evolutionary Theory of Economic Change*. Cambridge, MA: Harvard University Press.
Ramstad, Y. (1994): "Art. Veblen, Torstein", in Hodgson, G. M., Samuels, W. J. and Tool, M. R. (eds.), *The Elgar Companion to Institutional and Evolutionary Economics*. Aldershot, UK: Edward Elgar, 363–368.
Schefold, B. (1986): *Nachfrage und Zufuhr in der klassischen Ökonomie. Ökonomische Klassik im Umbruch*. Frankfurt am Main: Suhrkamp, 195–241.
Simon, H. A. (1977): "The Organization of Complex Systems", in Patte, H. H. (ed.), *Hierarchy Theory: The Challenge of Complex Systems*. New York: George Braziller, 1–27.
Simon, H. A. (1996): *The Sciences of the Artificial*. Cambridge, MA: MIT Press.
Simon, H. A. (2002): "Near Decomposability and the Speed of Evolution", *Industrial and Corporate Change* 11(3), 587–599.
Smith, A. (1979 [1776]): *An Inquiry into the Nature and Causes of the Wealth of Nations*. Vol. 2. Indianapolis, USA: Liberty Classics.
Veblen, T. B. (1949 [1899]): *The Theory of Leisure Class: An Economic Study of Institutions*. London: Allen & Unwin.
Vromen, J. (2007): "In Praise of Moderate Plurality: Teaching Pluralism in Economics", in Groenewegen, J. (ed.), *Teaching Pluralism in Economics*. Cheltenham, UK: Edward Elgar, 64–94.
Wall, K. D. (1993): "A Model of Decision Making under Bounded Rationality", *Journal of Economic Behaviour and Organization* 20(3), 331–352.

14 Functional income distribution in economic paradigms

The failure of the neoclassical approach and alternatives

Hansjörg Herr

1 Introduction

Functional income distribution shows how income is distributed between labour income and non-labour income. It is an important factor for personal income distribution as most of non-labour income flows to households with high income. Over the last decades the wage share in most countries decreased (see section 2) and substantially added to increasing personal income inequality (Piketty 2014). This chapter concentrates on functional income distribution. Different economic paradigms explain functional income distribution differently. In most textbooks and mainstream debates, only the neoclassical explanation of functional income distribution is discussed. However, in spite of its dominance in academic debates the neoclassical explanation is theoretically unsatisfactory and even inconsistent. The aim of this contribution is to show the weakness of the neoclassical explanation of functional income distribution and discuss alternative explanations.

When speaking about functional income distribution, it is obvious that many short-term effects like the business cycle can influence it. The main purpose of the chapter is to clarify the paradigmatic differences between different economic approaches. For this purpose not the whole paradigms are elaborated. Also governments and the external sector are excluded from the analysis. The focus is on the more long-term fundamental factors of functional income distribution and to show the nucleus of different paradigms in the field of functional income distribution. Section 3 discusses the neoclassical and section 4 the classical explanation of functional income distribution. The post-Keynesian paradigm follows in section 5, and especially John Maynard Keynes and Michal Kalecki are discussed. At the end conclusions are drawn. More technical elaborations are contained in boxes.

2 Development of functional income distribution

The wage share (wages as share of income) and profit share (profit as share of income) add up to 1. Under profit all non-labour income is subordinated, for example interest and dividend payments or undistributed profits. If Y is income, W the wage sum and Q the profit sum, it follows $Y = W + Q$ and $\frac{W}{Y} + \frac{Q}{Y} = 1$.

In empirical analyses, the wage or profit shares are usually shown as share of gross domestic product (GDP). This is also done in Figure 14.1, which shows the development of the adjusted wage share for a selection of countries in the OECD (Organisation for Economic Co-operation and Development).[1] It can be seen that wage shares in developed countries substantially dropped. In most countries, especially in the 1980s, big changes took place. In the United States, for example, an almost continuous fall of the wage share can be observed. Declining wage shares are very much connected with the crisis in the major capitalist countries in the 1970s and the changes of the capitalist model in the 1970s and especially in the 1980s towards a system with more deregulated financial and labour markets.

With the wave of deregulation of financial and labour markets, top management salaries including share options and other profit-related elements started to explode, especially in Anglo-Saxon countries. In 2015 CEOs of the S&P 500 Index earned 335 times more than an average nonsupervisory worker and 819 times more than the US federal minimum wage (AFL-CIO 2016). Though these payments have a close proximity to profit income, in the system of national accounts, they are classified as wages and salaries. Subtracting the wages of the top 0.1% income

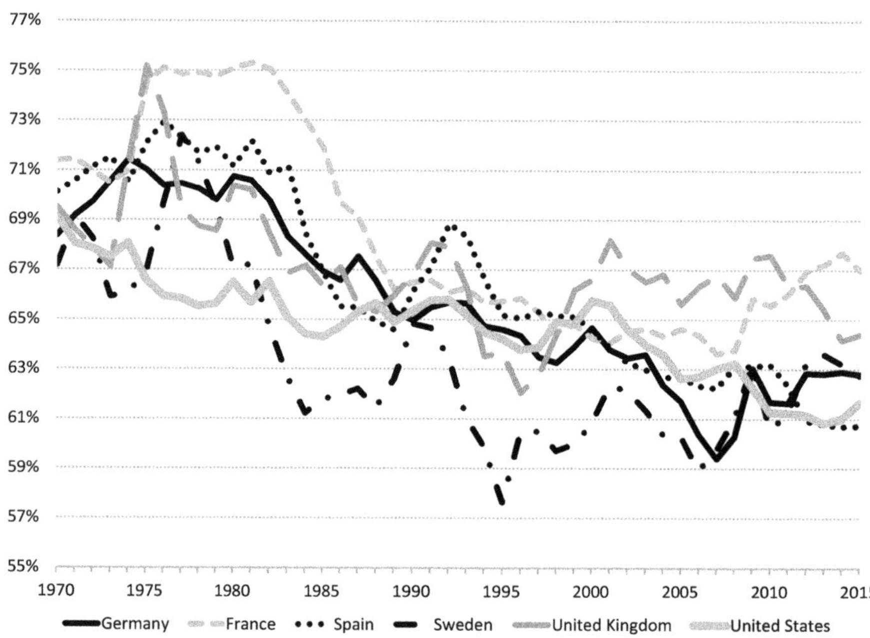

Figure 14.1 Adjusted wage share (labour income in percent of GDP)*; selected OECD countries; 1970–2015

Source: AMECO (2016); authors' calculations. Note: Data for Germany refer to West Germany until 1990.

* Compensation per employee as a share of GDP at factor costs per person employed. Labour's share includes both dependent and self-employed workers and GDP excludes taxes but includes subsidies.

earners from labour income produces a pronounced stronger downward trend of wage shares (Dünhaupt 2011).

3 The neoclassical paradigm

In the neoclassical paradigm, the marginal productivity theory of distribution explains functional income distribution. In this paradigm the so-called monetary sphere does not play any role. In the centre of the distribution model is the production function. The basic idea is that capital and labour as factors of production work together to produce an output.[2] Capital is the value of physical production inputs (except labour) embodying a certain technology. More precisely, a firm under perfect competition maximises profits under the condition that real wages are equal to the marginal product of labour and the rate of return on capital is equal to the marginal product of capital. The marginal productivity of labour and capital decreases under the condition that more labour or more capital is used. The law of decreasing returns holds, otherwise labour demand will not increase when wages fall and more capital is not invested when the interest rate goes down. In this approach, exploitation of workers does not exist. Each factor of production gets its fair share of output, including labour (see Box 14.1).

Box 14.1

The macroeconomic production function is given by $Yr = Yr(K, H)$, with Yr as real net domestic product or in a closed economy real income, K as real capital and H as labour input. With P as price index, total revenues are $P \cdot Yr(K, H)$; with w as wage per hour, wage costs are $w \cdot H$; and with i_r as the interest rate determined in the real sphere, interest costs are $i_r \cdot P \cdot K$ with $P \cdot K$ as the nominal value of capital. We follow here the neoclassical tradition to speak about an interest rate and not a profit rate. The interest rate i_r can be interpreted as the long-term equilibrium profit rate. The profit function is $Q = P \cdot Yr(K, H) - w \cdot H - i_r \cdot P \cdot K$, with Q as profit. With MPL as physical marginal product of labour (first derivative of the production function in respect to labour) and MPC as physical marginal product of capital (first derivative of the production function in respect to capital) a firm under perfect competition maximises profits when $\text{MPL} \cdot P = w$ and $\text{MPC} \cdot P = P \cdot i_r$. The profit-maximising conditions can also be written as $\text{MPL} = w/P$, with w/P as real wage and $\text{MPC} = i_r$. Real income is equal to the real wage sum and real interest sum $Yr = H \cdot \text{MPL} + K \cdot \text{MPC}$ or $Yr = (w/P) \cdot \text{MPL} + i_r \cdot \text{MPC}$. The interest rate determined in the real sphere determines the real money interest rate. The real money interest rate is the nominal money interest rate minus the inflation rate. If the interest rate of the real sphere determined by the marginal productivity of capital is different from the real money interest rate, economic development becomes distorted (Wicksell 1898).

To explain the falling wage share over the last decades, a specific technological development that privileges capital is assumed. Insufficient investment in "human capital" is also made responsible for a falling wage share. For example, the OECD argues that between 1990 and 2007, around 80% of the within-industry decline of wage shares stemmed from specific productivity developments.

> This is consistent with the idea advanced by many studies that the spread of information and communication technologies (ICTs) has created opportunities . . . for unprecedented advances in innovation and inventions of new capital goods and production processes, thereby boosting productivity.
>
> (OECD 2012, 110)

The neoclassical paradigm needs very specific assumptions about the production function. It is only consistent under the assumption of constant returns to scale. Otherwise, according to the model, the sum of wages plus profits distributed is bigger or smaller than the income created in the economy. There is no guarantee that constant returns to scale exist in reality. The opposite is the case. In many industries, economies of scale dominate. In addition, fundamental inconsistencies of the model were revealed during the Cambridge-Cambridge debate in the 1960s. It was shown that the model only works under the extremely unrealistic assumption of one capital good.[3] If these assumptions are not given, the whole model breaks down (Box 14.2).

Box 14.2

Usually a Cobb-Douglas production function, $Yr = T \cdot K^{\alpha} \cdot H^{\beta}$ with T as total factor productivity and α and β as output elasticities of capital and labour, is used to explain functional income distribution. Only if $\alpha + \beta = 1$ are wages and profits determined according to the marginal productivity theory equal to income and in equilibrium $Yr = H \cdot MPL + K \cdot MPC$ holds. In case of economies of scale $\alpha + \beta > 1$ more income is distributed than produced, and in case of diseconomies of scale $\alpha + \beta < 1$ the distribution rule does not distribute all income. Under the condition $\alpha + \beta = 1$, changing productivities of one of the production factors do not lead to changing wage or profit shares as the elasticities of substitution between capital and labour is per definition 1. The surprising result is that regardless of the amount of labour or capital used the share of labour will be α and the share of capital β (Rabbani 2016). This means the Cobb-Douglas production function under constant returns to scale cannot explain any change in functional income distribution. The only possibility to explain changes in income distribution is the exogenous "jump" from one production function to another one with a different α and β. It remains unclear what T is. In empirical estimations it is usually the "rest" which cannot be explained (Felipe and McCombie 2007).

The Cambridge (England)-Cambridge (USA) debate asked what *K* in the production function means. To calculate the marginal product of capital and labour, the stock of capital has to be known. In comparison to labour which can be measured in hours, capital has to be calculated in values. The value of a given stock of capital depends obviously on the structure of prices of capital goods. But the structure of prices depends on the distribution of income. Here, the model is tangled up in a circle as the stock of capital has to be known to determine functional distribution, and functional distribution has to be known to calculate the stock of capital. An example can make the problem clearer. Starting at equilibrium with equal profit rates in all industries and assuming increasing wages, then labour-intensive industries will suffer from a much bigger increase of wage costs than capital intensive industries. Profit rates become unequal. To come to a new equilibrium with equal profit rates the whole structure of prices has to change, whereas the complication is that the output of one industry is the input of another industry. The new equilibrium can show a lower or a higher value of the stock of capital even if the physical capital stock has not changed (capital reversing is possible). And under the new structure of prices, firms may choose a different profit-maximising technology which may be less or more capital intensive and employment may increase with increasing real wages (reswitching is possible). The neoclassical distribution model and the demand functions for capital and labour break down. Paul Samuelson (1966, 582 f.), one of the most famous US economists after World War II who first wanted to save the model, wrote:

> Reswitching . . . does alert us to several vital possibilities. Lower interest rates . . . can involve denial of diminishing returns and entail reverse capital deepening . . . There often turns out to be no unambiguous way of characterising different processes as more "capital intensive," more "mechanised" more "roundabout."

To sum up, the marginal productivity theory of distribution is theoretically not defendable (see Sraffa 1960; Garegnani 1970; Harcourt 1972; Lazzarini 2011).

4 The classical explanation

In the neoclassical world, the system of relative prices including real wages and the real interest rate and income distribution are determined in one model. Following Piero Sraffa (1960, 11), there is "one degree of freedom" in the system. Income distribution has to be explained by a sub-model. Only if income distribution is given by the sub-model can the overall model be developed. In the classical paradigm there is a sub-model to explain real wages.

Real wages are given by the reproduction needs of workers. Given real wages and the productivity of the economy, profits as the surplus are the remaining part. Thus under the condition of a given productivity, the profit share is determined by real wages. In more sophisticated approaches the power of the working class, in particular the power of trade unions, influences real wages. Productivity reflects

Box 14.3

The profit quota is $Q/Y = 1 - W/Y$. With $W = w \cdot H$ and $Y = Yr \cdot P$ we get $Q/Y = 1 - (w \cdot H)/(Yr \cdot P)$. Real wages are defined as $wr = w/P$ and productivity as $\pi = Yr/H$. Then the profit quota is given by $Q/Y = 1 - wr/\pi$. Given real wages, increasing productivity will increase the profit share as a surplus.

certain technologies and skills but also the intensity of labour or the structure of the economy. Under a long-term perspective an increase in productivity increases the profit share – at least as long as workers are not able to increase real wages (Sraffa 1960; Marx 1867) (Box 14.3).

In the classical paradigm all values are created by labour. However, capital only can earn a profit when labour does not get all its produced value. There must be a power source in capitalism which keeps real wages low. The power source of capital is unemployment which makes the working class weak. Unemployment is the usual state of affairs in a capitalist economy and is reproduced by the market mechanism. Let us assume a booming economy with GDP growth higher than productivity growth. Under this condition the resulting demand for labour reduces unemployment and increases the bargaining power of workers or trade unions. This leads to higher real wages and reduces profits. If profits become too low, the accumulation of capital stagnates resulting in low GDP growth, rising unemployment and finally falling real wages. Profits increase again and, at least potentially, can trigger a new wave of higher growth (Marx 1867, chapter 23). However, in this model the long-term level of real wages is given exogenously by reproduction needs and/or class struggle.

In this interpretation the falling wage share over the last decades is the result of a weaker working class. Indeed, many facts document a reduced power of the working class since the 1970s, for example a fall in union density, the deregulation of labour markets, aggressive government policies against unions or the threat of outsourcing or shrinking industries with traditionally high union density.

The classical model to explain functional income distribution is not very convincing. To fix exogenously real wages implies that *real* wages are determined in the labour market and not *nominal* wages (see below). And what kind of consumption basket should be assumed for workers? It is almost impossible to fix such a basket given by reproduction needs or class struggle. A group of workers may like to have a big car, others a nice flat and still others like to spend their income for holidays. The additional problem is that the consumption basket has to be fixed before relative prices are determined. This is not a very realistic assumption (Sraffa 1960, 33).

5 The post-Keynesian paradigm

From the post-Keynesian perspective, the neoclassical and classical paradigm falsely assume that *real* wages are determined in the labour market.[4] This violates the fact that in wage contracts only nominal wages are fixed.

Nominal unit labour costs for firms depend on nominal wages and productivity (see Box 14.4). There is no good argument why the price level should remain unchanged when the level of nominal unit labour costs changes. If the price of oil increases, companies roll over higher costs; if the value-added tax increases, prices will rise as well; and if wage costs for all companies increase, firms will increase prices as well. If costs fall – at least in competitive markets – prices will fall as well. The classical and neoclassical paradigm in "assuming that the wage bargain determines the real wage . . . have slipped in an illicit assumption." And if, for whatever reason, the working class wants to reduce the real wage level, "there may exist no expedient by which labour as a whole can reduce its *real* wage to a given figure by making revised *money* bargains with the entrepreneurs" (Keynes 1936, 13). In the short term there may exist various institutional factors like contractual commitments, adjustment costs for bargaining and changing prices, international competition and so forth which prevent price adjustments. However, in the medium and long run, these factors lose importance (Herr 2009).

In the following paragraph the relationship between increasing wage costs and changing prices is discussed in more detail. To which extent changing costs and, more specifically, changing unit labour costs are rolled over to prices or to which extent prices fall when costs fall, depends on the type of competition that exists in the goods markets. Under *pure competition* there are many small firms which produce a homogenous product. Firms have no influence on prices. Entry barriers of new firms in the market are low. In the long term firms earn low profits, which are simplified case equal to interest costs.[5] Increasing wage costs cannot bite into profits of firms under pure competition as there is no room to reduce profit. These firms will have to increase prices and roll over increasing costs otherwise they cannot survive. There is a direct cost-price mechanism in the framework of markup pricing. This means that there is no excess demand needed to increase prices. Under *monopolistic competition* also many small firms exist, but in this case they follow product diversification (e.g. different small restaurants offer different types of meals). Entry barriers in these markets are also low and in the long run the profit situation is the same as under pure competition.[6] In the case of *oligopolistic and monopolistic markets* only a small number or potentially only one firm dominates the market. Either homogenous or differentiated products can be produced. In the absence of legal restriction only economies of scale can explain oligopolistic and monopolistic markets. Entry barriers are high because big companies can produce more efficiently than small ones. In these markets, oligopoly or monopoly profits or quasi-rents can be earned.

Keynes (1930) developed his inflation mode in the *Treatise on Money*. He assumed implicitly pure or monopolistic competition. For the relation between wage costs and prices, this implies that increasing wage costs are completely rolled over. Wage cost and prices change in the same way – at least in the medium and long terms. The real wage level cannot be changed by changes in the nominal wage level (see Box 14.4).

Box 14.4

As $Y = W + Q$ and $Y = Yr \cdot P$, it follows that $P = W/Yr + Q/Yr$. Profits are given by the profit rate (q) multiplied with the nominal stock of capital $Q = q \cdot P \cdot K$. The term W/Yr expresses nominal unit labour costs. If nominator and denominator are divided by labour input (H) we get $W/Yr = w/\pi$ with w as nominal wage per hour and π as productivity. The definition of the price level then becomes $P = w/\pi + (q \cdot P \cdot K)/Yr$. If unit labour costs increase, a first round of price increases takes place. A second round is triggered as the nominal capital stock increases its value as firms pay now higher prices for their inputs. It is easy to show that a proportional relationship exists between increases of unit labour costs and the price level (Heine and Herr 2013). If, for example, nominal wages increase by 5% and productivity by 2%, unit labour increases by 3% and this increases the price level also by 3%. Of course, in this model many other factors which influence the price level are neglected. But this model gives the core of the Keynesian inflation model (Keynes 1930). Empirically a very close relationship exists between changes of nominal unit labour costs and price level changes.

Keynes argued, as the classical paradigm (which he called pre-classical), that all values are created by labour.[7] However, he did not believe in the surplus concept. In comparison to the classical paradigm, he developed an alternative sub-model to close the degree of freedom in the system. In his approach the profit rate is given exogenously whereas the profit rate is determined by the money interest rate.[8] It can be assumed that a company finances all its capital by credit and hence interest payments constitute actual costs or, more realistically, part of capital is financed by equity which earns a return equal to the interest rate.

Keynes (1936, chapter 17) developed a model in which the preference by wealth owners to keep money (which also stands for short-term monetary wealth as liquidity) is the key factor to determine the interest rate. In Keynes's thinking the subjectively felt advantage to hoard money creates a liquidity premium for their holders expressed in a percentage. With increasing liquidity holding the marginal liquidity premium decreases, however only to a certain level. The interest rate cannot fall below the marginal liquidity premium. "The rate of interest obviously measures . . . the premium which has to be offered to induce people to hold their wealth in some form other than hoarded money" (Keynes 1936, 216). And, as soon as interest exists a profit is enforced: "If, however, the rate of interest exceeds zero, a new element of cost is introduced which increases with the length of the process" (Keynes 1936, 216).

This model to explain the interest rate is sufficient to close the degree of freedom of the system but it is a bit queer. The main shortcoming is that the banking system is not included in the model and money is considered to be exogenously given by the central bank. In modern versions of the Keynesian paradigm, money is given endogenously and the interest rate depends on the refinancing rate of the central bank plus the interest rate spread demanded by commercial banks and private wealth owners for long-term credits (see Herr 2014). In addition, usually profit rates can and will be higher than interest rates. By how much profit rates exceed long-term interest rates depends on the power of the financial system, especially the corporate governance system.

One consequence of this analysis is that the wage share depends on the exogenously given profit rate and on factors which determine the capital coefficient (the capital-output ratio). Another consequence is that real wages are not determined in the labour market and are, at least in the medium to long terms, independent of developments of money wages. To increase real wages in the long run, productivity has to be increased (see Box 14.5).

Box 14.5

Profits in the long-run equilibrium are given by the profit rate multiplied with the nominal stock of capital. Wages are income minus profits: $W = Y - q \cdot P \cdot K$. Dividing both sides of the equation by Y and using the definition of the capital coefficient k as $k = (P \cdot K)/Y$ provides the follow definition of the wage share: $W/Y = 1 - q \cdot k$.

The capital coefficient can also be written as $k = (P \cdot K)/(P \cdot Yr) = (K/H)/(Yr/H) = b/\pi$ with b as capital intensity of production and π as productivity. Then we get $W/Y = 1 - q \cdot b/\pi$.

The wage share depends on the profit rate and the two technical variables capital intensity and productivity. It has to be taken into consideration that the capital coefficient and the capital intensity depend also on functional income distribution (see Cambridge-Cambridge debate).

What determines real wages? It holds by definition: $W/Y = (w \cdot H)/(P \cdot Yr) = wr/\pi$. Using this definition for the wage share it follows that $wr/\pi = 1 - q \cdot b/\pi$ and $wr = \pi - q \cdot b$.

Real wages depend on the macroeconomic level of productivity, labour intensity and the profit rate and not on the nominal wage development. As changes of q are limited and b is difficult to control and does also change slowly, the increase of productivity is the main factor for increasing real wages. Keynes (1936, 17) argues that in the short period, wages depend on the marginal product of labour. This is no contradiction to the above formula, which has a long-term perspective. Also, even if under perfect competition MPL $\cdot$ $P = w$ on a macroeconomic level, an increase of w will lead to an increase of P with an unchanged MPL.

In Keynes (1936) in a very simple model argued $l = i = q$, whereas the marginal liquidity premium determines the long-term money interest rate (i) and the interest rate the profit rate. In a more modern version the long-term interest rate depends on the short-term interest rate (is) determined by the central bank plus an interest rate spread or a risk premium (d). We obtain $is + d = i$. If p expresses the power of institutions and agents in the financial system to force companies to increase the profit rate above the interest rate, we get $q = i + p$ or $q = is + d + p$ (Herr and Ruoff 2016).

Let us turn to Kalecki (1971, 3), who thought that the assumption of pure competition (and we can add monopolistic competition) is a "dangerous myth." His theory of income distribution suggests that functional income distribution is determined by firms' price setting power. Firms impose a markup on unit variable costs depending on their *degree of monopoly* (Kalecki (1965; see also Hein 2014)). This means Kalecki assumes oligopolistic and monopolistic markets. Functional income distribution is then substantially influenced by the weighted markup of oligopolistic and monopolistic firms. The degree of monopoly depends on four factors, which are (a) the degree of economic concentration and price competition, (b) the role of non-price competition as for example advertising, (c) overhead costs, which also include interest and dividend payments[9] and (d) the bargaining power of trade unions.

The first two arguments are straightforward and influence the shape of the demand curve a firm is confronted with. The last two arguments deal with costs. When costs increase and firms do not increase prices, then profits will decrease. However, when firms increase prices, demand goes down according to the shape of the demand curve. It follows that the profit-maximising strategy might be a less than proportional increase of prices when costs increase. Under perfect and monopolistic competition, firms must roll over all cost increases because there are no profits which could be reduced. In oligopolistic and monopolistic markets, the situation is different. If firms in these markets are confronted with higher costs depending on their demand functions, prices might increase less than costs.

Strong trade unions bargaining on a firm level can exploit such a constellation:

> High mark-ups in existence will encourage strong trade unions to bargain for higher wages since they know that firms can "afford" to pay them. If their demands are granted but . . . [the mark-up is] not changed, prices also increase. This would lead to a new round of demand for higher wages and the process would go on with price levels rising. But surely an industry will not like such a process making its products more and more expensive and thus less competitive with the products of others industries. To sum up, trade-union power restrains the mark-ups.
>
> (Kalecki 1971, 161; see also Kalecki 1966, 18)

Under oligopolistic and monopolistic markets, Kalecki's argument is convincing. This is especially the case in stakeholder corporate governance systems in which management searches for a compromise between different stakeholders. For example, "extra-profit sharing" between unions and firms was widespread in big US corporations in the period after World War II, even in countries like the United States (Levy and Temin 2010).

In the Keynesian-Kaleckian approach the main reason for the falling wage share during the last decades can be found in the "conservative revolution" which started in the United Kingdom and the United States at the end of the 1970s (Harvey 2005). This revolution changed the type of capitalism towards a deregulated finance dominated model with far reaching deregulation of financial and labour markets and a market driven globalisation model with big financial institutions and multinational companies in the centre. A clear sign of this is the change in the corporate governance system from a stakeholder to a shareholder system from the 1980s onwards. Pioneers for the new corporate governance philosophy were Alfred Rappaport (1999) and Jack Welch, CEO of General Electric. Financialisation of the economy and the increasing power of agent in the financial system led to high pressure to increase profit rates. Stiglitz (2012) stresses that the excessive rent-seeking behaviour by companies through the creation of bigger and bigger companies, brand names, non-transparency, opaque pricing systems or political acceptance and support of very powerful firms increased profit markups. The proliferation of outsourcing of low-tech, labour intensive and ecologically problematic productions from developed to developing countries increased profits of lead firms in global value chains (Milberg and Winkler 2013). Trade unions were not able to oppose these developments. The opposite was the case, the power of trade unions erodes and also the possibility to "share" extra profits with big companies. Piketty (2014, 113 ff.) argues that the capital coefficient has been slowly increasing during the last decades. Together with the pressure and power to keep the profit rate high, the falling wage share can be explained.

There are a number of empirical investigations that stress the role of the factors mentioned above. According to these empirical studies, financialisation plays an important role as well as weaker bargaining power of labour and forces of globalisation (see Stockhammer 2015; Hein 2015; Dünhaupt 2016; Gallas et al. 2016). These arguments are very much in support of the post-Keynesian approach to explain functional income distribution.

6 Conclusion and policy consequences

The neoclassical paradigm is not very convincing in explaining functional income distribution. It assumes that real wages are determined in the labour market, which is obviously not the case. In addition, the neoclassical approach is caught up in contradictions within its own paradigm which are, however, concealed with great consistency and dishonesty. The failure of the neoclassical distribution model, including the breakdown of the inverse relationship between the stock of capital and the interest rate and falling wages and increasing labour demand, are not openly discussed and by no means included in textbooks. To save the model by assuming the existence of only one capital good is not an acceptable abstraction as it violates all empirical facts and already the existence of two capital goods destroys the model.

The other approaches stress different power sources which explain the existence of non-labour income. The classical paradigm stresses the power of capital based on unemployment. Keynes emphasises the power of wealth owners and the financial system. Kalecki argues with the oppressive power of companies to follow rent-seeking strategies whereas he assumed interest payments and dividends as part of overhead costs. From a post-Keynesian perspective, the classical approach is opaque because there is no convincing possibility to fix a basket of goods as reproduction needs. And there is no clear analysis how the wage bargaining process could directly determine a basket of goods independent of the structure of prices. The post-Keynesian approach is based on a clear market analysis. Keynesian and Kaleckian arguments complement each other.

What policies are suitable in the post-Keynesian approach to increase the wage share? The first area is the control of the financial system including institutions and regulations which reduce the power of financial agents. Keynes thought in a mature capitalist system real interest rates would fall to a level close to zero. This "would mean the euthanasia of the rentier, and, consequently, the euthanasia of the cumulative oppressive power of the capitalist to exploit the scarcity-value of capital" (Keynes 1936, 376). Keynes's expectations were probably overly optimistic, but policies to bring interest rates and dividend payments down and only reward innovative entrepreneurs and not rentiers who pocket interest and dividends go in the right direction.

A second area of policies to increase the wage share is to prevent the widespread rent-seeking behaviour of especially multinational companies. Anti-trust policies are needed, and all types of policies which reduce rents which are based on oligopolistic and monopolistic supply and/or demand positions and non-transparent markets.

A third area is the corporate governance system. The shareholder value corporate governance system has to be overcome. In a stakeholder corporate governance system in which management is forced to search for a compromise between the different stakeholders, not only rents become smaller and can be shared among the different stakeholders, but also the intensity of work and working conditions can be improved. Democracy has to include the management of big multinational companies which have turnovers that are almost comparable to small nation-states.

A fourth area of policies consists of socialising natural monopolies and establishing big state-owned or partly state-owned sectors, for example in the field of housing and public utilities.

Last but not least, it should be mentioned that inequality is a complex problem with many dimensions. Besides increasing the wage share wage dispersion, the distribution of profits among households and tax and expenditure policies of governments are also important. In the field of corporate governance and wage dispersion, strong trade unions play an important role to reduce inequality. In areas like reducing rent-seeking strategies, taxing obscenely high salaries, setting sufficiently high minimum wages or providing public goods government policies are needed. Only a whole package of policies can create a constellation which allows a stable, fair and sustainable economic system with high employment. Economics can only contribute to the development of such societies if it allows and supports open debates and recognises its own shortcomings. Mainstream economics, not least in textbooks and education, lacks such openness.

Acknowledgments

For comments I thank two anonymous reviewers.

Notes

1 Adjusted means that income of self-employed which is counted as non-labour income is divided in labour income and profits. The European Commission data base AMECO (2016) uses the following formula: (wages/GDP)·(active population/employees).
2 We abstract from land as an own production factor.
3 It also can be assumed that in all industries the capital intensity (ratio of capital to labour) is the same. This also implies in the end only one capital good.
4 There are other shortcomings. Neoclassical economists argue that at least in the long term demand does not influence economic development (Say's Law). In the post-Keynesian paradigm demand is important in the short and long terms. Another point is that money in the post-Keynesian paradigm is not neutral also in the long term.
5 When firms have own capital, this earns the same rate of return as the interest rate.
6 There is the general problem that it is unclear how prices under pure competition can change when all firms are price takers. For these reasons monopolistic competition can be assumed as the typical case.
7 "I sympathise . . . with the pre-classical doctrine that everything is *produced by labour* . . . . It is preferable to regard labour, including of course, the personal services of the entrepreneur and his assistants, as the sole factor of production, operating in a given environment of technique, natural resources, capital equipment and effective demand" (Keynes 1936, 213 f.)
8 Also Sraffa (1960, 33) follows this argument: "The rate of profits . . . is . . . susceptible of being determined from outside the system of production, in particular by the level of the money rate of interest."
9 Note that wages of accountants or costs for administration buildings and so forth are part of overhead costs. In Keynes's approach, overhead costs do not exist. Kalecki's analysis is based on a lower level of abstraction than Keynes's analysis. These differences do not affect the core of the arguments.

References

AFL-CIO (2016): *Pay Watch 2016*, www.aflcio.org/Corporate-Watch/Paywatch-2016, accessed 11 July 2016.

AMECO (2016): *European Commission*, http://ec.europa.eu/economy_finance/db_indicators/ameco/index_en.htm, accessed 11 July 2016.

Dünhaupt, P. (2011): *The Impact of Financialization on Income Distribution in the USA and Germany: A Proposal for a New Adjusted Wage Share*. Working Paper No. 7/2011. Macroeconomic Policy Institute.

Dünhaupt, P. (2016): "Determinants of Labour's Income Share in the Era of Financialisation", *Cambridge Journal of Economics* 4(1), 283–306.

Felipe, J. and McCombie, J.S.L. (2007): "Is a Theory of Total Factor Productivity Needed?", *Metroeconomica* 58, 195–229.

Gallas, A., Herr, H., Hoffer, F. and Scherrer, C. (eds.) (2016): *Combating Inequality: The Global North and South*. London: Routledge.

Garegnani, P. (1970): "Heterogeneous Capital, the Production Function and the Theory of Distribution", *Review of Economic Studies* 37, 407–436.

Harcourt, G. C. (1972): *Some Cambridge Controversies in the Theory of Capital*. Cambridge: Cambridge University Press.

Harvey, D. (2005): *A Brief History of Neoliberalism*. Oxford: Oxford University Press.

Hein, E. (2014): *Distribution and Growth after Keynes: A Post-Keynesian Guide*. Cheltenham, UK: Edward Elgar.

Hein, E. (2015): "Financialisation, Income Distribution and the Crisis", *Cambridge Journal of Economics* 39, 867–870.

Heine, M. and Herr, H. (2013): *Volkswirtschaftslehre: Paradigmenorientierte Einführung in die Mikro- und Makroökonomie*. München: Oldenbourg.

Herr, H. (2009): "The Labour Market in a Keynesian Economic Regime: Theoretical Debate and Empirical Findings", *Cambridge Journal of Economics* 33, 949–965.

Herr, H. (2014): "An Analytical Framework for the Post-Keynesian Macroeconomic Paradigm", *Izmir Review of Social Sciences* 1, 73–116.

Herr, H. and Ruoff, B. (2016): "Labour and Financial Markets as Drivers of Inequality", in Gallas, A., Herr, H., Hoffer, F. and Scherrer, C. (eds.), *Combating Inequality: The Global North and South*. London: Routledge.

Kalecki, M. (1966): *Studies in the Theory of Business Cycles: 1933–1939*. Oxford: Basil Blackwell.

Kalecki, M. (1971): "Class Struggle and Distribution of National Income", *Kyklos International Review for Social Sciences* 24, 1–9.

Kalecki, M. (2009 [1965]): *Theory of Economic Dynamics*. New York: Augustus M. Kelley Publishers.

Keynes, J. M. (1930): *Treatise on Money*. Cambridge: Cambridge University Press.

Keynes, J. M. (1936): *The General Theory of Employment, Interest and Money*. Cambridge: Cambridge University Press.

Lazzarini, A. (2011): *Revisiting the Cambridge Capital Theory Controversies: A Historical and Analytical Study*. Pavia: Pavia University Press.

Levy, F. and Temin, P. (2010): "Institutions and Wages in Post-World War II America", in Brown, C., Eichengreen, B. and Reich, M. (eds.), *Labor in the Era of Globalization*. Cambridge: Cambridge University Press, 15–50.

Marx, K. (1990 [1867]): *Capital*. Vol. 1. London: Penguin Books.

Milberg, W. and Winkler, D. (2013): *Outsourcing Economics: Global Value Chains in Capitalist Development*. New York: Cambridge University Press.

OECD (2012): *OECD Employment Outlook*, Paris.

Piketty, T. (2014): *Capital in the Twenty-First Century*. Cambridge: The Belknap Press of Harvard University Press.

Rabbani, S. (2016): *Derivation of Constant Labor and Capital Share from the Cobb-Douglas Production Function*. https://srabbani.com/cobb_douglas.pdf; accessed May 5, 2019.

Rappaport, A. (1999): "How to Link Executive Pay with Performance", *Harvard Business Review*, March–April, 91–101.

Samuelson, P. A. (1966): "A Summing Up", *Quarterly Journal of Economics* 80, 568–583.

Sraffa, P. (1960): *Production of Commodities by Means of Commodities: Prelude to a Critique of Economic Theory*. Cambridge: Cambridge University Press.

Stiglitz, J. (2012): *The Price of Inequality*. New York and London: W. W. Norton & Company.

Stockhammer, E. (2015): "Determinants of the Wage Share: A Panel Analysis of Advanced and Developing Economies", *British Journal of Industrial Relations* 55(1), 3–33.

Wicksell, K. (1936 [1898]): *Interest and Prices*. New York: Sentry Press.

15 The balance sheet approach to macroeconomics

Dirk Ehnts

1 Introduction

The Great Financial Crisis (GFC) has disrupted the rule of the neoclassical paradigm in monetary macroeconomics. New Keynesian macroeconomic equilibrium models with one representative agent do not feature debt and therefore are inappropriate to analyze the events leading to the GFC and after. Financial institutions and debt are not prominent in these models, as Adam and Vines (2009) point out.[1] While this might have come as a shock for many central bankers and economists, the practitioners probably were not moved much. Yglesias (2013) points out that the private sector has not used these "freshwater macroeconomics" models but instead relied on Keynesian models.[2] Weisenthal (2012) reports that the chief economist of Goldman Sachs, Jan Hatzius, claims that "the world's most important chart" is one that shows the financial (sectoral) balances for the United States. The chief economist of Nomura Investment pointed out in Koo (2008) that New Keynesian economics à la Woodford (2003) fails in a world of "balance sheet recession", where firms and households find themselves in a situation of unwanted levels of debt, often after a fall in asset prices. The private sector is concerned with repayment of debt and consequently ignores interest rates until some target level of net wealth or external debt is reached. There seems to have been a disconnect between academia and some central banks on the one hand and some other central bankers and practitioners on the other.

In the last few years, a new paradigm has emerged that looks at the (monetary) world through the lens of balance sheets. Even though it seems to be widely used and accepted, it has not yet been widely acknowledged. Smith (2016) claims that "heterodox economics hasn't really produced a replacement for mainstream macro". While he then points at stock-flow consistent (SFC) models, he is missing the larger picture: SFC models are very rigorous with respect to the account of stocks and flows (hence the name), but they are based on balance sheets and transactions. It is this that forms the new paradigm. In other words, accounting and identities are the new foundations of monetary macroeconomics, and behavioural assumptions are built on top. This is a methodology used not only by heterodox economists but also by mainstream economists. In this chapter I will argue that a replacement for the old neoclassical paradigm has already been in existence for some time and now evolves into a proper research program.

Among those working within the new framework are researchers from central banks (including the Bank of England and the European Central Bank), a few academic economists like Randall Wray, Bill Mitchell, Marc Lavoie and others, practitioners from the financial sector and international organizations like the International Monetary Fund (IMF). The approach has its roots in economic theory, with Knut Wicksell (1898) and Keynes (1936) all being early exponents. Wicksell can be singled out as the grandfather of the new paradigm as he verbally explains the process of credit creation by 'the stroke of a pen'. Even though he did not make it explicit, he was thinking about balance sheets! Schumpeter and Keynes knew about what later was called "endogenous" money, with post-war contribution coming from Jacques Le Bourva (1992 [1959, 1962]), Basil Moore (1988) and others.

The new methodology is presented in detail in section 2 and applied to some issues of relevance, including financial crises, quantitative easing, the TARGET2 payment system and the fiscal-monetary nexus relevant for the question of "fiscal space" in section 3. Section 4 concludes with a summary and a proposal for a research program.

2 What is the balance sheet approach to macroeconomics?

Defining a new paradigm obviously means to abstract from differences and find an overarching, general frame that would cover all the single instances that would fall under the new paradigm. My definition of the balance sheet approach would be the following:

> The balance sheet approach to macroeconomics focuses on assets and liabilities at different levels of the economy, from single units like households, banks, corporations and central banks up to aggregates like financial sector, private sector and public sector. Insights are derived through understanding the balance sheet movements of the past, both of single units and aggregates, and predicting those of the future in the form of conditional scenarios. It is explicitly recognized that because of the interdependence of balance sheets the economy is complex and that debt position matter for macroeconomic performance. The main use of the balance sheet approach is for questions of macroeconomics.

The last point is important, since it divides the balance sheet approach from accounting proper. No accountant in the real world working for a private firm would try to do the accounting in a way that allows the reader to understand the macroeconomic consequences. If this were so, the last crisis could have easily been foreseen by looking into the balance sheets of the big financial institutions! What divides the balance sheet approach from current models featuring "microfoundations" is the stress on the interdependence of balance sheets of the different actors of the economy. In models with a representative agent, this issue is invisible by definition.

The name "balance sheet approach" has been defined by Allen et al. (2002, 4) in the context of international financial crises:

> Unlike traditional analysis, which is based on the examination of flow variables (such as current account and fiscal balance), the balance sheet approach focuses on the examination of stock variables in a country's sectoral balance sheets and its aggregate balance sheet (assets and liabilities).

Dornbusch (2002), whose work is quoted in that paper, in his primer on emerging market crises has 37 mentions of "balance sheet". It seems fair to say that this line of research also falls under my definition of balance sheet approach.

The balance sheet approach to macroeconomics ultimately is primarily concerned with protecting the economy from a rise in unemployment and the recession or depression that normally goes hand in hand with it.[3] While the fall of investment is what causes problems in most developed nations, it is slow changes in the real exchange rate (caused by a fall in exports) that can be harmful to developing and developed economies. This was clearly visible when oil and other resource prices fell over the last few years, causing problems for exporters of those commodities. To understand these macroeconomic problems, knowledge of the way that "money" and its substitutes work is important. If a breakdown of the US interbank market has consequences for the amount of credit given by the banking system, then it would be useful to understand why this happened and how to ensure that either it does not happen again or that there is a proper strategy that bypasses this problem so that investment does not collapse. Also, if lack of demand is a problem in the economy, it would be useful to think about how to inject purchasing power in the economy. Often the private sector's wish to pay down debt leads to public deficits, which then stabilize the economy. Fewer taxes are drained from the private sector and more benefits are paid out, which is what we call the automatic stabilizer function of the state. If that is not enough, more spending needs to be forthcoming. This leads to the question of whether the state can go bankrupt or not – something which is central to the crisis in the Eurozone.

In order to provide an example for the balance sheet approach to macroeconomics, consider the question of whether a central bank can buy up all sovereign securities if it needs to. In Table 15.1 are the two balance sheets of Central Bank and Treasury after the central bank has bought up all sovereign securities from the market (balance sheets of the private sector are omitted).[4]

Table 15.1 Balance sheets of Central Bank and Treasury

Central Bank		*Treasury*	
sovereign securities	reserves		sovereign securities net debt

While this situation might have seen unthinkable before the Great Financial Crisis, many modern central banks today hold a significant share of outstanding sovereign securities of their government.[5] The central bank can create money by marking up deposits of the seller's bank's account at the central bank. It can do this without limit, as Wray (2012, 200) discusses. Note that in the extreme shown above, all investors would like sovereign securities as they can always sell them to the central bank. They would be judged riskless. What can also be seen is that when it comes to interest rate payments there is no problem at all. Treasury pays interest to the holders of sovereign securities, which in this case comes down to the central bank. Central bank profits are usually transferred to the Treasury. This means that whatever the interest rate on sovereign securities is, a government that issues sovereign securities in its own currency can never technically go bankrupt.[6]

Depending on the problem at hand, the balance sheet approach can be focused on single units and their interactions, on sectoral balances in the context of spending decision or on any other aggregated set of balance sheets in between up to balance sheets for a whole nation. The balance sheet approach hence covers the whole range between:

- *Micro*economic entities, like households, corporations, Central Bank or Treasury
- *Meso*economic entities, like a banking system or the financial sector[7]
- *Macro*economic entities, like the private or public sector or the rest of the world.

The balance sheet approach is scalable with respect to the aggregation of balance sheets, which provides some flexibility to adapt to different research questions. It can cover a wider range of issue than the New Keynesian paradigm, which is built on some rigorous assumptions like having a representative agent, using intertemporal optimization and assuming a non-changing link between interest rate and investment, among other things. Table 15.2 contrasts the new paradigm with the New Keynesian one.

The first line asks whether the two approaches deal with nominal or real variables. Nominal variables are about prices, whereas real variables are about quantities. Dynamic stochastic general equilibrium (DSGE) models rely on real wages and real marginal costs. Also, perhaps even more importantly, "the current output

Table 15.2 Comparison of balance sheet approach with New Keynesian paradigm

Issue	*Balance Sheet Approach*	*New Keynesian Paradigm*
nominal versus real	*nominal*	*real*
financial sector focus	yes	no
main problem	inter-temporal	intra-temporal
ontology, epistemology	realism	instrumentalism

gap is a function of the long term real interest rate" (Christiano et al. 2011, 304). To put it differently, investment reacts to the real interest rate. Clearly, the focus is on real variables. In contrast, the focus of the balance sheet approach is on nominal values. Changes in the net worth of single or aggregate balance sheets matter. This is why the variables are nominal and not real. For instance, financial problems can arise if nominal incomes fall, because this increases real debt. It takes longer to pay down any existing debts, and the risk of default is higher. If actors change their behaviour and try to spend less, then economic trouble will follow. Whether the price level during that episode went up or down is of secondary importance. A fall in nominal incomes can trigger a fall in aggregate demand, which probably would not be stopped even if the price level falls faster than the wage level. For a debt-deflation as described by Fisher (1933), the consumer price level is almost completely irrelevant, and the same goes for the leveraged financial positions taken up by speculators and investors as described by Minsky (1975, 1982, 1986, 1992).

The next line in Table 15.2 considers the focus on the financial sector. The balance sheet approach explains the way that debt works, including both public and private debt. There is a lot of work being done on the functioning of monetary policy, including Fullwiler (2010) and many authors from central banks. There is also Koo (2008, 2014), with his work on the so-called balance sheet recession in Japan and the failure of quantitative easing to provide economic stimulus. There are many more issues. A last one to point out is the neo-Chartalist perspective that combines both endogenous money and a Chartalist view of the economy. Authors of this kind, like Wray (2012) and also Ehnts (2016), are seen as proponents of the school of "Modern Mone(tar)y Theory". Not every author writing about and thinking in terms of balance sheets agrees with all others. Divisions inside the paradigm of the balance sheet approach mainly arise among the following views:

- (Neo-)Chartalist vs non-Chartalist (e.g. Wray [2012] vs. Mehrling [2010])
- Endogenous money vs loanable funds (e.g. Keen [2014] vs. Krugman [2014])
- Implications for the balance of payments, with a focus on the interactions of the current and financial account (e.g. Pettis [2013] vs. Ehnts [2016]).[8]

While credit spreads and other frictions in the financial system can be incorporated into DSGE models, as Cúrdia and Woodford (2010) show, the way it is done is rather ad hoc. There is no possibility of default in the New Keynesian models, which brings us to the next issue.

New Keynesian models feature intra-temporal problems and only those. This means that supply on the goods market does not equal demand, which creates a positive output gap. The problem is that there is not enough demand today, and the intertemporal optimization ensures that money not spend today will be spent tomorrow. So when savings are too high and demand is too low today, this translates into not enough savings and too much demand tomorrow. If the intra-temporal problem of spending versus non-spending decisions today would be solved, all future problems will be gone as well! Therefore, the problem in New Keynesian models is intra-temporal: savings and investment today are at values that are not compatible with full employment (because of a positive output gap) and maintaining the target inflation rate (because there is not enough demand).

The balance sheet approach considers intertemporal problems, namely the problem to transfer purchasing power from the present to the future. Saving requires holding some (real or financial) asset, and there might be problems with respect to future purchasing power: the debtor might default, the interest rate might lie below the inflation rate (so that the real interest rate is negative), the asset price or the banking system might collapse, so that bank deposits are gone or reduced.[9] Potential problems of repayment of debt can be targeted with the balance sheet approach because the evolution of important balance sheets can be tracked over time. This is why financial crises, quantitative easing, TARGET2 imbalances and the fiscal-monetary nexus, which are discussed in a later section, are natural fields of application for this paradigm. The last issue mentioned in Table 15.2, that of ontology and epistemology, is treated in section 2.1.

It is clear that the central bank sets only the interest rate and hence cannot determine the quantity of credit. This means that it is obvious that rules cannot work under all circumstances because there is no stable relationship between the change in private sector debt and the interest rate or interest rates set by the central bank. If the business cycle cannot be tamed on the downside by monetary policy, then the debate on rules regarding whether to target internal price stability (inflation) or external stability (current account, exchange rate, capital flows) becomes more relevant.[10] The discussion of negative equity at central banks is stopped dead by pointing out that "central banks are protected from insolvency due to their ability create money and can therefore operate with negative equity", as Bunea et al. (2016, 14) point out. The same goes for discussions of "fiscal space" when the government is indebted in domestic currency that the central bank can produce.

2.1 Ontology and epistemology

Ontology asks what we are exactly looking at when we engage in science. For the balance sheet approach, the answer is relatively easy: we look at balance sheets comprising assets and liabilities. They belong to an economic actor, an aggregate or something in between. The numbers in the balance sheet are nominal as opposed to real, so that the balance sheet approach has a nominal focus. Recent modern macroeconomics is built on real variables, as the name "real business cycle" implies. If one is not concerned with balance sheets, then real values might be preferred to nominal ones if growth in real GDP and other flows are the main focus. With the balance sheet approach, it is stocks that are put to the forefront: assets and liabilities of economic entities.

Epistemology is concerned with what exactly constitutes knowledge and what it is that we can (hope to) know. This is more open to debate than the question of ontology. Agreement is reached that balance sheets are interacting because assets are equal to liabilities and this means that changes in one balance sheet are causing changes in at least one other.[11] Accounting thus drives some changes in the economy, whereas others are driven by behaviour.[12] The latter are more difficult since no economic laws exist that would explain them. However, one can make reasonable assumptions when it comes to things like income and consumption, for instance. Nevertheless, not too much behaviour is allowed because otherwise the results "don't fit". For instance, if households want to save a positive amount of money but government wants to have a balanced budget and a balanced current account, then something will have to give. It is generally recognized that plans can collide and that this can lead to fallacies of composition where the behaviour of economic actors, while rational individually, leads to macroeconomic results that are catastrophic.

The balance sheet approach hence leads to more cautious claims about predictability of the future since the complexity of the economy is recognized in a proper way. Tomorrow's balance sheets are unknown because tomorrow's asset prices are unknown. These depend on tomorrow's debt arrangements, as pointed out by Hyman Minsky (1975). However, the liabilities of the future are a function of present expectations. The muddle is complete: we have reflexivity and there is no way to get rid of it! The answer is not to ignore the reality and dream up a world that is mathematically easy to handle, but instead to understand the past and the present through balance sheets and plausible assumptions about the structure of Leijonhufvud's "web of contracts" and behaviour. This, in very short terms, is the method applied by those practising the balance sheet approach.

3 Some issues in current macroeconomics

Work by the IMF's Mathisen and Pellechio (2006) finds that "recent improvements in statistical methodologies and data availability are facilitating detailed, high-frequency, timely macroeconomic balance sheet analysis". This is an answer to the challenge that has arisen from an increased opacity and complexity of financial markets. The times when central bankers, by looking at the Bank for International Settlements (BIS) statistics, could with confidence assess the country risk exposure of individual banking systems, are over. It seems that easier and cheaper access to more detailed and better data has been one of the drivers behind the ongoing paradigm shift. Another factor might be the flourishing of blogs and other internet platforms that allow for discussions of and publications on economic issues that journals would probably not accept since they are found to be "too descriptive" or that could not be found by colleagues because the journals are too obscure and very hard to find.[13]

Paradigm changes don't come out of the blue. The Great Financial Crisis (GFC) and the Eurozone crisis are what propel the balance sheet approach towards the status of an established paradigm. Most modern macroeconomic theories struggled to explain what a financial crisis is, what quantitative easing does to the economy, how the TARGET2 payment system works and what this means for the Eurozone's internal balance of payments, and what the fiscal-monetary nexus looks like. The balance sheet approach has offered new insights and also has done fairly well with hindsight. The next paragraphs shortly raise these issues without going into too much detail.

3.1 Financial crises

In DSGE models, a financial crisis can't happen because there is only one representative agent and debt is meaningless. If one goes back to the aggregate demand–aggregate supply (AD/AS) model and creates the curves in a way that the equilibrium implies a negative real interest rate, then at least something can be said – even though it is doubtful that this constitutes valuable insights, as Palley (2016) convincingly argues. Nevertheless, the financial crisis is a completely exogenous shock and is left unexplained. After hundreds of years of financial folly and crises, this seems a strange way to think about the economy.

In the balance sheet approach it is natural that financial crises shall result. The twin character of asset/liability (or wealth/debt) logically leads to defaults if one entity's income is not enough to service all debt payments. Promises are broken, and when that happens on a larger scale involving millions and probably billions of US dollars' worth of debt contracts, we call it a financial crisis. The balance sheet approach is much better suited to deal with financial crises and financial fragility or robustness than any other competing paradigm.

3.2 Quantitative easing (QE) and negative interest rates

The balance sheet approach has also performed well when it comes to QE and negative interest rates. Koo (2014) has brought forward the critique that QE won't increase consumption, not via higher holdings of deposits by the private sector and not via increased indebtedness due to lower long-term interest rates. It has also been pointed out that QE serves as an excuse to depreciate the currency in order to get a larger share of global demand. Discussion of quantitative easing for exchange rates requires knowledge of how dealers trade on the forex markets. Again, a proper knowledge of balance sheets is crucial to make qualified statements about QE.[14] Another case in point are negative interest rates, which are by now almost standard, as Palley (2016) argues. Again, the story is one involving balance sheets and their interactions, and not one about intertemporal optimization of one rational agent with full information who lives eternally and therefore has other reasons to be unhappy than to complain about low or negative nominal interest rates.

3.3 The TARGET2 payment system

When the Eurozone crisis was in full swing, Sinn and Wollmershäuser (2012) caused a lot of stir with their writings on the TARGET2 balances. Their view was disputed by a variety of authors, including Cesaratto (2013), Bindseil (2014), Whelan (2014) and Lavoie (2015). All of the latter authors went to some length in order to sort out the balance sheet mechanics, whereas Sinn and Wollmershäuser (2012) present only one balance sheet. The story of a current account transaction that they are using does not fit the balance sheets, which only means that using balance sheets is not enough.[15] One also has to understand transactions and behaviour to be able to interpret the balance sheets of the past. The TARGET2 payment system is the backbone of the euro, and hence understanding it is fundamental to anyone writing about monetary theory in the context of the Eurozone. The next issue also needs to be examined with a sound understanding of balance sheets.

3.4 The fiscal-monetary nexus

Monetary policy and fiscal policy have effects on each other, which can be easily understood from looking at balance sheets.[16] Moving interest rates up or down has an effect on government expenditure and hence the fiscal stance, defined as government spending minus taxes. On the other hand, a rise in government spending can lead to a fall in the money market short-term interest rate if the central bank does not intervene. This is because when government spends into the economy, the banks get additional reserves. Since almost all or all of them receive reserves, there is an increase in the supply of reserves and no increase in demand. On the interbank market, where reserves are traded between financial institutions and the central bank, this would lead to a fall in the short-term interest rate, as banks would ask for lower interest rates as they recognize that they cannot lend them out to market participants at the going rate. Most modern central banks intervene to keep the short-term interest rate on the money market close to their policy target. This is why the downward pressure that an increase in government spending exerts on the money market short-term interest rates is usually not visible. If it were, the idea of 'crowding out' in the investment-Saving/Liquidity preference-Money supply (IS/LM) model would probably have to be reworked. Public spending can crowd out private spending, but it is unlikely that the interest rate plays a major role in this. The proper channel would be the availability of resources.

4 Conclusion

The Great Financial Crisis (GFC) has pushed the focus of economics towards a different set of problems: financial fragility and crisis, deflationary problems, industrial policies and the financial implications of current account imbalances. It is obvious that the balance sheet approach to macroeconomics offers a new and exciting perspective that is both microeconomic and macroeconomic and can deal with these problems. Some work has already been started before the GFC hit; new work has since evolved. The approach has been used by a wide variety of authors and there is some disagreement on some issues. The research questions are developing into a literature quickly and in some years will probably trigger new and innovative textbooks that deal with the new questions that economists face in the 21st century. The balance sheet approach is a strong contender for the sub-discipline of macroeconomics.

What remains to be done? Certainly, the balance sheet approach is used to tackle different issues, like the understanding of financial crises, QE and negative interest rates, the fiscal-monetary nexus and others. Some of these issues fall into the field of monetary theory, others into macroeconomics or into the overlap between the two. The way that liability structures interact with asset prices and borrowing is a field that Hyman Minsky has worked on and that is still promising to bring more insights, given that the financial structure evolves constantly. Financial stability and instability are issues that with current institutional arrangements are very likely to stay with us.

Also, public finance is affected when it comes to the way government spends (and taxes). Different schools will probably evolve to drive the new paradigm forward, like the Modern Monetary Theory (MMT), which is a post-Keynesian offshoot focusing on balance sheets (and neglecting equilibrium models). Also, central bankers now have more and more balance sheets on their presentations, so probably there is some incentive to merge these two literature strands. The issues that I think worthy of further future work are the functioning of unemployment schemes, the way that inflation is affected by demand and the macroeconomic consequences of inequality.

The balance sheet approach features insights that will affect many more subfields, probably ecological economics because it shows a very clear dividing line between money and goods and services. As ecological economics has pointed out once and again, it is real resources that are or should be limited, not monetary resources! Of course, trying to limit the use of real resources might lead to changes in the monetary system, like higher taxes on some goods with externalities. Also, ideas about the rational agent and human behaviour should benefit from a closer look at the balance sheet approach because of the limitations that double entry bookkeeping impose on it. Where the new paradigm leads to is impossible to say today. Those working within it will be determining the future of economics.

Notes

1 It is notable that in a paper titled "Remaking Macroeconomic Policy after the Global Financial Crisis: A Balance-Sheet Approach", the authors do not show a single balance sheet!

2 "Freshwater" view stands for the University of Chicago, University of Minnesota and other US institutions away from the coast. The "saltwater" view was taught in the Boston area universities, Columbia University and University of California, Berkeley, among others.

3 This does not mean that people cannot use it for other purposes, and neither does it mean that other methods with the same goal are invalid.

4 The following shows how modern central banks work. See Desan (2014) for a history of money from a legal perspective and Vogl (2017) for a history of finance (fiscal issues). Balance sheets are stylized for improved readability.

5 This includes the Federal Reserve Bank, the Bank of England and even the European Central Bank, among others.

6 This would already follow from the first fact, that investors would not lose their appetite for sovereign securities because they are rightly perceived as riskless. The Eurozone is an exception because the ECB faces some legal – not technical – problems in its interventions. Governments might still declare bankruptcy for political reasons.

7 This is where Stützel (1978) and his "balance mechanics" have their comparative advantage. See Schmidt for arguments to include this kind of approach in the modern macroeconomics curriculum (2016).

8 Pettis (2013, 17–19) is particularly noteworthy here, because in the section 'Some Accounting Identities' he develops a very clear modern neoclassical position (featuring loanable funds, not endogenous money).

9 Usually there is some deposit insurance in most banking systems. However, in the case of a bail-in the depositors are set to lose some of their deposits.
10 See Barbaroux (2013, 19–35) for a discussion of Knut Wicksell in this context.
11 See Carrión Álvarez and Ehnts (2015) for more a longer explanation and more possibilities.
12 This connects to the structure and agency debate in sociology, where individual agency is limited by the structural constraints of accounting identities. See Giddens (1986).
13 The classic example of this is Leijonhufvud's (1998) paper published in the *Zagreb Journal of Economics*.
14 As seen in the example of the balance sheet approach for macroeconomics above, the central bank can buy any financial asset from the private sector for the currency it can create as long as there are willing sellers.
15 Sinn and Wollmershäuser mistakenly assume that the banks move to settlement at the end of the day, which is not how reality works. Banks have credit lines with each other and usually postpone settlement until balances return to zero or the counterparty is told to pay up if it is judged to be a risk.
16 Tymoigne (2014) shows the case of the United States.

References

Adam, C. and Vines, D. (2009): "Remaking Macroeconomic Policy after the Global Financial Crisis: A Balance-Sheet Approach", *Oxford Review of Economic Policy* 25(4), 507–552.

Allen, M., Rosenberg, C., Keller, C., Setser, B. and Roubini, N. (2002): "A Balance Sheet Approach to Financial Crisis", *IMF*. Working Paper No. 02/210.

Barbaroux, N. (2013): *Monetary Policy Rule in Theory and Practice: Facing the Internal vs External Stability Dilemma*. Abingdon, UK: Routledge.

Bindseil, U. (2014): *Monetary Policy Operations and the Financial System*. Oxford: Oxford University Press.

Bunea, D., Karakitsos, P., Merriman, N. and Studener, W. (2016): "Profit Distribution and Loss Coverage Rules for Central Banks", *ECB*. Occasional Paper No. 169/2016.

Carrión Álvarez, M. and Ehnts, D. (2015): *The Roads Not Taken: Graph Theory and Macroeconomic Regimes in Stock-Flow Consistent Modeling*. Working Paper No. 854. Levy Economics Institute.

Cesaratto, S. (2013): "The Implications of TARGET2 in the European Balance of Payments Crisis and Beyond", *European Journal of Economics and Economic Policies: Intervention* 10(3), 359–382.

Christiano, L., Trabandt, M. and Walentin, K. (2011): "DSGE Models for Monetary Policy Analysis", in Friedman, B. and Woodford, M. (eds.), *Handbook of Monetary Economics*. Vol. 3A. The Netherlands: North-Holland, 285–367.

Cúrdia, V. and Woodford, M. (2010): "Credit Spreads and Monetary Policy", *Journal of Money, Credit and Banking* 42(1), 3–35.

Desan, C. (2014): *Making Money: Coin, Currency, and the Coming of Capitalism*. Oxford: Oxford University Press.

Dornbusch, R. (2002): "A Primer on Emerging-Market Crises", in Edwards, S. and Frankel, J. A. (eds.), *Preventing Currency Crises in Emerging Markets*. Chicago: University of Chicago Press.

Ehnts, D. (2016): *Modern Monetary Theory and European Macroeconomics*. Abingdon, UK: Routledge.

Fisher, I. (1933): "The Debt-Deflation Theory of Great Depressions", *Econometrica* 1(4), 337–357.

Fullwiler, S. (2010): *Modern Monetary Theory: A Primer on the Operational Realities of the Monetary System*, http://papers.ssrn.com/sol3/papers.cfm?abstract_id=1723198, accessed 29 May 2018.

Giddens, A. (1986): *The Constitution of Society: Outline of the Theory of Structuration.* Berkeley and Los Angeles: University of California Press.

Keen, S. (2014): *The Keen-Krugman Debate*, www.opendemocracy.net/ourkingdom/steve-keen/keen-krugman-debate, accessed 29 May 2018.

Keynes, J. M. (1936): *The General Theory of Employment, Interest and Money*. London: Palgrave Macmillan.

Koo, R. (2008): *The Holy Grail of Macroeconomics: Lessons from Japan's Great Recession*. Singapore: John Wiley and Sons.

Koo, R. (2014): *The Escape from Balance Sheet Recession and the QE Trap: A Hazardous Road for the World Economy*. Singapore: John Wiley and Sons.

Krugman, P. (2014): *Frustrations of the Heterodox*, http://krugman.blogs.nytimes.com/2014/04/25/frustrations-of-the-heterodox/, accessed 29 May 2018.

Lavoie, M. (2015): "The Eurozone: Similarities to and Differences from Keynes's Plan", *International Journal of Political Economy* 44(1), 3–17.

Le Bourva, J. (1959): "La théorie de l'inflation, le rapport des experts et l'opération de décembre 1958", *Revue Économique* 10, 713–754.

Le Bourva, J. (1962): "Création de la monnaie et multiplicateur du crédit", *Revue Économique* 13, 29–56.

Leijonhufvud, A. (1998): "Two Types of Crises", *Zagreb Journal of Economics* 2, 39–54.

Mathisen, J. and Pellechio, A. (2006): "Using the Balance Sheet Approach in Surveillance: Framework, Data Sources, and Data Availability", *IMF*. Working Paper No. 06/100.

Mehrling, P. (2010): *The New Lombard Street: How the Fed Became the Dealer of Last Resort*. Princeton, NJ: Princeton University Press.

Minsky, H. (1975): *John Maynard Keynes*. New York: McGraw Hill.

Minsky, H. (1982): *Can "It" Happen Again?: Essays on Instability and Finance*. Armonk, NY: M. E. Sharpe.

Minsky, H. (1986): *Stabilizing an Unstable Economy*. New Haven: Yale University Press.

Minsky, H. (1992): *The Financial Instability Hypothesis*. Working Paper No. 74. Levy Economics Institute.

Moore, B. (1988): *Horizontalists and Verticalists: The Macroeconomics of Credit Money*. Cambridge: Cambridge University Press.

Palley, T. (2016): "Why ZLB Economics and Negative Interest Rate Policy (NIRP) Are Wrong: A Theoretical Critique", *IMK*, Working Paper No. 172.

Pettis, M. (2013): *The Great Rebalancing: Trade, Conflict, and the Perilous Road Ahead for the World Economy*. Princeton, NJ: Princeton University Press.

Schmidt, J. (2016): "Reforming the Undergraduate Macroeconomics Curriculum: The Case for a Thorough Treatment of Accounting Relationships", *International Journal for Pluralism and Economics Education* 8(1), 42–67.

Sinn, H.-W. and Wollmershäuser, T. (2012): "TARGET Loans, Current Account Balances and Capital Flows: The ECB's Rescue Facility", *NBER*, Working Paper No. 17626.

Smith, N. (2016): *Economics without Math Is Trendy, But It Doesn't Add Up*, www.bloomberg.com/view/articles/2016-08-08/economics-without-math-is-trendy-but-it-doesn-t-add-up, accessed 29 May 2018.

Stützel, W. (1978): *Volkswirtschaftliche Saldenmechanik: Ein Beitrag zur Geldtheorie*. Tübingen: Mohr Siebeck.

Tymoigne, E. (2014): *Modern Money Theory and Interrelations between the Treasury and the Central Bank: The Case of the United States*. Working Paper No. 788. Levy Economics Institute.

Vogl, J. (2017): *The Ascendancy of Finance*. New York: Wiley-Blackwell.

Weisenthal, J. (2012): "In Case You Haven't Realized, Goldman Sachs Is Predicting a Major Economic Turn to Happen in 2013", www.businessinsider.com/goldmans-2013-forecast-2012-12?IR=T

Whelan, K. (2014): "TARGET2 and Central Bank Balance Sheets", *Economic Policy* 29(77), 79–137.

Wicksell, K. (1936 [1898]): *Interest and Prices*. New York: Augustus M. Kelley Publishers.

Woodford, M. (2003): *Interest and Prices: Foundations of a Theory of Monetary Policy*. Princeton, NJ and Oxford: Princeton University Press.

Wray, R. (2012): *Modern Money Theory: A Primer on Macroeconomics for Sovereign Monetary Systems*. 2012th edition. Basingstoke, UK: Palgrave Macmillan.

Yglesias, M. (2013): *Freshwater Macroeconomics Has Failed the Market Test*, www.slate.com/blogs/moneybox/2013/12/18/freshwater_macroeconomics_has_failed_the_market_test.html, accessed 29 May 2018.

16 How to teach ethics and economics to undergraduate students?

Stefan Kesting

1 Motivation and resources

I have to start with a warning. What follows is not a conventional academic paper, presenting the evidence and reaching a logically derived conclusion. What I have written resembles more a personal memoir combined with some practical tips of how to teach ethics and economics. In a chatty tone, I report my motivation for and the development of my teaching economics students moral philosophy so they possess the instruments to apply normative evaluation to economic policies and company practices. And I do so in the hope that colleagues toying with such content in their courses can draw on my experience.

Before I provide some practical tips on how to teach ethics and economics as an economist in the second section of this chapter, I want to make a few remarks about my motivation and on what enabled me to do it. I have to admit, I received very little formal training in philosophy. However, I attended seminars taught by Beate Rössler (2015, 1996) on feminism when she was working at the University of Bremen and by Hans Joas on pragmatism (1993) when he was teaching for a year at the New School for Social Research in New York City where I happened to be at the time. Fortunately, the beauty of moral philosophy is that it does not create as many technical barriers of understanding as mainstream economics, with its emphasis on formal mathematical modelling, econometrics and a somewhat hermetic terminology. If prepared to read a lot and to wrestle with difficult texts, moral philosophy is fairly accessible for an amateur scholar. Unfortunately, most philosophers do not write as well as John Kenneth Galbraith! (1958, 1961, 1967, 1983).

Inspired and highly motivated by my PhD supervisor Adelheid Biesecker (1997), a major step to become half a philosopher was my PhD thesis (1998) on economics, power and Habermas's "Discourse Ethics" (1995 [1981], 1999 [1992], 2001). To answer the question, "What does it mean for *Homo oeconomicus* to learn to speak?" I decided my thesis had to be written with one foot standing on the shoulders of American critical institutional economists like Boulding (1956, 1969, 1990), Myrdal (1960, 1965 [1932], 1972 [1944]), Galbraith (1958, 1961, 1967, 1983) and Hirschman (1970, 1991, 1993a, 1993b, 1994); and with the other on the shoulder of the giant Frankfurt School philosopher Habermas (1995 [1981], 1999 [1992], 2001). Of great importance for me to understand American institutionalism was Geoff Hodgson's work (1993, 1999, 2001, 2004) and Wolfram Elsner's advice (Elsner et al. 2014). The discourse ethics element required a lot of critical reading of moral philosophy of its own. Moreover, very helpful were Ernst Tugendhat's essays (1992) and his lectures on ethics (1993) linking Kant's moral imperatives (Cassirer 1994 [1918]; Schulte 1996) to Adam Smith's *Moral Sentiments* (1976 [1759]).

During my nine years working with Adelheid Biesecker as her PhD student and post-doctoral assistant, we embarked on co-writing a microeconomics textbook from a social-ecological perspective (2003). Apart from studying feminist economics with Adelheid Biesecker in Bremen before I became her PhD student, I also received training in this sub-discipline of economics by Günseli Berik (Berik 2012; Berik et al. 2015) and the late David Gordon (1996) as an exchange student at the New School for Social Research in New York. This feminist foundation found its way into the pluralist textbook project and was further sustained by reading introductions to feminist philosophy, in particular the work of Virginia Held (1990) as well as introductions to feminist economics (e.g. Blau et al. 2006; Nany Folbre 2001; Julie Nelson 1996; Ferber and Nelson 1993). An excellent starting point to develop a critical ethical perspective on mainstream economics was provided by the contributions in J. J. Mansbridge's collection *Beyond Self-Interest* (1990). As part of the textbook project I also read Lutz and Lux's book on *Humanistic Economics* (1988) and delved into communitarianism. Most influential for me were Etzioni's *The Moral Dimension* (1988) and Charles Taylor's *Sources of the Self* (1989). However today, I would also recommend Michael Sandel's (2012) and Skidelsky and Skidelsky's (2012) books for their inspiring moral critique of economics.

To a certain degree my growing background in moral philosophy influenced the diverse range of microeconomic, macroeconomic and political economy classes I taught at Bremen University in Germany between 1995 and 2003 and at Auckland University of Technology (AUT) in New Zealand between 2004 and 2012. However, it was the AACSB accreditation process of AUT's business school and the same endeavour at Leeds University Business School (LUBS, my current employer) that led to the initial steps to design a specific course on ethics and economics and in the end enabled me to refine and implement it at LUBS. Association to Advance Collegiate Schools of Business's (AACSB) accreditation is of immense importance for business schools to boost their reputation. To get it, they need to first start from declaring their values in a mission statement and in the next step, based on this mission, to define what kind of skills, qualifications and capabilities students will have when they will have finished their education. Both AUT and LUBS decided to include ethics in their mission statement. The next and third step in the accreditation process required AUT business school and LUBS to demonstrate where ethics is taught in their programmes and how this learning goal is achieved by their students. This includes measuring the learning goal in specific assessments. As a consequence, while working at AUT, I was tapped by some leading figures in the business school and asked to try to introduce more education in ethics into the economics curriculum. I wrote a list of potential topics for a course on the back of an envelope including Etzioni's *Moral Dimension*, feminist approaches and Sen's (1987, 1995) and Nussbaum's (2000) capability approach and made a pledge for a course called "Ethics and Economics" during one of the next departmental meetings. My chair – a very clever, intellectually curious and well-read mainstream economist, but also proud and stubborn – was not having any of this. His response was twofold: first, we do not have the space for a course like this, we need our time and resources to teach our students standard microeconomics, macroeconomics and econometrics and second, we do not need such a course, we have welfare functions in economics. In his opinion, this was all the ethics our students needed.

2 Start and design of the course

Fortunately, when asked during my job interview four years ago by the dean of the business school at LUBS what I want to teach and mentioned "Ethics and Economics", the response was very positive. He leaned forward intrigued when I described the course, and he said this is exactly what the economics department at LUBS needs. The AACSB accreditation process was probably on his mind. And so, I tried to find some good practice to follow and received ample support from John B. Davis (2003; Davis and Boumans 2010, www.johnbryandavis.net/) and took advice from Jack Vromen (Vromen and Lanteri 2014; Vromen and Aydinonat 2015, www.jackvromen.nl/). While John provided me with the syllabus of his "Economics & Ethics" course, discussed the new course with me and suggested Sen's *On Ethics and Economics* (1987) as a basic text for the module, I found on Jack's website that he uses Hausman and McPherson (2006) as the textbook for his course in Rotterdam. Two other useful introductory texts I came across were Beckerman's *Economics as Applied Ethics* (2011) and Wright's *Ethics in Economics: An Introduction to Moral Frameworks* (2015). Wright's is probably as good as Dutt and Wilber's (2010) for the kind of module I am teaching, but the latter had the first mover advantage for me because of its publication date. While I took the label for my new module from Sen's book title, I decided not to use it as the basic reading material. Instead, I wrote a series of 11 lectures based on the third chapter in Dutt and Wilber's *Economics and Ethics: An Introduction* (2010) and on several chapters in Hausman and McPherson's book (2006; a new 2016 edition has just been published!). In addition, I assembled a reader with texts I expected the students to read in parallel to the lectures and to discuss in class.

This is the list of topics for the first semester where the module was taught in academic year 2012–2013 and the changed programme taught in 2016–2017:

Table 16.1 Lists of topics

2012–2013	*2016–2017*
Introduction to the module: Ethics and Economics	Introduction to the module: Ethics and Economics
Economics without Ethics?	Virtue, Deontological and Consequentialist Ethics
Approaches to Ethics and Justice	Utilitarianism (Harsanyi)
Individuals, Norms and Ethical Values	Libertarianism (Schmidtz)
Social Interaction and Ethical Values	Egalitarianism (Sen)
Markets and Ethical Values	Lutz and Lux's Humanistic Economics – a Kantian Perspective
The Morality of Markets and Government Intervention I	Etzioni's Moral Dimension, the Communitarian I and We Paradigm
The Morality of Markets and Government Intervention II	Sen's Capabilities Approach
Production, Income and Economic Growth	Feminist Ethics and Economics (Held and Nelson)
Fairness, Distribution and Equality	Nussbaum's Capabilities Approach
Ethics and Applied Economics	Discourse Ethics and its Critique (Habermas and Butler)

In its first round (2012–2013), the course was assessed by an oral presentation, a coursework essay and an exam. This initial combination of assessments was chosen based on John B. Davis's syllabus who uses a similar mix of exams, oral presentations and project essays. My approach to teaching "Ethics and Economics" is to familiarise students with the diverse strands of moral philosophy, that is, a structure emphasising types of theory and to expect students to apply one specific ethical approach of their choice in comparison with mainstream economics to a company practice or economics policy. John Davis approaches teaching our type of course from the opposite angle. He explicitly calls it an exercise in "Normative Economics, the part of economics that examines normative as opposed to positive judgments about economic outcomes, welfare, and economic policy" (Davis, syllabus Economics and Ethics ECON 4070–101 (5803), 2015) and organises his course along a range of moral issues, problems and conundrums and brings in economics and moral philosophy to evaluate them normatively. A similar approach to John's was applied by Mark Hayes (www.dur.ac.uk/theology.religion/staff/profile/?id=12961) when he started to teach an ethics and economics course at the University of Durham in 2015. Mark approached me to exchange notes when he was about to design his module at Durham and we had a very good discussion leading to fruitful mutual benefits for our teaching.

3 The performative learning outcome

There is certainly a pluralist undercurrent in the content of my module. In other words, one of its openly declared purposes is a critique of mainstream economics from a moral point of view. However, the main learning outcome of the course is a performance one. I want to provide students who will embark on a career as policy advisors, politicians, public servants, journalists, business consultants or managers of business companies and other organisations with moral frameworks to respond appropriately to ethical challenges and conundrums in their future professional life. So, my aim is that on completion of my module, students will be able to understand how moral philosophy can help economists to do economics better and how economics and ethics can help policy analysts to improve their evaluations of alternative policies and mangers to enhance their company and business practices from a moral point of view.

While teaching "Ethics and Economics" since 2013, I have come closer and closer in the course design to achieve this primary performative learning goal without completely losing the underlying goal of fostering a critical attitude towards mainstream economics among my students (see Table 16.1).

4 The assessment in stages

The core piece of assessment for this course is the final essay, which carries a weight of 60% of the overall mark (assignment brief in Appendix 1). The task for this research essay is to critically apply mainstream economics and a specific ethical approach to a particular case of economic policy or company practice freely chosen with my guidance by the students. Since over the first three years of running the module quite a number of students used either utilitarianism, libertarianism or egalitarianism as a foundation to conduct their normative analysis and evaluation of the case, I introduced texts and discussion sessions focussed on these brands of moral philosophy apart from feminism, communitarianism and the capability approach which were featured prominently already in the reader for the course and in class discussions right from the outset of the module. To make room for this content, I had to put discussions of Robert H. Frank's and Deirdre McCloskey's material on the back burner. I regret this to some extent and may try to reintroduce the discussion of these ethical approaches from a neoclassical and Austrian perspective in future semesters. In the very beginning, I had an exam at the end of the term to ensure that students do not opportunistically solely concentrate on one specific moral philosophy applied to their case but attend the lectures to get an overview of moral philosophy. However, I decided to replace the exam with a participation mark (10% of the overall mark) for contributions by students to class discussions (Vincent Roehling et al. 2010). This seems to work well to encourage lively debates in class and to widen the participation. Now it is no longer the same handful of individuals who talk in class, but a much larger group of students interact with me than before I had introduced the class participation mark. The discussions are based mainly on material I put in a reader which I hand out at the beginning of the semester. Students can find much more media and background reading material on the course specific Blackboard website (called VLE at Leeds).

In my experience, students find it challenging and somewhat unnerving to have to find a specific case (Velenchik 1995) and to decide on the most appropriate ethical approach to apply to it. They struggle to formulate a focussed research question which will allow them to develop the right kind of bite-sized piece for course work (the final essay). To guide them and provide feedback in this research-based learning process, there are two more pieces of assessment which carry less weight than the final essay. The first step is the proposal (10% of the overall mark), which focusses on finding and demonstrating a doable focussed case of the right size, demonstrates some research and familiarity with appropriate academic literature in a bibliography, provides a motivation for choosing the topic and shows a good attempt at formulating the first version of the research question. I mark these proposals (of 500 words each) and write a paragraph of critical feedback and advice for each student. In seminars with smaller groups of students, I provide general feedback on the proposals and discuss the difficulties they faced while embarking on their normative evaluation. Quite a number of students usually require some form of individual meetings and appointments to provide further guidance and advice. The next step is the oral (group) presentation (20% of the overall mark) in the last week of the semester. Based on the proposals, I try to match students with thematically similar topics in groups of ideally three and some in pairs. These groups will present in either blocks of 15 minutes (three students) or 10 minutes (pairs of students) on the progress of their research endeavour. This means each student has five minutes to present their case and garner feedback from me and a second marker (usually a moral philosopher working at Leeds). He or she will be mainly marked individually on his or her presentation skills. The aim of the group work aspect of the assessment is to encourage students to cooperate in designing their presentation, exchange tips about useful academic literature and to read each other's drafts to provide peer review and helpful feedback. The final essay is due a week after the last oral presentation is delivered. The distribution of marks across the four elements of assessment is: class participation – 10 marks (i.e. worth 10% of total grade), proposal – 10 marks (i.e. worth 10% of total grade), oral presentation – 20 marks (i.e. worth 20% of total grade) and the final essay – 60 marks (i.e. worth 60% of total grade).

5 Flipping the classroom

When I started teaching this course and until very recently, I gave four to five lectures in the first half of the semester introducing student to the main strands of moral philosophy. These lectures are based mainly on chapter 3 from Dutt and Wilber's *Economics and Ethics: An Introduction* (2010), several chapters of Hausman and McPherson (2006) and a diverse range of other texts and material. These lectures include a discussion of the distinction between virtue, deontological and consequentialist types of moral philosophy and utilitarianism, egalitarianism, libertarianism and contractarianism (including John Rawls's *Theory of Justice* [1971]). However, recently I decided to almost completely (apart from one lecture at the very beginning) "flip the classroom" (Findlay and Mombourquette 2014; Freeman Herreid and Schiller 2013). This means I recorded the introductory lectures (audio plus PowerPoint slides), and the students are supposed to listen to my presentations supported by the slideshow before they come to class to discuss with me what they have learned guided by specific discussion questions. All these learning resources can be found on the particular Blackboard intranet page for the course (Littlejohn and Pegler 2007). Moreover, these class discussions are based on a core text (contents page of the reader in Appendix 2). The class discussions in the larger second half (seven weeks) are solely based on core texts to be found in the reader. To further entice students to engage with me in class discussions, I added a series of films and plays (for the programme, see Appendix 3) which I show in voluntary sessions on the evening before the day of the class discussion. Most of the films are also available for the students to watch in their own time using links to Box of Broadcast National, YouTube and other websites. An example is the play "Professor Bernhardi" by Arthur Schnitzler (in an audio version in English produced by the BBC, 1971), which contains several scenes about moral conflicts and where the characters make either deontological or consequentialist ethical claims. An interpretation of these scenes discussing them with students helps their understanding of the distinction between these types of moral arguments.

Appendix 1

Assignment brief final essay

- Choose and describe an issue, policy or case to examine the relationship between economics and ethics, or how moral values and ethical reasoning are involved in both the science of economics and the operation of the economy. Generate and present a critical literature review.
- Critically discuss and compare how mainstream economics and at least one other ethical approach OR alternatively two (NOT MORE!) ethical theories (communitarian, consequentialist, contractual, deontological, discourse, egalitarian, feminist, libertarian, utilitarian, virtue or other); interpret, analyse and evaluate the issue, policy or case study.
- Assignments should be made up of 2,500 to 3,000 words in length. (This assignment is exceptional in that it DOES NOT have a word limit, only guidance).

Appendix 2

Reader, table of contents

John C. Harsanyi: Morality and the Theory of Rational Behaviour [*Utilitarianism*]
John Broom: Utility [*Utilitarianism*]
Amartya Sen: Inequality Re-examined,
ch. 1, Equality of What? [*Egalitarianism*]
David Schmidtz: The Institution of Property [*Libertarianism*]
Mark Lutz & Kenneth Lux: Humanistic Economics, ch. 6 [*Deontological*, Kant]
Amitai Etzioni: The Moral Dimension,
ch. 1 [*Deontological*, Communitarian]
Amartya Sen: Inequality Re-examined,
ch. 3 & 4, Functionings, Capabilities, Freedom, Agency and Well-Being [*Consequentialist*]
Martha Nussbaum: Women and Development – The Capability Approach, chs. IV, V, VI [Aristotelian]
Martha Nussbaum: Women and Development – The Capability Approach, cases
Robert and Edward Skidelsky: How Much Is Enough?, ch. 6 [Aristotelian]
Robert H. Frank: What Price the Moral High Ground?, ch. 1 [*Neoclassical*]
Deirdre McCloskey: Not by P Alone – A Virtuous Economy [*Austrian*]
Julie Nelson: Feminism, Objectivity and Economics, ch. 1 [*Feminist*]
Paula England: The Separative Self [*Feminist*]
Virginia Held: Mothering versus Contract [*Feminist*]
Hans Joas: Habermas's "Theory of Communicative Action", ch. 10 [*Discourse Ethics*]
Jürgen Habermas: Morality and Ethical Life: Does Hegel's Critique of Kant Apply to Discourse Ethics? [*Discourse Ethics*]
Judith Butler: Undoing Gender, ch. 10
Judith Butler: Gender Is Burning: Questions of Appropriation and Subversion, ch. 4 [*Feminist*]
Stefan Kesting: Boulding's Welfare Approach of Communicative Deliberation
George Akerlof: Labor Contracts as Partial Gift Exchange
James Konow: Which Is the Fairest One of All? A Positive Analysis of Justice Theories

Appendix 3

List of films and plays (2016)

Purpose	*Title*
Virtue ethics	*Antigone*, by Sophocles
Differentiate deontological and consequentialist ethics	BBC radio 4 audio play 1971, *Professor Bernhardi*, by Arthur Schnitzler.
Egalitarianism	*Made in Dagenham*, 2010 British film directed by Nigel Cole. OR: *Untouchable*, 2011 French buddy comedy-drama *film* directed by Olivier Nakache
Positive freedom critique of libertarianism	*The Singing Detective*, 1986 BBC television serial drama, written by *Dennis Potter*
Communitarianism and deontological duty ethics (Kant)	*High Noon*, 1953 classic Western written by Carl Foreman and directed by Fred Zinnemann
Utilitarianism, capabilities approach, discourse ethics, etc.	*Examined Life*, 2008 Canadian documentary film about philosophers directed by Astra Taylor (featuring Peter Singer, Martha Nussbaum, Judith Butler and others) + separate interview clips with Amartya Sen www.youtube.com/watch?v=Mre-lKWsRU4
	and Jürgen Habermas www.youtube.com/watch?v=jBl6ALNh18Q
Feminist economics	*Who's Counting, Marilyn Waring on Sex, Lies and Global Economics*, National Film Board Canada: www.nfb.ca/film/whos_counting/
Unethical business practices	*The Corporation*, documentary film written by University of British Columbia law professor Joel Bakan, and directed by Mark Achbar and Jennifer Abbott, 2003 www.youtube.com/watch?v=Y888wVY5hzw
Normative aspects of empirical research	*Kitchen Stories*, 2003 Norwegian comedy directed by Bent Hamer

References

Beckerman, W. (2011): *Economics as Applied Ethics: Value Judgements in Welfare Economics*. Houndmills, Basingstoke, UK: Palgrave Macmillan.

Berik, G. (2012): "What's Macroeconomic Policy Got to Do with Gender Inequality?", *Global Social Policy* 12(2), 183–189.

Berik, G., Beneria, L. and Floro, M. (2015): *Gender, Development, and Globalization: Economics as If All People Mattered*. London and New York: Routledge.

Biesecker, A. (1997): "The Market as an Instituted Realm of Action", *Journal of Socio-Economics* 26(3), 215–241.

Biesecker, A. and Kesting, S. (2003): *Mikroökonomik*. München: Oldenbourg.

Blau, F., Ferber, M. and Winkler, A. (2006): *The Economics of Women, Men, and Work*. Upper Saddle River: Pearson Prentice Hall.

Boulding, K. E. (1956 [1997]): *The Image: Knowledge in Life and Society*. Ann Arbor: University of Michigan Press.

Boulding, K. E. (1969): "Economics as a Moral Science, Presidential Address, American Economic Association, December 29, 1968", *American Economic Review* 59(1), 1–12.

Boulding, K. E. (1990): *Three Faces of Power*. Newbury Park, London and New Delhi: Sage.

Cassirer, E. (1994 [1918]): *Kants Leben und Lehre*. Darmstadt: Wissenschaftliche Buchgesellschaft.

Davis, J. B. (2003): *The Theory of the Individual in Economics: Identity and Value*. London and New York: Routledge.

Davis, J. B. and Boumans, M. (2010): *Economic Methodology: Understanding Economics as a Science*. Houndmills, Basingstoke, UK: Palgrave Macmillan.

Dutt, A. K. and Wilber, C. K. (2010): *Economics and Ethics: An Introduction*. Houndmills, Basingstoke, UK: Palgrave Macmillan.

Elsner, W., Heinrich, T. and Schwardt, H. (2014): *The Microeconomics of Complex Economies: Evolutionary, Institutional, Neoclassical, and Complexity Perspectives*. Amsterdam: Elsevier.

Etzioni, A. (1988): *The Moral Dimension: Toward a New Economics*. New York: Free Press.

Ferber, M. and Nelson, J. (eds.) (1993): *Beyond Economic Man: Feminist Theory and Economics*. Chicago and London: University of Chicago Press.

Findlay, S. and Mombourquette, P. (2014): "Evaluation of a Flipped Classroom in an Undergraduate Business Course", *Business Education & Accreditation* 6(1), 61–71.

Folbre, N. (2001): *The Invisible Heart: Economics and Family Values*. New York: The New Press.

Freeman Herreid, C. and Schiller, N. A. (2013): "Case Studies and the Flipped Classroom", *Journal of College Science Teaching* 42(5), 62–66.

Galbraith, J. K. (1958): *The Affluent Society*. Boston and New York: Houghton Mifflin.

Galbraith, J. K. (1961): *The Great Crash 1929*. Harmondsworth: Penguin Books.

Galbraith, J. K. (1967): *The New Industrial State*. London: H. Hamilton.

Galbraith, J. K. (1983): *The Anatomy of Power*. Boston: Houghton Mifflin.

Gordon, D. (1996): *Fat and Mean: The Corporate Squeeze of Working Americans and the Myth of Managerial "Downsizing"*. New York: Martin Kessler Books.

Habermas, J. (1995 [1981]): *Theorie des kommunikativen Handelns*. Frankfurt am Main: Suhrkamp.

Habermas, J. (1999 [1992]): *Between Facts and Norms*. Cambridge, US: MIT Press.

Habermas, J. (2001): *Kommunikatives Handeln und dezentralisierte Vernunft*. Stuttgart: Philipp Reclam jun.

Hausman, D. and McPherson, M. (2006): *Economic Analysis, Moral Philosophy, and Public Policy*. Cambridge: Cambridge University Press.

Held, V. (1990): "Mothering versus Contract", in Mansbridge, J. J. (ed.), *Beyond Self-Interest*. Chicago: University of Chicago Press, 286–304.

Hirschman, A. O. (1970): *Exit, Voice, and Loyalty: Responses to Decline in Firms, Organisations, and States*. Cambridge, US and London: Harvard University Press.

Hirschman, A. O. (1991): *The Rhetoric of Reaction: Perversity, Futility, Jeopardy*. Cambridge, US and London: The Belknap Press of Harvard University Press.

Hirschman, A. O. (1993a): "Exit, Voice, and the Fate of the German Democratic Republic", in Hirschman, A. O. (1995), *A Propensity to Self-Subversion*. Cambridge, US and London: Harvard University Press, 9–44.

Hirschman, A. O. (1993b): "The Rhetoric of Reaction; Two Years Later", in Hirschman, A. O. (1995), *A Propensity to Self-Subversion*. Cambridge, US and London: Harvard University Press, 45–68.

Hirschman, A. O. (1994): "Social Conflicts as Pillars of Democratic Market Societies", in Hirschman, A. O. (1995), *A Propensity to Self-Subversion*. Cambridge, US and London: Harvard University Press, 231–248.

Hodgson, G. (1993): *Economics and Evolution: Bringing Life Back* into Economics. Cambridge: Polity Press and University of Michigan Press.

Hodgson, G. (1999): *Evolution and Institutions: On Evolutionary Economics and the Evolution of Economics*. Cheltenham, UK: Edward Elgar.

Hodgson, G. (2001): *How Economics Forgot History: The Problem of Historical Specificity in Social Science*. London: Routledge.

Hodgson, G. (2004): *The Evolution of Institutional Economics: Agency, Structure and Darwinism in American Institutionalism*. London: Routledge.

Joas, H. (1993): *Pragmatism and Social Theory*. Chicago: University of Chicago Press.

Kesting, S. (1998): "A Potential for Understanding and the Interference of Power: Discourse as an Economic Mechanism of Coordination", *Journal of Economic Issues* 32(4), 1053–1078.

Littlejohn, A. and Pegler, C. (2007): *Preparing for Blended e-Learning*. London and New York: Routledge.

Lutz, M. and Lux, K. (1988): *Humanistic Economics: The New Challenge*. New York: The Bootstrap Press.

Mansbridge, J. J. (ed.) (1990): *Beyond Self-Interest*. Chicago and London: University of Chicago Press.

Myrdal, G. (1960): *Beyond the Welfare State: Economic Planning and Its International Implications*. New Haven and London: Yale University Press.

Myrdal, G. (1965 [1932]): *The Political Element in the Development of Economic Theory*. London: Routledge.

Myrdal, G. (1972 [1944]): *An American Dilemma: The Negro Problem and Modern Democracy*. New York: Pantheon Books.

Nelson, J. (1996): *Feminism, Objectivity and Economics*. London and New York: Routledge.

Nussbaum, M. (2000): *Women and Human Development*. Cambridge: Cambridge University Press.

Rawls, J. (1971): *A Theory of Justice*. Cambridge, US: Harvard University Press.

Rössler, B. (1996): "Feministische Theorien der Politik", in v. Beyme, K. and Offe, C. (eds.), *Politische Theorien in der Aera der Transformation*. Opladen: Westdeutscher Verlag, 267–291.

Rössler, B. (2015): "Feministische Gerechtigkeit", in Goppel, A., Mieth, C. und Neuhäuser, C. (eds.), *Handbuch Gerechtigkeit*. Stuttgart: Metzler, 92–98.

Sandel, M. (2012): *What Money Can't Buy: The Moral Limits of Markets*. London: Allen Lane and Penguin Books.

Schulte, G. (ed.) (1996): *Kant*. München: Eugen Diederichs Verlag.

Sen, A. (1987): *On Ethics and Economics*. Oxford: Blackwell.

Sen, A. (1995): "Equality of What, Chapter 1", in Sen, A., *Inequality Reexamined*. New York: Russell Sage Foundation and Oxford: Clarendon Press, 12–30.

Skidelsky, R. and Skidelsky, E. (2012): *How Much Is Enough? The Love of Money and the Good Life*. London: Allen Lane and Penguin Books.

Smith, A. (1976 [1759]): *The Theory of Moral Sentiments*. D. D. Raphael and A. L. Macfie (eds.). Oxford: Clarendon Press.

Taylor, C. (1989): *Sources of the Self: The Making of the Modern Identity*. Cambridge, US: Harvard University Press.

Tugendhat, E. (1992): *Philosophische Aufsätze*. Frankfurt am Main: Suhrkamp.

Tugendhat, E. (1993): *Vorlesungen über Ethik*. Frankfurt am Main: Suhrkamp.

Velenchik, A. D. (1995): "The Case Method as a Strategy for Teaching Policy Analysis to Undergraduates", *The Journal of Economic Education* 26(1), 29–38.

Vincent Roehling, P., Vander Kooi, T. L., Dykema, S., Quisenberry, B. and Vandlen, C. (2010): "Engaging the Millennial Generation in Class Discussions", *College Teaching* 59(1), 1–6.

Vromen, J. and Aydinonat, N. E. (eds.) (2015): *Economics Made Fun: Philosophy of the Pop-Economics*. London and New York: Routledge.

Vromen, J. and Lanteri, A. (2014): *The Economics of Economists*. Cambridge: Cambridge University Press.

Wright, J. B. (2015): *Ethics in Economics: An Introduction to Moral Frameworks*. Stanford: Stanford University Press.

17 Addressing controversies in economics instruction through interdisciplinary learning communities

The Evergreen experience

Peter Dorman

1 Introduction

Among those concerned with reforming the introductory economics course, there are two broad approaches to content. One advocates the purposeful incorporation of heterodox theoretical material from perspectives such as Marxism, post-Keynesian economics, feminist economics, institutional economics, and Austrian economics. The other sees the central problem as the closure of economics as a discipline and the remedy as the inclusion of linkages to adjacent fields of study like history, political science, psychology, ecology, and philosophy. There are reasonable arguments on all sides, and as we will see the approaches are not mutually exclusive. This chapter contributes a bit of empirical evidence to the discussion.

I will begin with a very brief gloss on the state of current debates over the teaching of introductory economics. My goal is not to weigh the arguments against one another but only to identify the main positions and their implications for reform strategies.

To provide a frame for assessment, I will review the complaints about the introductory course lodged by students in a series of protests primarily in North America and Europe. My goal will be to demonstrate that they can be distilled into a set of critical claims that cluster around three general concerns: that the discipline of economics is flawed, that the content of the introductory course does not accurately represent the state of the discipline, and that the methods used to present academic material to introductory students are stultifying, authoritarian, or otherwise inimical to reasonable educational goals. These will provide a basis for identifying the potential effects of reform practices.

The main part of the paper will review the experience of teaching introductory economics at Evergreen State College. Evergreen's approach to higher education is distinctive and provides a useful laboratory for observing the consequences of radical departures in economics instruction. I will document the forms that introductory economics takes at Evergreen, assess the extent to which it addresses the concerns of critical student groups, and indicate other issues this experience raises for the teaching and practice of economics. At the conclusion I will return to the larger debate over change *within* economics versus change *between* economics and other disciplines.

2 Two approaches to the reform of introductory economics

Economists whose perspective on the field is significantly non-mainstream or who value critical inquiry for its own sake are likely to have deep misgivings about the standard introductory curriculum, quite apart from the responses of students. The economics discipline has arguably marginalized dissenting traditions, foreclosing publication outlets in journals crucial for hiring and tenure decisions (Lee 2007; Lee and Elsner 2008). This marginalization is intensified in the principles courses, where only a particularly orthodox conception of economics, stripped of doubt or nuance, is on offer (Kwak 2017). Thus a heterodox, or even open-minded, economist experiences angst when placed in front of an introductory class with the expectation of adhering to the usual format.

Worse, mainstream introductory economics textbooks largely adopt an authoritarian intellectual posture, requiring students to parrot “the economic way of thinking”, with its emphasis on sweeping categorical judgments unaffected by historical or institutional context (Kwak 2017). Shielded from debate, students are not encouraged to weigh competing arguments, except within narrow limits. Empirical cases are selected to illustrate general principles, not to introduce students to grounded inquiry in the context of ambiguity or complexity. Thus the principles course is at odds with the ethos of critical thinking as it has developed elsewhere in the undergraduate curriculum.

Broadly speaking, there are two schools of thought on the nature of the problem and its remedy. The first emphasizes the role of pluralism: the core failure of introductory economics is its rigid orthodoxy, and the inclusion of heterodox material not only generates a body of knowledge more useful to the student but also necessitates and develops their capacity for critical judgment (Barone 1991; Garnett 2009; Knoedler and Underwood 2003; McDonough 2012; Nelson and Goodwin 2009; Peterson and McGoldrick 2009; Pluta 2006; Underwood 2004). An advantage of this approach is that it can be undertaken independently within existing institutional settings. An economics department can expand its offerings to embrace a more pluralist conception of the discipline, and an individual economist, if given autonomy, can expand the pluralism of her particular course offerings as well. This requires no coordination with any other academic entity.

The second approach is interdisciplinarity. Here the emphasis is on the connectedness that should exist between economics and related disciplines, recognizing the artificiality of their division (Caviglia-Harris 2003; Daley et al. 2013). This position has had fewer adherents in the literature, perhaps because movement toward true interdisciplinarity cannot be unilateral. Material from adjacent disciplines which economics might incorporate needs to be presented in a form and developed through applications which make them accessible to economics, and in particular to introductory students. Behavioral economics, for instance, is now internal within the economics discipline and can be incorporated unilaterally into entry-level courses. But economists have thus far drawn on only a portion of the literature in psychology pertaining to behavior in economic situations, largely adhering to the departures-from-rationality paradigm. True interdisciplinary would involve an encounter with a much wider spectrum of psychological research, but much of the latter is framed for non-economic audiences and difficult for introductory economics students to access. The same is also true in reverse, of course – psychologists wishing to incorporate more economics into their teaching will find much of the potentially relevant literature couched in terms and applied to issues that students without economics training will experience as inaccessible – with the result that reciprocity would impose demands on economists as well. The institutional structure to support such collaboration does not exist in most venues, nor are the disciplinary reward structures conducive to it. Nevertheless, as the literature demonstrates and as we will see shortly, such opportunities do arise.

Before moving ahead, it is important to note that these approaches are not mutually exclusive. Some strands of heterodox economics are directly inspired by developments in other disciplines; obvious examples include feminist economics, ecological economics, and political economy. Similarly, heterodox elements within economics are often sought out by practitioners in other disciplines precisely for their greater compatibility across disciplinary boundaries. There is no logical opposition, then, between pluralist and interdisciplinary strategies; the difference is one of starting point, emphasis and institutional context, and perhaps also pedagogical philosophy – inquiry versus discipline-centered – as we will see.

3 Student critiques of introductory economics

The first of the new wave of student critiques was launched by what became the "Post-Autistic Economics" movement in France. Its founding document was an "Open Letter from Economic Students to Professors and Others Responsible for the Teaching of this Discipline", which made a variety of points about the form and content of undergraduate economics instruction. Given the centralized control exercised over the university curriculum in France, this action was viewed as political in character and national in scope (Post-Autistic Economics 2000).

Similar sentiments were soon echoed in the English-speaking world. The Post-Autistic group extended their critique in the Kansas City Proposal, and similar attitudes were expressed at Cambridge University (Post-Autistic Economics 2001; The Cambridge 27 2001). Subsequent protests arose after the financial crisis of 2008. Students in Gregory Mankiw's introductory economics course (Econ 10) at Harvard staged a walkout in 2011 in a highly publicized episode (Concerned Students of Economics 10 2011). Similarly, a Post-Crash Economics Society was formed at the University of Manchester to criticize the presentation of economics at that institution (The Post-Crash Economics Society 2014). An umbrella group, the International Student Initiative for Pluralism in Economics, ISIPE, has been formed to coordinate student protests across multiple campuses; it currently claims to represent 82 local groups in 31 countries. Its founding document, issued in 2014, repeats many of the same criticisms voiced earlier (International Student Initiative for Pluralism in Economics 2014).

There are differences in content and emphasis between these groups, and what follows is not intended as a definitive summing up of their arguments. For the purposes of this paper, however, we need a composite list. I have organized it by dividing student criticisms into three levels: those that pertain to the discipline of economics itself, particularly its mainstream component; those that critique the content of introductory courses as biased or constricted even given the limitations of the discipline; and those that target the pedagogical methods used by economics instructors. Of course, the boundaries between these levels are porous, and critiques at one level have implications for others. Nevertheless, it is useful to work from a structure rather than a long list of scattered arguments. This distillation of student critiques is presented in Table 17.1.

Of course, to enumerate these objections is not to endorse them. All of them, however, are at least plausible in the sense that, if not categorical indictments of the standard principles course, each likely arises in particular contexts to one degree or another. For instance, to take only the first, while quantitative empirical methods are essential, particularly in an era of increasing data availability, it is true that in some situations economists tend to downplay the contribution that qualitative research can also make.[1] The rest of this chapter will therefore assume that there is validity to these criticisms, even if they are sometimes exaggerated by dissident students.

Table 17.1 Student critiques of introductory economics

Level 1: Critiques of the discipline

- A lack of critical perspective on quantitative methods; insufficient appreciation for qualitative methods.
- The lack of an explicit study of ethics in relation to economics.
- A perceived bias against a serious consideration of inequality.
- Excessive mathematical formalization in economic theory.
- Insufficient willingness of economists to accept uncertainty, especially in theory.
- The narrowness of the standard model of *Homo oeconomicus*, particularly as it obscures differences of gender and class.

Level 2: Critiques of the content of introductory economics courses

- A lack of empirical content regarding institutions, policies, and actual social behavior.
- Only neoclassical economics is presented, to the exclusion of alternative theoretical traditions.
- A lack of attention to epistemology or more general philosophical reflection on economics as a realm of knowledge.
- Insufficient coverage of the history of economic thought.
- Insufficient incorporation of economic history.

Level 3: Critiques of instructional methods in introductory economics

- Insufficient space for critical thinking
  - due to the narrowness of content.
  - due to teaching style (excessive lecturing).
- Insufficient connection to other social sciences and the humanities.
- Lack of exposure to classic primary texts.
- Insufficient attention to current issues.

4 The context of Evergreen State College

Evergreen State College opened its doors in 1971 as a nontraditional public undergraduate institution. As a public college it is subject to a board of directors appointed by the governor of Washington State as well as policies implemented by the state legislature and higher education regulatory bodies. It currently enrolls approximately 4,000 students (full-time equivalent) and offers bachelor's and master's degrees.

The college is internally diverse, with a main campus in Olympia and a satellite campus in Tacoma, a program of evening and weekend studies, a reservation-based program, and three graduate programs (education, environmental studies, and public administration). Nevertheless, for the purposes of this paper the focus will be on full-time, day undergraduate studies in Olympia, as this is the largest component of the college and constitutes the "purest" implementation of its approach to higher education.

At the outset the college adopted its "four no's": no academic departments, no academic requirements, no faculty rank, and no grades (Evergreen State College 2016). Students do not pursue majors, nor are there general education requirements such as mandatory credits in the humanities, sciences, and so forth. Students are free to study anything they wish, so long as they accumulate a sufficient number of credit hours to graduate. Faculty, instead of assigning grades, write a narrative evaluation of each student, and there are few criteria governing what these evaluations can say or how they say it.

The main venue for instruction is a "coordinated studies program", where a "program" is roughly equivalent to a course at more traditional institutions. These are full-time, offering 16 credit hours over the course of a quarter. (Evergreen operates on a system of three regular quarters during the academic year, plus the option of summer school, which operates under somewhat different rules.) A student takes just one such program in a given quarter, and faculty teach just one as well, although students can supplement it with an additional module (in math, foreign language, physical education, etc.), and faculty are also expected to sponsor internships and individual learning contracts. The graduation requirement is simply the successful accumulation of 180 credits, or slightly less than 12 quarters of full-time programs.

Most coordinated studies programs are team-taught by faculty from different disciplinary backgrounds. A few repeat regularly, but most are one-off or sporadic collaborations freely designed by their faculty. Faculty face few constraints on whom they can choose to teach with, so the structure of the curriculum is fluid. It is expected that most coordinated study programs will span a range of knowledges and skills, but administrators have little control over the extent to which the programs on offer during any given quarter encompass the typical range of academic specialties. Some programs have a one-quarter duration, while others extend for two or three quarters. Programs are generally scheduled two years in advance.

This structure has certain obvious implications for the teaching of economics and similar disciplines:

1 It is highly flexible, and faculty can experiment with many different contexts for instruction as well as selection of academic topics.
2 It enables planned interdisciplinarity. Rather than offering different subjects in parallel, as is common in most institutions, Evergreen allows teams of faculty the opportunity to design coordinated instruction linking multiple disciplines.
3 It allows for a wider variety of scheduling options within its 16-hour-per-week framework. Class periods can extend for several hours, and field trips are common.
4 It permits greater spontaneity within the program structure. Since faculty and student workload is largely restricted to just a single program, spur-of-the-moment decisions to alter activities, schedule, and content can be taken with few impediments.
5 Program flexibility can extend off-campus. Coordinated study programs can connect students to civic groups, government agencies, and businesses to enhance the real-world character of applied work.
6 The absence of a departmental structure removes nearly all external accountability from faculty decisions on whether and how to teach particular disciplines. This encourages innovation and diversity but limits coordination and predictability.
7 The lack of curricular standardization limits the ability of faculty to plan advanced programs with specified prerequisites.

Moreover, Evergreen is not neutral with respect to academic content. In general terms, two philosophies have guided the evolution of the college, each with important implications for how economics is taught. The primary influence is the self-cultivation approach associated with Alexander Mieklejohn, including the emphasis on seminars incorporating "great books" (Mieklejohn 2001). Indeed, since its inception Evergreen has attracted thousands of students seeking to find themselves and their path in life, and a substantial percentage of curricular offerings support this goal. These programs have minimal disciplinary content in the conventional sense and instead encourage introspection and the process of *Bildung*. Obviously, the most introspective programs do not encompass economics. Nevertheless, a substantial portion of the college is devoted to what might be called social self-discovery, finding one's place in the social and political world, and these may have economic content. Such programs are often centered on community studies or identity concerns, where economics plays a supportive role in helping students situate themselves. The predominance of education as self-discovery is exemplified by the central role played by seminars involving books faculty regard as profound: students are introduced to such seminars during their initial orientation upon matriculating, and they appear even in science-based programs where most of the effort is devoted to more traditional objectives.[2]

There is, however, a secondary tradition loosely associated with the approach of John Dewey, which emphasizes experiential learning, problem-solving, and an appreciation of academic disciplines as "tools".[3] Programs of this sort are typically structured around inquiry; often the program title states a question or a problem that the program content will attempt to answer or solve. Most programs encompassing economics fall into this portion of the curriculum; its logical home is in integrated social science studies centered on a pressing political or theoretical problem.

Despite these intellectual proclivities, Evergreen has also found it necessary to offer more traditional disciplinary options for its students. Much of the natural sciences, for instance, are taught in this manner: they are presented in packages that combine physics and chemistry or chemistry and biology, but their content is relatively similar to what is available elsewhere. Economics is also offered in this manner, as the next section will describe.

One characteristic of Evergreen plays an important role in economics instruction: since the college does not impose any general education requirement, and in particular no math requirement, it has become a magnet for students seeking to obtain a bachelor's degree while avoiding math entirely. Meanwhile, any inclusion of math within a coordinated studies program is at the discretion of the faculty teaching it, and since student resistance is substantial and the college offers few resources to support math instruction, there are strong incentives to exclude topics requiring quantitative or symbolic reasoning. Thus, while math does appear in the curriculum, and not only in the sciences, it does so to a much lesser degree than would be the case elsewhere. In particular, economics is usually presented with as little math as possible, a pattern that limits the topics that can be offered.

5 Economics at Evergreen

This section describes a selection of coordinated studies programs offered at Evergreen within the past decade that incorporate introductory economics, if sometimes in fragmentary form. It is based on an examination of the program syllabi as well as interviews with the instructors.

Broadly speaking, economics is taught in two contexts, either as a central component of a program whose main purpose is disciplinary, or as a service component of an inquiry-based program whose guiding question is not centered on economics.

5.1 Disciplinary treatment of economics

During the first decade of the college's existence it became clear that it was necessary to offer introductory micro- and macroeconomics in relatively traditional formats. There was student demand for this content, and many graduate programs required it. At the same time there was concern that conventional economics was too ideologically oriented in directions most of the faculty found uncongenial.

The solution was to create a regularly repeating program entitled either *Political Economy and Social Change* or *Political Economy and Social Movements* that combined mainstream economics and radical alternatives. A version of this program has been offered in most years since that time. Initially it enlisted a mainstream economist to teach the mainstream material, while Marxists and other radicals countered with their critiques. This agonistic format was not sustainable: mainstream economists were unwilling to be cast in the role of designated enemy. In recent decades the economics in this program has been taught by economists adhering to a more skeptical framework, lessening the intrinsic tension but also tending toward less incorporation of mainstream material. The extent to which conventional economics is made available has depended on which faculty is teaching it in a given year and ranges from relatively comprehensive to minimal.

A typical example of the "comprehensive" variety of this program is *Political Economy and Social Change* offered in the Fall and Winter quarters of 2010–2011, with faculty drawn from economics and communications studies. It employed textbooks in micro- and macroeconomics (chapter manuscripts in electronic format), embedded in a wide range of other materials. Readings in the first quarter included US history and various political topics (mass incarceration, racial inequality, the rise of conservatism); readings in the second quarter included modern world history, radical critiques of mainstream economics, and social movement theory. Students took part in audio and visual media production as well as the usual completion of shorter and longer written assignments; they also wrote exams on the economics content.

A different approach to the comprehensive presentation of economics is illustrated by *Macroeconomics, Money and Crisis*, offered during the Winter quarter of 2016, taught solely by an economist. As outlined in its syllabus, the program had four foci: introductory macroeconomics (taught from a textbook); basic skills in quantitative finance; critical inquiry into money, debt, and financial crises; and an exploration of epistemology and ideology as applied to economics in the context of social justice. Seven books were assigned in addition to the economics text, along with a variety of shorter readings. The goal was to present economics both as a resource for understanding the vulnerability of modern economies to financial crises and as itself an object for critique.

Sometimes more than one discipline is presented in a comprehensive way, so that the program they share approaches a traditional model of multiple independent courses; the natural sciences approximate this at Evergreen. An example incorporating economics, energy studies and climate change is *Global Meltdowns: Finance, Energy and Climate*, taught by an economist and a political scientist specializing in energy policy during Fall 2012 and Winter 2013. Here micro- and macroeconomics were taught from textbooks, while an energy policy textbook was also used along with numerous readings on climate change and contemporary political economy.

In some instances economics is central to the disciplinary content being presented, but via one of its applications. Typical of this case is *The Political Ecology of Land*, taught by an economist and an urban planner during the Fall of 2011 and

Winter of 2012. Here, rather than teaching economics from a textbook, a highly selective and condensed version of microeconomics was presented during the first three weeks in Fall, followed by more detailed applications to environmental, urban, and regional economics. Readings included classics in urban and environmental studies as well as political theory.

Another example of economics by application is *Alternatives to Capitalism*, taught solely by an economist during Spring 2013. Since the socialist calculation debate is the central pivot on which modern debates in this field turn, and since that requires at least a rudimentary understanding of general equilibrium theory, certain aspects of microeconomics were essential. The first three weeks were devoted to an intensive overview of the relevant portions of economic theory, and only then could economics be integrated with politics and history in a discussion of 20th-century experiences with non-capitalist (or variety-of-capitalist) institutions.

An example of both comprehensive and applied instruction in economics can be found in *Small World: Poverty and Development on a Shrinking Planet*, taught solely by an economist over Fall 2013 and Winter–Spring 2014. Originally intended as a boot camp for students interested in development internships, it included not only full treatments of introductory micro- and macroeconomics but also introductory statistics (also taught from a textbook), as well as other subject areas of particular importance to development practitioners: the history of colonialism and decolonization, cultural change, and development economics. The history and cultural theory elements constituted an ongoing critique of the standard economic material.

5.2 Economics as a service component

Here economics is of interest not in itself, but for what it can contribute to other topic areas. A typical and rather dramatic example is *Self-Determination in Latin America: Mexico*, offered in Winter of 2014. Faculty included an economist and two comparative literature professors with expertise in Latin America. Most of the readings were fiction and criticism, with some providing background in modern Mexican history. The role of economics in this context was to explain a set of forces and events central to the recent Mexican experience, such as the 1994 peso crisis, the impact of the North American Free Trade Agreement (NAFTA), and the general influence of relations with the United States on the Mexican economy. Economics readings were few and brief, and most of the instruction took the form of workshops.

A less radical subordination of economics can be found in a program like *Geopolitics: Energy, Economics and Stewardship of the Pacific Northwest*, taught during Spring 2015 by an economist and a business studies faculty. While economics is in the title of the program, its main thrust concerns regional energy and environmental disputes. Readings included books on environmental problems, land use planning, and entrepreneurship; there was little formal economics. A quick overview of the basics of market analysis was presented in lecture form, but its purpose was to support the other topics rather than introduce economics as such.

Because student self-discovery plays such a central role in the Evergreen experience, even a program in which only economists serve as faculty can put economics in a service capacity. This is the case with *Current Economic and Social Issues*, taught by two economists in Spring 2010. This program provided a light introduction to various academic content areas, but its main purpose was to help students situate themselves relative to current political debates. The issues addressed were economic inequality, the politics of education, immigration, and climate change. There was no formal economics instruction; workshops introduced students to basic skills in quantitative literacy. From an economics standpoint, the main purpose of the program was to evoke an interest in future economic studies rather than to present more than a passing glance at the subject area.

This is a partial survey of the programs on which the analysis in this paper is based. The full database can be found in the Appendix.

6 Discussion

At this point it will be useful to return to the student criticisms catalogued in section 3. I will take them up clustered by level.

Level 1: Critiques of the discipline

These criticisms are largely reversed. Evergreen programs incorporating economics are virtually drenched in discussion of inequality – not only in its economic form but also political and cultural. In many cases the main reason for bringing in economics is to support a broader analysis of inequality and social justice. *Homo oeconomicus*, to the extent he/she is allowed entry to the classroom, is held up to scrutiny from the perspectives of literature, cultural studies, and political theory. Conventional economics is on the defensive wherever it appears in the curriculum.

If anything, the problem at Evergreen is that quantification and formalization are deficient. Whenever discretion is exercised regarding what elements of the discipline to include or exclude from the syllabus (and in interdisciplinary team-teaching within a ten-week constraint, this is always), the choice is typically made to pare away the parts of theory that require more algebra and geometry. This is the case even where the theoretical material left out is germane to the noneconomic agenda of the program; an example is game theory, which hardly makes an appearance at the college despite its relevance to the social change mission of much of the curriculum. Instructors, to their credit, go against the grain – and their own incentives concerning workload and student relations – to introduce quantitative methods, but formal statistical analysis is seldom invoked. The problem, in other words, is *too little* formal modeling and quantitative empirical study.

Level 2: Critiques of introductory economics content

Here too the question is whether students' concerns apply to Evergreen in reverse. Evergreen programs typically center on historical, institutional, and political matters, and even those structured around an introduction to the discipline incorporate contextual material to the point where they begin to crowd out standard content. Alternative perspectives in economics are given substantial space, particularly Marxism and post-Keynesian theory when money and debt are at issue. Again, crowding out can be a problem. The embedding of economics in philosophy is a given: Evergreen economics faculty are attuned to the affinity between mainstream economics and the values of classical liberalism, and they bring both classic liberal texts and critiques of them into their syllabi. The literary bias in economics instruction favors primary sources from the 18th and 19th centuries, and a popular form of critique is to place these thinkers in their historical context, viewed through a more modern lens of economic and social egalitarianism.

It is difficult to imagine students protesting the academic content of the programs incorporating basic economics instruction at Evergreen as they have elsewhere. If they have grounds for activism, it has to do with the results of the various sources of crowding out: by the standards of other institutions, their exposure to conventional economics is minimal. This is especially the case in programs in which economics appears in a service capacity, despite the tendency for faculty in these programs to award credit equivalencies in economics. (While the internal structure of Evergreen is resolutely non-disciplinary, credits are given disciplinary equivalencies on student transcripts in recognition of the demands of external audiences.) Yet even where economics is the "star" of the curricular offering, its treatment is usually abridged relative to what occurs elsewhere.

Level 3: Critiques of instructional methods in introductory economics

Placing economics in the context of other disciplinary traditions and in the service of inquiries into political and theoretical controversies ensures that critical thinking will play a primary role in its presentation. Even when mainstream economics is offered as an intact element within a coordinated study program, its treatment has an aspect of role-playing: students are asked, for the time being, to put aside their doubts and absorb its concepts and techniques, but the boundaries of this "game" are invariably porous. Unlike a conventional structure, in which a single disciplinary course (like Econ 101) can maintain its boundaries from start to finish, elements of a coordinated study program share class time with one another, and programs have overarching themes that encourage students to look for synergies and conflicts between different disciplinary perspectives. Indeed, the struggle is often to persuade students to *withhold* critique, at least temporarily, until concepts can be presented in sufficient depth to be appreciated.

Given the large amount of time available to full-time Evergreen programs – up to 16 hours per week (plus field trips), whose scheduling is at the discretion of instructors – a variety of class activities is inevitable. Lectures may occupy as much as half of the allotted program time but rarely more; seminars, workshops, and project activities typically play a more important role. Moreover, since faculty must write detailed narrative evaluations for each student, they need more than exams to generate assessment data. Class discussion is useful for shedding light on each student's thinking about the program material, as are a range of assignments like short papers, research projects, and oral presentations. Evergreen students are encouraged to express themselves through multiple channels.

In fact, a difficulty that arises for economics instructors is sustaining student interest in studying the often-abstruse building blocks of mainstream economics in the face of competition from other, more immediately engaging program elements, such as current political controversies or the exploration of fiction and cultural narratives. Economics has a monopoly status in conventional economics courses, but the intellectual environment in coordinated studies programs is intrinsically competitive. It is more difficult to argue that an apparently hermetic subject should be studied because it will "someday" pay off, when class time and the weight of assignments can readily be shifted to subjects whose payoffs are immediate.

Thus, while little conscious effort has been made to "reform" mainstream economics or its teaching by faculty at Evergreen, the main criticisms students have raised against introductory economics classes have almost no purchase there. The format of coordinated studies programs and their orientation to themes of self-discovery and political or philosophical inquiry intrinsically promote conceptual flexibility, social relevance, critical thinking, and active learning. It is hardly possible to avoid problematizing the assumptions of mainstream economics and its usual packaging at the introductory level when students and faculty are simultaneously investigating history, philosophy, other social sciences, and current events. Collectively, Evergreen economists have created an "interdisciplinary economics" that strongly resembles what students protests implicitly favor.

Curricular reform and some drawbacks

Returning to the opening discussion of the two strategies of curricular reform in introductory economics, Evergreen represents a pathway that begins with interdisciplinarity and organically arrives at pluralism. Indeed, as we saw, the more direct approach to pluralism ventured in the early years of the college, in which faculty with competing theoretical commitments were enlisted to do battle with one another, has given way to a less agonistic model informed by the needs of a learning community engaged in interdisciplinary inquiry. To be sure, this has been aided by the fact that all the economics faculty at Evergreen are sympathetic in varying degrees to non-mainstream perspectives, but pluralism has been more effective for not being the main pedagogical focus.

Yet the drawbacks of Evergreen's approach are also apparent. Mainstream material, and especially the use of formal modeling and quantitative methods, is shortchanged: students only sporadically study economics from textbooks, and in many programs they are credited with exposure to introductory economics even though only a small portion of the standard topics is covered. There is very little intermediate economics offered at Evergreen; students who need intermediate theory courses or econometrics to qualify for graduate programs have to acquire them through independent study contracts – hardly a desirable vehicle. Applied subjects, like environmental economics, are taught concurrently with a smattering of introductory instruction rather than building on prior study since, in the absence of an overarching disciplinary framework, it is impossible to require prerequisites. While the specific forms taken by these drawbacks can be traced to the unique features of the Evergreen model, they reflect a more general problem that interdisciplinary approaches need to address: how to provide a sequential structure and standards for coverage when individual disciplines like economics are not able to formulate their own autonomous curricula?

At least two questions call for further exploration. First, on its own terms, how effectively is economics taught at Evergreen? Do its students acquire as much depth and mastery as those who study at more conventional institutions, or do they delve even more deeply due to their critical approach? Is retention greater, less, or about the same? To date there has been no assessment of student learning in economics that permits such comparisons.

Second, is it possible to preserve the advantages of the current system while facilitating more quantitative and advanced studies? If there is scope for reducing the tradeoff between disciplinarity and interdisciplinarity, it lies in greater coordination between individual faculty – difficult to engineer in the absences of academic majors and departments. Greater bottom-up standardization is clearly the key step, since it would reduce the cost of bringing more challenging material to the curriculum (avoiding much of the constant reinvention that characterizes the current system), while allowing for greater reliance on prerequisites. It would also create a larger pool of students who could serve as tutors and program assistants, reducing the draw on faculty workload that results from more quantitatively oriented teaching. The difficulties that economics, with its somewhat arbitrary assumptions and long detours through abstract elaboration, faces in a competitive intellectual environment would remain, however.

To a large extent, Evergreen has unintentionally served as a laboratory for testing the hypotheses put forward by both dissident students and their dissatisfied professors, but we need to know more about what the evidence is telling us.

Acknowledgment

The author would like to express appreciation to Ralph Murphy and Tom Womeldorff for providing much of the data on which this chapter is based.

Appendix

Table 17A.1 A set of Evergreen programs encompassing introductory economics

Title	*Quarters*	*Instructor*	*Textbook*	*Exams*	*Projects*	*Other material*
Alternatives to Capitalism	2013S	PD	Yes	Yes	Yes	history, political theory
Caribbean Cultural Crossings	2013F	TW+	No	No	No	literature, post-colonial studies, regional studies
Current Economic and Social Issues	2010S	PD, PB	No	No	No	contemporary politics
Ecological and Environmental Economics	2015F	RM	Yes	Yes	Yes	environmental studies, environmental and resource economics
Geopolitics: Energy, Economics, and Stewardship of the Pacific Northwest	2015S	RM+	No	Yes	Yes	entrepreneurship, energy systems, Pacific Northwest studies
Global Meltdowns: Finance, Energy, and Climate Change	2012F, 2013W	PD+	Yes	Yes	Yes	energy, political theory, climate change, modern world history
Macroeconomics, Money, and Crisis	2016 W	TW	Yes	Yes	Yes	financial crisis, political economy
Political Ecology of Land	2009S	RM	Yes	Yes	Yes	urban studies, regional studies, law
Political Ecology of Land	2011F, 2102W	RM+	No	Yes	Yes	urban studies, urban planning, political theory
Political Economy and Social Change	2010F, 2011W	PD+	Yes	Yes	Yes	political economy, media studies, history, social movement theory
Self-Determination in Latin America: Mexico	2014W	TW+	No	No	No	literature, post-colonial studies, regional studies
Small World: Poverty and Development on a Shrinking Planet	2013F, 2014W,S	PD	Yes	Yes	Yes	statistics, development, history, post-colonial studies
Understanding the Economic Crisis	2009F, 2010W	PD	Yes	Yes	Yes	finance, history, political economy

Economics instructors: Peter Bohmer (PB), Peter Dorman (PD), Ralph Murphy (RM), Tom Womeldorff (TW); "+" indicates other instructors were members of the teaching team.

Notes

1 The aversion to qualitative methods in economics is most clearly revealed by their occasional appearance. A well-known example is Bewley (2002). Prior to his work, economists had tried a variety of econometric strategies to test hypotheses about wage rigidity. Bewley's "innovation" was that he simply asked a cross-section of key labor market informants, such as managers, employment counselors, and union officials.

2 This predominance was recently enhanced by the introduction of an academic statement requirement, the only academic requirement imposed on students apart from their credit accumulation. This statement is a summative self-assessment by students of the "meaning" of their education; it is redrafted annually and appears in its final form in the student's transcript. Students are strongly encouraged to write statements that convey a journey via education to self-understanding.

3 Unlike Meiklejohn, Dewey is not primarily associated with higher education, although his ideas translate readily. A late statement of his position can be found in Dewey (1938); his approach to education is placed in the context of his broader political philosophy in Westbrook (1993).

References

Barone, C. A. (1991): "Contending Perspectives: Curricular Reform in Economics", *Journal of Economic Education* 22(1), 15–26.

Bewley, T. F. (2002): *Why Wages Don't Fall During a Recession*. Cambridge: Harvard University Press.

The Cambridge 27 (2001): "Opening up Economics: A Proposal by Cambridge Students", www.paecon.net/PAEtexts/Cambridge27.htm, accessed 25 September 2018.

Caviglia-Harris, J. L. (2003): "Introducing Undergraduates to Economics in an Interdisciplinary Setting", *Journal of Economic Education* 34(3), 195–203.

Concerned Students of Economics 10 (2011): "An Open Letter to Greg Mankiw", *Harvard Political Review*, 2 November.

Daley, M., Grumbling, O. and Peterson, R. (2013): *Teaching Undergraduate Economics in an Interdisciplinary Setting: The Green Learning Community*. SSRN Paper No. 2353553, accessed 25 September 2018.

Dewey, J. (1938): *Experience & Education*. New York: Kappa Delta Pi.

Evergreen State College (2016): *Historical Documents*, http://evergreen.edu/faculty development/keydocuments.htm, accessed 25 September 2018.

Garnett, R. F., Jr. (2009): "Rethinking the Pluralist Agenda in Economics Education", *International Review of Economics Education* 8(2), 58–71.

International Student Initiative for Pluralism in Economics (2014): *An International Student Call for Pluralism in Economics*, www.isipe.net/open-letter/, accessed 25 September 2018.

Knoedler, J. T. and Underwood, D. A. (2003): "Teaching the Principles of Economics: A Proposal for a Multi-Paradigmatic Approach", *Journal of Economic Issues* 37(3), 697–725.

Kwak, J. (2017): *Economism: Bad Economics and the Rise of Inequality*. New York: Pantheon Books.

Lee, F. S. (2007): "The Research Assessment Exercise, the State and the Dominance of Mainstream Economics in British Universities", *Cambridge Journal of Economics* 31(2), 309–325.

Lee, F. S. and Elsner, W. (2008): "Publishing, Ranking, and the Future of Heterodox Economics", *On the Horizon* 16(4), 176–184.

McDonough, T. (2012): "Integrating Heterodox Economics into the Orthodox Introductory Course", *International Journal of Pluralism and Economics* 3(4), 437–449.

Mieklejohn, A. (2001): *The Experimental College*. Madison, WI: University of Wisconsin Press.

Nelson, J. A. and Goodwin, N. (2009): "Teaching Ecological and Feminist Economics in the Principles Course", *Forum for Social Economics* 38(2), 173–187.

Peterson, J. and McGoldrick. K.-M. (2009): "Pluralism and Economic Education: A Learning Theory Approach", *International Review of Economics Education* 8(2), 72–90.

Pluta, J. E. (2006): *Integrating Evolutionary Economics into the Microeconomic Principles Course*. SSRN Paper No. 907119, accessed 25 September 2018.

Post-Autistic Economics (2000): "Open Letter from Economic Students to Professors and Others Responsible for the Teaching of This Discipline", www.paecon.net/PAEtexts/a-e-petition.htm, accessed 25 September 2018.

Post-Autistic Economics (2001): "The Kansas City Proposal: An International Open Letter to All Economics Departments", www.paecon.net/PAEtexts/KansasCity.htm, accessed 25 September 2018.

The Post-Crash Economics Society (2014): *Economics, Education and Unlearning: Economics Education at the University of Manchester*. University of Manchester, www.post-crasheconomics.com/economics-education-and-unlearning/, accessed 25 September 2018.

Underwood, D. A. (2004): "Principles of Macroeconomics: Toward a Multiparadigmatic Approach", *Journal of Economic Issues* 38(2), 571–581.

Westbrook, A. (1993): *John Dewey and American Democracy*. Ithaca: Cornell University Press.

Part III

Teaching for socio-ecological transformation

Economics as a transformative science?

18 Contours of a critical transformative science

Samuel Decker

1 Introduction

In the contribution "Towards a Critical and Interdisciplinary Economic Science?" in the related collection *Advancing Pluralism in Teaching Economics. International Perspectives on a Textbook Science* (Decker 2018), I argued that any serious challenger of mainstream economics must be able to link discursive-institutional change in science to a broader process of societal change. I reasoned that, without multiple forms of coordination and correspondence between science on the one hand and civil society (e.g. political parties, media organizations, social movements) on the other hand, the institutional-political network of mainstream economics could not be effectively dissolved and replaced. Further, I put forward the thesis that scientific pluralism, though being a desirable and highly advanced proposal in theory, lacks the political and strategic capacities to build such far-reaching alliances between science and civil society. The project of pluralist economics, though being very successful and far-reaching on its own terms, is thus not sufficient to radically transform economics and social sciences. It should – as I concluded in the mentioned article – be complemented by further approaches, as transformative science.

In this chapter, I want to proceed from this conclusion and take up the concept of transformative science, which attracts increasingly attention in German-speaking academia. The critical assessment of transformative science will take place against the background of the paradigm of Critical Theory, which was developed by the Frankfurt School during and after World War II. This contraposition in section 2 demonstrates that the concept of transformative science resembles characteristics of positivist science and should be developed further. In section 3, I introduce the concepts 'interior pluralism' and 'second-order transformation' that are supposed to contribute to the paradigm of a *critical transformative science.* In section 4, I will present a few topics that could present primary projects of a critical transformative science.

2 Positivist and critical elements of transformative science

In their foundational text "Pledge for a Transformative Science: A Conceptual Framework" Schneidewind et al. (2016) describe transformative science as a "specific type of science that does not only observe and describe societal transformation processes, but rather initiates and catalyzes them" (ibid., 6). The text argues that the functional differentiation of modern societies "resulted in a system where its various sub-systems are more and more isolated from each other" (ibid., 4.). Digitalized communication via social media, the development of high-risk technology or 'dis-embedded' financial markets provide examples of the 'isolation' of societal sub-systems. As a result, "humanity [. . .] has to find a way of dealing with . . . social-ecological transformation processes and learn how to organize societal systems differently" (ibid.). In other words, societal problems of functional differentiation necessitate a normative, interventionist type of science. To "re-integrate societal sub-systems, science needs to transcend its descriptive analytical functions and cooperate with non-academic actors to achieve shared, normative goals" (ibid.).

The concept of transformative science received criticism for blurring the line between science and politics (e.g. Strohschneider 2014). The normative goal of sustainability "overrides the epistemic and institutional autonomy" (my translation) of science according to Strohschneider (ibid., 182). Voss (2013) warned against a 'technocratization' (ibid., 28) (my translation) of science, where political statements are disguised as scientific truths.

The debate about transformative science should be read as an episode of a more fundamental controversy in social sciences between positivist and critical approaches. The method dispute (*Werturteilsstreit*) before World War I and the positivism dispute (*Positivismusstreit*) between Critical Rationalism and Critical Theory in the 1960s can be interpreted as episodes of this controversy (Strunz and Gawel 2017). Notwithstanding this recurring controversy about the role of value judgements in social sciences, which plays a formative role in political science or sociology until today, economic thought became dominated by a positivist method already at the end of the 19th century, when the neoclassical paradigm started to supersede the classical paradigm together with the institutionalization of 'economics' as an academic discipline (Jäger and Springler 2015).

On a basic level, positivism can be understood as an epistemological tradition that understands science as *separated from its object*. As a neutral (or 'value-free') observer, the scientist can and should develop accurate descriptions of reality without choosing sides for one particular social group. Critical approaches understand science *as interrelated with its object*. As a societal actor that is shaped by social relations and in turn exerts influence on them, the scientist should reflect on its role in society and take a position. It is crucial to point out that a positivist or a critical understanding of science does not determine the role of empirical arguments. Epistemology (the understanding of knowledge) and methodology (the justification of knowledge) are separated things. To characterize economics as a positivist approach does not imply that it favours empirical analysis to unfounded political statements; on the contrary, economics has been criticized as a system of deductive-mathematical models that are detached from the real world and defy empirical testing (Freeman and Kliman 2005; Lawson 2013). At the same time, economics transmits a pro-growth, pro-market, pro-capitalist, pro-extractivist bias via creating an apolitical, allegedly 'value-free' model that naturalizes the 'economy' as an autonomous sphere strictly separated from history, society and the environment (Jäger and Springler 2015).

The critique of positivist, 'value-free' science was most comprehensively formulated by the Frankfurt School and the paradigm of Critical Theory. As summarized by Honneth (2006), Critical Theory understands science as a societal practice that is shaped by competing interests and expresses power structures that are inherent to society. Critical Theory is a form of science that keeps itself aware of its societal context of formation *and* usage. It is opposed to positivist science, which sees itself as detached from practical interests and thus has lost consciousness of the societal roots and practical objectives that produce science in the first place. While positivist theory pretends to stand in a neutral and value-free relationship to society as it exists (and thus implicitly legitimizes it), Critical Theory focuses on the socially produced character of science and thus is able to analyze the ideological functions of (mainstream) science and to develop scientific knowledge for emancipatory goals that exceed the existing organization of society. Crucially, positivist epistemology conceptualizes society as a homogenous whole, where all interests are justified and equally able to make themselves heard. Critical Theory understands society as divided by power structures, for example regarding to the position different societal groups hold in the economic process, and sides with those interests that are directed against various kinds of oppression in an emancipatory way (Honneth 2006).

With this short exposition of Critical Theory in mind, does the concept of transformative science follow the lines of Critical Theory or rather resembles positivist science? Interestingly, transformative science holds characteristics of both epistemological traditions. On the one hand, it commits itself to emancipatory learning processes and progressive objectives that, at least partially, question existing societal institutions and structures. On the other hand, it develops the justification for these normative goals on positivist ground. The problem of 'unmanageable' differentiation of societal sub-systems – which is clearly borrowed from the disputed paradigm of systems theory – as well as the diagnosis of an already unfolding process of social-ecological transformation that needs to be managed are presented as empirical facts. Transformative science as developed by Schneidewind et al. (2016) argues for the introduction of normative goals into scientific reasoning a posteriori due to objectively postulated problems that are external to science. Put simply, due to the challenge of social-ecological transformation, science is supposed to develop a normative and interventionist dimension and support the transformation towards sustainability. Critical Theory, on the contrary, assumes the normativity of science a priori. Science is a societal practice that is shaped by competing interests and expresses power structures that are inherent to society.

This specific conceptualization of transformative science inherits the theoretical problems of positivism: science is reassured as an objective problem-solver that stands in a neutral relationship to society – or even 'humanity' (Schneidewind et al. 2016, 4) – which is understood as a homogenous entity. Instead of considering competing societal interests that originate different kinds of understandings of problems and solution strategies, one specific set of interpretations and solutions is defined in advance. As Voss (2013) has pointed out, this version of transformative science runs the risk of leveraging a certain interpretation of 'sustainability' and 'transformation' that is tied to powerful societal interests. Brand and Wissen (2017) have pointed out that the transformation discourse that is put forward, for example, by the German Advisory Council on Global Change (WBGU 2011), which orients itself at the 2030 Agenda for Sustainable Development (Agenda 2030) (UN 2015), neglects more radical notions of transformation and thus can be described as a 'new critical orthodoxy' (Brand and Wissen 2017). While Critical Theory adhered to the principle possibility of an emancipatory transformation beyond capitalism, the standpoint of transformative science is unclear in this regard. The proclaimed transformation to sustainability rather resembles the aim of an ecological modernization of capitalism alongside Agenda 2030 and the UN Sustainable Development Goals.

This concept of transformative science supports societal goals as the horizon of scientific inquiry, without fully recognizing the societal and power-driven nature of the scientific process itself. From the perspective of Critical Theory, it is impossible to 'introduce' normative interests (of domination, utilization, emancipation, transformation, etc.) ex post into the scientific process, because those interests are vital in *creating science in the first place*. When following emancipatory goals, science can therefore only expand on existing societal conflicts in the form of *immanent critique*. Transformative science, however, follows the logic of *external critique*, where predefined objectives and solution paths are developed in vitro and then injected into the societal discourse. Societally produced and constructed processes and goals (transformation, post-growth, etc.) are thus naturalized and excluded from debate. In Critical Theory, normative judgements result implicitly from the analysis in the form of analytical critique (Pühretmayer 2010). Transformative science, on the contrary, seems to follow a superficial understanding of normativity, where value judgements are explicitly assumed by the scientist.

Despite these problems, the concept of transformative science contains interesting approaches to reorganize science and especially economics, and thus is worthy of being developed further. The hands-on approach of transformative science points a finger at a weak spot of Critical Theory, which often remains in the abstract realm of critique and theoretical self-referentiality. Transformative science shifts the focus on actual influencing and shaping societal developments in the "tradition of pragmatism, where the strict separation of knowledge and experience disappears" (Schneidewind et al. 2016, 8). In what follows, I will therefore try to develop a more reflexive and (self-)critical version of transformative science that follows the lines of Critical Theory and at the same time retains its interventionist and pragmatist impetus.

3 Interior pluralism and second-order transformation

To formulate critical concept of transformative science that overcomes its connections to positivism, both the justification for and the formulation of value judgements must be conceptualized in a different way.

Science – also critical or transformative science – is socially produced and contested. State legislation and finances, corporate finances and hegemonic discourses influence the scientific process massively (Freeman and Kliman 2005). There is no possibility to formulate a normative position as starting point or conclusion of a scientific argument that could have universal validity, because every aspect of science takes place within a normative structure. This is not to be misunderstood with a constructivist argument, which claims that the concept of 'truth' is a mere linguistic construction, of which prime function consists in ordering hegemonic discourses and reproducing asymmetrical power relations. In a critical epistemology truth is understood as an ambivalent social phenomenon, which can occur *both as a technique of domination and a means of emancipation.*

In order to clarify this point, a few fundamental ontological considerations have to be made. Positivism presupposes the existence of an objective world that is independent of those who observe it. A critical ontology does *not* proceed from the opposite assumption, as an extreme version of constructivism would, that no objective reality exists outside the symbolic constructions of language. The notion of truth is not abandoned, however with an important restriction. Truth claims are elements of theories, which are conceptualized as *condensations of societal practices*. These practices that operate in the medium of language can establish contingent yet relatively *durable relations* between signifiers and their referents in the objective world. The durability of these relations is determined by *both the characteristics of the objective world and societal power relations as aspects of this objective world* (Carroll and Ratner 1994, 15; Sayer 1992).

A critical ontology must consider both the societal materiality of science and the emancipatory role science nevertheless can and must play – not only via deconstructing hegemonic truth claims but also via creating truth claims that are helpful for progressive struggles. Since those truth claims can be neither universal nor clean of power relations, there must be a form of *interior pluralism* that allows different truths to claim this progressive function for themselves. The analysis of differentiating societal sub-systems that necessitate an integrative function of science is only one specific justification of transformative science; the 'sustainability transformations' Schneidewind et al. (2016, 11) propose is only one possible idea of social change. What is needed is a critical pluralist discourse that allows different problem analyses and objectives to exist in parallel to each other. The justifications and objectives of transformative science then could develop organically on the ground of open, unfinished debates within progressive societal spectres and in society at large. Transformative science would gain the function of a democratic forum for the analysis of societal problems and the discussion of (transformative) solutions strategies and would in this way become a form of a public science (see e.g. Neun 2018). At the same time, it must be clear that transformative science cannot escape the powerful interests that shape societal discourses and must be critically aware of those interests and – in turn – of its own performative impact on societal and political discourses due to its aura of scientific legitimation (Voss 2013; Barth and Rommel in Chapter 19).

When coupled with the concept of interior pluralism, transformative science can refrain from its positivist elements via developing its scientific questions and answers in an open, competed discussion process. However, when opening up the epistemic terrain of transformative science, the question occurs which notions of transformation and transformative science can be accepted and which can be not. The existing version of transformative science is, as mentioned above, strongly influenced by the German Advisory Council on Global Change (WBGU 2011) that in turn orients itself at the 2030 Agenda for Sustainable Development (Agenda 2030) (UN 2015). The concept of transformation plays a prominent role in various reports and policy proposals that orient themselves at Agenda 2030. The meaning or definition of the term 'transformation' in these reports, however, remains highly vague and seems to be used synonymously to expressions as 'influential', 'far-reaching' and 'altering'.

Brand (2016) has put forward a powerful systematization of the transformation discourse as well as a critique of the usage of the term by the German Advisory Council on Global Change (WBGU). Brand (2016) criticizes that conscious and intended acts of change are one-sidedly understood as the subjects of transformation. Instead, individual actors, companies or governmental institutions should not only be understood as (potential) actors of positive change, but as "co-constitutive with societal processes and structures" that have to be transformed (ibid., 7). In other words, state policies and investment strategies must be understood as part of the problem and only under certain circumstances as part of the solution (Greven 2008). Additionally, he criticizes a naturalistic understanding of the object (or drivers) of transformation, for example as "demographic trends, the globalization of production, [. . .] technological progress and digitalization" (Brand 2016, 6).

Brand argues for a comprehensive understanding of transformation, in which the capitalist growth economy is depicted as a crucial driver of transformation. In this theoretical setting, transformation – observable in changing modes of living and production, shifting patterns of political regulation and discursive changes – is a general characteristic of societies in which the capitalist mode of production is dominating. Following this comprehensive understanding of transformation, the crucial question for any political strategy of transformation is not "how could a transformation (e.g.: towards sustainability) be induced" but "how could the current mode of transformation be replaced by a different mode of transformation that builds on other mechanism of economic reproduction". Brand's conceptualization of transformation is pioneering, because he acknowledges the importance of systemic patterns of (political-economic) reproduction (e.g. cycles of investment and credit, geopolitical competition) that have to be considered in order to analyze and change the current mode of transformation.

This concept of *second-order transformation* – the transformation of a preexisting pattern of transformation – can help to distinguish between approaches that use the term 'transformation' on a rhetoric level and approaches that aim at altering deeper-seated structures of economic and social reproduction. The project of transformative science could then be defined as a coordination of social practices of knowledge creation that contribute to the systemic transformation of the currently dominant mode(s) of transformation. What those modes of transformations are, how they work and what has to be changed about them would be subject of pluralist discussions. Approaches, however, that deny taking capital accumulation, credit creation, market mechanisms, (transnational) corporations and state policies into account as disruptive and transformative processes that need to be transformed in order to reach progressive goals would not belong to the project of transformative science.

In conclusion, this concept of transformative science differs profoundly from the one Schneidewind et al. (2016) have presented. Schneidewind et al. proceed from already existing processes of transformation (digitalization, social-ecological change, climate change and de-carbonization, etc.) that have to be steered in a sustainable direction. In this understanding of transformation, policy makers, managers and other influential actors of society have to be equipped with scientific proposals that support the transformation towards sustainability. The critical version of transformative science developed here proceeds from already existing processes of transformation as well (capital accumulation, economic crisis tendencies and counter-mechanisms, eco-imperial rivalries between nation-states, etc.). They are, however, not interpreted as inherent necessities but as the manifestation of social relations that can and have to be transformed in order to develop alternative systems of economic and social reproduction.

4 Key areas of a critical transformative science

The vision of transformative science implies a long-term scientific project that contributes to an emancipatory, social-ecological transformation of neoliberal and fossil capitalism. This scientific project can only be realized via a collaboration of critical spectres in social and technical sciences as well as through a wider transformative alliance within (transnational) civil society. This alliance must be part of a broader political dynamic within the context of an organic crisis of global capitalism in which new collective subjectivities emerge. Transformative science would be the intellectual operating system of a non-dogmatic and plural 'Progressive International' (Varoufakis 2016a) that not only analyzes flaws but develops concrete pathways for systemic change.

Currently, various processes of political-economic transformation are unfolding. The decades-long expansion of capitalist and legal structures and their integration into a system of Western-based global governance seems to have decelerated or even reversed. The global financial and economic crisis of 2007–2009, the disintegration of the European Union or the currency and trade wars the US government has become involved in are visible signs of the limits of capitalist globalization in its current form. Capitalist globalization creates contradictory trends – on the one hand, it leads to the economic penetration of former peripheral countries and their *integration* into a global economic framework. On the other hand, these countries rise to own-standing capitalist hegemons that compete for export markets, credit, dividends, financial power, oil and other key natural resources. This multilayered dynamic of competition (on company, nation-state and regional levels) leads to a *dis-integration* of the international order. The systemic lack of aggregate demand, the inflating global credit bubble and historical trade imbalances are driving these international conflicts. At the same time, the transnationalization of ownership, investment, production and consumption as well as persisting international hierarchies prohibit a rapid erosion of the international order. This *concurrence of continuity and crisis* leads to a profound process of transformation of the current political and economic order (Decker and Sablowski 2017).

Critical transformative sciences (e.g. transformative economics, transformative legal studies, transformative political science, transformative computer science, transformative geography) should locate themselves in these historical processes and develop progressive strategies for the de-construction and re-construction of the international order. I want to propose key areas that should stand at the centre of a critical transformative science.

- *Breaking with neoliberalism*: Governments are caught in international economic and legal frameworks where the regulation and taxation of capital, the protection of workers' rights and wages and other aspects of progressive economic policy are legally prohibited (as in the European Union) and economically toxic, as they bring competitive disadvantages (Schneider 2017). Policy tools are needed that reduce the dependence of national economies from international capital, financial markets and trade. The debates fostered by the British Labour Party under Jeremy Corbyn (Labour Party 2017a) or within the *Democracy in Europe Movement* (DiEM25 2017) could be interesting points of reference for an anti-neoliberal economics. Amon these proposals are classical social democratic ideas, as the taxation of profits and capital revenues or the socialization and strengthening of public welfare systems and infrastructures. But there are also more transformative concepts, as the general basic dividend (Varoufakis 2016b) or alternative models of ownership (Labour Party 2017b).
- *Building a transformative block*: Such radical social democratic policies would provoke immense political resistance by companies, other governments and international organizations and therefore can only be implemented by a government that is carried by an anti-neoliberal hegemony that is anchored in society. Nation-based transformation strategies, however, have so far not failed due to political reasons in the first place, but due to economic crisis symptoms that flip the public opinion. There is the need for an international transformation strategy, where progressive governments and central banks, unions, non-governmental organizations and social movements support each other and build a transnational network (a 'transformative block') in which anti-neoliberal policies can be stabilized.

The European Union (EU), where deep-seated economic disparities have contributed to massive economic and political crisis symptoms, serves as an excellent example. Caught between a desperate hope in national economic independence via exiting from the common currency, the euro, and not less unpromising attempts to reform the EU's fundamental structure, critical science should point out options of selective dis-integration and reintegration (Wahl 2017). The discourses on regional (dis-)integration (ibid., Candieas and Demirović 2017; Streeck 2018; Ehrlich 2011), de-financialization (Sawyer 2017; Christophers 2015) and de-globalization (Bello 2013; Novy 2017) present interesting starting points for a transformative science that supports the creation of a transformative block.

- *Moving beyond capitalism*: As Patnaik (2010) has shown, economic policies that come into conflict with capital interests create an ambivalent dynamic. To be sustained, more far-reaching policies have to be implemented that increase the dysfunctionality of capitalism even further. If those policies cannot be executed in the face of corporate or public resistance, a backward dynamic ensures that the measures implemented so far are taken back. There is either a dynamic of intensification or of disintegration of capitalism, but there can be no stable plateau with a mixed economy. This argument rejects the reformist strategy taken by social democracy in the first half of the 20th century. Proceeding from this argument, a critical transformative science should investigate both transitory and post-capitalist economic systems. The concepts of degrowth (Kallis 2011), digital transformation and post-capitalism (Mason 2016), de-commodification (Gerber and Gerber 2017), economic pluralism (Garnett et al. 2010) and digital economic coordination (Huckle and White 2016) are important starting points in this regard.

This sketch of a transformative science research agenda remains incomplete as well as highly unrealistic when compared to the current state of science and political discourses that currently witness a shift to the right rather than to the left. The international rise of the far right can be interpreted as the result of an ideological vacuum left by the centre and the left. On the one hand, the (neo)liberal utopia of unhampered deregulation and globalization failed to deliver a stable and inclusive model of capitalist development. One the other hand, socialist and social democratic strategies for the transformation of capitalism have not led to alternative models of economic regulation either. The far right fills this ideological gap via promising protection from international economic rivals, transnational corporations and migrants as potential competitors in the labour market. The (not yet existent) Progressive International so far offers no alternative economic narrative, which would combine mid-term anti-neoliberal measures with a long-term post-capitalist vision. Internationalism and nationalism can be interpreted as different strategies of workers to defend their interests – "and nationalism in the form of protection against migrants as additional competitors and against all other impositions of globalization currently appears more realistic than internationalist strategies" (Sablowski 2017) (my translation). The prime task of a transformative science should be to develop this internationalist strategy. Only a radical vision that on the one hand builds on the achievements of liberal democracy and on the other hand transcends its limits has the potential to create a new political dynamic. Only a scientific approach that – contrary to pluralist economics – both follows scientific methods *and* allies with a political project can be part of a 'Progressive

International' and at the same time create the political dynamic that would be necessary to push back mainstream economics.

References

Bello, W. (2013): *Capitalism's Last Stand? Deglobalization in the Age of Austerity*. London: Zed Books.

Brand, U. (2016): "How to Get Out of the Multiple Crisis? Contours of a Critical Theory of Social-Ecological Transformation", *Environmental Values* 25(5), 503–525.

Brand, U. and Wissen, M. (2017): *Imperiale Lebensweise*. München: Oekom.

Candieas, M. and Demirović, A. (ed.) (2017): *What's Left? Die EU zwischen Zerfall, Autoritarismus und demokratischer Erneuerung*. Hamburg: VSA-Verlag, 151–174.

Carroll, W. K. and Ratner, R. S. (1994): "Between Leninism and Radical Pluralism: Gramscian Counter-Hegemony and the New Social Movements", *Critical Sociology* 20, 3–26.

Christophers, B. (2015): "From Financialization to Finance: For 'De-Financialization'", *Dialogues in Human Geography* 5(2), 229–232.

Decker, S. (2018): "Towards a Critical and Transdisciplinary Economic Science?", in Decker, S., Elsner, W. and Flechtner, S. (eds.), *Advancing Pluralism in Teaching Economics*. London and New York: Routledge, 245–263.

Decker, S. and Sablowski, T. (2017): *Die G20 und die Krise des globalen Kapitalismus*. Berlin: Rosa-Luxemburg-Stiftung.

DiEM25 (2018): *European New Deal: A Comprehensive Economic & Social Policy Framework for Europe's Stabilisation, Sustainable Recovery & Democratisation*, https://diem25.org/wp-content/uploads/2017/03/European-New-Deal-Complete-Policy-Paper.pdf, accessed 1 February 2018.

Ehrlich, R. T. (2011): "Global Inequalities, Alternative Regionalisms and the Future of Socialism", *Journal für Entwicklungspolitik* 27(1), 72–94.

Freeman, A. and Kliman, A. (2005): "Beyond Talking the Talk: Towards a Critical Pluralist Practice", *Post-Autistic Economics Review* 40, 26–53.

Garnett, R. F., Jr., Olsen, E. K. and Starr, M. (eds.) (2010): *Economic Pluralism*. New York and Abingdon: Routledge.

Gerber, J.-D. and Gerber, J.-F. (2017): "Decommodification as a Foundation for Ecological Economics", *Ecological Economics* 131, 551–556.

Greven, M. T. (2008): "'Politik' als Problemlösung – und als vernachlässigte Problemursache. Anmerkungen zur Policy-Forschung", in *Die Zukunft der Policy-Forschung. Theorien, Methoden, Anwendungen*. Wiesbaden: Springer.

Honneth, A. (2006): "Traditionelle und kritische Theorie", in Honneth, A. (ed.), *Schlüsseltexte der Kritischen Therie*. Wiesbaden: VS Verlag für Sozialwissenschaften, 229–232.

Huckle, S. and White, M. (2016): "Socialism and the Blockchain", *Future Internet* 8(4), 49.

Jäger, J. and Springler, E. (2015): *Ökonomie der internationalen Entwicklung. Eine kritische Einführung in die Volkswirtschaftslehre*. Wien: Mandelbaum Verlag.

Kallis, G. (2011): "In Defence of Degrowth", *Ecological Economics* 70(5), 873–880.

Labour Party (2017a): *For the Many Not the Few: The Labour Party Manifesto 2017*, https://labour.org.uk/wp-content/uploads/2017/10/labour-manifesto-2017.pdf, accessed 1 February 2018.

Labour Party (2017b): *Alternative Models of Ownership*. Report to the Shadow Chancellor of the Exchequer and Shadow Secretary of State for Business, Energy and Industrial Strategy, https://labour.org.uk/wp-content/uploads/2017/10/Alternative-Models-of-Ownership.pdf, accessed 1 February 2018.

Lawson, T. (2013): "What Is This 'School' Called Neoclassical Economics?", *Cambridge Journal of Economics* 37(4), 947–983.

Mason, P. (2016): *Post-Capitalism: A Guide to Our Future*. London: Penguin Books.

Neun, O. (2018): "'Public Sociology' und 'Public Understanding of Science' (PUS) bzw. 'Medialisierung' der Wissenschaft", in Lettkemann, E., Wilke, R. and Knoblauch, H. (eds.), *Knowledge in Action: Neue Formen der Kommunikation in der Wissensgesellschaft*. Wiesbaden: Springer Fachmedien, 3–19.

Novy, A. (2017): "Emancipatory Economic Deglobalisation: A Polanyian Perspective", *Revista Brasileira de Estudos Urbanos e Regionais* 19(3), 558–579.

Patnaik, P. (2010): "Socialism or Reformism?", *Social Scientist* 38(5/6), 3–21.

Pühretmayer, H. (2010): "Zur Kombinierbarkeit von Critical Realism und Poststrukturalismus: Eine Reformulierung der Struktur-Handlungs-Frage", *Österreichische Zeitschrift für Politikwissenschaft* 39, 9–26.

Sablowski, T. (2017): "Die Widersprüche der europäischen Integration und die Linke Europa", in Candieas, M. and Demirović, A. (eds.), *What's Left? Die EU zwischen Zerfall, Autoritarismus und demokratischer Erneuerung*. Hamburg: VSA-Verlag, 151–174.

Sawyer, M. (2017): "The Processes of Financialisation and Economic Performance", *Economic and Political Studies* 5(1), 5–20.

Sayer, A. (1992): *Method in Social Science*. New York: Routledge.

Schneider, E. (2017): *Raus aus dem Euro – rein in die Abhängigkeit? Perspektiven und Grenzen alternativer Wirtschaftspolitik außerhalb des Euro*. Hamburg: VSA-Verlag.

Schneidewind, U., Singer-Brodowski, M., Augenstein, K. and Stelzer, F. (2016): "Pledge for a Transformative Science: A Conceptual Framework", *Wuppertal Papers*, No. 191, http://nbn-resolving.de/urn:nbn:de:bsz:wup4-opus-64142, accessed 1 February 2018.

Streeck, W. (2018): "Taking Back Control? The Future of Western Democratic Capitalism", *Efil Journal of Economic Research* 1(3), 30–47.

Strohschneider, P. (2014): "Zur Politik der Transformativen Wissenschaft", in Brodocz, A., Herrmann, D., Schmidt, R., Schulz, D. and Schulze, W. J. (eds.), *Die Verfassung des Politischen*. Wiesbaden: Springer Fachmedien.

Strunz, S. and Gawel, E. (2017): "Transformative Wissenschaft: eine kritische Bestandsaufnahme der Debatte", *GAIA: Ecological Perspectives for Science and Society* 26(4), 321–325.

UN-United Nations (2015): *Transforming Our World: The 2030 Agenda for Sustainable Development*, Resolution adopted by the General Assembly, 25 September, www.un.org/ga/search/view_doc.asp?symbol=A/RES/70/1&Lang=E, accessed 1 February 2018.

Varoufakis, Y. (2016a): "Building a Progressive International", *Project Syndicate*, 31 July, www.project-syndicate.org/commentary/building-a-progressive-international-by-yanis-varoufakis-2016-07?barrier=accessreg, accessed 1 March 2017.

Varoufakis, Y. (2016b): "The Universal Right to Capital Income", *Project Syndicate*, 31 October, www.project-syndicate.org/commentary/basic-income-funded-by-capital-income-by-yanis-varoufakis-2016-10?barrier=accesspaylog, accessed February 1 2018.

Voss, J.-P. (2013): "Technikwissenschaftliches Wettrüsten für nachhaltige Entwicklung? Wo transformative Wissenschaft hinführen könnte", *Ökologisches Wirtschaften* 2013(2), 28–29.

Wahl, P. (2017): "Between Eurotopia and Nationalism: A Third Way for the Future of the EU", *Globalizations* 14(1), 157–163.

WBGU (German Advisory Council on Global Change) (2011): *World in Transition: A Social Contract for Sustainability*. Berlin: WBGU, www.wbgu.de/en/flagship-reports/fr-2011-a-social-contract/, accessed 1 February 2018.

19 Transformative economics – calling for a more conscious relationship between economics and society

Jonathan Barth and Florian Rommel

1 Introduction

One cannot make it clearer than MacKenzie (2008) in his title: economic science has become "an engine not a camera". It means that economics does not simply depict the driving mechanism of the economy, like the textbook distinction of positive and normative statements implies (Mankiw 2014, 17). Instead, the idea of positive statements can prevent economists from reflecting about their perspective and impact on society.[1] This is analyzed by scientists on the issue of the "performativity of economics". The understanding emerging from this debate that economics feeds back onto society in various ways can provide a chance to move towards a self-reflexive economic science. Such a science would contrast the idea of an engine, blindly driving a restructuring of institutions.

Especially the Pluralist Economic movement should resolve the above fallacy. The aim should never be to solely produce "better pictures" but to increase the awareness of dealing with multiple pictures.

As economics contributes to the world, we need to cultivate a reflexive knowledge culture in which we are conscious for the perspective utilized (Davis and Klaes 2003; Mäki 2013). In addition, economics should be put back into the responsibility of democracy and enable a deliberate and participative decision process. We argue that the appeal for economics as a transformative science is a first step towards a more conscious relationship with society and a contribution to the public debate that necessitates concrete institutional changes in academic economics.

2 Awakening from the machine dream

The equilibrium concepts of modern textbook economics have their origin in classical mechanics. They are co-created by the dream to provide accurate descriptions and guidance for interventions in the social science, as physics has provided for engineering (Brodbeck 1998; Mirowski 2002; Mankiw 2006). As a consequence, economics adapted a very *specific scientific attitude towards society* starting from the end of the 18th century (Graupe 2007; Ross 2010). It has come to define itself by virtue of its method (Mäki 2009a; Graupe 2012) and thereby conforms with a mechanistic explanatory model (Hempel and Oppenheim 1948) that is widely contested for the domain of social science (Hedström and Ylikoski 2010). The aspiration is to isolate mechanisms through positive analysis that are the basis for normative judgements of political interventions.[2] A successful isolated mechanism seems to make methodological reflection obsolete: the moment we had a working description of gravity, we had a "true picture" of it. A positive statement about the world implies a safe ground to act upon.

However, this mechanistic abstraction has an endogenous moment, as economics cannot avoid that with its descriptions and pictures of society, economics adds to society. It adds knowledge that was not there before and that *can be used as a program for individual action and institutional pattern.* These manifests themselves in formal economic and societal institutions, as the design of financial markets (MacKenzie 2008), of accounting standards (Perry and Nölke 2006; Rommel 2015a) or the educational system (Krautz 2007). Economics also set informal institutions as "paradigms of thought" (Campbell 2004) for journalists, teachers, decision makers and policy makers (Fischer and Zurstrassen 2014; Pühringer and Hirte 2014). While the former are engraved in laws and regulations, the latter restrict as "cognitive locks" (Blyth 2011) the way decision makers and societal actors perceive their social and economic reality and affect what these actors interpret as an appropriate solution (Block 1990; Block and Heilbroner 1996). The methodological basis of current economics entails an epistemic norm, which leads to serious distortions of these pictures (Cartwright 1999; Alexandrova 2006; Grüne-Yanoff 2011). In mechanically applying this epistemic norm on various societal contexts, *economics becomes an engine powering a specific type of transformation, called economization* (Çalışkan and Callon 2009, 2010).

Thereby current economics often lacks the moment to reflect upon the desirability of the direction of the transformation it is contributing to.[3]

3 Imagining conscious transformative economics

Many heterodox positions that indeed contribute important perspectives on society and the economy should not commit the fallacy of solely offering better pictures. Consequently reflections of pluralism should not just praise pluralism for its superior explanatory potentials (Bigo and Negru 2008; Dobusch and Kapeller 2012) but must also address the normative dimension of pluralism (Dow 2004; Rommel 2015b).

Up to now the calls and claims for pluralism have covered the need for alternative views and the reflection on perspectives in economic research. The appeal for *transformative economics* (Schneidewind, Pfriem et al. 2016; Schneidewind, Singer-Brodowski et al. 2016) adds the reflection of the performative dimension of economics. Thereby it opens the horizon for a different mode of science by raising a central question: what would an economic science look like that is conscious about its performative impact, and how it could increase the societal capacity for self-reflection? At the current stage, we can only suggest some criteria of a more conscious way of conducting economics and point out some institutional changes we regard as important. Both should just provide a basis for discussion and shall not overlay the openness and importance of the question raised here.

Motivated by the ever-increasing challenges faced by today's society regarding ecological depletion and increasing social inequality, and recognizing the particular role of economics in this regard, the call for "transformative economics" presents five criteria for transformative economic science. First, economist must be *transparent* on normative assumptions and methodological approaches to foster awareness of the strength and weaknesses of different research approaches. Second, economic research must *reflect* the performative potential of economic research and the contextuality of knowledge production within time-dependent value frames to avoid propagating unfeasible one-size-fits-all solutions. Third, scientists must be *conscious on their values* that might guide economic research to provide feasible solutions for today's challenges, complementing the pursuit for exhaustive explanations of economic phenomena, as economics is not an end in itself. Fourth, *participation* of non-scientific actors is required to obtain socially important questions and societal values, spread economic knowledge and include other forms of economic knowledge.

The above encloses the request for a *plurality* of theories and methods to foster the creation of new innovative ideas and reflect on the shortcomings and potentials of different approaches. In addition, it takes the performative potential of economics as given. Consequently, economics is not only perceived as a discipline that provides positive explanations, which narrows down the possibilities decision makers can act upon and thereby enacts an undemocratic societal transformation, as captured by the metaphor of the "engine". Instead economics may be thought of as a producer of ideas for societal orientation that is fueling democratic debates and itself reflects societal problems and a democratic will in the way it proceeds. Conducting "transformative economic research" is about elaborating a colourful bouquet of courses for political and societal action, which reflect societal needs such as the distributive and ecological effects of economic policy measures.

We argue that this understanding of an *integral reflexive epistemic plurality* combined with the mission to elaborate solutions for the challenges society is tackling today, is crucial in addition to the pluralistic aim for more perspectives and better pictures. However, its realization will necessitate a dramatic alteration of the institutional setting of today's economics.

4 Promoting change in economics

We have pointed out elsewhere (Barth and Rommel 2017; see also Dobusch and Kapeller 2009) that economics as a discipline itself is locked in an institutional vicious cycle. Scientific self-reproduction in economics stabilizes itself by multiple institutions: the standardization of teaching materials limits both the way young economists think and what they perceive as interesting research questions. Evaluation criteria, such as impact factors, restrict access to the scientific arena. Social norms define what is accepted as "sound economic research" and the availability of resources supports certain research approaches and career tracks only. To break this circle, it seems reasonable to focus on two kinds of strategies: one targeting change from within science and the other aiming at gathering support from outside the discipline.

As resources and power are unequally distributed within economics (Heise et al. 2017), the most promising way of changing economics from within is by *complementing* existing scientific institutions with new ones instead of aiming at their complete *substitution* in the short run. Regarding teaching, it might be an important first step to create *new teaching materials and textbooks*, which provide an easy opportunity for critical researchers to teach students different perspectives on the economy and different goals of economics in general. Additionally, *new forms of knowledge transfer* are needed to reach out to students solely confronted with mainstream thinking.[4] These offer an important opportunity for the acquisition of critical economic knowledge independently of teaching programs at universities. Regarding research, heterodox economists should finally overcome their internal (mostly content-related) battles and concentrate on a constructive collaboration and mutual learning. *New networks* are needed that not only provide a safe space for economic debates besides the mainstream but also strategically concentrate actions targeting change in economics. These networks may serve as fruitful ground for the establishment of *institutional entrepreneurs*, which contribute to a further institutionalization of a "transformative" approach of economics. These pioneers have the potential to motivate *young scholars* to choose different research tracks and commit themselves to pluralist and transformative research.[5] Concentrated actions of institutional entrepreneurs and networks could successfully advocate new economic thinking and communicate the issue beyond the borders of science.

Exactly this public communication will be important, as pioneers of change within the system heavily depend on the support of actors outside the economic discipline (Heise et al. 2017). Consequently, initiatives promoting change in economics must inform non-scientific actors about the current state of economics to create public pressure for an alteration of existing institutions and release resources that support these actions.[6] We need a democratic debate about what is the aim of economic research, which seems to prove itself as the politically most powerful social science. As citizens and societal subjects, we have to ask ourselves whether we want economics to be this powerful and if so, whether there is a particular responsibility arising from it, and what does it need to fulfill it. Do we agree that economics should not solely understand itself as a descriptive science responsible for providing better "pictures" of the economy? Should economists also act as producers and reflectors of societal solutions that are fuelling public debates on possible courses for political action? The narrowness of economics today is not only limiting science in the pursuit for better explanations. In the definition of what is a better picture and what pictures we want to produce and consequently act upon, value judgements are contained. The judgements contained in economic models as a norm for transforming our societies deserve public attention. Science can deal with epistemic pluralism, but value pluralism needs a democratic process and a conscious relation among science and society.

For sure, there are other and complementary strategies at hand. Nonetheless, the proposed measures might be a starting point to discuss what is needed to put the concept of "transformative economics" into practice. By acting on distinct levels, change might come into reach. To bridge the existing gap between science and society, we propose that economics not only understands itself as positive but also as transformative science. Claims for pluralism often fall short of the impact economics has always had on society. Instead of solely offering a better engine that unconscious transforms society, economics must reflect its societal impact and offer multiple competing solutions for dealing with the challenges of the 21st century. Only the availability of several alternatives can facilitate a democratic debate and public discourse about the appropriate path for the future development of our societies.

Notes

1 By making this point we do not want to solely blame economists, as there are plenty who cautiously refrain from naïve applications of mathematical models. We would rather wish to point at the consequences of the way of teaching economics by serious omissions to create a reflexive knowledge culture (Graupe 2012, 2017). As Rodrik (2015) points out in a survey for his blog, Mankiw asked whether economists agree with statements like "Fiscal policy (for example, tax cut and/or government expenditure increase) has a significant stimulative impact on a less than fully employed economy". Over 90% of the economists agreed with this statement, though the assumptions necessary for these statements to be true have not been outlined.

2 Whether these mechanisms are taken to isolate real mechanisms or are just instrumentally working abstractions remains an issue of debate (Friedman 1953; Mäki 2009b).

3 The economist Edward Lazear (2000) is a noteworthy exception. He reflects the impacts of economics and thereby provides a good overview. But instead of reflecting economics preconditions, he provides a good example for how a normative judgement can become a measuring rod for scientific progress.

4 One good example in this regard is the publicly available open-access online platform "Exploring Economics".

5 The master's program "Plurale Ökonomik" in Siegen and the "Cusanus Hochschule" with its alternative and transformative bachelor's and master's programs in economics need to be mentioned here as existing pioneers.

6 The efforts of Kate Raworth (2017) provide a promising example here. With her book and campaign, which outline the shortcomings and political implication of the current state of economics for the "interested citizen", she successfully increased awareness on the topic.

References

Alexandrova, A. (2006): "Connecting Economic Models to the Real World: Game Theory and the FCC Spectrum Auctions", *Philosophy of the Social Sciences* 36(2), 173–192.

Barth, J. and Rommel, F. (2017): "Auf dem Weg zu einer transformativen Wirtschaftswissenschaft. Ein Wissenschaftsverständnis und die Strategien seiner Institutionalisierung", in R. Pfriem et al. (eds.), *Transformative Wirtschaftswissenschaft im Kontext nachhaltiger Entwicklung*. Marburg: Metropolis.

Bigo, V. and Negru, I. (2008): "From Fragmentation to Ontologically Reflexive Pluralism", *The Journal of Philosophical Economics* 1, 127–150.

Block, F. L. (1990): *Postindustrial Possibilities: A Critique of Economic Discourse*. Berkeley: University of California Press.

Block, F. L. and Heilbroner, R. (1996): *The Vampire State: And Other Myths and Fallacies about the US Economy*. New York, USA: The New Press.

Blyth, M. (2011): *Great Transformations: Economic Ideas and Institutional Change in the Twentieth Century*. Cambridge: Cambridge University Press.

Brodbeck, K.-H. (1998): *Die fragwürdigen Grundlagen der Ökonomie: Eine philosophische Kritik der modernen Wirtschaftswissenschaften*. Darmstadt: WBG.

Çalışkan, K. and Callon, M. (2009): "Economization, Part 1: Shifting Attention from the Economy towards Processes of Economization", *Economy and Society* 38(3), 369–398.

Çalışkan, K. and Callon, M. (2010): "Economization, Part 2: A Research Programme for the Study of Markets", *Economy and Society* 39(1), 1–32.

Campbell, J. L. (2004): *Institutional Change and Globalization*. Princeton, NJ: Princeton University Press.

Cartwright, N. (1999): *The Vanity of Rigour in Economics Theoretical Models and Galilean Experiments*. London: LSE, Centre for the Philosophy of the Natural and Social Sciences.

Davis, J. B. and Klaes, M. (2003): "Reflexivity: Curse or Cure?", *Journal of Economic Methodology* 10(3), 329–352.

Dobusch, L. and Kapeller, J. (2009): "'Why Is Economics Not an Evolutionary Science?' New Answers to Veblen's Old Question", *Journal of Economic Issues* 43(4), 867–898.

Dobusch, L. and Kapeller, J. (2012): "Heterodox United vs. Mainstream City? Sketching a Framework for Interested Pluralism in Economics", *Journal of Economic Issues* 46(4), 1035–1058.

Dow, S. C. (2004): "Structured Pluralism", *Journal of Economic Methodology* 11(3), 275–290.

Fischer, A. and Zurstrassen, B. (2014): *Sozioökonomische Bildung*. Bonn: Bundeszentrale für Politische Bildung.

Friedman, M. (1953): *The Methodology of Positive Economics*. Chicago: University of Chicago Press.

Graupe, S. (2007): *The Basho of Economics: An Intercultural Analysis of the Process of Economics*. R. Gathman (trans. and intro.). Berlin: Walter de Gruyter.

Graupe, S. (2012): "The Power of Ideas: The Teaching of Economics and Its Image of Man", *Journal of Social Science Education* 11(2), 60–84.

Graupe, S. (2017): "Beinflussung und Manipulation der ökonomischen Bildung – Hintergründe und Beispiele", in *FGW-Studie, Neues ökonomisches Denken 05*. Düsseldorf: FGW – Forschungsinstitut für gesellschaftliche Weiterentwicklung e. V.

Grüne-Yanoff, T. (2011): "Isolation Is Not Characteristic of Models", *International Studies in the Philosophy of Science* 25(2), 119–137.

Hedström, P. and Ylikoski, P. (2010): "Causal Mechanisms in the Social Sciences", *Annual Review of Sociology* 36, 49–67.

Heise, A., Sander, H. and Thieme, S. (2017): *Das Ende der Heterodoxie?* Wiesbaden: Springer Fachmedien.

Hempel, C. G. and Oppenheim, P. (1948): "Studies in the Logic of Explanation", *Philosophy of Science* 15(2), 135–175.

Krautz, J. (2007): *Ware Bildung: Schule und Universität unter dem Diktat der Ökonomie*. Kreuzlingen and München: Diedrichs.

Lazear, E. P. (2000): "Economic Imperialism", *The Quarterly Journal of Economics* 115, 99–146.

MacKenzie, D. (2008): *An Engine, Not a Camera: How Financial Models Shape Markets*. First MPI Press paperback ed. Cambridge, MA: MIT (Inside technology).Mäki, U. (2009a): "Economics Imperialism: Concept and Constraints", *Philosophy of the Social Sciences* 39(3), 351–380.

Mäki, U. (2009b): "MISSing the World: Models as Isolations and Credible Surrogate Systems", *Erkenntnis* 70(1), 29–43.

Mäki, U. (2013): "Performativity: Saving Austin from MacKenzie", in Karakostas, V. and Dieks, D. (eds.), *EPSA11 Perspectives and Foundational Problems in Philosophy of Science*, 443–453.

Mankiw, G. (2006): "The Macroeconomist as Scientist and Engineer", *The Journal of Economic Perspectives* 20(4), 29–46.

Mankiw, G. (2014): *Economics*. Boston: Cengage Learning EMEA.

Mirowski, P. (2002): *Machine Dreams: Economics becomes a Cyborg Science*. Cambridge: Cambridge University Press.

Perry, J. and Nölke, A. (2006): "The Political Economy of International Accounting Standards", *Review of International Political Economy* 3(4), 559–586.

Pühringer, S. and Hirte, K. (2014): "ÖkonomInnen und Ökonomie in der Krise. Eine diskurs- und netzwerkanalytische Sicht", *Wirtschafts- und Sozialpolitische Zeitschrift des ISW (WISO)* 37(1), 159–178.

Raworth, K. (2017): *Doughnut Economics: Seven Ways to Think Like a 21st Century Economist*. Vermont: Chelsea Green Publishing.

Rodrik, D. (2015): *Economics Rules: The Rights and Wrongs of the Dismal Science*. New York and London: W. W. Norton & Company.

Rommel, F. (2015a): "Ökonomische Theorie und Rechnungswesen. Wie Marktfakten geformt werden", in Ötsch, W., Hirte, K., Pühringer, S. and Bräutigam, L. (eds.), *Markt? Welcher Markt? Der interdisziplinäre Diskurs um Märkte und Marktwirtschaft*. Marburg: Metropolis, 253–280.

Rommel, F. (2015b): *Performing Pluralism: A Discourse in Need of the Performative Turn?* Mark Blaug Student Essay Prize of FEED. Unpublished manuscript.

Ross, D. (2010): "The Economic Agent: Not Human, But Important", in Mäki, U. (ed.), *Elsevier Handbook of Philosophy of Science*. Vol. 13, *Economics*, 627–671.

Schneidewind, U., Pfriem, R., a.o. (2016): "Transformative Wirtschaftswissenschaft im Kontext nachhaltiger Entwicklung", *Ökologisches Wirtschaften* 31(2), 30–34.

Schneidewind, U., Singer-Brodowski, M., a.o. (2016): "Pledge for a Transformative Science: A Conceptual Framework", *Wuppertal Papers*, No. 191.

20 Tackling the roots

(Economic) education for social-ecological transformations and degrowth societies

Christoph Sanders

1 Introduction

Education allows humans to deal with themselves and the world in a reflexive and ethical manner (Bieri 2012). In this regard, education is inherently connected with social and individual change (Bieri 2012; Koller 2010). (Economic) education isn't a neutral endeavor: whatever a society declares to be relevant for (economic) education on the premises of its power structures, moral standards, cultural repertoire, economic necessities and scientific findings will determine individual and social perceptions of the world and respective behaviors.[1] Against this background, fundamental assumptions about education should be as transparent as possible; they should respect pluralism and equip subjects with critical thinking so they can analyze their worldviews and become self-determined in their conduct. Today's mainstream economic education fails to do so while strongly focusing on the growth-oriented neoclassical school of thought. Moreover, it increasingly seeks to equip humans with capabilities that allow them to contribute to economic growth. In addition, this narrow perspective of mainstream economics generally veils its own ontological foundations (Graupe 2013).

In order to adequately confront the ongoing violence of the multiple crises that are connected with economic growth,[2] economic education (and teaching economics) needs to be embedded in an education for social-ecological transformations which departs from a critical review of growth and its cultural foundations. Especially the latter is of primary importance as the teaching of mainstream economics still supports the unconscious internalization of growth dogmas (see sections 2 and 3) that can be labeled as mental infrastructures of growth (Welzer 2011).[3]

By consequence, economic education has to be transformed on the level of contents as well as on the level of didactics. On the level of contents, a more pluralist approach to economics is key. This includes the fundamental questions of why we pursue economic activities and for the benefit of whom. To answer these questions, it's crucial to debate different perceptions of a good life.[4] On the level of contents, economic education needs to deal with the challenge of how to make a good life possible for all. Furthermore, transparency regarding ontological premises is important in order not to turn education into ideological manipulation. From a growth-critical perspective, the prime challenge for economic education on the level of didactics is to support the transformation of modern mental infrastructures of growth. As the latter are deeply embodied, economic education needs to develop more integral ways of learning which go further than cognitive thinking.

This chapter focuses on the cultural, ontological and psychosocial dimensions of (economic) education that are fundamentally connected with the social and political realm. In that perspective it prioritizes the level of didactics without ignoring the intrinsic nexus to content. The emphasis of the entire chapter lies on carving out the contours of an education for social-ecological transformation based on a theory-driven analysis. This analysis is largely based on the degrowth discourse.[5] Although the contours of an education for social-ecological transformation are formulated regarding education in general, throughout the chapter I explicitly stress why this is highly important for the teaching of economics and economic education.

The chapter is structured as follows. First, I will analyze the interconnectedness of modern world relations and of current social, economic and ecological crises. Therefore, I will refer to concepts that are rooted in the depicted degrowth discourse, especially dealing with cultural as well as psychosocial dimensions of economic growth (mental infrastructures). Second, I will outline how mainstream economic education, its organization and structure prepare individuals for growth societies. The stressing of the concept of human capital in the context of the most recent reform of the European education system will be used as a primary example. Moreover, the nexus is examined between a mechanic worldview, the domination of nature as a central characteristic of modern cultures and the neoclassical theory. Third, after this critical analysis I will address how to change education to enable social-ecological transformations. Therefore, I will refer to Hartmut Rosa's concept of resonance (Rosa 2016) and to Marcel Hunecke's suggestion of a set of six psychic resources for degrowth societies (Hunecke 2013). These concepts argue for a self-transformative process that goes further than cognitive learning by including more integral ways of embracing the world in an educational process. However, they don't ignore the relevance of social structures. Finally, I will outline a possible education for social-ecological transformation with explicit implications for economic education.

2 The culture of growth: mental infrastructures as the basis for modern world relations

The last decades have clearly shown that the ongoing global crises require a fundamental change of ways of life in the Global North.[6] It has not been possible to attain a sustainable level of resource consumption via technological solutions (efficiency and consistency) while maintaining economic growth without exploiting humans and nature (especially in the Global South).[7] Yet a cultural change towards sufficiency requires a change of modern mental infrastructures.

At the moment, mental infrastructures are strongly shaped by a growth-oriented pattern which is linked with central aspects of the European and thus globalized "modernity" (Sanders 2016).[8] Against the background of the ethical foundations of the modern world, this is most plausible: modern thinking explicitly stresses the individual freedom to choose between lifestyles and convictions. The freedom of choice is both a central promise and a challenging task for most individuals (Rosa 2016, 37–45). Due to this openness, it seems wise to accredit oneself with as many (non-)material goods as possible to be able to choose, or as Rosa puts it: "To ensure the own rights and positions, to enlarge the own range of action via money, knowledge and relations, to expand the own capabilities and to widen the proper networks proves to be the most appropriate strategy of living" (Rosa 2016, 45; own translation).

If we consider that in competitive accelerating societies passiveness and pausing means to fall behind, this strategy gives incentives for endless enhancement.[9] Although the depicted strategy doesn't in itself guarantee a good life, in the course of modernity the obsession with the enhancement of (non-)material goods shifts away from being just a prerequisite for a good life to the perception that it is the good life itself (Rosa 2016, 46). Consequently, we don't change our imperial ways of life towards more sufficiency, but we reproduce exploitation of nature and human labor, since the cultural growth paradigm is so deeply rooted in our mindsets and so "normal" that we are mostly unable to question or even perceive it.[10] As our mental infrastructures are heavily constructed by education, the latter is a primary arena for cultural change.

In the following, three dominant psycho-social growth imprints are suggested. Understanding them helps to sketch an education for social-ecological transformations.

2.1 The mental infrastructure of acceleration

So far, I have given a cultural explanation for endless enhancement that is characteristic for mental infrastructures of growth in general. It is, as shown above, closely linked with the phenomenon of social acceleration (ethical indetermination in combination with the fear of falling behind in competitive and accelerating societies). The structural necessity to increase the individual pace of life that results from technological acceleration and the acceleration of social change (see note 9) is also closely related to the growth paradigm, which calls for the increase of the cash value of all produced goods and provided services within a fixed time period (one year).

Yet Rosa identifies another cultural explanation for individual acceleration. Modern people tend to have "a conception of life in which the good life is the fulfilled life, a life that is rich in experiences and developed capacities" (Rosa 2009, 90). The reason for this lies within the cultural problem that the time of the world dramatically diverges from our individual lifetime. In the premodern era, the solution for this problem was provided by religions offering the concept of the endless afterlife. However, with secularization the hope for eternity lost its strength and was replaced by the ideal of the fulfilled life – the idea of living as many lives as possible within one lifetime (Rosa 2009, 91). We strive to realize as many experiences as possible: as much consumption, as many social contacts, journeys and so forth as possible. This promise of acceleration is complemented by the promise of prosperity, since money allows fulfilling the wish for acceleration and is also able to compensate for those uncertainties that a high-speed society involves (Rosa 2012, 285) – as society and technologies change with increasing pace, uncertainties about the future increase.

2.2 *The mental infrastructure of the "enterprising self"*

The "enterprising self" (Bröckling 2007) is a widespread model for the governing of ourselves within competitive capitalist societies, allowing us to understand how modern individuals are governed from within.[11] The enterprising self basically consists of two major elements. The first is *Homo oeconomicus* as developed in the human capital theory of Gary S. Becker and Theodore Schultz of the Chicago School. *Homo oeconomicus* is designed as a rational agent who tries to optimize his/her decisions regarding costs and benefits. In that sense, Becker and Schultz universalize egoistic rational thinking and acting in the name of the maximization of individual utility beyond the economic sphere into all spheres of human behavior. This expansion of economics is indeed a characteristic development of the last century (Graupe 2013, 88f.). By consequence and according to Schultz, the "human agent becomes ever more a capitalist by virtue of his personal human capital" (Schultz 1982, 76). The second element of the enterprising self is the *entrepreneur*. In contrast to *Homo oeconomicus*, the *entrepreneur* overcomes the threshold of uncertainty: he/she cannot translate uncertainty into calculable risks as the prototype of the manager does, since he/she acts against the background of insecure information and lacking pathways, which he/she compensates by restless activities and constant change (Bröckling 2007, 116–123).

Both (contradictory) elements are put into effect via processes of subjectivization. This means that individuals first need to change their self-interpretations and behaviors (governing of themselves) according to the enterprising self. Only then may it materialize in their actions. As to changing self-interpretations, in order to translate the premises of the capitalist economy into our mentalities, structural incentives and constraints are important. Yet Bröckling stresses the softer power of so-called interpellation (Bröckling 2007, 27–31): We are asked to understand ourselves as enterprising selves and to act accordingly – but only if this call resonates in us, it becomes powerful and the process of subjectivation takes place. Often, we unconsciously react to calls that are vastly present in our daily lives – for example in discourses, advertisements, party platforms, guidebooks, economic textbooks or simply in the actions of our peers. Finally, the interpellations of the enterprising self produce the feelings of lack and guilt (ibid., 290) – in competition we have never done enough; our position is always threatened. These feelings are powerful drivers for action.

Just as the wish for acceleration can be described as being often unquestioned, since it is linked to our cultural ideal of the good life, the economic and instrumental view on ourselves and fellow human beings becomes an increasingly dominant and unconscious mentality. It perfectly fits the logic of social acceleration and is a structural necessity for the realization of increasing productivity and thus of economic growth. Consequently, the enterprising self has spread across various social spheres since the welfare state has been transformed into a neoliberal enabling state in which human capital is seen as a primary vehicle to generate economic growth.[12]

2.3 The domination of nature as a mental infrastructure of growth

The domination of nature is a central characteristic of modern societies and a way of relating to the world that bases on a specific perception. Modern people tend to see themselves apart from nature: mind versus body; culture versus nature. This separation and dualism was strongly promoted by modern scientists since the 17th century (see e.g. Descola 2013). They assumed that the behavior and characteristics of nature could be computed: if nature has no mind, and thus no possibilities for individual decisions, there can't be intentional behavior. By consequence, it needs to behave according to constant and rational laws; it must be predictable, calculable and controllable.

> This elimination of any kind of nonmeasurable aspects like perceptions (colors, smells, sounds) and emotions, as well as teleological implications and activities, implied a complete exclusion of experience, which had to be cast out of nature in order to render it easily describable in quantitative terms.
>
> (Muraca 2007, 166)

For the French anthropologist Philippe Descola, modern scientists thus "depict the world according to the image of a machine whose wheel-work can be disassembled by the savants" (Descola 2013, 105; own translation).

Yet the necessary outcome of this process was not only a fixed and objectified nature that could only speak through scientific channels but also "a free, percipient subject, defined at first only through the remains of that process of exclusion" (Muraca 2007, 167). As a result of the perception of separation, modern societies seek to dominate, exploit and instrumentalize nature (the inner human and outer one) for their own purposes. This attempt is closely linked to the modern understanding of freedom, progress and development that promises humans emancipation from nature and to be less vulnerable in the light of natural forces (Görg 2006, 192). The last 300 years have shown that the radical objectification and instrumentalization of the animated and non-animated nature triggered economic growth and allowed the increase of human life expectancy (primarily in the Global North). Indeed, economic growth is unthinkable without the perception of nature as a resource pool at humanity's disposition. Yet this understanding of progress is currently challenged by the existential threat of climate change. It becomes clear that increasing domination of nature doesn't emancipate humans indefinitely from nature (Görg 2006). The current situation rather suggests the opposite.

2.4 The crisis of modern world relations

Due to their strong connection to economic growth and enhancement, the depicted mental infrastructures are currently connected with global crises (see above, especially note 2). Rosa explicitly claims that the global crises are a result of the crises of the fundamental ways of how modern subjects relate individually and collectively to other humans, beings and things (Rosa 2016, 707; see also Plumwood 2001).

The refined and presented concept of mental infrastructures of growth helps us to understand this claim. Moreover, it helps us to understand why modern ways of life also reach psychic and political limits (Rosa 2012; Ehrenberg 2009): People are in danger of feeling unworthy as their efforts never seem to be enough. A significant number of people experience exhaustion and burnout. Yet stressed-out humans tend to have no capacities for others and tend to be more afraid. This is not only a problem for solidarity in society but also for democratic politics, which require time. As people lack time and as the political system is pressured by the faster modes of the economy and technology, politics increasingly react to already existing phenomena instead of designing new social life (Rosa 2012, 391–427). As a reaction, politicians tend to save time by bypassing citizens – politics get more authoritarian and vulnerable to lobbying (ibid.). This triggers peoples' feelings of disconnection, anxiety and anger (Rosa 2016). The world may appear to be increasingly mute or even hostile.

This is also the case, since acceleration increases the number of superficial experiences. We have less time for every (sense) contact – be it with humans or nature. The world may not only appear mute due to lacking possibilities for intense experience, but also due to the feeling of being in constant competition with others (enterprising self). Finally, it may appear mute due to the separation between nature and humans.[13]

But how are the mental infrastructures of growth reproduced in standard (economic) education and how does education therefore contribute to the depicted crises? The next section provides some answers.

3 The internalization of the mental infrastructures of growth in mainstream (economic) education

This section analyzes how mainstream (economic) education gives strong incentives to modern people to internalize the depicted mental infrastructures of growth. It thereby provides valuable insights for possible alternatives. As to the spreading of the enterprising self, I primarily would like to refer to the work of Silja Graupe (2012, 2013). She analyses how the role-model of *Homo oeconomicus* colonized our thinking via economic textbooks and social discourses.

Another way of how economic thinking and incentives for acceleration were spread beyond the economic sphere was by the latest reform of the European mainstream education system in the last 20 years. After briefly interpreting the reform process, I deal with the relation between the domination of nature and the ontological foundation of neoclassical thinking.

3.1 Education as human capital

The reform of the European education system since the end of the 1990s was heavily driven by the wish to maintain the competitiveness of the European economy in the light of globalization. In the 1990s, the underlying fear of important economic actors and interest groups such as the Organisation for Economic Co-operation and

Development (OECD 1996) or the European Roundtable of Industrialists (ERT 1995; Kauppinen 2014) was that Europe could become less innovative and less competitive and would therefore fail to uphold economic growth. Against this background, the crucial question was, what kind of knowledge and competences does the economy need to stay competitive and innovative? This was quickly picked up by politicians. The EU strategy of Lisbon of 2000 reads: "The Union has today set itself a new strategic goal for the next decade: to become the most competitive and dynamic knowledge-based economy in the world capable of sustainable economic growth" (European Council 2000). Nearly at the same time, the Bologna Process was kicked off by the Bologna Declaration to reform the higher education system, also with a strong focus on knowledge and competitiveness (The Bologna Declaration 1999). Another key word in the reform context was employability, since the economization of education implies that individuals improve their knowledge, skills, contacts, networks – in short, their human capital – in order to be fit to participate in the ever-changing job market. The turn towards education as human capital caused a fundamental shift in the functioning of educational institutions. It concerned not only the reform of organizational structures but also the way of learning itself. The shift went along with the installation of respective tools, instruments and incentives to guarantee specific outputs (knowledge and capabilities) to be used in the economy (Hepp 2011, 41–48, 188). This also affected the design of education for sustainable development, which neither challenges economic growth nor the dominant mental infrastructures (Getzin and Singer-Brodowski 2016).

Regarding mental infrastructures, the reform tends to push students, teachers and scientists to internalize the idea of education as human capital (see also Masschelein and Simons 2005). It gives incentives to turn people into enterprising selves, able to survive in the hostile environment of competitive market societies. Moreover, the reform included, at least in Germany, a significant reduction of study times in university and school in order to better connect the educational system with the needs of the economy. Thereby, the reform gave incentives for acceleration (for details, see Sanders and Jacobs 2014). We can sum up the reform process as follows: "Education gets reframed merely as a means to an end. It is subordinated to economic growth" (Graupe 2016, 90f.; own translation).

3.2 The reproduction of the human-nature dualism in (economic) education

The teaching of mainstream economics stresses the separation between nature and humans, since neoclassical theory has a strong connection to the mechanic worldview depicted above. "'I rationalize; therefore I am' might well be the credo of everyman as an economist" (Samuelson 1966, 1731). This quote of bestselling economic textbook author Paul Samuelson puts it in a nutshell. "I rationalize; therefore I am" is the central epistemological claim of René Descartes. It marks the radical separation of a thinking mind (*res cogitans*) from the non-thinking material (*res extensa*) and strongly kicked off the mechanic worldview of the 17th century, which was then adopted by early neoclassical thinkers. They were scientifically and biographically influenced by important physicists and successfully stripped off real-world components (social, experiential and political aspects) from economic thinking at the end of the 19th century. Thereby they established a purely abstract thinking about economic activities on the basis of mathematic formulas and equations (Graupe 2016, 78).[14] This was explicitly framed as a positive development.[15] The depicted line of thought continued to influence thinkers like Paul Samuelson, whose standard textbooks are today read by millions of people (for details on the continuation of thinking, see his Nobel Prize–winning work, *Foundations of Economic Analysis* [Samuelson 1983]). Samuelson neither veiled his enthusiasm for physics and thermodynamics nor masked his ambitions to influence political dynamics by teaching economics: "One of the most joyful moments of my life was when I was led by listening to E. B. Wilson's exposition of Gibbsian thermodynamics" (ibid., xix); "I don't care who writes a nation's laws – or crafts its advanced treatises – if I can write its economics textbooks" (Samuelson quoted in Weinstein 2009).[16]

Although more research on the connection between neoclassical theory and the separation of humans and nature is needed, the hitherto analysis clearly suggests that the current teaching of mainstream economics is constantly reproducing the mental prerequisites for the domination and exploitation of nature. By adopting the mechanic worldview of early physics and transferring it into mathematical formulas, which are still at the basis of neoclassical economics, millions of students and economists are manipulated to reproduce the separation of nature and humans. For Rosa, this also applies for the teaching of mathematics and natural sciences, in which the objectification of non-human creatures and things is systematically justified and practiced until it seems to be a natural stance towards the world (Rosa 2016, 382). Finally, education for sustainable development also reproduces this worldview (Getzin and Singer-Brodowski 2016).

4 Education for social-ecological transformations and degrowth societies

Up to this point, the chapter has shown the problematic aspects of mainstream (economic) education. This section provides a theoretical concept for alternatives and from there outlines an ideal type of education for social-ecological transformations. A central endeavor for future (economic) education is to contribute to the ending of global social-ecological crises and to a good life for all. In order to do so, it needs to provide the basis for the change of modern world relations and for the searching as well as practicing of other mental infrastructures. Therefore, frames of references are urgently needed that are transparent and compatible with the ethical foundations of modernity. In the following I will introduce Rosa's concept of "resonance" (2016) as a normative and analytical frame of reference for a social-ecological transformation that allows people to live well and self-determined within the moral and ecological boundaries. In that regard it is also meant as a frame of reference for education, teaching economics and the transformation of modern mental infrastructures.

4.1 Frame of reference I (individual and collective level): resonant world relations

Resonance is a relationship that focuses on the connection between subjects and the world (humans, creatures and things) that isn't determined in its content. It is not identical with harmony or unison.

> Resonance may be defined as a specific cognitive, emotional and corporal world relation in which subjects are moved by certain parts of the world. Yet, in this relationship they are also able to act, to respond and to exert influence on other world entities. Subjects experience themselves thereby as self-efficient. This is the nature of the responding relationship or of the "vibrant" connection between subject and the world.
>
> (Rosa 2016, 279; own translation)

Resonance is explicitly understood as a phenomenon that exists before the emergence of subjects and objects, since these categories only evolve in a dynamic relationship between entities of the world (Rosa 2016, 61–70). As such, phenomenologically, Rosa understands resonance as a basic experience, a basic need and a basic capability (ibid., 293). In that regard the concept is descriptive. However, resonance is also designed as a normative conceptual frame of reference for the good life that tries to diminish the separation of mind and body (or nature) that has been established by strict rationalism (ibid.).[17] Rosa sees it as an opposite of "alienation" (a basic analytical category of the Critical Theory of the Frankfurt School). Against this background, a critical analysis of the socio-economic situation that influences the realization of resonance is of great importance. A large part of it – although from a slightly different angle than Rosa's approach – has been described above.

Resonance requires free entities that are able to speak with their proper voice. Yet humans and other beings need to stay accessible for each other in order be able to allow a relation of interconnectedness. This implies three prerequisites: (1) On the individual level, subjects need to be enabled to allow the mode of resonance to arise. Mental infrastructures of growth are the main hindrances for such a mode: on the one hand, they impede subjects themselves from being capable of allowing resonance; on the other hand, mental infrastructures give incentives to subjects to mute their counterparts (humans, nature) by exploitation and instrumentalization. (2) Resonance can only take place if an independent counterpart – be it humans, creatures or things – responds in his/her/its own voice, in his/her/its own manner. (3) As already made clear, the relationship of resonance is not free of collective aspects. If the social sphere is dominated by structures that involve exploitation, stress and anxiety, individual efforts are limited. What is needed is thus an enabling space for resonant world relations (ibid., 294).[18]

The three prerequisites for resonance show that we won't be able to change our world relations without changing our socio-economic structures; yet we won't change our socio-economic structures without changing our world relations. This clearly shows why the concept of resonance comports well with a degrowth perspective. Both concepts, degrowth and resonance, strive for a good life for all. Both concepts stress that the members of our societies have to get active on the collective and the individual level in order to live a better life, and in order to stop the destruction of human and non-human lives.[19] (Economic) education is an excellent approach to do so, since it significantly shapes our world relations (Rosa 2016, 402). In the following, I will refine the individual approach of transformation by turning to the question of what it means to be individually capable of resonant relationships to occur.

4.2 Frame of reference II (individual level): psychic resources for sustainable ways of life

Deeply internalized habits and culturally embedded routines are difficult to transform – especially because they seem to perfectly fit the structural requirements of our competitive and capitalist societies. Yet we already dispose of many insights whose realization would greatly help in experiencing more resonant world relations. In this article, I limit myself to presenting Marcel Hunecke's approach (2013) of psychic resources for sustainable ways of life.

Hunecke names six psychic resources that may contribute to the transformation towards a degrowth society. If all resources are strengthened, according to Hunecke, they are helpful to cope with the exigencies of growth societies, to live a more sustainable life and to increase individual well-being. They also provide opportunities for integral (embodied) and positive experiences. For Hunecke, the resources have the potential to mutually strengthen but also stimulate each other (ibid., 120f.). The six resources are not postulated from a normative perspective but derived from empirical research. Hunecke's work is largely based on results of positive psychology but also environmental psychology, resource-based coaching and social-ecological research. The six resources are:

1. The *capability to enjoy* facilitates experiencing more intense moments of life instead of just increasing the quantity of consumed world options. Here wealth of time and regional and seasonal consumption are important concepts to connect this psychic resource with a possible degrowth lifestyle, resonance and altered concepts of the good life.
2. *Self-acceptance* prevents people from compensating perceived dissatisfaction by material consumption to increase their social status. As shown above, the feeling of unworthiness can be perceived as a consequence of the extension of competition and the enterprising self.
3. *Self-efficacy* strengthens the conviction to be able to contribute to the change of personal and societal environment. Self-efficacy allows to open oneself to the world and to make positive experiences. In that regard it is also an important prerequisite for resonance.
4. *Mindfulness* is a mental strategy to adopt a conscious non-judging attitude with the aim to be aware of the needs of oneself and of other beings. It is conducive to experiencing joy and helps to realize self-acceptance.

Mindfulness facilitates the reduction of egoism: via the focus on immediate experiences, mindfulness expands the awareness for questions of sense beyond our subjective well-being to the well-being of other persons. Mindfulness thus renders the characteristics of other humans and creatures visible to us and allows a change in our relationships to them. Mindfulness is a bridge between us and the world and allows resonance to occur.

5 By becoming aware of one's own needs and those of others, mindfulness also opens the way to more general questions about the sense of life. By *searching comprehensive explanations for our being*, we may see a meaning in life beyond our individuality. The searching and construction of sense therefore has the potential to bring people in contact with the world and to positively impact on their well-being.

6 Finally, *solidarity* allows orientating ourselves according to the values of social justice and the conviction that social justice may be realized in common acting. It cuts through the dominant paradigm of competition and empowers and connects people.

Taking into account the strengthening of the depicted resources within educational processes covers many suggestions of other research and approaches. This also applies for transformative learning (Getzin and Singer-Brodowski 2016) and brain research. The latter's findings show that human brains constantly change and learn on the basis of past experiences. In that regard every brain structure is unique and the establishment of new routines and habits is difficult. Departing from these insights, the suggestion for learning and education is that learning is an individual process that is enhanced if individuals learn integrally and if they make positive experiences that are related to older ones (Kafka and Krause 2011).

4.3 Sketches of (economic) education for socio-ecological transformation

What do education and teaching economics look like which enable the world relation of resonance in order to realize social-ecological transformations? In the following, I will lay out contours of an ideal type:

1 *Integral learning*: Economic education provides spaces in which the growth-related crises of our ways of life can be experienced in an integral way, in which individual change, altered attitudes and routines can be practiced. Thereby, psychic resources are strengthened and useful skills taught (e.g. for care work or repairing). For economic education, this would mean explicitly taking into account the social and individual implications of doing economics. Economic education should thereby focus on the day-to-day problems of learners that are connected with economics.

2 *Wealth of time*: Individuals pass through educational spaces without the lack of time and without being stressed by the density of curricula (Matzen 2005).

Failures (the loss of time) are accepted and it is possible to perceive them as enriching phenomena.

3 *Democracy, interest and joy*: Teachers and learners are, as far as possible, on par with each other.

Both groups are motived by an intrinsic interest for specific aspects of the socio-economic world – also because their individual lives are concerned (Masschelein and Simons 2010, 41). Intrinsic interests or even joy as well as the absence of fear are crucial to allow resonance in the context of education to arise. Regarding the school context, Rosa thus assumes that the curriculum is of minor importance as world relations are shaped within the interactions of the classroom and the school yard (Rosa 2016, 403). Young people make the experience of recognition and joy instead of repulsion. They react with intrinsic interest towards school and its contents instead of indifference and aversion. These are key experiences for world relations that are characterized by resonance instead of alienation (for details, see Rosa 2016, 402–419). Interest only arises if students embrace education. Therefore, enthusiastic teachers are important who guide a learning process which is as autonomous as possible. Students are able to democratically participate (together with teachers and staff) in the shaping of the public educational space, not only but also in order to identify with it. Finally, they are able to connect education with their lives as education is useful for their orientation in the world.

4 *Pluralism and multidisciplinarity*: Personal affectedness is one reason why teaching economics is not an isolated discipline but is embedded in greater socio-ecological dynamics and research. Another reason is that teaching economics heavily impacts on other parts of the social life. By consequence, economic education is connected with them by feedback loops and constant exchange processes. Economic education focuses on understanding the fundamental mechanisms of the economy and of capitalism as well as its social and psychological implications. Mechanisms of exploitation in the globalized world are analyzed and debated. Economic education thus respects a wide array of theories and approaches to the economy. These aspects point to a better connection with other societal actors and real-life experiences (see point 1).
5 *Critique and emancipation*: Against this background, teaching economics serves as understanding of education that stresses critical, emancipatory and reflexive thinking as part of its social responsibility. As such, education is positioned in a tension between resistance and adaption (Frost 2008). Adaption, in the sense of an orientation towards economic outputs, is limited to a minimum to contain the reproduction of the enterprising self.
6 *Relations to nature*: Regarding relations to nature, economic education integrates various philosophical positions as well as pedagogical approaches and techniques that allow integral and positive experiences as well as changes in the human-nature relationship to reduce the gap between humans and other creatures and things. This serves to contain the exploitation of

inner and outer nature as well as strengthen resonant world relations. Outdoor education, wilderness awareness, environmental education or theater pedagogy serve as pilot techniques to do so and to build psychic resources for sustainable ways of life. These techniques are tested regarding their potential to establish more peaceful relationships towards nature (see notes 19 and 21).

4.4 *Where to start?*

In the medium term, established actors will not significantly push for such a form of (economic) education. This is why actors should be addressed and supported that already provide educational spaces in the outlined sense or who can potentially do so. Today this is especially true in out-of-school and non-formalized education. Providers of political education, global learning, education for sustainable development or the just mentioned approaches to reduce domination of nature are promising allies for (economic) education for social-ecological transformations. This also applies to higher education where niches also exist: extracurricular programs, student initiatives and student councils are just some examples. The establishment of new universities, alternative textbooks, new study programs and the flexible interpretation of existing possibilities are others. It is crucial to experiment on this niche level to use existing alternatives as arguments in the parallel struggle to change the formalized institutional contexts.[20] In this regard, lessons can be learned from research on transformations that stress the levels of culture and niches in order to change the mainstream (see e.g. Narberhaus 2013; Geels 2002).

5 Conclusion

This chapter summarized the current debate on education for social-ecological education with a focus on teaching economics. It made clear how the current mainstream (economic) education reproduces mental dispositions, habits and ways of life that are closely connected to ecological, humanitarian, psychic and political crises. In a second step, it used the theoretical concepts of resonance and psychic resources for degrowth ways of life as a descriptive and normative base to derive an ideal type of (economic) education for social-ecological transformation. Thereby, a focus lay on the interconnectedness of individual and collective change. In the future, it is of great relevance to bring forward more efforts to respect this nexus within (economic) education. Guiding questions could be: How should (economic) education be designed in respective contexts in order to meet its relevance for social change without curtailing the free educational process of students? Which methods are most apt to connect cognitive learning with integral and embodied experiences? What kind of formats do we need at university and (secondary) school to integrate economic and educational content and real-life experiences? What kind of skills do teachers and facilitators need in this regard?

Answering these questions is crucial for potential success in the transformation of mainstream educational institutions against the resistance of established interest groups. Although realistic alternatives to the current (economic) education will be shaped in societal niches, it is likewise necessary to continue addressing the institutional level.

Finally, answering these questions is also vital for the formulation of a more comprehensive and differentiated version of the concept of (economic) education for social-ecological transformations.

Notes

1 In this chapter, education refers not to parental education but to the process of cultural, personal and professional maturation that is mastered by the individual with or without assistance.

2 For the nexus between economic growth, climate change and the destruction of the planet's biodiversity, see for instance Jackson (2009). Importantly, economic growth can't be decoupled (fast enough to cope with climate change) from the exploitation of nature. For an inspiring ethical approach to the humanitarian crises of ongoing global poverty, see Pogge (2008). Economic growth is extremely inefficient in reducing global poverty (NEF 2006). At the same time, and as happiness research reveals, "economic growth [. . .] has only an indirect and limited impact on well-being in the long-run" (Barrington-Leigh 2017). Brand and Wissen identify multiple crises of climate change, financial markets, exhaustion of natural resources, liberal democracy and social reproduction (Brand and Wissen 2017, 21–27).

3 Harald Welzer is a German sociologist. According to him, mental infrastructures are a person's psychological, social and cultural settings or imaginaries. They (unconsciously) affect our concepts of a good life, of social and individual development, our desires and thus also our daily routines. We can go as far as stating that they fundamentally determine our most basic relations to the world (Sanders 2016). Welzer assumes, in a similar way as Latouche or Castoriadis (2009) do, that these basic perceptions and relations to the world are strongly shaped by the paradigm of growth.

4 The ratification of the Sustainable Development Goals (SDGs) by the UN member states stress the interpretation that societies should strive for a good life for all humans within the existential boundaries of nature. The main page of the SDGs reads: "On September 25th 2015, countries adopted a set of goals to end poverty, protect the planet and ensure prosperity for all as part of the new sustainable development agenda" (www.un.org/sustainabledevelopment/sustainable-development-goals/).

5 Degrowth challenges the dominant ways of doing and thinking economics that are strongly linked with economic growth, destroying nature and the reproduction of social exclusions. With respect to global justice and considering post-development perspectives, it focuses on the early industrialized countries of the Global North. In these countries a cultural transformation towards more sufficiency needs to complement the strategy of efficiency (and consistency). Resource intensive sectors of the economy need to shrink, while other sectors that are basing on values such as cooperation, democracy, solidarity and care may grow. (Technological) innovations take place, but their aim is no longer the increase in the gross domestic product but a contribution to the good life for all (see www.degrowth.de/en/what-is-degrowth/). Degrowth inspires a wide range of actors from decision makers and civil society actors to scientists.

6 Ulrich Brand and Markus Wissen describe the ways of life of the Global North as being imperial, since they are based on the (often unconscious) access to cheap labor, resources and products of the Global South as well as on the protection of this access (Brand and Wissen 2017). In distinction to the terms *lifestyle* and *conduct of life*, the

concept stresses the connection between the daily lives of individuals, power structures and exploitations (ibid. 2017, 46–47).

7 For the question of decoupling economic growth from the exploitation of nature and greenhouse gas emissions, see e.g. Jackson (2009).

8 In this chapter, the term *modernity* is used in accordance with Rosa. According to him, those influential and classic interpretations that analyze modernization as a process of individualization (Simmel), rationalization (Weber), differentiation (Durkheim) and increasing domination of nature (Marx) all focus on one aspect: the experience of tremendous acceleration, mobilization and dynamization of social life (Rosa 2012, 101).

9 Rosa's theory of social acceleration links technological with social acceleration and the increase of the speed of life. The rates of technological innovations are pushed by competition. The faster the technology changes, the greater the pace of changes within social institutions (work, life, cultural techniques). Rosa describes the latter with the phenomenon of the shrinking present: the future as a time of uncertainty is getting closer and closer. The acceleration of social change demands individuals to stay flexible for these approaching future changes and to adapt to the ever-transforming social and technological environment. This increases the pace of life. Moreover, individuals increasingly feel as if they are standing on slippery slopes or walking on downward escalators (Rosa 2012). In this context, fear is very important, since "people feel pressed to keep up with the speed of change they experience in their social and technological world in order to avoid the loss of potentially valuable options and connections" (Rosa 2009, 88).

10 Power structures and the particular design and logic of organizations and institutions are other important obstacles for more peaceful ways of life.

11 Bröckling largely bases his work on Foucault's *Governmentality*.

12 See for example the OECD: "The term 'knowledge-based economy' results from a fuller recognition of the role of knowledge and technology in economic growth. Knowledge, as embodied in human beings (as 'human capital') and in technology, has always been central to economic development. But only over the last few years has its relative importance been recognized, just as that importance is growing" (OECD 1996).

13 The transformation of the welfare state into an enabling state thus also concerns the educational system. As German Chancellor Angela Merkel put it in 2008: "A republic of education is the best welfare state" (CDU/CSU Fraktion 2008; own translation).

14 "Pure mechanics surely ought to precede applied mechanics. Similarly, given the pure theory of economics, it must precede applied economics, and this pure theory of economics is a science which resembles the physico-mathematical sciences in every respect. [. . .] If the pure theory of economics [. . .] is a physico-mathematical science like mechanics or hydrodynamics, then the economists should not be afraid to use the methods and language of mathematics. The mathematical method is not an experimental method; it is a rational method" (Walras 2003, 71).

15 For example, Irving Fisher (1867–1947), a prominent representative of neoclassical theory whose doctoral thesis supervisor was an influential physicist (Josiah Willard Gibbs), claimed: "There is higher economics just as there is a higher physics, to both of which a mathematical treatment is appropriate. [. . .] The introduction of mathematical method marks a stage of growth – perhaps it is not too extravagant to say, the entrance of political economy on scientific era[. . .] . Up to this time political economy had been the favorite field for those persons whose tastes were semi-scientific and semi-literacy" (Fisher 1965, 109).

16 For understanding the link between the mechanic worldview and neoclassical theory, I would like to thank Lukas Bäuerle (Cusanus University). This passage is written on the basis of his non-published papers.

17 Generally, the concept is not free of substantial critique. It is formulated against the romantic turn of Rosa's Critical Theory (reconcile mind and material). Moreover, he is criticized for suggestive arguing, especially when it comes to the question whether

resonance can really be seen as a basic capability that is pre-cognitive but not pre-social (Rosa 2016, 234, 244f.; Neuhann and Kaczynski 2016; Brumlik 2016).

18 It is important to note that instrumentalization is not per se problematic. According to Rosa, economic, technocratic and scientific instrumentalization also guarantee quality of life and thereby provide the possibilities for resonance. However, it turns into an impediment for resonance when it becomes dominant.

19 Although the establishment of more peaceful relationships to nature are a key challenge for a social-ecological transformations, their development is a delicate enterprise. How can we find ways to reduce the domination and exploitation of nature without endangering the achievements of reason and supply the tipping into post-factual societies? Against this background, the critique against Rosa's concept of resonance needs to be taken very seriously (see note 19).

20 For a general account on degrowth politics for more resonant world relations on the basis of changed mental infrastructures, see Sanders (2017).

References

Barrington-Leigh, C. (2017): "Sustainability and Well-Being: A Happy Synergy", http://greattransition.org/publication/sustainability-and-well-being, accessed 5 April 2017.

Bieri, P. (2012): "Wie wäre es gebildet zu sein?", in Hastedt, H. (ed.), *Was Ist Bildung?* Stuttgart: Reclam, 228–243.

"The Bologna Declaration of 19 June 1999: Joint Declaration of European Ministers of Education", www.ond.vlaanderen.be/hogeronderwijs/bologna/documents/MDC/BOLOGNA_DECLARATION1.pdf, accessed 24 November 2016.

Brand, U. and Wissen, M. (2017): *Imperiale Lebensweisen – Zur Ausbeutung von Mensch und Natur im globalen Kapitalismus*. München: Oekom.

Bröckling, U. (2007): *Das unternehmerische Selbst – Soziologie einer Subjektivierungsform*. Frankfurt am Main: Suhrkamp.

Brumlik, M. (2016): "Resonanz oder: Das Ende der Kritischen Theorie", Blätter für deutsche und internationale Politik 5, 120–123.

Castoriadis, C. (2009): *Gesellschaft als imaginäre Institution. Entwurf einer politischen Philosophie*. Frankfurt am Main: Suhrkamp CDU/CSU Fraktion (2008): "Die Bildungsrepublik ist der beste Sozialstaat: Generaldebatte zum Bundeshaushalt 2009", www.cducsu.de/themen/bildung-und-ausbildung/bildungsrepublik-ist-der-beste-sozialstaat, accessed 24 November 2016.

Descola, P. (2013): *Jenseits von Kultur and Natur*. Frankfurt am Main: Suhrkamp.

Ehrenberg, A. (2009): *The Weariness of the Self: Diagnosing the History of Depression in the Contemporary Age*. Montréal: McGill-Queen's University Press.

European Council (2000): "Lisbon European Council 23 and 24 March 2000: Presidency Conclusions", www.europarl.europa.eu/summits/lis1_en.htm, accessed 24 November 2016.

European Roundtable of Industrialists (1995): "Education for Europeans: Towards the Learning Society", www.ert.eu/sites/ert/files/generated/files/document/1995_education_for_europeans_-_towards_the_learning_society.pdf, accessed 24 November 2016.

Fisher, I. (1965): *Mathematical Investigations in the Theory of Value and Prices*. New York: Kelley.

Frost, U. (2008): "Bildung als pädagogischer Grundbegriff", in Mertens, G., Frost, U. and Böhm, W. (eds.), *Handbuch der Erziehungswissenschaft. Grundlagen Allgemeine Erziehungswissenschaft*. Paderborn: Schöningh, 297–311.

Geels, F. (2002): "Technological Transitions as Evolutionary Reconfiguration Processes: A Multi-Level Perspective and a Case-Study", *Research Policy* 31(8–9), 1257–1274.

Getzin, S. and Singer-Brodowski, M. (2016): "Transformatives Lernen in einer Degrowth Gesellschaft", *Socience* 1, 33–46.

Görg, C. (2006): "Natur und Gesellschaft", in Scherr, A. (ed.), *Soziologische Basics*. Wiesbaden: Springer VS, 124–129.

Graupe, S. (2012): "Humankapital – Wie der ökonomische Imperialismus das Denken über Bildung bestimmt", in Kraus, K. (ed.), *Wozu Bildungsökonomie?* Berlin: Deutscher Lehrerverband, 35–50.

Graupe, S. (2013): "Die Macht ökonomischer Bildung", in Frost, U. and Rieger-Ladich, M. (eds.), *Demokratie setzt aus. Gegen die sanfte Liquidation einer politischen Lebensform. Vierteljahresschrift zur wissenschaftlichen Pädagogik*. Paderborn: Schöningh , 85–112.

Graupe, S. (2016): "Wirtschaftswachstum und Bildungswiderstand", in Sánchez de Murillo, J. (ed.), *Facetten des Wachstums*, in *Aufgang – Jahrbuch für Denken, Dichten, Kunst*. Vol. 13. Stuttgart: Kohlhammer,70–95.

Hepp, G. F. (2011): *Bildungspolitik in Deutschland – Eine Einführung*. Wiesbaden: Springer VS.

Hunecke, M. (2013): *Psychologie der Nachhaltigkeit – Psychische Ressourcen für Postwachstumsgesellschaften*. München: Oekom.

Jackson, T. (2009): *Prosperity without Growth*. London: Routledge.

Kafka, B. and Krause, J. (2011): *Transformatives Lernen in der Internationalen Zusammenarbeit*. Berlin: GIZ.

Kauppinen, I. (2014): "The European Roundtable of Industrialists and the Restructuring of the European Higher Education", *Globalisation, Societies and Education*, 498–519.

Koller, H. C. (2010): "Grundzüge einer Theorie transformatorischer Bildungsprozesse", in Liesner, A. and Lohmann, I. (eds.), *Gesellschaftliche Bedingungen von Bildung und Erziehung*. Stuttgart: Kohlhammer, 288–300.

Masschelein, J. and Simons, M. (2005): *Globale Immunität oder Eine kleine Kartographie des europäischen Bildungsraums*. Zürich and Berlin: Diaphanes.

Masschelein, J. and Simons, M. (2010): *Jenseits der Exzellenz. Eine kleine Morphologie der Welt-Universität*. Zürich and Berlin: Diaphanes.

Matzen, J. (2005): "Grundrecht Bildung: Lernen auf Dauer in Zeiten der Beschleunigung", in *Oldenburger Universitätsreden 160*. Oldenburg: Bibliotheks- und Informationssystem der Universität, 11–37.

Muraca, B. (2007): "Getting Over 'Nature': Modern Bifurcations, Postmodern Possibilities", in Kearns, L. and Keller, C. (eds.), *Ecospirit: Religions and Philosophies for the Earth*. New York: Fordham University Press, 156–177.

Narberhaus, M. (2013): "How to Break Out of the System, Smart CSO's Lab, Berlin", www.smart-csos.org/images/Documents/How%20to%20break%20out%20of%20the%20system%20trap%202013.pdf, accessed 24 November 2016.

Neuhann, E. L. and Kaczynski, R. (2016): "Rezension von Rosa, Hartmut: Resonanz", *Zeitschrift für philosophische Literatur* 4(3), https://zfphl.de/index.php/zfphl/article/view/140/244, accessed 5 April 2016.

New Economics Foundation (2006): "Growth Isn't Working", http://b.3cdn.net/nefoundation/7b6f36cb5e380aff0c_wsm6b1a5l.pdf, accessed 5 April 2017.

OECD (1996): "The Knowledge Based Economy", www.oecd.org/sti/sci-tech/1913021.pdf, accessed 24 November 2016.

Plumwood, V. (2001): *Environmental Culture: The Ecological Crises of Reason*. London: Routledge.

Pogge, T. (2008): *World Poverty and Human Rights*. 2nd edition. Cambridge: Polity Press.

Rosa, H. (2009): "Social Acceleration: Ethical and Political Consequences of a Desychronized High-Speed Society", in Rosa, H. and Scheuerman, W. E. (eds.), *High-Speed Society: Social Acceleration, Power, and Modernity*. University Park: Pennsylvania State University Press, 77–112.

Rosa, H. (2012): *Beschleunigung – Die Veränderung der Zeitstrukturen in der Moderne*. 9th edition. Frankfurt am Main: Suhrkamp.

Rosa, H. (2016): *Resonanz – Eine Soziologie der Weltbeziehungen*. Frankfurt am Main: Suhrkamp.

Samuelson, P. A. (1966): "Economic Thought and New Industrialism", in Stilitz, J. (ed.), *The Collected Scientific Papers of Paul A. Samuelson*. Vol. 2. Cambridge and London: MIT Press, 1729–1750.

Samuelson, P. A. (1983): *Foundations of Economic Analysis*. Enlarged edition. Cambridge and London: Harvard University Press.

Sanders, C. (2016): "Mentale Infrastrukturen revisited – Analyse der Wachstumskultur", in *Politische Ökologie 146*. München: Oekom, 132–135.

Sanders, C. (2017): "Degrowth-Politik, Resonanz und mentale Infrastrukturen", in Schachschneider, U. and Adler, F. (eds.), *Postwachstumspolitiken*. München: Oekom, 103–116.

Sanders, C. and Jacobs, S. (2014): "Die beschleunigte Hochschule – Eine Bildungskritik", in Tremmel, J. (ed.), *Generationengerechte und nachhaltige Bildungspolitik*. Wiesbaden: Springer VS, 293–325.

Schultz, T. W. (1982): *Investing in People: The Economics of Population Quality*. Berkeley, Los Angeles and London: University of California Press.

Walras, L. (2003): *Elements of Pure Economics*. Reprinted edition. London and New York: Routledge.

Weinstein, M. (2009): "Paul A. Samuelson, Economist, Dies at 94", *New York Times*, 13 December, www.nytimes.com/2009/12/14/business/economy/14samuelson.html?pagewanted=all&_r=0, accessed 24 November 2016.

Welzer, H. (2011): "Mentale Infrastrukturen", in *Schriften zur Ökologie*. Vol. 14. Berlin: Heinrich-Böll-Stiftung, www.boell.de/sites/default/files/Endf_Mentale_Infrastrukturen.pdf, accessed 24 November 2016.

21 Pluralist economics is taking shape. But further steps have to follow – conclusion

Samuel Decker, Wolfram Elsner and Svenja Flechtner

1 The multiple crisis of globalization and the need for a pluralist economics

It is now more than 25 years since a petition of 44 leading economists called for "a new spirit of pluralism in economics, involving critical conversation and tolerant communication between different approaches" in the *American Economic Review* (Abramowitz et al. 1992). The petition continued to demand pluralism in "scientific debate, in the range of contributions in its journals, and in the training and hiring of economists".

What has been achieved since then? While the global political and economic order as well as social, ecological, and technological conditions have changed rapidly and considerably, it is questionable if economics curricula have changed accordingly and appropriately to address new realities. The recent crisis of (neo-liberal) globalization, diverse forms of economic, social, and ecological disintegration and deterioration, the increases of poverty, climate downgrade, widely felt deprivation, perceived over-turbulence, fundamental uncertainty and disquiet, and the related political revolt of the far right as its concomitant in the leading developed countries of the "West" are visible aspects of a multiple crisis, as we have argued in some more detail in the introduction to this volume.

In the context of apparent economic, social, ecological, and political limits to growth and globalization, and to development more broadly understood, the lasting lack of pluralism, alternatives, and deep and ongoing discussion in economics turns out to be not only an academic, epistemological, teaching, textbook, and policy-advice problem, but a societal problem more generally. Alternative economic explanations, solutions, systems, worldviews, but also textbooks, curricula, study programs, research consortia, and so forth remain underdeveloped, and this gap makes itself noticeable also as the well-known lack of political alternatives. Pluralism is a crucial requisite not only for democracy but also for the mere quality of political decision-making. It is not surprising, then, that the lack of pluralism in the perhaps leading academic discipline, which influences policy makers and the public opinion, everyday rhetoric, general consciousness, and ideology, has brought various reactionary and far-right political tendencies into the arena, even in the established, richer countries of the "West", which somehow reflect the crises mentioned, without of course curing its root causes.

Though pluralism in economics is more indispensable than ever, an overall pluralist and then also more innovative and real-world-oriented economics discipline is still not in sight. Although a number of new topics as well as theoretical and methodological elements from behavioral and experimental to complexity economics are making inroads into mainstream scientific research, sometimes also into teaching and textbooks, the general state of the mainstream of the discipline is not much better than 25 years ago, or even 10 years ago, when the outbreak of the financial crisis sparked a debate on economics reform, including curriculum reform.

A comprehensive transformation of economics towards a pluralist and thus, overall, more critical and more problem-solving science will not come by itself, but has to be actively promoted and constructed. With the complementary volume *Advancing Pluralism in Teaching Economics* (Decker et al. 2018) and the present volume we intend to address key issues and problems of pluralist economics. While the former volume has focused on "structural" problems – the lack of a modern, well-developed, state-of-the-art scientific and epistemological program, the lack of a truly multinational perspective, and the lack of alternatives to the mainstream textbooks system – this collection has addressed more applied, down-to-earth or "practical" perspectives on and approaches to pluralist teaching, along with a more political and strategical final discussion on the transformative capacities and potentials of the economics discipline in general.

2 Remaining empty spaces of a pluralist economics

This volume has presented a number of diverse *principles* (Part I), a rich variety of practiced, if sometimes only experimental, *specific teaching approaches* and *building blocks of pluralist study programs* (Part II), and finally, reflections on the potential of (a pluralist) economics of a *social-ecological transformation* (Part III).

Transversely to this structure, we had sorted the 20 chapters of this volume, which of course stem from a *diverse practical heterodox space* and in fact are *multidimensionally interrelated*, in an ideal but simplifying scheme.

As has become apparent with the help of this display, an emphasis of quite a few contributions has been on *didactical principles and approaches*. Although principles and approaches have been divided into the first and the second parts of this book, the great bulk of these chapters widely share their didactical and educational perspectives. Five chapters in this horizontal category of the table have a *comparative focus*, with *interdisciplinarity* (Panther, Dorman) and *interparadigmatic* comparisons (Derrer, Dimmelmeier et al., Jäger). Another subgroup in this horizontal category is related to particular substantial *fields* of economics (often at the same time also course themes), such as *microeconomics* (Beckenbach), *political economy* and *post-Keynesianism* (Jäger and Springler), *income distribution* (Herr), *ecological economics* (Söderbaum), and *feminist economics* (Miller). *Meta-theoretic* contributions focused on the method of an organized dialogue between *second opinions* (Freeman), *economics and ethics* (Kesting) and the concept of *understanding* in teacher's education (Lenger, Keipke and Goldschmidt).

Table 21.1 Contributions in this volume and empty spaces of pluralism

Thematic Focus (Discipline-, Paradigm-, and Field-Related) / *Field of Application (Didactic-, Method-, Course-, and Praxis-Related)*	*Meta-Theoretic*	*Inter-disciplinarity*	*Disciplinary*				
			Paradigms Comparing	*Field-Related*			
				Micro Economics	*Macro Economics, Political Economy, Post-Keynesianism, Money*	*Ecology Sustainability, Degrowth*	*Feminist Economics*
Didactic Principles and Approaches	Kesting, Ethics and Economics Freeman, Second Opinion Lenger, Keipke, Goldschmidt, A Social Theory of Teaching Teachers	Panther, De-Othering Sociology	Derrer, Dissenting Views; Dimmelmeier et al., Comparative Approach; Jaeger, Multi-Paradigmatic Perspective	Beckenbach, Micro-Economic Textbook Approach	Jaeger/ Springler, Political Economy and Post-Keynesianism in EU-Integration Herr, Income Distribution	Söderbaum, Ecological Economics	
Method-Related:							
Stock-Flow/ Input-Output					Richters/Barth, Monetary and Ecological Economics		

(*Continued*)

Table 21.1 Continued

Thematic Focus (Discipline-, Paradigm-, and Field-Related) / *Field of Application (Didactic-, Method-, Course-, and Praxis-Related)*	*Meta-Theoretic*	*Inter-disciplinarity*	*Disciplinary*				
			Paradigms Comparing	*Field-Related*			
				Micro Economics	*Macro Economics, Political Economy, Post-Keynesianism, Money*	*Ecology Sustainability, Degrowth*	*Feminist Economics*
Balance-Sheet Approach		**Empty spaces of pluralism**			Ehnts, Macro-Economics		
Qualitative methods							Miller, Feminist Economics
Course-Related		Dorman, Interdisciplinary Learning Communities	Betz, Comparing Paradigms;		Reardon/Madi, Macroeconomics and Sustainability		
Praxis/ Trans-formative Science	Barth/ Rommel, Trans-formative Economics, Economics and Society		Decker, Critical transformative Science			Sanders, Transformation and Degrowth	

There are three further horizontal categories: "*method-related*", "*course-related*" and "*praxis/transformative science*". Although aspects of all these four horizontal categories (didactics, methods, courses and socio-political considerations) appear in different relative weights in almost every chapter, there is generally a key focus out of those in each chapter. Three chapters are anchored in a specific *method* (Barth and Richters, Ehnts, Miller), three in specific *courses* (Dorman, Betz, Reardon and Madi). Finally, three chapters reflect the socio-political *transformative potential* of the discipline, one with a perspective on economics and society (Barth and Rommel, Decker, Sanders).

Having mapped the coverage in this in the multidimensional structure of a future pluralist economics, at the same time empty spaces of economic teaching become visible, which we could not cover with practical and practiced approaches so far. To identify these empty spaces and the related need for future developments in pluralist teaching, we just may follow the vertical columns (discipline-, paradigm- and field-related contribution).

With respect to the column "*interdisciplinarity*", we may state that concrete suggestions for interdisciplinary *courses* as well as the interdisciplinary teaching along a *method* are weak spots. It does not appear to be really surprising that an interdisciplinary method application or interdisciplinary courses still are "uncharted territory", since "neighboring" social sciences usually deploy qualitative or mixed methods, while "quantitative" methods are usually assigned to economics. On the other hand, an integration of mainstream economics with the methods of the modern complexity (natural and computer) sciences (complex modeling, interactions on networks and social network analysis, or agent-based computational simulations) is proceeding only rather inertly, and particularly so in mainstream economics teaching. To overcome this methodological divide between economics and the other (social) sciences and to compare and *integrate methods of different disciplines in economics teaching* will be an appropriate work site for the further development and an establishing practice of pluralist economics.

Also, with regard to the category of "*paradigmatic comparison*", method-related inter-paradigmatic comparisons still appear rather underinvestigated. The contribution by Dimmelmeier et al., for instance, includes a part on a methodological comparison between different economic schools of thought. This perspective and approach has been further developed, for instance, on the pluralist online platform Exploring Economics (www.exploring-economics.org/en/), where entries compare broad sets of methods used by different economic paradigms and schools. But nevertheless, experience-based knowledge on how *methodological pluralism* can be taught has yet to be further collected. Method-conscious approaches, too, still are not well covered in this volume, when it comes to teaching microeconomics, for instance.

In the "*field-related*" columns, socio-political applications (as reflected in the category of *praxis/transformative science*) are also generally missing – except for the field "*ecology, sustainability, degrowth*". Since the conception of and debate on "transformative economics" is quite new, it is not surprising that the transformative aspects and potentials of the different fields of economics are not yet developed and reflected in pluralist teaching approaches. Especially in the field of macroeconomics and political economy and so forth, more detailed investigations on the performative impact of economics and the possibilities of macroeconomic transformation and problem-solving will be of great value.

Course-related contributions that set out concrete options and approaches to include pluralist teaching in economics curricula are still rare as well. This volume mirrors some *mismatch* between the quite good availability of alternative, paradigm-comparing and pluralist *textbooks* on the one hand and missing teaching forms (courses) and course experience to apply those contents on the other hand. To close this gap and to provide more specific handouts for pluralist teaching (entire programs and individual courses) and related teaching material (also in digital and online form) will be a key task in the further building of a pluralist teaching in economics.

3 A potential fragmentation of pluralism and the need for alternatives

Besides that schematic display of the content of this volume (and its still "empty spaces"), additional "blind spots" or shortcomings of pluralist economics may be identified. On the one hand, many *entire alternative paradigms* – such as Austrian, behavioral, complexity, evolutionary, or institutionalist economics – and their teaching have not been included in the form of a particular paradigm-related chapter.

On the other hand, and related to this plurality of existing perspectives, which could only be represented partially in this volume, a more fundamental question arises. As important as it is to present different perspectives and paradigms in parallel, and even to work out possibilities of teaching paradigms and methodologies transversely, this will not be sufficient to transform the economics discipline towards some fruitful, integrated and *proactive pluralism*. What then is needed are more integrated *cross-paradigm approaches* to teaching that include, compare and discuss a number of perspectives, methodologies and perhaps even disciplines. It is still unclear how the manifold alternatives to neoclassical economics could *converge* to some more *fruitful interaction*. Several broader such "meta-paradigm projects" may then have the scientific and organizational capacities to develop into true challengers of mainstream economics, both in research and teaching. The affluence of alternative heterodox theories in its current quite *fragmented* form reflects an ongoing dominance of mainstream economics rather than a serious threat of its monoparadigmatic and dogmatic ruling. In fact, such fragmented diversity should be understood as the expression of a rather early phase of the development of a pluralist economic discipline. And in face of the multiple real-world crises, as mentioned, such fragmented state of plural heterodoxies is a problem.

We have picked up and discussed the concept of "*transformative economics*" as a current attempt to overcome the fragmentation of alternative economic thought and to develop a rich and diverse integrated (meta-)paradigm, which may establish common ground among different paradigms and even disciplines and is directed to a shared vision of socio-economic and socio-ecological transformation. There still are a number of open questions and ambiguities that come along with the concept of transformative science, but for the further development of the discipline, there should be a discussion on *"meta-paradigmatic" projects* and their potential to challenge the institutional-political power of mainstream economics.

As we pointed out in our complementary volume, *Advancing Pluralism in Economics*, the economics discipline is at a critical juncture. With economic, political, social, and ecological crisis symptoms that have accompanied the process of capitalist globalization, economics faces the decision of whether to ignore or at least let linger on the multiple crises, or to become a seriously problem-solving force. As in the 1930s and 1940s, in the wake of the Great Depression and the rise of the international far right, economics has to radically renew itself in order to contribute to the development of economic and political alternatives. Institutionalism, Marxist political economy, and later mainly Keynesianism tried to do parts of that job. What additionally comes into play in the first half of the 21st century are manifold ecological failures and aberrations – including the close possibility of cataclysmic climate change – that reinforce the economic, (geo)political, and social crises. The structures of the economic model of the past and present are deteriorating. It is therefore high time that economics develops enabling structures for broad, participatory, and inclusive problem-solving processes. This may start with pluralist economic teaching.

Appendix

Documentation: practicing pluralism through study program accreditation

Promoting economic pluralism – PEP

An extract from an overview of PEP
provided by
Henry Leveson-Gower
Founder and CEO, PEP

Summary

We believe that a more pluralist approach to economic analysis, research and teaching would provide a wider set of analytical tools to draw on, and more capacity to apply them to understand and address the pressing social, environmental and economic challenges we face. For an important instance, a more pluralist analytical approach might have helped policy makers to better understand the possibility of the 2007/8 Crash and maybe to have avoided it. If you assume that markets tend toward equilibrium as standard macro-economic models do, it is difficult to "see" the possibility of crashes even if you manage to represent the finance sector in models.

However the economics profession face a huge transformational challenge to move from a situation where analysis, research and teaching is dominated by the single approach of neoclassical economics to one embracing a pluralist approach. There is though a growing consensus that this is necessary, indicated for instance by the ESRC funding of a new centre for *Rebuilding Macroeconomics* as well as Paul Romer, the ex-World Bank's Chief Economist's, reflections on the problems of macro-economics.

We are a growing coalition of economic researchers, practitioners and users, who are already developing, applying and using a pluralist approach and working with other disciplines to develop transformative approaches to tackling social, environmental and economic challenges. We are supported by experts in organisational and cultural transformation. We believe that we can help support the transformation of the economics profession towards pluralist economics.

Our main current project is to develop an international accreditation system for master's courses that take a pluralist approach to economics teaching. We intend to co-create an accreditation system to establish a common international identity and "brand", which is widely understood and supported. Then potential students can easily and confidently find these courses and employers can understand their significance.

We already have some influential supporters in policy, finance and business as you can see at our website (https://economicpluralism.org/supporters/). They include the Chief of Staff at the OECD, the Chair of the biggest European investment management company and the UK Trade Union General Secretary. They are not just the usual suspects and cross the political spectrum.

The point of this is not to determine what economics is "right" or which courses are "best". It is to build a shared sense between those inside and outside of academia, including employers, of what economic teaching looks like that fosters creativity and critical thinking to address real world issues, i.e. prepares students to take on 21st century challenges.

What are our objectives?

To develop and implement a transformation strategy to catalyse learning and innovation across the economics profession, and its policy customers, that promotes analysis, research and teaching that:

- develops and delivers a pluralist approach to economics applying "fit for purpose" methodologies to best inform different social, economic and environmental challenges;
- promotes creative cross-fertilisation between the whole range of available methodological approaches in economics; and
- engages with other disciplines to ensure a whole systems approach to problem understanding and solving, i.e. an engaging economics.

In order to support our understanding of and equip future economic practitioners and researchers to understand and respond to the complex, multidimensional social, environmental and economic challenges that we face.

In short, we want the economics profession to move from focusing on applying a theory to whatever problem is presented to focusing on understanding the economic system utilizing fit for purpose theories, methodologies and techniques both from economics and other disciplines.

Why is reform needed?

Mainstream economic research has for some decades become increasingly narrowed to focus on one theoretical approach, that of neoclassical economics. Economics curriculums generally only include neoclassical economics and the interaction with other disciplines is very limited. The Institute for New Economic Thinking have dubbed this a Crisis of Conformity.

Many graduates may not even be made aware of the existence of other schools of thought and if they are, are not encouraged to engage with them. Much of economics is taught in terms of theoretical mathematical models with very limited use of real world applications. This is in spite of neoclassical economics being widely criticised for many years for its unrealistic assumptions such as rationality, individualism and markets tending to equilibrium, the weaknesses of which were particularly highlighted in the profession's inability to envisage the 2007/08 Crash.

Practising economists use this training and research, either within government, universities or consultancies, to inform decision making across governments. While economists are particularly influential in economic departments such as the Treasury, Bank of England and the Department of Business, Innovation and Skills, they are also important contributors to policy in social and environmental departments.

In practice, good economic practitioners do seek to add a more practical real world "common sense" understanding to the insights that neoclassical economic models provide recognizing their limitations due to the required assumptions of rationality etc. However a more pluralist approach can provide a more systematic, evidence based approach to bringing wider considerations into problem understanding and policy by directly adding such considerations as:

- institutional design and evolution (institutional, Marxist and evolutionary economics);
- human behaviour and values (behavioural and post-Keynesian economics);
- interactions with ecosystems (ecological economics);
- gender dimensions (feminist economics); and
- uncertainty and complex systems (complexity and post-Keynesian economics).

[. . .]

Why is reform such a significant challenge?

Many initiatives have been started over the last decade since the Crash to seek to address the lack of pluralism in economics with the following being the most notable:

- the Royal Economic Society (RES) and Government Economic Service (GES) set up a process to review the direction of economics as a result producing a book "What is the Use of Economics?";
- the Institute for New Economic Thinking (INET) has been established with substantial funding to promote research outside neoclassical economics and promote economics curriculum reform;
- economics students have set up *Rethinking Economics* to promote economics curriculum reform internationally and raise awareness of economic schools of thought outside neoclassical economics both amongst students and more widely amongst the public;

- "early career" economics lecturers have set up *Reteaching Economics* to respond to student demands for pluralist teaching; and
- the CORE curriculum has been developed and promoted by a wide range of economists and has been taken up by a number of universities.

However the economics profession faces a huge innovation challenge given its narrow focus on neoclassical methodology for some decades:

- The RES lead process was unable to develop a consensus on a way forward except that there was a need for more teaching of economic history and use of real world applications;
- the CORE curriculum, although more problem focused and including a broader historical perspective, is still dominated by neoclassical based theory and methodologies (e.g. explaining behavior in terms of preferences and not referencing leaders in other schools of thought such as Geoffrey Hodgson in the unit on institutions);
- it will be very challenging for current economics lecturers to move from teaching a traditional neoclassical curriculum to any agreed pluralist one, as they haven't been trained in such and may not even be aware of many of the schools let alone have respect for them;
- the UK Research Excellence Framework, which assesses economics research quality based on peer review, does not include recognised non-neoclassical economists on the assessment panel suggesting actual or perceived risks of bias towards neoclassical research;
- there is a widespread perception that top economic journals will only publish articles within the neoclassical framework;
- economic practitioners will also find it challenging to move from a single approach to economic analysis, which they were trained in, to a more pluralistic approach; and
- policy users may find it challenging to receive analysis which may not provide the same sort of answers that they are used to from neoclassical economists.

Hence reform of the economics profession involves a major process of transformation in which all will have to play their part. To date there is little evidence of change leading to the Institute of New Economic Thinking declaring that there is a "Crisis of Conformity" in the economic discipline.

What can we offer to the process of reform and innovation?

As we are economic researchers, practitioners and users whose primary focus and expertise is on applying economics to inform the achievement of policy outcomes to serve the public interest, we

- understand the types of tools and analysis economics needs to produce to be practically useful;

- understand the type of teaching and study future practitioners need;
- are already involved in the innovation process of developing better understanding of complex adaptive economic systems to achieve policy goals;
- understand and have implemented processes of transformative change;
- are not tied to the status of a particular school of economic thought but are looking for a range of tools and approaches to be used on a "fit for purpose" basis to inform policy, programmes and projects; and
- are able to motivate and link in effectively to wider interests in change outside academia within the policy community, social movements, media and wider public, while also being able to work with the academic community.

We are supported by experts in transformational change of organisations and cultures.

Why are we acting now?

- ***There is increasing recognition amongst leaders within the profession that change is needed in economics.*** Following the 2007/08 Crash, economists, represented by the Royal Academy, admitted to the Queen that economic models had been inadequate to represent and understand the possibility of a crash. The ESRC, while issuing its recent call for proposals to develop new approaches to understanding macro-economics, noted that there is "a consensus that there was some substance to many, if not all, of the issues that have been highlighted by critics of mainstream macroeconomics." The IMF recently published a paper entitled "Neoliberalism – oversold" questioning the benefits of some key policy directions derived from neoclassical economics.
- ***There are increasing growing movements for change outside the economics profession.*** Students have a developing and growing international campaign to reform economics teaching to deliver a more pluralist curriculum. The sustainable development community are promoting the need to develop understanding of a sustainable economy. Social movements have coalesced around such issues as tax and housing policy reform as "standard" economics is seen as delivering tax avoidance and pricing the youth out of housing. Many influential people, as seen by the range and diversity of our supporters, believe reform is needed in how economics is taught.

References

Abramowitz, M. et al. (1992): "Plea for a Pluralist and Rigorous Economics", *American Economic Review* 82(2), xxxv.

Decker, S., Elsner, W. and Flechtner, S. (eds, 2018): *Advancing Pluralism in Teaching Economics. International Perspectives on a Textbook Sciences.* London and New York: Routledge.

Index

Note: numbers in *italic* indicate figures and numbers in **bold** indicate tables on the corresponding pages.

For Product Safety Concerns and Information please contact our EU representative GPSR@taylorandfrancis.com
Taylor & Francis Verlag GmbH, Kaufingerstraße 24, 80331 München, Germany

www.ingramcontent.com/pod-product-compliance
Ingram Content Group UK Ltd.
Pitfield, Milton Keynes, MK11 3LW, UK
UKHW022008180926
475701UK00003B/263
* 9 7 8 0 3 6 7 7 8 5 6 0 4 *